陳夢家著作集

General Study of Chinese Bronzes

中 華 書 局

圖書在版編目(CIP)數據

中國銅器綜述＝General Study of Chinese Bronzes：英文/陳夢家著.—影印本.—北京：中華書局,2019.4
(陳夢家著作集)
ISBN 978-7-101-13774-3

Ⅰ.中…　Ⅱ.陳…　Ⅲ.銅器(考古)-研究-中國-英文
Ⅳ.K876.414

中國版本圖書館 CIP 數據核字(2019)第 034087 號

書　　名	General Study of Chinese Bronzes
著　　者	陳夢家
叢 書 名	陳夢家著作集
責任編輯	李碧玉
出版發行	中華書局
	(北京市豐臺區太平橋西里 38 號　100073)
	http://www.zhbc.com.cn
	E-mail:zhbc@ zhbc.com.cn
印　　刷	北京瑞古冠中印刷廠
版　　次	2019 年 4 月北京第 1 版
	2019 年 4 月北京第 1 次印刷
規　　格	開本/787×1092 毫米　1/16
	印張 38¾　插頁 2　字數 650 千字
印　　數	1-800 冊
國際書號	ISBN 978-7-101-13774-3
定　　價	280.00 元

陳夢家著作集
出 版 説 明

　　陳夢家先生(1911—1966)是我國現代著名的詩人、古文字學家和考古學家,浙江上虞人。1932年於中央大學畢業後,先後在青島大學、燕京大學、昆明西南聯大任教。1944—1947年在美國芝加哥大學講授中國古文字學,並蒐集流散在歐美的商周青銅器資料。歸國後,擔任清華大學教授,1952年調至中國科學院考古研究所任研究員。

　　陳夢家先生因研究古代宗教、神話、禮俗而治古文字,再由研究古文字而轉入研究古史及考古學。在甲骨學、西周銅器斷代及簡牘研究方面,均卓有建樹,爲國内外學術界所推重。

　　我們此次出版陳夢家先生的著作,除收有《殷虚卜辭綜述》、《西周銅器斷代》、《中國銅器綜述》及其英文稿 GENERAL STUDY OF CHINESE BRONZES、《漢簡綴述》、《尚書通論》、《西周年代考》、《六國紀年》、《中國文字學》(附英文稿 AN INTRODUCTION TO CHINESE PALAEOGRAPHY) 等專著,《海外中國銅器圖録》與美國、加拿大、北歐所藏《中國銅器集録》等圖録,以及新詩集《夢家詩集》外,另將陳夢家先生已刊和未刊的文章,分别輯爲《夢甲室存文》(散文集)、《陳夢家學術論文集》和《陳夢家詩文補編》出版。

　　“陳夢家著作集”的出版,得到陳夢家先生内弟趙景心、景德、景倫三先生的鼎力支持,我們表示由衷的感謝。中國社會科學院考古研究所爲陳夢家先生遺稿的整理付出了巨大的努力和艱辛的勞動,謹致謝忱。

　　謹以此書的出版,紀念陳夢家先生和趙蘿蕤女士。

中華書局編輯部

2018年6月

目　録

CONTENTS

CHINESE BRONZES IN AMERICAN COLLECTIONS: A CATALOGUE AND A COMPREHENSIVE STUDY OF CHINESE BRONZES

BY

Ch'en Meng-chia

Professor of Chinese Archaeology and Palaeography,
National Tsing Hua University, Peiping, China

A Project under the Auspices of the
Harvard-Yenching Institute
Harvard University
Cambridge, Massachusetts
July, 1945-June, 1947

Directions for Printing

1. The consecutive page numbers of the fifteen chapters of "The Introduction" are at the top of each page on the right side beginning with "L" 1 and ending with 553, and from 554 to 1732 for the "Catalogue."

2. The numbers of the illustrations of the vessels and figures of the small prints are marked in purple ink on the back of each print (U.S. 1-850; figs. 1-79).

3. The table of contents of the book is in the front of the book. There is also a list of contents before each chapter.

4. I prefer collotype for the plates of illustrations. If you do not have collotype, please use very fine half-tone. I prefer $8 \times 10''$ (original size of the print) for the size of the illustration.

5. There are eight large size prints in a large folder. In printing, please make them $8 \times 10''$ like the others.

6. The plates for the inscriptions, which are in natural size, should remain the original size, $8 \times 10''$.

7. The Chinese characters, with few exceptions, in the text are common ones.

8. The text of parts one and two (the fifteen chapters and the Catalogue) may be printed in one volume if it is not too thick, and the plates of the vessels and the inscriptions may be printed in one volume if it is not too thick. Otherwise, make them into four volumes.

CHINESE BRONZES IN AMERICAN COLLECTIONS: A CATALOGUE AND A

COMPREHENSIVE STUDY OF CHINESE BRONZES

BY

Ch'en Meng-chia

Professor of Chinese Archaeology and Palaeography
National Tsing Hua University, Peiping, China

A Project under the auspices of the
Harvard-Yenching Institute
Harvard University
Cambridge, Massachusetts
July, 1945-June, 1947

Part I   General study of Chinese Bronzes dealing with
method and materials, historical background, important publications, excavations, finds, geographical distribution, terminology, classification,
typology, palaeography, inscriptions, forgery,
casting, cultural background, chronology, style,
decoration and dating. Altogether fifteen chapters,
plus chronology tables and translations of important references.

Part II   Eight hundred and fifty sacrificial vessels selected
from thirty-seven museums and institutions, and
seventy-six private collections, including art dealers.
Arranged according to type, subtype and date.
Altogether thirty-five classes of various types
from Shang to the Han dynasty. The following infor-

~~Arranged according to type, subtype and date.~~
~~Altogether thirty-five classes of various types~~
~~from Shang to the Han dynasty.~~ The following
information is given for each vessel: the dimensions, the inscription's English translation,
references, provenance, geographical distribution, date, the former and present collectors,
notes and a detailed discussion concerning the
vessels and the sets.

Part III   Illustrations of the Vessels
                There is a picture of each vessel plus seventy-
                nine figures which have been discussed in the
                Catalogue.

Part IV   Rubbings of Inscriptions
                There are four hundred and forty-six rubbings
                of the eight hundred and fifty vessels. There
                are also other rubbings.

CHINESE BRONZES IN AMERICAN COLLECTIONS: A CATALOGUE AND A
COMPREHENSIVE STUDY OF CHINESE BRONZES

CHINESE BRONZES IN AMERICAN COLLECTIONS: A CATALOGUE AND A COMPREHENSIVE STUDY OF CHINESE BRONZES

PREFACE

Chinese bronzes are not only objects of great beauty
and of artistic importance, but they are relics of a very old
civilization. Therefore, they are valuable as source material
for the study of the ancient culture and history of China, and
are of great interest to students of history, anthropology,
and archaeology.

A large number of these valuable objects are now found
in American collections; although they have furnished much
toward the understanding of the culture in the Far East, they
have not been utilized to the fullest extent. It is my desire,
therefore, to make a complete survey of Chinese bronzes in
various public and private collections, so that such material
might be made known to the scholarly world; at the same time,
such a survey would contribute to a better knowledge of particular objects with regard to their authenticity, dating, and
historical significance. Incidentally, it would also be useful
in the promotion of mutual understanding and cooperation between
China and the United States.

In the Autumn of 1944, I came to the United States under
the arrangement made by the Rockefeller Foundation and the University of Chicago to teach and to do research work. From July 1,
1945 to June 30, 1947, a grant was given to me by the Harvard-Yenching Institute of Harvard University to compile a corpus of
Chinese Bronzes in American collections. In 1946, another grant

was given by the Rockefeller Foundation for the extension of this project to include the bronzes in the Ontario Museum, Toronto, Canada.

During my stay in America, the Oriental Institute of the University of Chicago has given me free access to the reference books that I needed and a spacious room for work. Therefore, I would like to take this opportunity to express my sincere thanks to Dr. David H. Stevens, Director of the Humanities of the Rockefeller Foundation, and to Dr. John A. Wilson, Director of the Oriental Institute, The University of Chicago, until the Spring of 1947. I am indebted to Professor Serge Elisseeff, Director of the Harvard-Yenching Institute for his full help and confidence in me which has made this project possible. I am also deeply grateful to President Mei Yi-chi and to Professor Feng Yu-lan of the National Tsing Hua University for granting me a three years' leave. I also wish to acknowledge my thanks for the assistance and cooperation given to me by the Museums, private collectors and friends whose names are listed in the front of the catalogue.

This project has been successfully completed in two years. We have in our possession the necessary material and information concerning the objects. However, because of the time limit, the tremendous quantity of material which is far beyond our estimation and because the author is bound to do almost everything himself, we are not able to publish all of the valuable collections at once. The author is glad to see the growing interest in Chinese bronzes and hopes that the publication of the corpus might be of some significance for the further study of Chinese art.

I wish to dedicate this work to my dear wife, Chao Lo-jui, in remembrance of the hardships we suffered together during the war. For without her endurance and her wise inspiration, I would not have been able to continue my research in those dark years during which we had to fight against the war and starvation. The very detailed discussions on so many problems which appear here and there in this work were mostly written in a simple hut in a small village outside the city of Kunming. They were not done without sacrifices. I, therefore, feel that my wife should share in the credit for this work which I am now dedicating to her.

Ch'en Meng-chia

314 Oriental Institute
The University of Chicago
Chicago, Illinois
June 30, 1947

ACKNOWLEDGMENT

I take this opportunity to express my grateful thanks
to all of the museum staffs, private collectors and many other
friends who helped me directly or indirectly in the compilation
of this work. The Fogg Museum, under the curatorship of Mr.
Warner, has cooperated with this project from the beginning to
the end. Among the other museum directors and curators, my
special thanks go to Messrs. Wenley, Priest, Kelley, Sickman,
and to Mr. Plimpton for their various kinds of help in giving
me every facility to study the collections. I also extend my
thanks to Messrs. Tomita, Hollis, Pope, Schenck, Stubbs,
MacLean, Hobby and to Misses Lee, Magurn, Gentles, Hughes,
Blair, Simmons, Tupper, and to Mrs. Sirich and Mrs. Cross.
Among the private collectors, I give special thanks to Messrs.
Pillsbury, Brundage, Knapp, Bidwell, Roberts, McAlpin, Falk,
Hoyt, Hovey, Mayell, Plumer, Thacher and to Mrs. Kahn, Mrs.
Moore, Mrs. Meyer and Mrs. Hirschland.

I am indebted to Mr. C. T. Loo for his great help in
collecting the material and in finding the whereabouts of many
private collections, large or small. Many free copies of photographs were provided by him. I must, at the same time, express
my deep thanks to Mr. Frank Caro who worked with great patience
and skill and an excellent technique in photographing Loo's
complete collection and other collections. He took photographs
for me of the complete collections of Mr. David Weill, Mrs.

Kahn, Miss Duke, Dr. Knapp, Mr. Wacker and many others. My

thanks also go to Mr. C. F. Yao for helping me with the Holmes

Collection; to Mr. Wacker for giving me every facility to work

on the bronzes now in the Chinese Gallery where he is the sec-

retary and treasurer; to Mr. Daniel E. Newell for providing

photographs; and to Mr. Komor for showing me many interesting

pieces.

Many of the photographs were given to us, that is,

without any charge, by the following museums: Fogg, Honolulu,

Albright, Pittsburgh, Baltimore, Rhode Island, Herron, Beloit,

and Portland. The following private collectors also gave us

free copies of photographs: d'Ancona, Beckmann, Bidwell,

Brundage, Falk, Forman, Gumps, Heerameneck, Hirschland, Hochs-

tadter, Hoogs, Hovey, Hoyt, Loo, Low-Beer, Luquiens, Mather,

Mayer, Mayell, McAlpin, Moore, Osgood, Roberts, Simkhovitch,

Thacher, Worch and Yao. The photographs marked "photographed

by Frank Caro" in the catalogue were given by C. T. Loo.

I also want to thank my assistants and my former stu-

dents in the University of Chicago, Mr. Harry Mist who was with

me when I started to work on the project and Mrs. Ellen West Capiz

who with patience and great care typed the last draft of the

manuscript.

CHAPTER I

Method and Materials

I have always had a great admiration for the scholarship of the Han and the Ch'ing members of the p'u-hsüeh
school. It was first called p'u-hsüeh by Han Wu Ti
(cf. Han shu: Ju lin chüan) and later it was also called k'ao
chü   hsüeh. P'u means 'plain', 'simple', 'substantial'.
Its original meaning was 'a rough gem'. K'ao means 'to test',
'to examine', 'to investigate', 'to scrutinize', 'to prove',
and 'to criticize'. Chü means 'evidence', 'proof' and
'source'. Therefore, the so-called p'u-hsüeh can be defined
as: A substantial research ascertaining the origin, nature,
and history of a given object by gathering all available
material and by critically and minutely investigating the
evidence and arriving at the facts.

I believe that this was the way that past scholars
treated the classics and history, and I hope that it can be
used to advantage in the study of bronzes. We are going to
find facts rather than create theory or make conjecture. It
is even worse if a theory is held in mind before approaching
a study of the bronzes.

About fifteen years ago the writer became interested
in ancient religion and then realized that comparative anthropology alone could not solve the problem. It needed the two

tools of palaeography and archaeology, especially for the study
of the original materials, the oracle bones and the bronzes.
Since the object of our research is the historical period of
Shang and Chou, ancient history is also required. It is natural
then to study the pre-Ch'in classics and books. For these a
knowledge of textual criticism, catalogues and editions are of
major importance. After all of these are acquired, if we approach a certain bronze the date and the authenticity of that
vessel must be proved before it can be admitted as evidence in
historical reconstruction and as criteria of stylistic study.
In dating and reading the records in the written documents we
can not avoid the difficult and complex problems of chronology.
Astronomy and astrology were always confused in ancient times.
Astrology can not be neglected, and further, it is often connected with philosophy. In preparing for these studies we can
not depart for a moment from the method of <u>K'ao</u> <u>chü</u> <u>hsüeh</u>.
Although we sometimes need explanations or make deductions because the histories are incomplete and there are lapses between successive reigns, we must first consider the facts.

      It is obvious that any single bronze is not itself
isolated, but belongs to a certain period, a certain area and
to a certain class of people. Its shape, decoration and inscription connect it with other bronzes and groups of bronzes.
Therefore, a certain bronze will show relations which can be
tabulated, in part, as follows:

           (1) Period

           (2) Geographical distribution

           (3) Social class represented

           (4) Shape

(5) Decoration

(6) Inscription

Divisions (1) and (2) can be determined by (4) to (6) and provenance and the special treatment of surface, the ornament and
the method of casting. For these things we must have a group
of vessels which can be dated and given a provenance and then
make them the criteria or standard for determing the dates of
uncertain bronzes. These bronzes must be studied individually,
and from the knowledge of many individual pieces a system may
be established. During the time of research this knowledge is
corrected and edited by new materials and by new facts of excavation, by new factors gotten from a critical study of written
documents and by the increasing results of comparative archaeology derived from pottery, jade, bones, stone objects, etc.

When we start to study one single bronze we must first
try to find out its provenance and the year in which it was
unearthed, the collectors, its records in various catalogues
and the historical facts shown in its inscription. Then from
the style of the shape, decoration and inscription we determine
its relation to other bronzes. If the inscription connects it
with other bronzes, we then form them into a "set" and study
them together. If the characteristics of shape and decoration
are connected with other bronzes, and if one of the other bronze's,
which came from an excavation or find, date and geographical
distribution can be ascertained then we can date the one bronze
with which we began our study.

It is obvious that the bronzes we have seen are our
first hand materials; the photographs and good collotypes are

second; the line drawings of the Sung catalogues, which are reliable because the number of forgeries at the time was small,
are third; the woodcuts and lithographs of the line drawings,
in the Ch'ing catalogues, which should be used with great care,
because the drawings are inaccurate and this period abounds in
forgeries, are fourth. Of all of these materials those bronzes
which have come from excavations are the best, because there is
no question as to their provenance or their authenticity. Unfortunately, very few of these materials have been published.
We have to use the materials which we ourselves must investigate
both as to provenance and to authenticity.

The present book is an enlargement of my former work
"Outline Study of Chinese Bronzes" which I wrote in the spring
of 1940. It was published in both Chinese and in English in
the first volume of my Chinese Bronzes in Foreign Collections.
At that time I made a general survey of Chinese bronzes and
thought that it would be helpful to scholars if a certain datum
and problems could be stated in details. I was glad to find out
later that in 1941, Professor Yung Keng published his work entitled The Bronzes of Shang and Chou with the same intention.
However, that book was written in Chinese and I differ on many
points with his opinions. In 1945, when I was asked to work on
the Catalogue of the Buckingham Collection of Chinese Bronzes,
I followed my outline and made some new arrangements. In com-
piling this book I have revised almost everything from my
former works with many changes and corrections.

Appendix

Princeton University Bicentennial Conference
"Far Eastern Culture and Society"
(Chinese Art and Archaeology)
Morning Session   April 2, 1947

Some Suggestions for the Study of Chinese Bronzes

by

Ch'en Meng-chia

I want to take this opportunity to say a few words on Chinese bronzes --
a subject about which I have thought for many years and on which I have worked
during the past two years preparing my corpus for Harvard University.

First, with regard to dating. It is obvious that the stylistic study
could help us to a certain extent in determining the date of bronzes. However,
the first important process is to acquire a group of vessels which can be dated
and which can be used as criteria. We do not have many specimens which can
function as such, and only by further study and with new materials can we hope
to build on a more reliable and satisfactory basis which will enable us to do
a definitive work. We have difficulties in the study of Western Chou chronology,
and if we do not go too far as to ascertain a date about which we are not sure
we might be able to date the bronzes with a certain accuracy, not under each
reign but rather under a more definite period of time such as, for the Western
Chou bronzes we could divide them into early, middle and late periods. In this
way, we can make our dating more specific.

Second, geographical distribution. This consists of knowledge about the
provenance of the bronzes -- where they were found, and the provenance of the
bronzes -- where they were made. From this we might find out the difference
between Shang and Early Chou, or we might fail to find out whether there is any
great difference between them. But one thing is certain, that during the
Eastern Chou period the movement of a certain style could be traced by the
movement of a certain strong state. Take Chin for instance, it was a strong
state, and later it was divided into three states by its three chiefs, Han,
Chao and Wei. Chin was situated in the present Shansi province where the
famous Li-yü bronzes were found. Then it extended its territory southward.
First to Northern Honan and then to Central Honan. We can see the typical
Li-yü style that was brought to these areas by their invaders. Again let us
take Yüeh for example, it became a strong power at the end of the Ch'un Ch'iu
period and began contact with the Central states. On the weapons and musical
instruments of that state a bird-shaped script often appeared and it was
usually inlaid with gold or silver. Soon this peculiar script also appeared on
the vessels in the central area. Thus, these two instances show that the
cultural contact between the Southern and Northern states is more important than
that between the Western and Eastern states, as in the pre-Chou period.

Third, the sets. When we refer to a set of bronzes we mean that they
were made by or made for the same person or the same family. They were, in
many cases, found in the same tomb or they bore the same inscription (usually
a clan name). The study of the set gives us a group of contemporaneous vessels,
which in some cases contain different types of vessels and different motifs of
designs. For instance, we know that there are four archaic types of ting,
that is, the round ting, the rectangular ting, the tripartite ting and the

Ch'en Meng-chia   - 2 -

ting with animal legs. In some sets these four types existed at the same time
(i.e. during the same period). From these examples of set we learn that there
were three types of decorations, namely: (1) the all-over decoration (or ornate
decoration), (2) the frieze decoration (or moderate decoration), and (3) the
simple decoration, which were used on different vessels in the same set.
Furthermore, the number and composition of groups of vessels such as the wine-
vessel group, the food-vessel group, or the combination of wine and food vessel
group may be found in the study of sets. Thus we know that during Shang and
Early Chou a ting and a kuei formed a food vessel group, while in the Late
Western Chou period often ten ting or eight kuei formed a group.

        Fourth, the inscription. The number of the characters or the appearance
of a special character many times cannot be used as a criterion for dating.
When we determine a Shang inscription, it may be longer than twenty characters,
and a bronze of Western Chou may consist of only one single clan name. It is
the style of writing, the composition, the grammar (especially the pronouns
and particles) which determine the date. Also in the inscription the historical
facts which are referred to indicate the dates. Thus the study of inscription
is in the field of palaeography and history. Former scholars have studied
inscriptions of the bronzes individually, i.e., each inscription is studied
separately (or under isolated conditions) without taking into consideration the
whole to which it belongs. They lack the sense of the evolution of the style
of writing, the grammatical differences during the Eastern Chou period and
the relations among vessels which originally belonged to one set. Here I would
like to emphasize one point, i.e., when we go into the study of bronzes we must
first have a thorough knowledge of the entire historical background as well as
special knowledge of each vessel. The latter is the result of a study of every
aspect of the vessel, but especially that of the correct interpretation of
the inscription.

        We are now in a far better position than we were before. Ancient histori-
cal sites have been scientifically excavated and we hope more may be done.
We have a better printing method to reproduce vessels and designs in detail.
We have scholars everywhere who are interested in the subject. It is time for
us to do some solid and constructive framework, with the materials that we have
at hand, that may be followed by later generations. I hope that we shall not
try to delay this by trying to do what is beyond our power. The art of a
country is the soul of the people and in studying it other aspects of their
lives should also be considered. We are very fortunate indeed, in this Conference, to have experts of Chinese philosophy, sociology and the other arts.
I consider it a good beginning for the cooperation among scholars of the East
and the West.

∠ /2

CHAPTER II

The Historical Background

To this day we do not know when the Chinese actually began to cast bronzes. In some later books, not earlier than Late Eastern Chou, there are various stories about those who, in ancient times, first cast bronzes. These, however, are legends and can have no archaeological value. Perhaps future scientifically conducted excavations will disclose the origins of this art, but we can only definitely know that during the second half of the Shang dynasty, vessels of such high technical and artistic merit were being produced that a long pre-history of development must be inferred.

The earliest written document to mention the bronzes was the Tso chuan , a commentary on the Ch'un ch'iu , the latter being a fragment, all that is extant, of the history of the Lu State, supposed to have been compiled by Confucius. Although the Tso chuan was compiled during the Late Chan Kuo period, it preserved materials pre-dating its compilation. In the fourth year of the Ting Kung it quotes the sayings of Chu T'o (Tzu-yü) that when Wu Wang conquered Shang, Chou Kung was helping the royal family. He gave Lu Kung (the Duke of Lu State), officers and sacrificial vessels. He gave K'ang Shu (the Duke of Wei State), and T'ang Shu (the Duke of Chin State), some musical instruments. Although there is no incontrovertible proof that these statements are authentic and correct, we believe it possible, since,

in the inscriptions of the Western Chou bronzes we discover that
when the king ordered the high officials to a territory he often
presented them with musical instruments, ceremonial robes and
lower class officers.

As we know, the bronzes were used in rites and ceremonies,
and since they were regarded as precious during the Ch'un Ch'iu
period they were sometimes used in other ways. The vessel
ting   was regarded as a symbol of sovereignty and the Tso
chuan (Huan 2) says, "When Wu Wang conquered Shang, he moved the
nine ting to the Lo city." It is also said that when the last
king of the Shang dynasty fell, the ting were moved to Chou. In
the third year of Hsüan Kung, Chuang Wang of Ch'u State asked
ting of Chou (Tso chuan). It was also recorded in the Chan kuo
ts'e   , Tung chou chapter, that the Ch'i asked nine
ting from Chou. There is also a legend that when the Chou empire was overthrown by Ch'in the nine ting of the Chou were lost
in the river. (cf. Fung shan shu and Ch'in shih huang pen chi of
shih chi).

Bronzes also had their role as gifts, bribes and spoils
of war. The Tso chuan further says, in the second year of Huan
Kung that Sung Tu bribed Huan Kung of Lu with a large ting from
the Kao State.... In the twenty-first year of Chuang Kung that
the king gave Cheng Po the p'an of the Queen, and gave Kuo Kung
a chüeh.... In the second year of Ch'eng Kung that Ch'i Hou
bribed a Chin troop with hsien from Chi   .... In the tenth
year of Ch'eng Kung that the Cheng State bribed Chin State
with Hsiang bells.... In the eleventh year of Hsiang Kung
that the Chen State bribed Chin Hou with two sets of bells....
In the twelfth year of Hsiang Kung that Lu got the bells from

Yün State and made a p'an for Lu Kung.... In the nineteenth year
of Hsiang Kung that Lu got weapons from the Ch'i State and made a
bell.... In the same year of Hsiang Kung that Lu bribed a high
official of the Chin State with a ting from Wu State.... In the
twenty-fifth year of Hsiang Kung that Ch'en Hou bribed Cheng State
with their temple vessels.... In the same year Ch'i bribed Chin
Hou with temple vessels and musical instruments.... In the
seventh year of Chao Kung that Chin Hou gave Tzu-ch'an of Cheng
State two square ting from Ch'ü   .... In the same year of Chao
Kung that the Yen State bribed Ch'i with a chia.... In the six-
teenth year of Chao Kung that Hsü State bribed Ch'i State with
the Chia Fu ting.

        The bribes referred to were used in negotiations of peace
conferences during wars and in the manoeuverings connected with
the political turmoil of the times, one state frequently bribing
the high officials of another. It should be noted that the vessels offered as bribes were very often from a state other than
the one offering the bribe. It is also recorded for the sixth
and twenty-ninth years of Chao Kung that the Chin State cast
their law on an iron ting.

        These findings in the Tso chuan are corroborated by the
inscriptions on the bronzes themselves. During the Chan Kuo
period people tried to reconstruct the unknown ancient history.
An ideal pre-Shang history was systematically established and
inventions were attributed to various ideal kings and emperors.
In the Tso chuan, for the third year of Hsüan Kung, it is said
that the Hsia began to cast the bronze ting. When the Hsia was
ended the ting was moved to Shang. In the Lü shih ch'un ch'iu
the decoration on the ting is discussed. It also recorded the

robberies of the royal tombs.

The history of the study of bronzes falls into four very
clearly demarcated periods, which had their rise during the Han,
Sung, Ch'ing and the Republic.

The high degree of technical excellence shown in Shang
vessels was maintained until Late Eastern Chou, when, during the
confusion and upheaval of the times, the art was evidently lost,
for when the Han bronzes begin to appear, the technique of casting is less sure and the line and decoration of the vessels
simply stated and unelaborated. That they had, however, a pro-
found respect and admiration for the older vessels is evidenced
by the fact that the discovery of one of them was considered an
event so noteworthy as to justify the changing of the reign
title to commemorate it. In 116 B.C., during the reign of Han
Wu Ti, a _ting_ was recovered from the Fen River and the reign
title was changed to _Yüan-ting_   (_Wu ti chi, Han shu_). It
is recorded in contemporary histories that bronzes at that time
were beginning to be collected and treasured. Han Wu Ti had
"an old bronze vessel of Ch'i Hüan Kung" (_Feng shan shu, Shih chi_),
and "Liang Hsiao Wang had a _tsun_ and other precious vessels"
(_Wen er wang chüan, Han shu_). Han Hsüan-ti's reign (73-49 B.C.)
marked the discovery of a _ting_ from Mei-yang and "Chang
Ch'ang   could read the inscriptions" (_Chiao shih chih, Han
shu_). In the later Han, during the reign of Han Hou-ti (89-
105 A.D.), a _ting_ was found in the Hsiung-nu territory (_Tou
hsien chuan, Hou Han shu_). At this time scholars began to decipher the inscriptions on these vessels. Hsü Shen's   ,
(ca. 58-147 A.D.) preface to the _Shuo wen chieh tzu_
said, "Commanderies and states often recovered _ting_ and other

vessels from mountains and rivers. Their inscriptions were in
the old script of early dynasties and were all alike." Yüan
K'ang   of the Later Han dynasty in the eleventh volume of
the Yüeh chüeh shu   , divided the weapons of ancient
times into four periods:

     (1) Shen Nung's time: Stone weapons

     (2) Huang Ti's time: Jade weapons

     (3) Hsia Yü's time: Bronze weapons

     (4) Hsia Yü's time: Iron weapons

Although the dates are wrong, he is quite right in the development of the materials used to make the weapons.

From Han to Sung many chung and ting were recovered.
The discoveries were considered auspicious omens and since
chung and ting were often mentioned and because chung was an
important musical instrument and ting an important sacrificial
vessel, during the Sung dynasty these two names were combined
to form the term for the study of bronzes, chung-ting
Another term used was chin-shih   (bronzes and stone monuments), because of the interest, dating back to the beginning
of T'ang (which period marked their rediscovery) in the stone
monuments. The Sung scholars regarded these stone inscriptions
as of equal importance with the bronzes.

It should be noted that during the Sung dynasty the
approach of scholarship to the study of these antiquities underwent a change. Instead of regarding them primarily as talis-
manic as had those of the earlier periods, Sung scholars were
cognizant of their artistic merit and of the historic importance of the inscriptions. The inscriptions also became the
most admired and emulated models for calligraphy. By the time

of the Sung dynasty, the method of making rubbings had been
evolved and so, copies of the inscriptions were made available
for general study. An important point is that the study of
bronzes ran parallel to the study of palaeography. As we know,
the Sung dynasty also saw the revival of interest in the study
of the Shu wen. The publications of Chin-shih in the Sung
dynasty can be divided into two schools, one of which emphasized
the shape, decoration and design of the vessels. This school
was principally interested in the relationship between the
bronzes and the ritual. The other directed its attention to the
inscriptions, its purpose being calligraphy and historical
studies.

The Imperial Collection was begun in the third year of
Hsien-p'ing   (1000 A.D.) when a magistrate got a hsien and
presented it to his majesty (K'ao ku t'u: 2. 17-18). In 1501 A.D.
Yang Yüan-ming   was ordered by the Emperor, Jen Tsung, to
compile a catalogue of the Imperial Collection which contained
eleven vessels; it was called Huang yü san kuan ku ch'i t'u
                , a catalogue of the antiquities of the Three
Galleries in the Huang-yü period. In 1063 A.D. Liu Ch'ang
compiled a book called Hsien ch'in ku ch'i chi
a catalogue of pre-Ch'in antiquities which also contained
eleven pieces carved on stone. From then on there were many
bronzes presented to the throne by the people. These two catalogues were lost. Before 1092 the famous K'ao ku t'u was published which contained the Three Galleries of the Imperial
Palace and the bronzes of thirty-seven private collections;
altogether two hundred and eleven bronzes and eleven jades.
During the period 1107-1110 A.D., Sung Hui Tsung ordered the

compilation of the Po ku t'u which contained five hundred and
twenty-seven vessels. During the Hsuan Ho period, between 1123
and 1125 A.D., this catalogue was revised and the number of
bronzes increased to eight hundred and thirty-nine. At this
time the private collectors presented their collections to the
Imperial Palace. This collection was lost only a few years
later when the Sung dynasty was compelled to move to the south
in 1126 A.D.

After the Sung dynasty, the study of bronzes fell into
desuetude until the Ch'ing dynasty. During the reign of Ch'ien
Lung in 1755 A.D., there began to be published the important
catalogue of Palace bronzes and scholars began to collect and
study them. The first important book was published by Jüan Jüan
in 1804. He was at that time a great collector and held
the highest position in the government. He was also one of the
prominent scholars of the day. This work had a great influence.
After that the scholars began to study the inscriptions and
vessels and published many catalogues on both in woodblock and
stone carving and later in lithograph. In the late Ch'ing
period when forgeries began to appear Ch'en Chieh-ch'i
(1813-1844 A.D.) was the best scholar who could make rubbings
and judge authenticity. In 1884 Wu Ta-ch'eng   (1835-1902 A.D)
published a dictionary of bronze characters calling it a supplement to the ancient characters of the Shuo wen. It changed
the attitude of the scholars toward the Shuo wen and showed
that the bronze characters have a greater value than those recorded in the Shuo wen. Sun I-jang   (1848-1908 A.D.) a
great scholar of Chinese ritual and classics, studied the bronze

inscriptions and was the first to decipher the oracle bones thus
opening a new road in palaeography. By the end of the Ch'ing
dynasty, the study of bronzes was recognized as an important
element in the study of palaeography.

During the last twenty years, the Chinese scholars have
begun to use scientific methods to excavate in various areas,
and we are now able for the first time to verify and establish
with certainty the dates of vessels. During the Sung many
bronzes were arbitrarily dubbed 'Shang' with no corroborating
evidence. The results of the excavations by the Academia Sinica
at An-yang include, besides the oracle bones, pottery and other
objects, the real Shang bronzes, which can be used as models
from which to date others discovered by accident or with history
unknown.

For the past thirty years many good catalogues have
been published in collotype. The late Lo Chen-yü contributed
most in this field. Tung Keng, Shang Ch'eng-tso, Yü Sheng-wu,
Sun Hai-po and Huang Chün published many good catalogues with
details of design and the inscriptions, sometimes with a commentary. Both Kuo Mo-jo and Professor T'ang Lan   have contributed a great deal on the dates and deciphering of the inscriptions.

In the Western world, Professor Karlgren of Stockholm,
Professor Yetts of London and Bishop White of Toronto have
published some catalogues with their researches, forming a
large contribution to the study of Chinese bronzes.

L 20

CHAPTER III

I. Works in Chinese

 A. Collotypes of Vessels

 B. Drawings of Vessels

 C. Rubbings of Vessels

 D. Inscriptions

 E. Dictionary and Catalogue Index

II. Works in Japanese

III. Works in English

 A. Published in England

 B. Published in America

 C. Published in Sweden

 D. Published in China

 E. Published in France and Belgium

 F. Published in The Hague

IV. Works in French

V. Works in German

VI. Works in Swedish

CHAPTER III

Important Publications

In this chapter the following bibliography is included of works in Chinese and in other languages because of the great importance of materials used in research work. Comments are given on each of the Chinese illustrated catalogues, especially those with collotypes of the vessels, for the convenience of Western scholars. The Chinese catalogues may be divided into three categories:

  (1) Collotypes of the vessels (C)

  (2) Drawings of the vessels

    (a) Woodblocks (W)

    (b) Lithograph of whole-shape rubbing (R)

    (c) Lithograph of line drawing (L)

    (d) Stone carving of line drawing (S)

  (3) Inscriptions only

    (a) Woodblock (W)

    (b) Lithograph (L)

    (c) Collotype (C)

    (d) Transliteration

For the study of shape, decoration and authenticity the first category is more important. Under careful consideration the second category is also useful. Occasionally it is necessary, because of limitations in material, to use just the inscription of a vessel when an illustration cannot be located. The Four

Imperial Catalogues (38)-(41) of the Ch'ing dynasty involve
forgeries and these catalogues must be used with great care.
I shall give no details, except in special cases, on books published in Western languages. For Chinese works the abbreviation in romanisation is placed before the Chinese title in
characters, and is followed by a letter showing whether the work
is a woodblock (W), or a collotype (C), etc. For important
Western works the abbreviation is placed before the title. The
catalogues of the transliterations of the inscriptions are not
listed here.

I. Works in Chinese

A. Collotypes of vessels

1. <u>Shuang</u> <u>yü</u> 双王

Chou An, <u>Shuang</u> <u>yü</u> <u>hsi</u> <u>chai</u> <u>chin</u> <u>shih</u> <u>t'u</u> <u>lu</u>. In series of
<u>I</u> <u>shu</u> <u>ts'ung</u> <u>pien</u>, Shanghai, 1916, pp. 1 to 30, altogether
thirty-one vessels. There are two seals, twenty-six bronzes,
one Han pottery, one iron vessel of the Ch'in dynasty, one ink-
stone of the Sung. Among the bronzes there are spurious
examples, and the photographs are not very good. It was the
first book to reproduce the bronzes in collotype.

2. <u>Lei</u> <u>cheng</u> 数徵

Chou An, <u>I</u> <u>shu</u> <u>lei</u> <u>cheng</u>. In series of <u>I</u> <u>shu</u> <u>ts'ung</u> <u>pien</u>,
Shanghai, 1916-1920. The first volume, pp. 1 to 36 contains
eighteen sacrificial vessels, weapons, Buddhist figures, etc.

3. Meng yi I 夢鄩

Lo Chen-yü, Meng yi ts'ao t'ang chi chin t'u, in 3 ts'e, 1917.
Ts'e 1, plates 1 to 56; ts'e 2, plates 1 to 40; ts'e 3, plates
1 to 55. Lo's collection. This contains the ex-collections
of Tuan Fang, Ch'en Chieh-ch'i, Sheng-yüeh, Wu-yün, Liu Ê, Wu
Ta-ch'eng, Liu Hsi-hai, Fei Nien-tz'u, Shen Ping-ch'en, Lu
Hsin-yüan et al. Ts'e 1, plates 1 to 3, musical instruments;
plates 4 to 51, sacrificial vessels; plates 52 to 56, chariot
fittings and miscellaneous. Ts'e 2, plates 1 to 25, military
instruments; plates 26 to 40, credentials and weights of the
Ch'in dynasty. Ts'e 3, plates 1 to 33, Han bronzes (30), Wei
bronzes (2), Shu of the Three Kingdoms bronze (1); plates 34
to 55, bronzes from the Six dynasties to the Ming dynasty (21),
mostly Buddhist figures.

4. Meng yi II 夢圓續

Lo Chen-yü, Meng yi ts'ao t'ang chi chin t'u hsü pien in 1 ts'e.
Plates 1 to 66. Lo's collection. Supplement of the previous
book. Plates 1 to 30, sacrificial vessels; plates 31 to 36,
military instruments; plate 37, buckle; plates 38 and 39, unknown objects; plate 40, weight of the Ch'in dynasty; plates 41
to 66, bronzes of Han and later.

5. Hsin cheng t'u 新鄩圖

Chin Yün-p'eng, Hsin cheng ch'u t'u ku ch'i t'u chih, in 3 ts'e.
In the collection of the Honan Provincial Museum at Kaifeng.
These were found in the Hsin-cheng hsien of Honan province in 1923.

They are poor photographs, but they retain the original condition
of the objects before restoration. (The other catalogues of this
group were taken after the restorations.) The first ts'e contains twenty-one musical instruments, sixty-six sacrificial vessels, two fragments of vessels, six hundred and thirty-five
other fragments, three jade objects and two small pottery pieces,
all of which were unearthed by the landlord and the army before
September 12, 1923. The second ts'e contains five sacrificial
vessels, one musical instrument, three military instruments, nine
chariot fittings and miscellaneous objects, thirty-five fragments
of bronzes, nine jade objects, five pottery objects, six tiles
of the Ch'ing dynasty, three porcelains of the Sung dynasty, three
hundred and seventeen cowries and eight of another variety of
cowry. These were found after September 12th, to the end of the
month. The second ts'e also contains other later articles of
pottery and two Buddhist figures which were contributed by the
native people to the government. At the end of this ts'e there
is a drawing which is a reconstruction of the tomb with the
objects in situ. The third ts'e, pp. 1 to 66, contains tele-
grams, letters, official announcements regarding this find and
some of the records of the excavation. This book is important
for the study of the history of the Hsin-cheng finds because it
contains the first-hand original material.

6. Pao yün 寶蘊

Jung Keng, Pao yün lou yi ch'i t'u lu, in 2 ts'e, Peiping, 1929.
Ts'e 1, pp. 1 to 61, ts'e 2, pp. 62 to 119.   Formerly in the
Feng T'ien Palace   collection. About 1914 or 1915 the

collection in Feng T'ien moved to Peking and was exhibited in
Pao Yun Lou of the Palace, the National Museum. In 1927, the
Museum appointed a committee of twenty scholars to examine these
bronzes. The author belonged to the Committee. These bronzes
of the Feng T'ien Palace which are catalogued in the Hsi ch'ing
hsu chien i pien were altogether nine hundred. This book
selected ninety-two vessels from the whole collection. This and
the Wu Ying are the only two catalogues of the Palace Collection
published in very good collotype, besides the Four Imperial
Catalogues of drawings. Has measurements, transliterations and
comments.

7. Hsin cheng ku 新鄭古

Kuan Po-i, Hsin cheng ku ch'i t'u lu, in 2 ts'e, Shanghai, Commercial Press, 1929. Ts'e 1, plates 1 to 57, contains ninety-
three of the one hundred and ten objects included in the Hsin-
cheng finds. These photographs are better than those in (5).
Ts'e 2 contains notes and commentaries. In 1928, the same
author published ten vessels of Hsin-cheng finds in whole-shape
rubbings in series one of Ch'uan ku pieh lu   , 1st.
series.

8. Sung chai I 頌齋

Jung Keng, Sung chai chi chin t'u lu, in 1 ts'e, Peiping, 1933.
Plates 1 to 39. Former Jung's collection. Records and commentary, pp. 1 to 25; important details of the designs are inserted in the text. Plates 1 to 21, sacrificial vessels,

plates 22 to 25, musical instruments; plate 26, chariot fittings;
plates 38 and 39, miscellaneous, plate 39 being later than Han.
This is a small collection and the vessels are not as important
as those in his second book, the Sung chai II. The vessel in
plate 1 is now in the National Library of Peiping. The vessel in
plate 5 is now in Academia Sinica. The rest are now in the collection of the National Central Museum.

9. Honan 河南

Kuan Po-i, Ho nan chin shih chih t'u, series 1, vol. 1, Shanghai,
1933. This book contains both bronzes included in the Hsin-cheng
finds and the stone monuments found in Honan province. It shows
only one musical instrument and thirteen sacrificial vessels,
with thirty-six plates of details. This is a selection of the
best of the bronzes and the photographs are the best appearing
in any book on the subject.

10. Wu ying 武英

Jung Keng, Wu ying tien yi ch'i t'u lu, in 2 ts'e, Peiping, 1934.
Ts'e 1, pp. 1 to 86, ts'e 2, pp. 87 to 169. Jehol Palace
collection. Publication of the Harvard-Yenching Institute. About
1914 or 1915 the collection in Jehol moved to Peking, and was
exhibited in the Wu Ying Tien of the Palace, the National Museum.
The author selected one hundred vessels, almost all sacrificial
vessels, from the eight hundred and fifty-one vessels of the
original collection. It has measurements, transliterations and
comments. This book is better than (6). It has better photographs and details of the important designs.

11. Shuang chien I 双吉

Yü Sheng-wu, Shuang chien i ch'i chin t'u lu, in 2 ts'e, Peiping, 1934. Ts'e 1, pp. 1 to 53, ts'e 2, pp. 1 to 60. Yü's collection. Ts'e 1, plates 1 to 53, sacrificial vessels; commentary, pp. 1 to 12. Ts'e 2, plates 1 to 51, military instruments; plates 52 to 60, bronzes of the Ch'in and Han, pp. 1 to 15, commentaries. Altogether there are fifty-three sacrificial vessels, fifty-two weapons, one Ch'ing weight and eight Han objects. It has measurements, transliterations and comments.

12. Chen sung 贞松

Lo Chen-yü, Chen sung t'ang chi chin t'u, in 3 ts'e, Mo yüan t'ang, Ta-lien, 1935. Ts'e 1 contains fifty-eight vessels and ts'e 2 contains seventy-seven vessels. These are all of the pre-Han period. Ts'e 3 contains sixty-three vessels and objects of the post-Ch'in period. No text.

13. Ta hsi 大系

Kuo Mo-jo, Liang chou chin wen tz'u ta hsi t'u lu, in 5 ts'e, Tokyo, 1935. Ts'e 1 contains illustrations of two hundred and fifty-three sacrificial vessels and musical instruments. These were reproduced from other catalogues, including photographs, rubbings and drawings arranged by classification. In ts'e 2 to ts'e 5 are the inscriptions, on which he comments. The commentary, Liang chou chin wen tz'u ta hsi k'ao shih, is his main work, while the T'u lu is the supplement to his K'ao shih. In the K'ao shih he selected two hundred and fifty Western Chou

bronzes and two hundred and sixty-one Eastern Chou bronzes,
altogether five hundred and eleven vessels of the whole Chou
dynasty.   There are three hundred and twenty-four inscriptions
from these five hundred and eleven vessels which he published
in the T'u lu, ts'e 2 to 5.   The arrangement of the inscriptions
for Western Chou is chronological, for Eastern Chou, geographical.
From the five hundred and eleven vessels he got two hundred and
forty-six illustrations which he published in ts'e 1 of the T'u lu
with a few additions.   The K'ao shih is in 3 ts'e, published at
the same time with an introduction in English, translated by
John C. Ferguson.   Ts'e 1 to 2, pp. 1 to 156 for Western Chou;
ts'e 3, pp. 153a to 156a, 157 to 252 for Eastern Chou.   In 1931
the same author published Yin chou ch'ing t'ung ch'i ming wen yen
chiu in Shanghai which was the result of his initial research
into Chinese bronzes.   In the same year he published Liang chou
chin wen ts'u ta hsi (one volume) in Japan, which later he corrected and enlarged and which formed the basis for the T'u lu
and the K'ao shih as mentioned above.   In 1932, he published
Chin wen ts'ung k'ao in 4 ts'e which discussed some general problems and some special research on individual vessels.   In the
same year he published a supplement to that book called Chin
wen yü shih chih yü in 1 ts'e.   In 1933, he published the Ku tai
ming k'e hui k'ao in 3 ts'e.   One ts'e was devoted to special
research on individual vessels.   In 1934, he published the
Hsü pien, a supplement to that book, partly devoted to the discussion of some of the bronzes.   Kuo's work had a great influence both in China and abroad because of his systematic
arrangement and dating of the Chinese bronzes.

14. <u>Shih er</u>   ⼗⼆

Shang Ch'eng-tso, <u>Shih er chia chi chin t'u lu</u>, in 2 <u>ts'e</u>, Nanking, 1935. Twelve private collections. Series A of the Institute of Chinese Culture Studies, University of Nanking.

<u>Ts'e</u> 1: <u>Shuang chien i</u> (Yü Sheng-wu's collection), pp. 1 to 8.
4 objects.

Pao ch'u chai (Fang Huan-ching's collection), pp. 1 to
16. 10 objects

Chiu yü lou (Fang Jo's collection), pp. 1 to 10.
8 objects.

Ch'u an (Wang ch'en's collection), pp. 1 to 30. 31 objects.

Chü chen ts'ao t'ang (Chou chin's collection), pp. 1 to
30. 19 objects.

Hsüeh yüan (Sun Chuang's collection), pp. 1 to 25. 17
objects.

<u>Ts'e</u> 2: <u>Shih ku chai</u> (Sun Cheng's collection), pp. 1 to 15. 13
objects.

Ching han hsieh (Chang Wei's collection), pp. 1 to 8.
5 objects.

Pu lo an (Chang Chih-ho's collection), pp. 1 to 4. 3
objects.

Tsun ku chai (Huang Chün's collection), pp. 1 to 29.
23 objects.

Ch'i chai (Shang Ch'eng-tso's collection), pp. 1 to 35.
28 objects.

Hsia an (Yeh Kung-ch'ao's collection), pp. 1 to 12.
8 objects.

Thirteen musical instruments, one hundred and thirty-four sacrificial vessels, seventeen military instruments, and five
miscellaneous objects. Only the two drums and three of the
miscallaneous objects are later than Han. Besides Yü Sheng-wu
and Huang Chün, who have large collections in their own catalogues; and Fang Huan-ching who published his collection

entitled <u>Ch'u</u> <u>pao</u> <u>chai</u> <u>ts'ang</u> <u>ch'i</u> <u>t'u</u> <u>shih</u> in 1934, the other
collectors have only a few things each.   They all belong to
modern collectors.   It has measurements, transliterations, comments, and details of the important designs.

15. <u>Yeh</u> <u>I</u>   鄴一

Huang Chün, <u>Yeh</u> <u>chung</u> <u>p'ien</u> <u>yü</u>, 1st. series, in 2 <u>ts'e</u>, Peiping,
1935.   <u>Ts'e</u> 1, plates 1 to 50; <u>ts'e</u> 2, plates 1 to 50.   All are
bronzes except as noted:

    1. 34-41   Pottery mother moulds.

    2. 15-23   Jades; 24-47 Oracle bones; 48-50 Carved
               bones.

The bronzes are said to have come from An-yang together with
the other objects.   No text.

16. <u>Hai</u> <u>wai</u>   海外吉金

Jung Keng, <u>Hai</u> <u>wai</u> <u>chi</u> <u>chin</u> <u>t'u</u> <u>lu</u>, in 3 <u>ts'e</u>.   Monograph #3 of
the Archaeological Society of China, Peiping, 1935.   Plates 1 to
126, sacrificial vessels; plate 127, credentials; plates 128 to
145, musical instruments; plates 146 to 155, Han and later vessels; plates 156 to 158, miscellaneous of later objects.   Altogether one hundred and fifty-eight pieces collected from seven
Japanese catalogues of Chinese bronzes.   One vessel from <u>Shina</u>
<u>kodo</u> <u>ki</u> <u>shu</u>; one hundred and one from <u>Sen-oku</u> <u>sei-shō</u>; ten from
<u>Sen-oku</u> <u>sei-shō</u> <u>besshū</u>; thirteen from <u>Sen-oku</u> <u>sei-shō</u> <u>zokuhen</u>;
five from <u>Hakkaku</u> <u>kikkin</u> <u>shū</u>; sixteen from <u>Shū</u> <u>kan</u> <u>i</u> <u>hō</u>; twelve
from <u>Shina</u> <u>kōgei</u> <u>zukan</u>. Commentary at the end of <u>ts'e</u> 3, pp. 1
to 27.   The most important Chinese bronzes in Japanese collec-
tions can be found in this book.

17. <u>Ch'u</u> <u>ch'i</u> 楚器

Liu Chieh, <u>Ch'u</u> <u>ch'i</u> <u>t'u</u> <u>shih</u>, in 1 <u>ts'e</u>. Publication of the
National Library of Peiping, Peiping, 1935. Found in Shou-
hsien in 1933. Plates 1 to 9; pp. 1 to 21, commentaries with
an appendix by Professor T'ang Lan on the finds. These photographs appear in <u>Shih</u> <u>er</u>: <u>tsun</u>: 17 to 29.

18. <u>Shan</u> <u>chai</u> 善齋

Jung Keng, <u>Shan</u> <u>chai</u> <u>yi</u> <u>ch'i</u> <u>t'u</u> <u>lu</u>, in 3 <u>ts'e</u>. Published by
the Harvard-Yenching Institute, Peiping, 1936. Liu T'i-chi's
collection. Mr. Liu was a well known collector in China. In
recent years his collection was dispersed, the best of the
pieces going to Academia Sińica. Before this publication, in
1934 Liu himself published the <u>Shan</u> <u>chai</u> <u>chi</u> <u>chin</u> <u>lu</u>, of drawings which contained more vessels, but also more forgeries.
The present book selected from Liu's collection one hundred
and seventy-five vessels. Plates 1 to 19, musical instruments;
plates 20 to 167, sacrificial vessels; plates 168 to 173,
measuring devices; plates 174 and 175, vessels of the Sung and
Yüan dynasties. Commentaries at the end of <u>ts'e</u> 3, pp. 1 to
45. It has measurements, transliterations, and comments.

    In 1936 Liu sold his entire collection, the distribu-
tion of which is as follows: Plates 1 to 12, Sumitomo; plate 107,
Freer; plate 123, Fogg; plates 13-18, 20, 23-25, 27-30, 34-35,
37-38, 41, 43-46, 50, 53-54, 57, 59-62, 64-65, 68-71, 76-77, 81,
83, 87, 90, 95-96, 103-105, 108, 110, 115-17, 124, 127, 131-32,
137-38, 140, 143-45, 147, 149-150, 152, 154, 156-157, 159-160,

163-164, 169-175, National Central Museum; plates 19, 49, 55, 63, 100, 112, 119, 139, Yung Keng; plates 31, 47, 129, 155 Yü Sheng-wu.

19. Tsun ku 尊古

Huang Chün, Tsun ku chai so chien chi chin t'u, 1st. series, in 4 ts'e, fifty pages to each ts'e, Peiping, 1936. Dealer's collection. Ts'e 1, nine musical instruments and thirty-nine sacrificial vessels. Ts'e 2, forty-six sacrificial vessels, pp.24 and 25, four animal figures; pp. 26 to 45, eighteen measuring devices from Ch'in to Sui dynasties; pp. 47 to 50, four Han vessels. Ts'e 4, pp. 1 to 24, twenty-three Han vessels; p. 25, Chin vessel; pp. 26 to 33, eight T'ang ingots; pp. 34 to 47, fourteen miscellaneous objects of pre-Han; pp. 48 to 50, three credentials of Yüan and Ch'ing. Altogether one hundred and ninety pieces. No text. Some of the vessels are now in the United States of America.

20. Hun yüan 渾源

Shang Ch'eng-tso, Hun yüan yi ch'i t'u, in 1 ts'e, pp. 1 to 28, Nanking, 1936. Series A of the Institute of Chinese Culture Studies, University of Nanking. Found in Li-yü village of Hun-yüan Hsien in Shansi province in 1923. Plates 1 to 26, sacrificial vessels; plate 27, chariot fittings. Mr. Shang took eighteen photographs from Mr. Shih Po-chai, and added nine plates from Umehara's photographs in Shina kodo seikwa (plates 164-172). Mr. Shih's photographs include seventeen vessels,

plates 24 and 25 being two views of the same vessel. These are
only a part of the twenty-six vessels now in the possession of
the Hun-yüan district government. Some of the photographs are
poor. It has measurements, descriptions and other pertinent
information.

21. International exhibition 考倫

Illustrated Catalogue of the Chinese Government Exhibits for the
International Exhibition of Chinese Art in London. Vol. I,
Bronzes. Edited by the Chinese Organizing Committee. Nanking,
China, 1936. Commercial Press, Shanghai.

This volume is divided into six parts:

  (1) Plates   1 - 38: cooking utensils and food vessels.
  (2) Plates   39 - 80: containers, heating and drinking
                            vessels.
  (3) Plates   81 - 89: vessels for ordinary use.
  (4) Plates   90 - 96: musical instruments.
  (5) Plates   97 -104: bronzes from Hsin-cheng.
  (6) Plates   105 -108: bronzes from Shou-hsien.

(5) is in the collection of the Honan Provincial Museum, and (6)
is in the Anhui Provincial Library. The other bronzes are
from the National Palace Museum and the National Museum. The
collection of the National Museum may be found in (6) and (10)
above, and the National Palace Museum Bronzes may be found in
(34) below. The plates are small with introduction, descriptions
and measurements in both Chinese and English.

22. Yeh II   鄴二

Huang Chun, Yeh chung p'ien lu, 2nd. series, in 2 ts'e, Peiping, 1937. Ts'e 1, pp. 1 to 49; ts'e 2, pp. 1 to 51. All are bronzes except as noted:

    1. 42-49   Pottery mother moulds.

    2. 1-5   Pottery mother moulds; 23-24, Jades
                    and marbles; 35-42, Oracle bones;
                    43-51, Carved bones.

The bronzes are said to have come from An-yang together with the other objects. No text.

23. Hsin cheng   新鄭

Sun Hai-po, Hsin cheng yi ch'i, in 2 ts'e; ts'e 1, pp. 1 to 65; ts'e 2, pp. 66 to 139. Series of Honan Provincial Histories, Peiping, 1937. All of the bronzes here are in the Honan Provincial Museum at K'aifeng except two li, 10th and 11th, pp. 64 and 65, which were taken from Umehara's Shina kodo seikwa: 97. These two vessels are now in the State Museum of Berlin. This is the ~~fifth~~ fourth publication of the Hsin-cheng finds, with details of the important designs, records and commentary. The preceding volumes include three of photographs and one of drawings. This new volume is the best. It includes thirty-three musical instruments, sixty-six sacrificial vessels, three military instruments and three miscellaneous articles. This covers the important finds, but it is not complete.

24. Sung chai II   欣齋

Jung Keng, Sung chai chi chin hsü lu, in 2 ts'e, Monograph #14

of the Archaeological Society of China, Peiping, 1938. Ts'e 1,
plates 1 to 70; ts'e 2, plates 71 to 134. The commentary is on
pp. 1 to 20 at the end of ts'e 2. Jung's collection. Seventy-
five vessels were formerly in Liu T'i-chih's collection. It has
important details of the designs, measurements, transliterations,
and comments. Sacrificial vessels, plates 1 to 103; musical instruments, plates 104 to 122; chariot fittings, plates 123-125;
military instruments, plates 126 to 129; miscellaneous, plates
130 to 134, the last three are Buddhist sculptures of a later
period.

25. Chün hsien 濬縣

Sun Hai-po, Chün hsien yi ch'i, in 1 ts'e, pp. 1 to 75. Series
of Honan Provincial Histories, Peiping, 1938. Collection of the
National Central Museum. In 1932-35, the Honan Archaeological
Research Institute made an excavation in Chün hsien headed by
Kuo Pao-chün. Mr. Kuo published his Preliminary Report on the
Excavations on the Ancient Cemetary at Hsin Ts'un, Hsün Hsien,
Honan, in the T'ien Yeh K'ao Ku Pao Kao, No. 1, Academia Sinica,
1936. Before the publication of Mr. Kuo's completed report,
Mr. Sun compiled his book, based almost entirely on Mr. Kuo's
records and materials, and added to it his own opinions. All
of the important bronzes found in this excavation are included:
fifteen sacrificial vessels; nineteen military instruments,
thirty-nine chariot fittings, and five miscellaneous objects,
the last being of jade.

26. Sheng kao   勝稿

Sun Hai-po, Ho nan chi chin t'u chih sheng kao, in 1 ts'e,
plates 1 to 50. Monograph #19 of the Archaeological Society of
China, Peiping, 1939. The author published Hsin-cheng and
Chün-hsien under the series of Honan Provincial Histories. This
book comprises the remainder of those materials. The materials
used in this book came from the following places:

    The Society for the Preservation of Antiquities, Anyang,
    (plates 10, 23, 24, 41, 44), found in An-yang;

    the Honan Archaeological Research Institute, (plates 13
    to 19, 45 to 50), found in Chi-hsien;

    the Honan Provincial Museum,(plates 2 to 5, 7 and 28);

    Shina kodo,(plates 8, 11, 12, 22, 25 to 27, 30, 33 to 37,
    42, 43);

    Hakkaku,(plates 31 and 32);

    Cull Bronzes,(plate 20);

    Yu and Kuang,(plate 40);

    Old Lo-yang,(plate 21);

    Tsun ku chai,(plate 29); and from

    private and other unindicated sources,(plates 1, 6, 9,
    20, 29, 38, 39, 48).

Commentaries on pp. 1 to 14. They are almost all sacrificial
vessels, except plate 48; chariot fittings; plate 49; military
instruments, and plate 50, a set of tools used on chariots.
The bronzes found in Chi-hsien, An-yang, and those bronzes now
in the collection of the Honan Provincial Museum were never
before published. They are important. The author ascribes the
locale of the Chi-hsien vessels to Hui-hsien.

27. <u>Shuang chien</u> II 双古

Yü Sheng-wu, <u>Shuang chien yi ku ch'i wu t'u lu</u>, in 2 <u>ts'e</u>,
Peiping, 1940. Yu's collection. <u>Ts'e</u> 1, plates 1 to 40, sacrificial vessels, and plates 41 to 52, military instruments.
<u>Ts'e</u> 2, plate 1, Late Chou chariot fittings; plates 2 to 9,
Han bronzes; plate 10, a T'ang buckle; plates 11 to 16, seals
from Shang to Chin; plates 17 to 22, musical stones; plates 23
to 25, stone; plates 26 to 30, jade; plate 31, imperial seal
of the Sung dynasty; plates 32 to 34, oracle bones; plate 35,
bone ruler of the Chou dynasty; plates 36 to 39, bone and
ivory; plates 40 to 45, clay. No text.

28. <u>Ch'ih an</u> 痴庵

Li Te-fen, <u>Chih an ts'ang chin</u>, in 1 <u>ts'e</u>, plates 1 to 70,
Peiping, 1940. Li's collection. Plates 1 to 31, sacrificial
vessels; 32 to 70, military instruments. This book contains
many spurious or doubtful articles. Part of the collection is
now in Ch'i Lu University.

29. <u>Hsi ch'ing shih yi</u> 西清拾遺

Jung Keng, <u>Hsi ch'ing yi ch'i shih yi</u>, in 1 <u>ts'e</u>, plates 1 to
20. Monograph #20 of the Chinese Archaeological Society of
China, Peiping, 1940. In 1932, when the Palace Museum moved
their important vessels to the south they left behind bronzes
that were considered to be of secondary importance or doubtful.
Of these, the author selected twenty sacrificial vessels from
the collection of Yi Ho Yüan   , the Summer Palace in the

west of Peiping, which rightly were considered to be authentic
and good. It has two pages of commentary.

30. Shang chou 商周

Jung Keng, Shang chou yi ch'i t'ung k'ao, 2 vols., Yenching
Journal of Chinese Studies, Monograph Series #17, The Bronzes
of Shang and Chou, published by the Harvard-Yenching Institute,
Peiping, 1941. Book I of vol. I, part I, chapter 1, "Origins;"
chapter 2, "Discoveries;" chapter 3,"Classification;" chapter 4,
"Dating;" chapter 5, "Inscriptions;" chapter 6, "Designs;"
chapter 7, "Casting;" chapter 8, "Value;" chapter 9, "Methods
for Removing Patina;" chapter 10, "Rubbings;" chapter 11,"Imitations;" chapter 12, "Forgeries;" chapter 13, "Destructions;"
chapter 14, "Collectors;" chapter 15, "Catalogues." Part II,
chapter 1, "Food Vessels;" chapter 2, "Wine Vessels;" chapter 3,
"Water Vessels and Miscellaneous;" chapter 4, "Musical Instruments." Figures 1 to 294, intertextual illustrations. It has
a bibliography. Vol. II, pp. 1 to 10, additional plates 1 to
18, pp. 11 to 520, plates 1 to 991. Two vessels on one page,
half-tone. This book was carefully done with the general summary of all current knowledge on bronzes. It is very useful
and convenient for students beginning to study bronzes, although
the information is not without errors. The photographs included in the second volume were collected by the author, He did
not examine many of the original vessels, therefore there were
some mistakes.

31. <u>Yeh</u> III 戳三

Huang Chün, <u>Yeh chung p'ien yü</u>, 3rd. series, in 2 <u>ts'e</u>, Peiping,
1942. <u>Ts'e</u> 1, pp. 1 to 50; <u>ts'e</u> 2, 1 to 50. All are bronzes
except as noted:

       22-23, Clay musical instruments; 24-26, White
           pottery; 27-31, Jades; 32-33, Marbles; 34-50,
           Oracle bones.

The bronzes are said to have come from Anyang together with
other objects. No text.

32. <u>Yen k'u</u> 巖窟

Liang Shang-ch'un, <u>Yen k'u chi chin t'u lu</u>, in 2 <u>ts'e</u>, Peiping,
1944. <u>Ts'e</u> 1, pp. 1 to 66, plates 1 to 66; <u>ts'e</u> 2, pp. 1 to
59, plates 1 to 76. <u>Ts'e</u> 1, sacrificial vessels; <u>ts'e</u> 2,
plates 1 to 65, weapons; plates 66 to 72, chariot fittings;
plate 73, chains from a <u>p'an</u>; plates 74 to 76, Han and T'ang
objects. It has measurements, transliterations, provinces and
comments.

33. <u>Foreign collections</u> 海外銅器

Ch'en Meng-chia, <u>Hai wai chung kuo t'ung ch'i t'u lu</u>, in 2 <u>ts'e</u>,
<u>Chinese Bronzes in Foreign Collections</u>, 1st. series, National
Library of Peiping, Commercial Press, Shanghai, 1946. This was
compiled in 1940-41. <u>Ts'e</u> 1, pp. 1 to 96, Chinese text; pp. (1)
to (15), "Outline Study of Chinese Bronzes" in English, with
English catalogue, pp. (1) to (5). <u>Ts'e</u> 2, plates 1 to 150.
Plates 1 to 73, sacrificial vessels; plates 74 to 83, weapons;

plates 84 to 106, chariot fittings; plates 107 to 139, mirrors;
plates 140 to 150, figures of animals. Collections in America,
England and Europe. The second series, still in the press, contains 160 bronzes, no. 151-310.

34. Ku kung   故宮

Ku kung yüeh k'an, published monthly by the Palace Museum, Peiping, from 1929 to 1933. Number 1 to 45. It has about one
hundred and eighty sacrificial vessels.

B. Drawings of vessels
35. K'ao ku (W)   考古圖

Lu Ta-lin, K'ao ku t'u, in 10 chüan. Author's preface dated
1092 A.D. Reprinted in 1892 from a Ming copy edition.

36. Po ku (W)   博古

Wang Fu et al., Po ku t'u lu or Hsüan ho po ku t'u lu, in 30
chüan.   Compiled between 1107 and 1110 A.D., revised between
1123 and 1125 A.D. Reprinted in 1891 from a Ming edition.

37. Hsü k'ao ku (W)   續考古

Anonymous, Hsü k'ao ku t'u, in 5 chüan. Sung dynasty. Twenty-
seven collections. Reprinted in 1887.

38. Hsi ch'ing (W) 西清

Liang Shih-ch'eng et al., Hsi ch'ing ku chien, in 40 chüan.
Peking, compiled by an Imperial Commission between 1749-1751.
Woodblock edition by order of the Imperial Government in 1755.
Copper plate edition in 1888. Lithograph small size edition
in 1888 and 1908.

39. Ning shou (L) 寧壽

Anonymous, Ning shou chien ku, in 16 chüan. Compiled by an
Imperial Commission and published in 1913 by the Commercial
Press, Shanghai. This book was compiled before 1781.

40. Hsi ch'ing chia (L) 西清甲

Wang Ch'ieh et al., Hsi ch'ing hsü chien chia pien, in 20
chüan, supplement in 1 chüan. Compiled by an Imperial Commission between 1781 and 1793. Published in 1910 by the
Commercial Press, Shanghai.

41. Hsi ch'ing i (L) 西清乙

Wang Ch'ieh et al., Hsi ch'ing hsü chien i pien, in 20 chüan.
Feng T'ien Palace collection. Compiled by an Imperial Commis-
sion between 1781 and 1793. Published by the National Museum,
Peiping, 1931.

42. Shih liu (W) 十六

Ch'ien Tien, Shih liu ch'ang lo t'ang ku ch'i k'uan shih k'ao,
in 4 chüan, 1796. Reprinted by K'ai Ming Bookstore, Shanghai, 1933.

43. Ch'iu ku (W) 求古

Ch'en Ching, Ch'iu ku ching shê chin shih t'u, in 4 chüan, 1813.
Twenty-two bronzes in chüan 1.

44. Chin so (W) 金索

Fung Yün-p'eng and Fung Yün-yüan, Chin shih so, in 12 chüan, 1821.
In two sections, the first section in 6 chüan is the Chin so,
the bronze section.

45. Ch'ang an (W) 長安

Liu Hsi-hai, Ch'ang an huo ku pien, in 2 chüan. Compiled during
1821-1850. Published in 1905 by Liu Ê.

46. Huai mi (S) 怀米

Ts'ao Tsai-k'uei, Huai mi shan fang chi chin t'u, in 2 chüan.
Soochow, 1839. A Japanese woodblock edition in 1882. A stone
edition was reprinted in lithograph in 1922.

47. P'an ku (W) 攀古

P'an Tsu-yin, P'an ku lou yi ch'i k'uan shih, in 2 ts'e, 1872.

48. Liang lei (W) 兩罍

Wu Yün, Liang lei hsien yi ch'i t'u shih, in 12 chüan, 1872-73.

49. Heng hsien (W) 㤭軒

Wu Ta-ch'eng, Heng hsien so chien so ts'ang chi chin lu, in 4 ts'e, 1885.

50. T'ao chai I (L) 闰斎

Tuan Fang, T'ao chai chi chin lu, in 8 chüan, 1908.

51. T'ao chai II (L) 闰廣

Tuan Fang, T'ao chai chi chin hsü lu, in 2 chüan and supplement, 1909.

52. Shan chai (d) (L) 善斎吉金

Liu T'i-chih, Shan chai chi chin lu, in 28 ts'e, Shanghai, 1934. The bronze vessels are in Li ch'i lu   , 8 chüan; the musical instrument is in Yüeh ch'i lu   1 chüan; and the Han and daily used vessels are in Jen ch'i lu

53. Cheng chung (L) 鄭冢

Kuan Po-i, Cheng chung ku ch'i t'u k'ao, in 4 ts'e. Chung Hua Press, Shanghai, 1940. In the beginning of the book he lists a catalogue of the Hsin-cheng finds, comprising twenty-two musical instruments, seventy-six sacrificial vessels, five military instruments, eight miscellaneous objects, and six hundred and seventy-one fragments of bronzes. It covers almost all of the bronzes of the Hsin-cheng finds, together with five pottery pieces, eight jade objects, twenty-four animal teeth, three hundred and seventeen cowries, three skull frag-

ments, and one jaw fragment.   It has drawings of selected objects, records, and commentaries.

C. Rubbings of vessels

54. Ch'eng ch'iu (R) 澂秋

Sun Chuang, Ch'eng ch'iu kuan chi chin t'u, in 2 ts'e, Peiping,
1931. Ch'en Cheng-ch'iu's collection. Pp. 1 to 53, forty-
seven sacrificial vessels; pp. 54 to 56, four military instruments; pp. 57 to 63, seven Han vessels; pp. 64 to 75, twenty-
four mirrors; pp. 76 to 78, three miscellaneous articles.
Altogether eighty-five pieces, with measurements and occasional
notes made by Lo Chen-yü and Wang Kuo-wei.

55. Yi lin (R) 移林

Ting Lin-nien, Yi lin kuan chi chin t'u shih, in 1 ts'e, 1910.
Reprinted by Sun Hai-po, Peiping, 1940.

D. Inscriptions

56. Hsüeh shih (S) 薛氏

Hsieh Shang-kung, Li tai chung ting yi ch'i k'uan shih fa t'ieh,
in 20 chüan, 1144. Reprinted by Yü Sheng-wu in lithograph in
Peiping, 1935, and is based on Chu's woodblock edition of 1633.

57. Hsiao t'ang (W) 嘯堂

Wang Ch'iu, Hsiao t'ang chi ku lu, in 2 chüan. Postface made in
1176. Reprinted by the Commercial Press, Shanghai, in recent
years, from a Sung edition.

58. Fo chai (W) 復齋

Wang Hou-chih, Chung ting k'uan shih, in 1 chuan, Sung dynasty.
Reprinted by Jüan Jüan in 1802. It contains only sixty vessels.

59. Chi ku (W) 積古

Jüan Jüan, Chi ku chai chung ting yi ch'i k'uan shih, in 10
chüan, 1804. It included five hundred and fifty-one vessels
with commentary. At the beginning of the book there are two
chapters on the general study of Shang and Chou, and one chapter on a discussion of weapons.

60. Ch'ing ai (W) 清愛

Liu Hsi-hai, Ch'ing ai t'ang chia ts'ang chung ting yi ch'i
k'uan shih fa t'ieh, in 1 chüan, 1838. It has only thirty-
five vessels of the author's collection.

61. Yün ch'ing (W) 筠清

Wu Yung-kuang, Yün ch'ing kuan chin wen, in 5 chüan, 1842.

62. Ch'ung ku (L) 從古

Hsü T'ung-po, Ch'ung ku t'ang k'uan shih hsüeh, in 16 chüan,
1886.

63. Chün ku (W) 攈古

Wu Shih-fen, Chün ku lu chin wen, in 3 chüan, 9 ts'e, 1895. This book is one of the important books of inscriptions. It contains some 1334 inscriptions of vessels of Shang and Chou. Most of the private collections of the Ch'ing dynasty were included in this book.

64. Chin wu (L) 敬吾

Chu Shan-ch'i, Chin wu hsin shih yi ch'i k'uan shih, in 2 ts'e, 1908.

65. Chui i (L) 綴遺

Fang Chün-i, Chui i chai yi ch'i k'uan shih k'ao shih, in 30 chüan. The author began work on this book in 1869 and finished it in 1894. It includes 1382 vessels of Shang and Chou. The author was one of the most prominent scholars of the late Ch'ing dynasty. His work, however, was not published until 1935 when the Commercial Press of Shanghai put it out. It has a very good commentary, and three chapters on a general study of vessels at the beginning of the book. Yenching University of Peiping has the complete MSS of this work which has four to five hundred more inscriptions than the publication.

66. Ch'i ku (L) 奇觚

Liu Hsin-yüan, Ch'i ku shih chi chin wen shu, in 20 chüan, 1902. It contains 2203 vessels with some forgeries.

67. <u>Chou</u> <u>chin</u> (L) 周金

Chou An, <u>Chou</u> <u>chin</u> <u>wen</u> <u>ts'un</u>, in 6 <u>chüan</u>. Series of <u>I</u> <u>shu</u>

<u>ts'ung</u> <u>pien</u>, Shanghai, 1916-1921.   This book includes 1545 ves-

sels with a supplement and notes.   The book is not arranged in

good order, although it was an important work before Lo pub-

lished his work.   Sometimes it reproduces whole-shape rubbings.

68. <u>Yin</u> <u>wen</u> (L) 殷文

Lo Chen-yü, <u>Yin</u> <u>wen</u> <u>ts'un</u>, in 2 <u>chüan</u>, 1917.   The inscriptions

listed in this work are supposed to be Shang.

69. <u>Chia</u> <u>chai</u> (L) 客齋

Wu Ta-ch'eng, <u>Chia</u> <u>chai</u> <u>chi</u> <u>ku</u> <u>lu</u>, in 26 <u>ts'e</u>. Commercial Press,

Shanghai, 1918. This is one of the important works.   It in-

cludes some 1000 inscriptions of vessels.   In the second edition,

1921, Commercial Press of Shanghai, a supplement called <u>Shih</u>

<u>wen</u> <u>sheng</u> <u>kao</u>   in 1 <u>ts'e</u> was added; it was also pub-

lished separately in 1919, by the same company.

70. <u>Fu</u> <u>chai</u> (L) 簠齋

Teng Shih, <u>Fu</u> <u>chai</u> <u>chi</u> <u>chin</u> <u>lu</u>, in 8 <u>chüan</u>, 1918.   Rubbings of

Ch'en Chieh-ch'i's collection. Occasionally, there are some of

Ch'en's own notes.

71. Ch'ing i (L) 清儀

Chang T'ing-chi, Ch'ing i ko so ts'ang ku ch'i wu wen, in 10 chüan. Commercial Press, Shanghai, 1925. Only the first chüan has bronzes.

72. I wen (L) 集古遺文

Lo Chen-yu, Chen sung t'ang chi ku i wen, in 16 chüan, 1930. Before the publication of San tai, this book was the most important for studying inscriptions. In 1931 Mr. Lo published Pu i, a supplement to this work in 3 chüan. In 1934 he published Hsü pien, another supplement in 3 chüan. Altogether 21 chüan, 2217 vessels, transliterations and notes. One chuan of the Hsü pu is a supplement to the supplement.

73. Hsü yin (L) 續殷

Wang Ch'en, Hsü yin wen ts'un, in 2 chüan. Peiping, 1935. This book was compiled as a continuation of Lo's Yin wen ts'un. It contained 1668 vessels.

74. Hsiao chiao (L) 小校

Liu T'i-chih, Hsiao chiao ching ko chin wen t'o pên, in 18 chüan. Shanghai, 1935. This work included 6456 vessels with some forgeries.

75. San tai (C) 三代

Lo Chen-yü, San tai chi chin wen ts'un, in 20 chüan, 1937.

This includes 4831 vessels of Shang and Chou. It is the most important and complete collection of inscriptions. It should be read together with I wen and San tai ch'in han chin wen cho lu piao. In our catalogue all references of inscriptions are taken from San tai, except those not appearing in the work.

76. Shan tung (L) 山东

Tseng Yi-kung, Shang tung chin wen chi ts'un, in 3 chüan. Chinan, 1940. This work contains the vessels that were found in Shantung or made by states once located in that area.

D. Dictionary and Catalogue Index

77. Chin wen pien (L) 金文編

Jung Keng, Chin wen pien, in 3 ts'e. Supplement in 2 ts'e. Monograph of the Academia Sinica, Commercial Press, Shanghai, 1939. It contains 1804 characters in the first 3 ts'e, the duplicates numbering 12,736. In the supplement he lists those characters that are still undeciphered, 1165, and duplicates 966. This is a revised edition of a work which was originally published in Peiping in 1925. The characters that were found on the vessels of Shang and Chou are listed here. The characters that were found on the vessels of Ch'in and Han were published by the same author in Chin wen hsü pien in 2 ts'e. Monograph of the Academia Sinica, Commercial Press, Shanghai, 1935. In 1844 Wu Ta-ch'eng published Shuo wen ku chou pu in 14 chuan. Jung adopted Wu's method and enlarged it. The arrangement is under the order of the Shuo wen chieh tzu.

78. San tai piao   三代表

Lo Fu-i, San tai ch'in han chin wen cho lu piao, in 8 chüan,
with supplement, 1933. This book is based on Wang Kuo-wei's
Kuo chao chin wen cho lu piao, in 6 chüan, 1914. Wang's
tables were based on the materials of (42), (45), (46-51),
                                        and
and (59), (61-64), (66), (72). It recorded pre-Han vessels
          3569
3568, Han vessels 616, post-Han vessels 110; altogether 4295,
including 312 spurious and doubtful vessels. Lo's table·was
added to the materials of (3-4), (38-41), (43), (54), (55),
and (69). He also added page numbers, the collector's name
and provinces. It recorded pre-Han vessels 4699, Han vessels
961, post-Han vessels 120; altogether 5780, including 357
spurious and doubtful vessels. It is an index to the above
mentioned catalogues.

79.

John C. Ferguson, Li tai cho lu chi chin mu, in 1 volume.
Catalogue of the Recorded Bronzes of Successive Dynasties, 1939.
Commercial Press, Shanghai. This is a larger index than (77)
and includes additional material published before the end of
1935. However, this book is not a scholarly work, and the
arrangement is very confusing.

80.

Wang Kuo-wei, Sung tai chin wen cho lu piao, in 6 chüan, 1914.

This is the index for the Sung Catalogues: (35-37), (57), (58),
and other catalogues of transliteration made in the Sung
dynasty. There are 643 vessels, including some vessels of Han
and later than Han.

            81.

Lo Fu-i, Nei fu ts'ang ch'i cho lo piao, in 2 chüan, supplement
1 chüan, 1933. This is the index for the Imperial collection
which appeared in (38-41) and in catalogues (3), (4), (47),
(49), (50), (51), (54), (55), (59), (62), (63), (64), (66),
(68), (69), (72). It recorded pre-Han vessels 1236, Han vessels 58, and post-Han vessels 7, altogether 1301 vessels.

            II. Works in Japanese

        82. Kodoki

田島 志一   支那 古銅器 集
Tajima, Shiichi. Shina kodōki shū. Collection of Chinese Bronze
Antiques, Tokyo, 1910, with English preface and notes.

        83. Sumitomo I or Senoku I   泉屋

濱田 耕作   泉屋清賞
Hamada, Kosaku. Senoku-seishō. Part I of the Collection of the
Chinese Bronzes of Baron Sumitomo, Kyoto, 1919 and 1924. Three
volumes with separate explanatory notes in English.

84. Sumitomo II   泉屋倩

泉屋 清賞 續編

Hamada, Kosaku. Senoku-seishô zokuhen, Kyoto, 1927. Additional
volumes of the Collection of Old Bronzes of Baron Sumitomo.
Part I, vases, images, etc. There are notes in Japanese and in
English.

85. Sumitomo III   泉屋別

泉屋 清賞 別集

Hamada, Kosaku. Senoku-seishô besshû, Kyoto, 1922. Ten Bronze
Bells formerly in the Collection of Ch'en Chieh-ch'i, being
a special volume of Senoku-seishô, or the Collection of the
Chinese Bronzes of Baron Sumitomo. It has explanatory notes in
Japanese and in English.

86. Sumitomo IV   泉屋删

删訂泉屋清賞

Hamada, Kosaku. Sen-oku sei-shô, Kyoto, 1934. A New and Revised
Edition of the Collection of Old Bronzes of Baron Sumitomo. It
has notes in Japanese and in English.

87. Kakko   攷古

大村 兩屋   攷古 圖録

Ômura, Seigai. Kakko zuroku. Catalogue of an Exhibition in
Ôsaka in 1923 by Yamanaka and Company, Ôsaka, 1923. Volume I,
bronzes and jades. Many of Tuan Fang's bronzes are in this work.

88. Shu kan

原田 淑人   矢島 恭介   周漢遺寶

Harada, Yoshita and Yashima, Kyosuke. Shû kan i hô. Relics of

Han and pre-Han dynasties. Catalogue of the Exhibition held in
May, 1932, in the Imperial Household Museum, Tokyo, Japan. Published by the Otsuka Kogeisha, Tokyo, with English titles.

89. Kogei

工芸

雪取秀真   支那 工藝 圖鑑

Katari, Shushin. Shina Kôgei zukan. Illustrations of Chinese
Technology, Metal Artifacts, Kyoto, 1933. 3 volumes. Vols.
1-2, plates; vol. 3, notes.

90. Shina kodo

菁華

梅原末治   支那古銅菁華

Umehara, Sueji. Shina kodo seikwa. Selected Relics of Ancient
Chinese Bronzes from Collections in Europe and America. Published by Yamanaka and Company, Ôsaka, 1933. Part I, bronze
vases; vols. 1-3 have English notes.

91. Pien-chin

枝黹

枝黹の 考古學 的 考察

Umehara, Sueji. Henkin no kôkogaku teki kôsatsu. Étude
Archeologique sur le Pien-chin, ou serie de Bronzes avec une
table pour l'usage rituel dans la Chine antique, with French
abstract. The Academy of Oriental Culture, Kyoto, 1933.

92. Chan kuo

戰國式

戰 國 式 銅器 の 研究

Umehara, Sueji. Sengoku shiki dôki no kenkyû. Étude des Bronzes
des Royaumes Combattants. (Studies on Chan kuo Bronzes)   The
Academy of Oriental Culture, Kyoto, 1936. It has a French
preface and titles.

93. Chin ts'un   金村

洛陽 金村 古墓 聚英

Umehara, Sueji. Rakuyō kinson kobō shūei. (Selected Relics
found at Chin-ts'un of Lo-yang). Kobayashi, Kyoto, 1937. It
has English titles. The revised edition has additional
plates, Kobayashi, Kyoto, 1944.

94. An-yang treasures   遺宝

河南安陽遺寶

Umehara, Sueji. Kanan anyō ihō. Selected Ancient Treasures
found at An-yang, Yin sites, Kobayashi, Kyoto, 1940. It has
English titles.

95. Shapes   形態学

古銅器 形態 の 考古學 的 研究

Umehara, Sueji. Kodoki keitai no kōkogaku teki kenkyū. On the
Shapes of the Bronze Vessels of Ancient China: An Archaeologi-
cal Study. The Institute of Oriental Culture, Kyoto, 1940.
It has an English abstract.

96. An-yang finds   遺物

河南 安陽 遺物 の 研究

Umehara, Sueji. Kanan anyō ibutsu no kenkyū. (A Study of
An-yang Finds). Kyoto, 1941. It has English titles.

97.

支那 考古学 論攷

Umehara, Sueji. Shina kōkogaku ronkō. (Articles on Chinese
Archaeology). Tokyo, 1938. It has plates.

98. Hakkaku

嘉納治兵衛　白鶴　吉金集

Kano, Jihei. Hakkaku kikkin shū. (Kano Collection of Chinese
Bronzes in Hakuzuru Museum). Sumiyoshi, 1934, with notes by
S. Umehara. Some of the bronzes also appeared in Hakkaku jô

白鶴帖　, vol. 1, Sumiyoshi, 1917.

99. Horaikyo

内藤虎次郎　朋来居清賞

Naito, Torajiro. Hôraikyo seishô. In Naito's collection with no
date, place, or name of publisher.

100. Teishitsu

帝室　博物館　鑑賞録

Teishitsu hakubutsukwan kanshô roku (2 vols.) Tokyo, 1906.

III. Works in English

A. Published in England

101.

Bushell, S. W. Chinese Art: Victoria and Albert Museum.
London, 1924. The bronzes are in volume 1, pp. 59-95, with
illustrations.

102. Koop

Koop, Albert J. Early Chinese Bronzes. Ernest Benn, London
and Charles Scribner's Sons, New York, 1924.

103. Eumo　献民

Yetts, W. P. The George Eumorfopoulos Collections. Catalogue of
Chinese and Corean Bronzes, Sculpture, Jade, Jewelry, and Miscellaneous, (3 vols.) Ernest Benn, London, 1929-1932.

104. London　倫敦

The Chinese Exhibition, A Commemorative Catalogue of the International Exhibition of Chinese Art, Royal Academy of Arts,
November, 1935 - March, 1936. London, 1936. Selected illustrations in large sizes. The Catalogue of the International
Exhibition of Chinese Art, 1935-36, is more complete, but the
illustrations are small in size.

105. Cull　柯尔

Yetts, W. P. The Cull Chinese Bronzes. Courtauld Institute of
Art, London, 1939.

106.

White, W. C. "The Richest Archaeological Site in China: The
Elephant Tomb," Illustrated London News, March 23, 1935.

107.

White, W. C. "Sacrificial Knives and Weapons from Ancient China:
Further Bronzes from the 'Elephant Tomb,'" Illustrated London
News, April 20, 1935.

108.

Timperley, H. J. "The Awakening of China in Archaeology: Further Discoveries in Honan Province - - Royal Tombs of the Shang Dynasty," Illustrated London News, April 4, 1936.

109.

Pelliot, Paul. The Royal Tombs of An-yang. Lecture in Studies in Chinese Art and Some Indian Influences, chapter IV. The India Society, London, 1938.

110.

Ancient Chinese Bronzes. Bluett and Sons, London, 1938. Dealer's catalogue.

111. Siren

Siren, Osvald. A History of Early Chinese Art-the Prehistoric and Pre-Han Periods. London, 1929. Original edition in French, see (148).

B. Published in America

112. Holmes catalogue

Selected Ancient Chinese Bronzes from the collection of Mrs. Christian R. Holmes. Orientalia, New York.

113. Waterbury

Waterbury, Florance. Early Chinese Symbols and Literature:
Vestiges and Speculations. E. Weyhe, New York, 1942.

114. Freer catalogue 费利亚

Lodge, John E., Wenley, A. G. and Pope, John. A Descriptive
Illustrated Catalogue of Chinese Bronzes, acquired during the
administration of J. E. Lodge. Oriental Studies, no. 3.
Freer Gallery of Art, Washington, D. C., 1946.

115. Buckingham collection 柏晨美

Kelley, C. F. and Ch'en Meng-chia. Chinese Bronzes from the
Buckingham Collection. The Art Institute of Chicago, 1946.
The preparation of the plates and the descriptions by Kelley;
the chronology, dating, translations of inscriptions, commentary and notes by Ch'en.

116.

First Exhibition of Chinese Art. Friends of Far Eastern Art.
Mills College, Oakland, California, 1934.

117.

Priest, Alan. Chinese Bronzes of the Shang through T'ang
Dynasty. An exhibition lent by American Collectors and
Museums and shown in Gallery D 6 from October 19 through
November 27, 1938, Metropolitan Museum, New York.

118. Loo catalogue (1939) 虜目

An Exhibition of Chinese Bronzes. C. T. Loo and Company, New York, 1939.

119. Loo catalogue (1940)

An Exhibition of Ancient Chinese Ritual Bronzes. Loaned by C. T. Loo and Company, to the Detroit Institute of Art. New York, 1940.

120. Loo catalogue (1941)

Exhibition of Chinese Art. C. T. Loo and Company, New York, 1941.

121.

Ancient Chinese Bronzes and Chinese Jewelry. Selected from C. T. Loo's collection in the special exhibition galleries of the museum from February 19 to March 2, 1941. Toledo Museum of Art, 1941.

122. Masterpieces

Masterpieces of Ancient Chinese. Jan Kleijkamp Collection. Exhibited in the Santa Barbara Museum in 1941 and in the Detroit Institute of Arts in 1942. Kleijkamp Inc., New York, 1941.

123. *Leventritt*

Mortimer <u>C</u>. <u>Leventritt</u> <u>Collection</u>. Far Eastern and European
Art. T. W. Stanford Art Gallery, Stanford University, California, 1941.

124. <u>Yamanaka</u> <u>catalogue</u> (1925)   山中日

<u>Exhibition</u> <u>of</u> <u>Early</u> <u>Chinese</u> <u>Bronzes</u>. Yamanaka and Company,
New York, 1925.

125. <u>Yamanaka</u> <u>catalogue</u> (1926)

<u>Exhibition</u> <u>of</u> <u>Early</u> <u>Chinese</u> <u>Bronzes</u>, <u>Stone</u> <u>Sculptures</u> <u>and</u>
<u>Potteries</u>. Yamanaka and Company, New York, 1926.

126. <u>Yamanaka</u> <u>catalogue</u> (1938)

<u>Exhibition</u> <u>of</u> <u>Ancient</u> <u>Chinese</u> <u>Bronzes</u> <u>and</u> <u>Buddhist</u> <u>Art</u>.
Yamanaka and Company, New York, 1938.

127. <u>Yamanaka</u> <u>catalogue</u> (1939)

<u>Collection</u> <u>of</u> <u>Far</u> <u>Eastern</u> <u>and</u> <u>Other</u> <u>Chinese</u> <u>Art</u>, assembled by
Yamanaka and Company, Inc. Catalogue for auction held by the
Alien Property Custodian of the U. S. A., New York and Chicago,
1943.

128. <u>Yamanaka</u> <u>catalogue</u> (1944)

<u>Oriental</u> <u>Art</u>. This includes the entire stock of the New York

Store with additions from the Chicago Store of Yamanaka and Company, Inc. Catalogue for auction held by Alien Property Custodian of the U. S. A., New York, 1944.

C. Published in Sweden

129.

Karlbeck, O. Notes on the Archaeology of China. BMFEA, vol. 2, 1930.

130.

Exhibition of Early Chinese Bronzes. BMFEA, vol. 6, 1934.

131.

Karlgren, B. On the Date of the Piao-bells. BMFEA, vol.6, 1934.

132.

Anderson, J. G. The Goldsmith in Ancient China. BMFEA, vol. 7, 1935.

133.

Karlbeck, O. Anyang Moulds. BMFEA, vol. 7, 1935.

134.

Karlbeck, O. Anyang Marble Sculpture. BMFEA, vol. 7, 1935.

135. <u>Yin and Chou</u>   啟用銅王

Karlgren, B. Yin and Chou in Chinese Bronzes. <u>BMFEA</u>, vol. 8, 1936.

136. <u>New studies</u>

Karlgren, B. New Studies on Chinese Bronzes. <u>BMFEA</u>, vol. 9, 1937.

137.

Sylwan, V. Silk from the Yin Dynasty. <u>BMFEA</u>, vol. 9, 1937.

138.

Karlgren, B. Notes on a Kin-ts'un Album. <u>BMFEA</u>, vol. 10, 1938.

139.

Karlgren, B. Huai and Han. <u>BMFEA</u>, vol. 13, 1941.

140.

Karlgren, B. Some Early Chinese Bronze Masters. <u>BMFEA</u>, vol. 16, 1944.

141.

Karlgren, B. Some Weapons and Tools of the Yin Dynasty. <u>BMFEA</u>, vol. 17, 1945.

142.

Karlgren, B. Once Again the A and B Styles in Yin Ornamentation. <u>BMFEA</u>, vol. 18, 1946.

D. Published in China

143. Lo-yang 洛陽

White, W. C. Tombs of Old Lo-yang. Kelly and Walsh, Shanghai, 1934.

144.

Ferguson, J. C. Survey of Chinese Art. Vol. 1, Bronzes. Commercial Press, Shanghai, 1939.

E. Published in France and Belgium

145.

Rostovtzeff, M. Inlaid Bronzes of the Han Dynasty, in the collection of C. T. Loo. G. Vanoest, Paris and Brussels, 1927.

F. Published in The Hague

146.

Visser, H. F. E. The Exhibition of Chinese Art, Amsterdam, 1925, of the Society of Friends of Asiatic Art. The Hague, 1926.

IV. Works in French

147. Loo catalogue (1924)

Tch'ou, Tö-yi. Bronzes Antiques de la Chine Appartenant à

C. T. Loo et Cie. Paris, 1924.

148.

Sirén, Osvald. Histoire des Arts Anciens de la Chine. Vol. 1,
L'Époque Préhistoriques. G. Vanoest, Paris and Bruxelles, 1929.
English edition see (111).

149.

Salles, Georges. Bronzes Chinois des Dynasties Tcheou, Ts'in
et Han. Musée de l'Orangerie, Mai-Juin, Paris, 1934.

150.

Grousset, René. L'Évolution des Bronzes Chinois Archaïques.
D'après l'Exhibition Franco-Suedoise du Musée Cernuschi, Mai-
Juin, 1937. Paris, 1937.

151.

Monod-Bruhl, Odette. Guide-catalogue du Musée Guimet. Paris,
1939. China: pp. 156-190, historical sketch, no illustrations.

152. RAA

L'Exposition de Bronzes Chinois. Revue des Arts Asiatiques:
Annals du Musée Guimet. Tome VIII, numéro iii. Paris.

V. Works in German

153.

Voretzsch, E. A. Altchinesische Bronzen. Berlin, 1924.

154. Berlin state

Chinesische Bronzen aus der Abteilung für Ostasiatische Kunst
an den Staatlichen Museen Berlin. Berlin, 1928

155. Yu and Kuang

Trübner, J. Yu und Kuang. Zur Typologie der Chinesischen
Bronzen. Leipzig, 1929.

156.

Salmony, Alfred. Asiatische Kunst. Ausstelung, Köln, 1926.
Verleg F. Bruckmann, München, 1927. It has notes by Paul
Pelliot.

157

Kümmel, O. Chinesische Kunst. Berlin, 1930.

158.

Kümmel, O. Jörg Trübner zum Gedächtnis. Berlin, 1930.

159. Burchard Catalogue

Reidemeister, L. Chinesische Kunst. Berlin, 1935. Die Bestände
der Firma Dr. Otto Burchard and Company. (2 vols.) Dealer's
catalogue.

160. Trautmann

Ecke, Gustav. Frühe Chinesische Bronzen aus der Sammlung Oskar
Trautmann. Peking, 1939. 入中口

161.

Huggler, M. and v. Tscharner, E. H. Asiatische Kunst aus
Schweizer Sammlungen. Kunsthalle Bern, 1941.

162.

Itten, J. Ausstellung Asiatische Kunst aus Schweizer Sammlungen.
Kunstgewerbemuseum Zürich, 1941.

163.

Asiatische Kunst, Indien Tibet China Korea Japan. Kunstgewerbemuseum Zürich, 1941.

164. Lochow

Ecke, Gustav. Sammlung Lochow, *Chinesische Bronzen* ~~Chinese Bronse~~. Hans Juergen v.
Lochow's Collection. Peiping, 1943
入中口

VI. Work   in Swedish

165.

Sirén, O. Kinas Konst, under tre årtusenden. Stockholm, 1943.
(2 vols.) English edition is in preparation.

Additional

A. Works in English

1. Chinese Bronzes of the Shang, Chou and Han Periods.   In the
        collection of Mr. Parish-Watson.   Notes by Berthold
        Laufer.   New York, 1922.

2. The Four Bronze Vessels of the Marquis of Ch'i by John C.
        Ferguson.   Peking, 1928.

3. A Loan Exhibition of Chinese Art.   Detroit Institute of
        Arts, 1929.

4. Catalogue of the Sunglin Collection of Chinese Art and
        Archaeology.   New York, 1930.

5. A Collection of Ancient Chinese Bronzes, Bluett and Sons,
        London, 1937

6. Recent Accessions in American Museums, Oriental Arts in America, the New Or
                                                                    society o
                                                                    Ameri
6. Early Chinese Art, section II, University Prints, Oriental   Chic
        Art, Series O, by L. Sickman.   Newton, Massachusetts,   19
        1938.

7. Catalogue of the Fine Collection of Important Early Chinese
        Bronzes, Rare Archaic Jades, Ceramics and Works of
        Art.   The property of H. K. Burnet, London, 1941.

8. Chinese Collections, University Museum, Philadelphia, 1941.

9. Anyang: A Restrospect by Yetts.   China Society Occasional
        Papers, London, 1942.

10. A Short History of Chinese Art by Ludwig Bachhofer, Pantheon,
        New York, 1946.

B. Works by the Same Author

"The Sacrificial Systems as Found in Ancient Inscriptions of
        Shang and Chou," Yenching Hsüeh Pao, no. 19.

"Myths and Witchcraft during the Shang Period," Ibid., no. 20,
        1936.

"A Study of the Hu of King Yu Han," Ibid., no. 21, 1937.

"The Origin of Wu-hsing, or the Doctrine of the Five Elements,"
        Ibid., no. 24, 1938.

"The Names of the Kings of Shang," Ibid., no. 27, 1940

"A Study of Kao-mei, Chiao-she and Tsu-miao," Tsing Hua Hsüeh Pao,
        Vol. 12, no. 3, 1937.

"The Seat of Learning and the Site of Heaven-Worship in Ancient
        China," Ibid., Vol. 13, no. 1, 1941.

"Notes on Archaic Chinese," Ibid., Vol. 13, no. 2, 1943.

"The Authorship of Ku-wen Shang-shu," Quarterly Bulletin of
Chinese Bibliography (National Library of Peiping), New Series,
        Vol. 4, no. 3, 1943.

"A Study on the Discovery of the Bamboo Books in the Chin
        Dynasty," Ibid., Vol. 5, no. 2, 1944.

A Palaeographical Study on the Book of Lao Tzu, Commercial Press,
        1945.

"Style of Chinese Bronzes," Archives of the Chinese Art Society
        of America, 1, 1945-1946.

        (All of the above are in Chinese except the last one)

Study on Western Chou Chronology, Commercial Press, 1945-

L 70

CHAPTER IV

Excavations and Finds

Honan Province

      I. An-yang Excavations

         Date of An-yang Finds

      II. Chün Hsien Excavations

         Date of Chün Hsien Finds

     III. Chi Hsien Excavations

     IV. Chin-ts'un Finds

         Date of Chin-ts'un Finds

      V. Ma-p'o Finds

     VI. Hsin Cheng Finds

         Date of Hsin Cheng Finds

Hopei Province

     VII. I Hsien Finds

    VIII. Lai-shui Finds

Shantung Province

     IX. Shou-chang Finds

      X. Ch'ang-ch'ing Finds

     XI. Huan-t'ai Finds

     XII. Lin-tzu Finds

    XIII. I-tou Finds

    XIV. Shou-kuang Finds

     XV. Yi-shui Finds

    XVI. Huang Hsien Finds

   XVII. Chiao Hsien Finds

  XVIII. Hsin-t'ai Finds

CHAPTER IV

Excavations and Finds

The provenance of a bronze can be ascertained from
the reports of scientific excavations and from the records of
collectors and dealers. It is obvious that the first is the
most reliable but, unfortunately, there are not many published
reports on the various excavations. The Sung catalogues were
the first to record the provenance of the bronzes and most of
them are quite reliable. During the Ch'ing dynasty scholars
neglected the provenance until the latter part of the dynasty
when a few records appeared. If we treat this information
with our knowledge of other phases we can arrive at a more accurate decision. In the following sections, I shall discuss
the excavations and the finds. As to the finds, I wish to
emphasize two points. First, those finds which form a significant archaeological group and second, those finds which do not
form a group but which have a significance for geographical distribution. Therefore, the following list of finds is not exhaus-
tive but the most important information is recorded. The excavations are limited to those conducted by the Academia Sinica.
The Hsin-cheng finds, though carried on publically, can not be
properly classed as scientific excavations.

I. An-yang Excavations

As early as 1092 A.D. when Lü Ta-lin compiled the K'ao
ku t'u he mentioned five bronzes which had been found in what

is now called An-yang   of Honan province. They are:

(1) Ting, vol. 1, p. 21 - two characters - "Obtained at
T'an-chia city of Yeh commandery.... If we study the style, the
inscription and the place of origin, it should be a Shang vessel."

(2) Ting, vol. 1, p. 23 - one character - "Obtained at the
bank of the Chang River   of the Yeh commandery... the inscription is of such archaic style that it can not be deciphered.
It is also a Shang vessel."

(3) Yu, vol. 4, p. 5 - twenty-four characters - "Obtained
at Yeh.... The Ho-t'an-chia lived in Shang in what is now Yeh
commandery. The inscription speaks of nine sacrifices (the
Shang called 'year', 'sacrifice'). Therefore, it is no doubt
a Shang vessel."

(4) Ku, vol. 5, p. 12 - "Obtained at T'an-chia city of
Yeh commandery. No inscription."

(5) Ying, vol. 4, p. 44 - one character - "This vessel was
said to have been found near the Huan River   bank near the
tomb of T'an-chia."

From the results of recent excavations, we know that
these five vessels were found near the Huan River in what was
the site of the ancient Shang capital.

T'an-chia (the full name was Ho-t'an-chia) was a Shang
king six generations removed from T'ang, the first Shang king.
The so-called T'an-chia city or T'an-chia tomb is only in a
vague sense a city of a Shang king.

From the Chu shu we know that Ho-t'an-chia moved to a
place called Hsiang   . Five generations later P'an Keng
moved to Yin   , which is now called An-yang city.

During the Northern Wei dynasty, An-yang belonged to
Hsiang Chou   which was founded in 400 A.D. During
the Sui dynasty, Hsiao-t'un became apart of Hsiang Hsien as
shown on a stone epitaph excavated at Hsiao-t'un in 1929 by
Academia Sinica. This is dated 603 A.D. and partly reads,
"Buried at the east of the brushwood at Ting-yen village, 7
li northwest of Hsiang Hsien of Hsiang Chou." Because of this,
later scholars confused the old Hsiang (capital of T'an-chia)
with An-yang (one time Hsiang Hsien). Thus Lu shih (Kuo ming
chi IV) says "The old site of T'an-chia was 5 li northwest of
An-yang. T'an-chia's tomb was outside of the northwest corner
of the city, on the south bank of the Huan River."

Comparing the inscriptions and designs of the bronzes
found at T'an-chia city during the Sung dynasty with the vessels which were scientifically excaved by the Academia Sinica
on the same site, it has been shown that they are indubitably
Shang vessels. And the same excavations reveal that the tombs
had been robbed, not only in recent years, but also in very
ancient times. In the Yüan dynasty Na Hsiang   , in his
book, Ho su fang ku chi   wrote:

> Five li and forty paces northwest of An-yang
> hsien, at the south bank of the Huan River,
> lies the Ho-t'an-chia city. There are a
> group of tombs which by tradition are said to
> be the place where Ho-t'an-chia is buried.
> The old people said that in the second year
> of Yüan-feng of the Sung dynasty (1079 A.D.,
> fourteen years before the compilation of the
> K'ao ku t'u) during the summer there were
> great rains and Anyang had a flood. The
> waters inundated the bank and the tomb was
> sundered, the peasants ransacked the tomb
> and carried away ancient bronze vessels.
> Body and inscription were complete and nothing
> was eroded. People feared the law and dared
> not sell all of these things in the market.
> Therefore they broke them and sold the frag-
> ments and then resealed the tomb to erase all

traces of their guilt. From than on there
were no more bronzes unearthed. (Quoted
from Kuei T'ai's An-yang hsien chih, vol. 15).

It is also recorded in the original notes of the above

mentioned Lu shih that"In the seventh year of Yüan-feng

(1084 A.D.) An-yang had a flood. The people found bronzes on

the bank and melted them."

The description of the location was so accurate that it

proved to be the identical site at which the Academia Sinica

made its excavations, the locality now called Hsiao-t'un   .

Considering the date of the Sung discovery of the bronzes, we

may suggest that some of the five bronzes catalogued in the

K'ao ku t'u may have come from the 1079 or 1804 period.

From that time on, Hsiao-t'un was disregarded until the

beginning of the Kuang-hsü reign (1875-1908) of the Ch'ing

dynasty when the discovery of the oracle bones at An-yang, then

the capital of Chang-te fu   , aroused great interest in

that neighborhood. The oracle bones were first recognized to be

of archaeological value in 1899, but they were actually un-

earthed some thirty years earlier. In the interim the farmers,

on whose land they were discovered, had found a ready market

in Peiping medicine shops and the local market where they were

sold as dragon bones for medicinal purposes. When the interest

of scholars and collectors became aroused, the dealers in

possession of what promised to be a storehouse of profit, took

pains to conceal their whereabouts. In addition, early books

of the period noted that the oracle bones were found in T'ang-

yin   , the neighboring district of An-yang. This error

occurred by reason of the fact that there are two villages

called Hsiao-t'un in the nearby districts, one called Ch'ien

Hsiao-t'un (Hsiao-t'un is a common term meaning 'small village')
the Upper Hsiao-t'un in the T'ang-yin district and the other, Hou
Hsiao-t'un, the Lower Hsiao-t'un in the An-yang district. By
1910 Lo Chen-yü had gotten information from a dealer that the
oracle bones were found not in T'ang-yin, but in An-yang, 5 li
northwest of the city. By 1911, however, when Lo Chen-yü sent
his brother to Hsiao-t'un to collect oracle bones, the location
had been properly identified, and in 1915 Lo himself visited
Hsiao-t'un. While the peasants dug for oracle bones they also
turned up bronzes and other artifacts.

The Peiping-Hankow Railway station lies at the northwest
of the city of An-yang. If we start from the station and walk
along the railway northward and turn west until we come to Kao-
lou chuang   , the next village to the west is Hsüeh-chia
chuang   . Then we turn and follow a path northwest
until we come to the Hsiao-t'un ts'un. To the northwest of
Hsiao-t'un lies the villages of Hua-yüan chuang   , Hsiao-
chuang   and Wang-yü-k'ou ts'un   . Hou-chia
chuang   is about 12 li northwest of An-yang city, on the
north side of the Huan River. The Huan River has its source in
the north and flows past the west side of Ch'iu-k'ou ts'un
and Hou-chia chuang, then comes down and turns to the east pas-
sing Wu-kuan ts'un   and Hsiao-ssu-k'ung ts'un
to Ta-shih-k'un ts'un   , to the west of which it again
turns to the south. When it reaches Hsiao-t'un the river
curves eastward where it meets the railway, to the west of which,
on the south bank of the river is located the mound called Hou-
kang   , north of Kao-lou chuang. As may be seen, the Huan
River follows a convoluting serpentine course, sometimes flowing

southward and sometimes flowing eastward. Hou-chia chuang is on the east side of the river, but on the north bank, and Hsiao-t'un is on the west side of the river on the south bank. Where the Huan River crosses the railway it forms a U-curve, and in the mouth of the curve lies Kuo-chia wan   . There is another village, Fan-chia chuang   , which lies on the west bank of the Huan River opposite Hou-chia chuang.

The scientific excavation was made by the Academia Sinica (Archaeological Department, Division of History and Philology). The excavations were made under the leadership of Tung Tso-pin   , Li Chi   , and Liang Ssu-yung   . The first expedition was made in the autumn of 1928, and the fifteenth in the spring of 1937. The work was interrupted by the onset of the Sino-Japanese war in that same year. The general report of the An-yang excavations has not been published. Here I base the materials on the preliminary reports and other sources in order to make a general sketch of the important excavations.

We can divide the excavations into three periods: (1) from the autumn of 1928 to the spring of 1934, from the first expedition to the ninth; (2) from the autumn of 1934 to the autumn of 1935, from the tenth expedition to the twelfth; and (3) from the spring of 1936 to the spring of 1937, from the thirteenth to the fifteenth expedition. During the first period the excavations were principally concentrated on the Hsiao-t'un village, although occasional excavations were made across the river on the north bank. From the autumn of 1934 to the autumn of 1935 the excavations were concentrated at Hou-chia chuang on the north bank. In the third period they returned to work at Hsiao-t'un again. The excavations made on

the south bank were meagre until the spring of 1936 when they uncovered a store of oracle bones. The total number of inscribed
bones was 17,804, of which some two or three hundred were complete and unbroken. The meagreness of the yields on the south
bank may be accounted for by the years of repeated digging in
this famous area by the peasants of this locality.

    The south bank further revealed a clue to the casting
of the bronzes. Early in the spring of 1929 a pottery mould for
bronze casting was unearthed. In the autumn of the same year
they found moulds still attached to bronzes, as well as the remains of some charcoal mingled with the residue of molten copper. Here was a simple statement of proof that the Shang bronzes
were made in Shang territory. We find in the <u>An-yang</u> <u>hsien</u> <u>chih</u>,
vol. 5, that:

> According to <u>Yeh</u> <u>ch'en</u>, T'ung shan
> lies 40 <u>li</u> northwest of the city. In
> olden days it produced copper.

    From the excavations in the first period they found
some tombs with a few bronzes, most probably of the mortuary
type, and some military instruments; but as has been noted, early
lootings had robbed the tombs on the north bank of the fine
Shang bronzes.

    Some bronzes were found in the spring of 1931 in Hsiao-
t'un, although there were still more weapons than sacrificial
vessels. The expedition also excavated the east side of a village
called Ssu-p'an -mo   west of Hsiao-t'un, more than a
mile on the south bank opposite the village of Wu-kuan ts'un
on the north bank. This place was well known to robbers as a
lucrative source for bronzes. The excavators recovered little
more than a few weapons. In the spring and autumn of that year

they made an experimental excavation at Hou-kang where they found pottery of the three strata, Liang-shao, Lung-shan, and Hsiao-t'un. In the following year, the spring of 1932, they achieved the same results at Kao-chin-t'ai-tzu   , northwest of Hou-chia chuang near the river. During the same season they also made another experimental excavation on the east side of Wang-yü-k'ou and Huo-chia hsiao-chuang (sometimes called Hsiao chuang), southwest of Hsiao-t'un, an area also well known to looters. The excavations uncovered a few bronzes.

In the autumn of 1932 the remains of a platform of a house, 28.4 meters long, 8 meters wide and 1 meter high with three rows of pillar bases of natural round stone were found at Hsiao-t'un. The building was oriented with the length running from north to south. On the same site they found a few bronzes, moulds and the slag of earlier castings. In the following autumn season, 1933, again at Hsiao-t'un, they uncovered a single row of pillar bases running north and south, 31 meters long with each pillar two and a half meters apart. Atop the pillar bases were found bronze bases for wooden columns which were evidenced by charred remains.

In the winter season of 1933 and the spring season of 1934 the third and fourth expeditions were made at Hou-kang where they found one large undisturbed Shang tomb and two smaller tombs, all containing bronzes. In the same season they crossed the river to the north bank and excavated Nan pa-t'ai   , northwest of Wu-kuan ts'un, recovering only a few uninscribed oracle bones. In the autumn of 1929 a small expedition was sent to Pa-t'ai near Wu-kuan ts'un which found six tombs, and on the south side of Hou-chia chuang an excavation

recovered only a few bronzes and seven complete tortoise shells.
This closed the first period and, except for the last three excavations mentioned above, they were all on the south bank and
the main efforts concentrated on Hsiao-t'un and its environs.

The second period began in the autumn of 1934 at the
site on the northwest mound of Hou-chia chuang, which we may
call the Royal Tombs of Shang. The excavation covered an area
close to eight acres and from that season until the autumn of
1935 there were three expeditions to the site uncovering ten
large tombs and eight hundred and fifty-eight small tombs. The
large tombs can be divided according to their shapes into cruciform, square, and rectangular. The largest had a surface area of
464 square yards being a wooden chamber in the middle of a pit
with four flights of stairs at the main points of the compass
running down to it. It is similar to the large tomb found in
Hou-kang, but the latter has only two flights of stairs, at the
north and the south, and the arms of the cruciform chamber
measure 4.4 meters and 3.5 meters. All of the tombs are oriented ten to sixteen degrees east of true north. All of the
larger tombs contained a variety of bronzes. Near the tombs
were found pits in which were buried the remains of birds and
animals, one yielding the bones of an elephant. In those tombs
sets of sacrificial vessels were found, some of the bronzes
forming sets of food vessels and others forming sets of wine
vessels.

In the autumn of 1934 a small excavation was made at
T'ung-lu chai   , southwest of Ch'iu-k'ou ts'an. The
three strata were also uncovered at Hou-kang. In the autumns
of 1935 and 1936 there was an expedition to the south side of

Ta-shih-k'ung ts'un. It unearthed some bronzes. In the autumn
of 1935 a small excavation was made at the north side of Fan-chia
chuang, and it uncovered no more than a small tomb already rifled.
This closed the second period. Almost all of the excavations
were made on the north bank.

In the third period, except for the excavation at Ta-shih-
k'ung ts'un, all of the work was concentrated on a thorough uncovering of the Hsiao-t'un village. In the autumn of 1936 and
the spring of 1937 the expedition recovered various bronze vessels which formed sets. The out-break of the Sino-Japanese war
forced an untimely conclusion to these excavations.

These fifteen expeditions excavated twelve sites in an
area to the northwest of the city of An-yang covering about 170.2
square kilometers. The results are given in tabulated form below:

Hsiao-t'un: Shang capital, temple, palace, and pre-Shang
          residences.

Hou-kang: Shang residences and pre-Shang and Liang-shao
          residences.

Ssu-p'an-mo: Shang residences and burials.

Wang-yü-k'ou: Hsiao chuang: Shang residences and burials.

Hou-chia chuang(northwest mound): Shang Royal Tombs.

Hou-chia chuang(south sites): Shang residences and burials.

Kao-chin-t'ai-tzu: Shang residences and Liang-shao residences.

T'ung-lo chai: Shang burials and pre-Shang and Liang-shao
          residences.

Fan-chia chuang: Shang burials.

Nan pa-t'ai: Shang residences and burials and pre-Shang
          residences.

Pa-t'ai: Shang residences and burials.

Ta-shih-k'ung ts'un: Shang residences and burials.

These excavations also discovered tombs which were dated after Shang. They are as follows:

Chan Kuo	Hou-kang and Ta-shih-k'ung
Han	T'ung-lo chai
Sui	Hsiao-t'un
T'ang	Hsiao-t'un and Hou-kang
Sung	Hsiao-t'un and Hou-kang
Ming	Hsiao-t'un
Ch'ing	Hsiao-t'un

There was a preponderance of Sui tombs in this group and it should be carefully noted that not a single Western Chou tomb was found in this area. Since traces of the wooden columns found by the Academia Sinica were charred and other objects discovered by various collectors showed such marks, it may be suggested that this city was burned, probably at the beginning of the Chou dynasty. As we know, at the beginning of the Chou or in the last years of the Shang, Chün-hsien was the real capital of the Shang. Therefore there is little danger in calling these bronzes, found in An-yang, "Shang bronzes."

Besides the knowledge gained from the excavations of the Academia Sinica, we also know the location of the sites from which bronzes were unearthed:

1. Hou-chia chuang: An-yang treasures - 34, 38, 39, 40, 41, 48.

2. Kuo-chia wan: Ontario NB 3213 - 3218; NB 3193 - 3196.

3. Ta-shih-k'ung ts'un: Collection of Ontario Museum, so-called "Elephant Tomb" find. Illustrated London News, April 20, 1935.

The Society for the Preservation of the Antiquities of
An-yang has bronzes that were found at the following places:

1. Hsueh-chia chuang: two rectangular ting, two kuei,
   one yu, one broken tsun, one ku, one chih, one
   chüeh, and one chia. (cf. Sheng kao: 10, 34, 44).

2. Wu-kuan ts'un: one decorated rectangular ting, three
   bow-string ting, one hsien and two plain ku.

3. Ta-shih-k'ung ts'un: two bow-string ting, one plain
   ting, one plain hsien, one decorated ting, two
   hsien, two ku, two chüeh, and one fang-i

4. Fan-chia chuang: one plain ting, one decorated ku, and
   one Shang bell.

5. Hou-chia chuang: one plain Shang bell.

There were other remains unearthed with the bronzes;
white and grey pottery, carved bone, ivory, jade, shell objects,
and stone or marble sculptures. There were also quite a few
military instruments and chariot fittings found, both by Academia Sinica and others.

Date of An-yang Finds: We know that the Shang people lived at
An-yang for two hundred and seventy-three years and the bronzes
found there should be dated in this period (1300 - 1028 B.C.).
It seems to me that the bronzes were used only in the latter part
of the Shang dynasty. On the white pottery found at Hou-chia
chuang and Hsiao-t'un the shape and decoration were different
from and earlier than the bronzes. Only a small part of the
decoration of the white pottery also appears on the bronzes.
Judging from the very few inscriptions incised on the white
pottery, they are similar to those on the oracle bones from the

period of Wu Ting who was ruler during the early days of Shang.
The technique and the decoration on the stone and marble vessels,
on the carved bones and ivory were quite similar to the bronzes.
It seems to me that after the Shang craftsmen had had some experience on carving the mother moulds, then they transferred that
technique to stone, marble, jade, bones and ivories. It is now
too early to divide the Shang bronzes into early and late, but
when there are more materials and the stratification is completely
known this should prove an easy task. The divisions can not be
made only on a basis of a simple or a complex decoration since
most of the bronzes are from the Royal family, some are from the
nobles and the feudal lords and some are from the common people.

There is one point on which I wish to place emphasis,
viz., that the An-yang site is the only place which has Shang
pieces or comparatively late pieces, but it has no relics at
all from Western Chou. As has been mentioned before, Academia
Sinica excavated twelve sites in that large area and found
nothing other than Shang earlier than Chan Kuo. This gave strong
support to the supposition that the Shang capital at An-yang was
ruined during its late days when it was conquered by the Chou.
The burned pillars and the oracle bones and other relics showing
traces of fire may give us a little hint. In the study on the
N1 set I have already pointed out that the Shang capital, attacked
by Wu Wang and Ch'eng Wang twice, was at Ch'ao-kê. It is very
strange that all of those bronzes said to be from An-yang are of
the early type and can be easily distinguished from those of
Middle Western Chou, although there is some similarity with
Early Western Chou pieces. From the Sung dynasty on those
bronzes said to be from An-yang and are attributed to Shang are

not so far from the truth. Jung Keng says, "In 1934 the Academia
Sinica excavated the Shang Royal tombs in An-yang and got a
great deal of bronzes. Comparing them with those bronzes in the
old catalogue they proved the earlier scholars 'statements on
the Shang bronzes to be most reliable." (Shang chou: 1.31) Hsü
Chung-shu (Notes on Yin Bronzes and Yeh chung p'ien yü, K'ao ku
#2, 1935, pp. 34-38) also pointed out that the bronzes which
were excavated at An-yang were very similar to those bronzes
shown in Yeh chung, a catalogue made by a dealer for those bronzes
said to have been found in An-yang.   At that time both of these
scholars were connected with Academia Sinica and saw the bronzes
from the excavations. I myself believe, with very few exceptions,
that the three series of Yeh chung are good examples of Shang
bronzes although they were not found by excavation.

II. Chün Hsien Excavations

The excavations were made in Hsin-ts'un   in the
southwest corner of Chün-hsien   city of Honan province.
The station of the Peiping-Hankow railroad is about 6 li east
of that site. The tombs are located on a gentle slope near
the Ch'i River   . These tombs are located as above mentioned, and were first robbed in the very early days, probably
just after the burial. In recent years they have been robbed
many times. The excavation was made by Kuo Pao-chün under the
auspices of the Honan Archaeological Research Institute which
was conducted, the Academia Sinica and the Honan Provincial
Government. They made four expeditions:

(1) From April 16 to May 26, 1932. Excavated tombs #1 and 2.

(2) From October 11 to December 6, 1932. Excavated
        tombs #3 to 13.

(3) From April 1 to May 24, 1933. Excavated tombs
        #14 to 34.

(4) From October 20 to December 12, 1933. Excavated
        tombs #35 to 88.

More chariot fittings, trappings and weapons were recovered
than sacrificial vessels because the tombs had been robbed
many times and because there were horse pits. There were fifteen sacrificial vessels illustrated in Chün hsien yi ch'i;
these pieces were from six tombs, and there were chariot fittings from these six and other tombs. The larger robberies
were made just a year before the excavations started and a
group of very important bronzes were found, probably in a single tomb. The finds of this group have been listed under the
Ni set and the K'ang Hou set. The Freer Gallery got twelve
weapons (34. 3-14) said to have been found in the same place.
A note, in Chinese, was made by Ch'u Te-i   which says:

> In the 6th month of 1931 at Wei-hui fu
> (the old name of present Chi Hsien) of Honan
> near An-yang district the local people dug in
> the earth and uncovered a pit of ancient wea-
> pons. There were six kê, one mao, two fu and
> three tao. One tao has the two characters
> K'ang Hou inscribed on it. K'ang Shu was the
> younger brother of Chou Ch'eng Wang. Wei-hui
> fu and An-yang district were his fief. There-
> fore, I decided that these twelve weapons were
> relics of K'ang Hou of the Chou dynasty. In
> this group the Ch'ih-yu tao, the sickle-shaped
> tao, the kê with the ox-head and the kê inlaid
> with shells had a remarkable and archaic shape
> and technique. They have never been seen be-
> fore. By those who study early Chou history they
> must be treated as really great treasures.
> Twelfth year of the Republic, 10th month, 11th
> day. Notes by Ch'u Te-i. (No seal or signature).

A copy of this note is now in the Freer Gallery (cf.
Freer Catalogue, p. 91). The contents of this group were

illustrated in <u>Freer Catalogue</u>, pts. 45-49. The date is probably
right; the location is different from that given by Yü Sheng-wu
and other scholars who record Chün-hsien as the place. I believe
that they were found somewhere in the Chi Hsien and Chün Hsien
areas, The tombs of the Ni and the K'ang Hou sets are those of
the ruler of Wei State, which were said to have been found at
Wei-hui or Hui Hsien. They do not belong to any of the eighty-
eight tombs excavated. There are other weapons and chariot
fittings which can be determined as coming from Hsin-ts'un if
we compare them with the Hsin-ts'un finds.

      1. Hou <u>chih</u>   <u>Chün hsien</u>: 29

          a. <u>Sung chai</u>: 33

          b. <u>Shih er</u>: <u>Ch'i</u>: 31

          c. <u>Shan chai ku ping lu</u>: 1.40

          d. Ontario

      2. Pole top jingle   <u>Chün hsien</u>: 61

          a. <u>Tsun ku</u>: 4.38, inscribed 'Hou'

          b. <u>Sung chai</u> II: 124, inscribed 'Hou'

          c. <u>Sung chai</u> II: 125, inscribed 'Hou'

      3. Kê with dragon on blade. <u>Chün hsien</u>: 24

          a. Freer: 34.7

      4. Chariot fitting   <u>Chün hsien</u>: 69

          a. <u>Tsun ku</u>: 4.45, inscribed as above pieces.

    The Ontario Museum got some pieces from Chün-hsien, in-
cluding a helmet (NB 3153). All of the finds were early Western
Chou.

<u>Date of Chün Hsien Finds</u>:   The site of Hsin-ts'un was first
known as "Shang tombs." This designation was later rejected by
excavators. The latter, in the preliminary report, dated it

between 1112 and 600 B.C. according to the traditional chronology, from the beginning of Chou to the last years of Ch'en
Kung of Wei State.   The date given for the close of this period
is quite wrong.   As will be discussed later, the latest period
was not as late as 600 B.C.   The author of the Chün Hsien (catalogue) dated the inscribed tsun (pp. 12-14) to Wu Kung of Wei
State, according to the traditional chronology 812-258 B.C.,
making the early bronzes of this find as late as Late Western
Chou, which is a great mistake.   Based on the limited materials
which were published in that catalogue, I now date them as follows: The relics of nineteen important tombs are in the Chün-
Hsien (catalogue).   A detailed map of the tombs is not given
and only the simple statements of the preliminary reports can
be used.   Taking the village of Hsin-ts'un as a centre, the
tombs excavated outside of the village were in the four directions as follows:

    1. East side

        Tomb 1   In a wheat field.

        Tomb 25   (Horse pits) Near the village east side wall.

    2. Further East

        Tomb 3   (Horse pits: robbed) San chiao wa, further
                        east of the village.

        Tomb 5   Northwest of Tomb 3.

    3. Southeast side

        Tomb 2   Near Ai-t'ou.

        Tomb 42   North of Tomb 2, near the village wall.

        Tomb 4   South of the highway.

        Tomb 8   Twenty meters north of Tomb 4.

        Tomb 19   North of Tomb 8.

4. Northeast side

    Tomb 29   (Undisturbed) Northeast, outside the village.

    Tomb 68   East of Tomb 29.

    Tomb 51   (Undisturbed) Northeast of Tomb 29.

    Tomb 38   At the northeast side of the village.

    Tomb 76   (Undisturbed) Southeast of Tomb 38.

    Tomb 55   (Undisturbed) Southeast of Tomb 29.

    Tomb 60   (Undisturbed) West of Tomb 29.

    Tomb 62   Southeast of Tomb 55.

    Tomb 67   East of Tomb 29.

These nineteen tombs are dated in three periods: the number following the name of the vessel in the parenthesis is the page reference to Chün hsien yi ch'i:

a. Earlier period: not later than Early Western Chou

    Tomb 76   ting (3)

    Tomb 51   plain ho (17)

    Tomb 21   horse bell (68)

b. Early Western Chou

    Tomb 60   ting (4); plain kuei (8); plain hsien (6) tsun (12); yu (15); chüeh (18); fu (weapon) (32c); kê (weapon) (22).

All of these sacrificial vessels were buried at the same time since this tomb was undisturbed. The tsun has the characters for Tsung chou on it. Therefore it is Chou. The ting and the plain kuei may be earlier. The latter is very similar to the pottery kuei (Ontario: NA 2123 and 2157) found at An-yang. These kuei are plain and have no pendant under the ears.

    Tomb 29   plain ting (1); hsien (7); plain kuei (9-10)

This tomb also yielded more than ten kê.   The plain kuei has
pendants under the ears; perhaps it is a little bit later than
Tomb 60.

        Tomb 55   plain ting (2)

The style of the ting is the same as the ting in Tomb 29;   they
are contemporary.

        Tomb 42   plain kê (20, 23-26); openwork mao (31b);
                           fu (32a, b); chih (33, 34) The last three
                           are weapons.
                           chariot fittings(58); yoke (62); mask(73)
                           jade ornament (74).

The kê (25) has the inscription of Ch'eng chou on it, and the
two chih are of a new type. Some of the kê (viz., 20 and 21) remain in the Shang style and some (viz., 23 and 24) are of a typical Chün-hsien style.   Therefore they are dated as Early Western
Chou.

        Tomb 2   chih (27-29) weapons

The chih is contemporary with the one in Tomb 42 which has the
top turned at an angle and is sharpened on one side. Those in
Tomb 2 are sharpened on both sides and are straight upward.   The
latter are a bit later.

        Tomb 8   chih(weapon) (30); chariot fittings (53);
                           mask(71-72)

The chih is contemporary with Tomb 2 and the masks are similar
and may be a bit later than Tomb 42.

        Tomb 1   openwork mao (31a); chariot fittings (50-
                           51); pole top jingle (61); horse bits(66g)

The mao is similar to that in Tomb 42. The jingle of this type
sometimes has the inscription hou on it as often appeared on the
chih of Tomb 2.   Therefore this tomb is contemporary with

Tombs 2 and 42.   In Tomb 1 was found a man buried face down
which practice was also known in the Hsiao-t'un tombs.

       Tomb 68   chariot fittings (69)

This round piece is plain and has the same inscription as found
in the buffalo-head shaped fitting (Tsun ku: 4.45) which shows
that they are Early Chou. The three characters contain a Wei
which is the name of a state.

       Tombs 38, 62, 67, 60, and 4 each show only a single ob-
ject, unimportant, and are tentatively dated under period b.

   c. Late Western Chou

       Tomb 5   chariot fitting (35, 37, 39, 41)

             square toilet case (19)

The pattern is without a doubt of the Late Western Chou. The excavators called this tomb a woman's tomb. A station master,
T'ang Yi-yün   , got a li said to be from this tomb, and
having the inscription "Wen Chùn, the wife of Wei State." If
this information is right, this should be a Wei tomb.

       Tomb 3   chariot fitting (43, 45, 47, 59, 60, 64)

               yoke (63); dog ornament (70).

Although this tomb was disturbed the excavators got almost
twelve complete chariots.

       Tomb 25   chariot fitting (56, 65)

The chariot fitting of (56) is similar to (54) of Tomb 3.

       These three tombs show no direct evidence to prove they
are later than Late Western Chou. It is quite safe to place
them within the Western Chou period.

       In giving the b period I have here and there pointed
out relations and similarities to Shang bronzes. These sites
were occupied by Shang people during the Late Shang and the
Early Chou. Therefore it is natural that the Shang technique

should be evident. The yu (15) has an inscription which gives
a clan name, Ya-Ni, at its close. There are many vessels from
An-yang with the same clan name and therefore it may be said
that this yu was made by some descendant of the Shang. Although
most of the bronzes belong to the Western Chou, it is possible
that there were some Shang bronzes.

III. Chi-hsien Excavations

Shan-piao chen   is a town located on the highway
between Chi   Hsien and Hui   Hsien in Honan province. The
finds here are sometimes referred to as Hui Hsien.   Chi Hsien
was called Wei-hui fu during the old days. At the beginning of
August, 1931, Kuo Pao-chün investigated this site under the auspices of the Honan Archaeological Research Institute and worked
about one month. I saw the report on this excavation some ten
years ago; it has not yet been published.   The bronzes found
are as follows:

Chien	2	Sheng kao: 14-15.
Tou	4	Sheng kao: 13.
Hu	4	Sheng kao: 16-19.
Stand	2	Sheng kao: 45.
Shao	4	Sheng kao: 46.
Ladle	1	Sheng kao: 47.
Chariot fittings		Sheng kao: 48, inscribed.
Weapons - more than 100		Sheng kao: 49, inscribed.
Chariot tools one set		Sheng kao: 50
Hu with swing handle 1		
Ting	5	(Honan Provincial Museum
		has two of the same set).
Kuei	1	

Fu	1
Animal-form tsun	1
P'an	2
Tseng	1
Li	3
Lei	1
Yi	2
Pi	2
Fu(heating vessel)	1
Chung	4
Miscellaneous	

These finds can be dated in the Chan Kuo period. The pair of
Hu (Sheng kao: 16-17) is similar to the Hu in Chan Kuo: 76,
which can be dated 340 B.C. (cf. Chin ts'un finds below).

IV. Chin-ts'un Finds

Loyang   is located in west central Honan near the
Shansi border. During these hundred years there have been many
bronzes uncovered in this area. In many instances the exact
place remains unknown. The statement on Chin-ts'un
is based on Bishop White's book, "Tombs of Old Loyang" and the
information is given by Bishop White.

During 1928-31 the local people robbed the old tombs
on the east side of Chin-ts'un. This place was called, by the
local people, Li-mi city   , a name acquired in the Sui
dynasty from the rebel Li-mi who made it his headquarters. It
is thirteen miles northeast of present Lo-yang. The tombs are
situated in the northeast angle at the northern foot of the
Mang-shan

Bishop William C. White of the Anglican Church of Honan province, who was at that time in K'ai-feng   , through a dealer, Lin Shih-an   , got some of the finds from this site. He himself did not visit the site, but got his information through the dealer and the head of the village of Chin-ts'un, Chang Tzu-mei, and from a carpenter in that same village. From the information of the latter he drew the plan of the Han tomb. A sketch map of Li-mi ch'eng was made by a Chinese engineer. According to Bishop White's statement there were eight tombs in two rows. The first row was 250 feet south of the remains of the old city wall and the distance between the tombs was 200 feet. Some 350 feet further north there were two other tombs. On the east side, between the first and the second tombs , was the so-called Tomb A. Tomb VI was at the west end, and at its north and south were tombs B and C, about 350 feet from Tomb VI. The tombs A, B and C were unvaulted.

The finds from this site are usually called Chin-ts'un finds. This is, however, inaccurate. The materials shown in Bishop White's book are now in the Ontario Museum. They were excavated from Tombs V and VII and Tomb A. The materials are so mixed up that it is not possible to distinguish which piece came from which tomb. Umehara published a book entitled "Select Relics from Chin-ts'un at Lo-yang" which is supposed to show pieces from that site. There are many other bronzes scattered over the whole world.

Date of Chin-ts'un Finds: In Bishop White's book he remarks that the eight tombs are nearly identical, and he calls these tombs "Han (state) tombs." This contention is based on two points: (1) the long inscription on a set of bells which

stated that the owner, Piao Ch'iang, was a subject of the Han
State, and (2) a tou (Lo-yang 109) with two characters Han chün

which he translated as "Prince of Han." These evidences
are very weak. As I shall discuss later, the Piao Ch'iang is
rather earlier than the others. The character he read as Han
on the tou is quite different from the character Han on the bell;
it is in fact not Han. I shall now investigate it and try to
determine its date.

The locality of the so-called Li-mi city, which is also
now called Chiu-t'u ch'eng   , meaning "an old earth-
walled city," It was the old Lo-yang before the Wei-Chin dynasties and probably was the original site of Ch'eng chou during
the Chou dynasty. According to the Shui ching chu
vol. 16, the chapter Ku shui says "Wei Li-wang (425-402 B.C.) of
the Eastern Chou dynasty was buried at the southeast corner of
Lo-yang city. The tomb of Ching Wang (544-520 B.C.) was in the
middle of the great granary."Although the locality of Wei Li-
wang's tomb was somewhere near the eight tombs, which the local
people call 'the five pits'   or 'the five separated tombs',
we have nothing to prove that these tombs are connected with
the Royal tombs. The same source says, "In the Ch'in dynasty
the prime minister, Lü Pu-wei   , was given the incomes
of 100,000 families in Lo-yang. He extended the city and included the tomb of Chin Wang. His (Lü's) tomb was there."
The commentary on the biography of Lü Pu-wei in the Shih chi
quoted the Huang lan saying, "Lü Pu-wei's tomb was in Honan
(district), north of Lo-yang on the highway of Mang-shan. It
is the great westerly tomb." According to the Shui ching chu,
same as mentioned above, "Ming Ti of the Wei dynasty(227-240 A.D.)

built the Chin-yung   city at the northwest of Lo-yang city."
In the same source it is also said that it was later called Chin-
shih   . This is the present location of Chin-ts'un, and the
five pits are between Chin-ts'un and Ti-chüan chen   •
During the Chan Kuo period this place was probably within the borders of the Han State.

The finds at Chin-ts'un cover a long period which can be
divided into several parts:

(1) Hsin-cheng period: a large _ting_, fragments of the
ear, rim and leg (_Lo-yang_: 235) are its remains and they are similar
to a large _ting_ found in Hsin-cheng (_Hsin cheng_: 28-31).   The
covered oval vessel (_Lo-yang_: 321) is similar to the Hsin-cheng
piece (_Hsin cheng_: 124-5) which might tentatively be dated as
Middle Ch'un Ch'iu. The _li_ (_Lo-yang_: 237) is similar to
Hsin cheng, though later.

(2) Piao Ch'iang period: the sets of bells, Piao
Ch'iang _chung_, with the help of the inscription can be dated
404 B.C. with certainty (cf. Chronology, sec. 8).   These Piao
bells have a comma pattern which also appears on a square vessel
(_Lo-yang_: 252), a fragment (_Lo-yang_: 244) and a pair of _hu_
with a crown (_Lo-yang_: 253). We must here notice that a Fu ch'a
chien, a basin, in the Berlin Museum für Volkerkunder (_BMFEA_: 8,
pl. 52), whose inscription dates it to 514-496 B.C., was unearthed in Tai chou   of Shansi province during 1862-1874.
This vessel is puzzling, in that from the inscription it is
one hundred years older than the Piao bells, but from the decoration it is younger. A sword Fu ch'a _chien_ (_Shuang chien_ II: 1.40)
was also found in Chin-ts'un. The characters for _Wu_ and _fu_ are
different from those on the basin. Therefore, I suppose that
the inscription on the basin is unreliable and so place the

comma-pattern around 400 B.C., unless it is some hundred years
before.

(3) T'ien chang hu period; In Lo-yang; 248 there is
a hu. Its whereabouts is unknown. A similar piece is in the
Pillsbury collection (40.45), whose decoration is similar to the
T'ien chang hu of the University Museum (C243). The latter, a
piece of booty from Yen, with the aid of the inscription can be
dated as from the war of 314 B.C. between the Yen and Ch'i
States, and it was made before 314 B.C. This type of pattern
is the forerunner of the patterns found on the inlaid bronzes.

(4) Chin-ts'un period; The Chin-ts'un period is the
name designated for the inlaid vessels having a variation of
the new pattern, the Chin-ts'un style. One of the chariot fittings is in the Ontario Museum (NB 2883) and it has a single
character in rather late Chan Kuo script. These fittings are
shown in Lo-yang 003-017 and 051, and in Chin ts'un (revised);
71-90. The best examples for the inlaid vessels found at
Chin-ts'un were listed in our catalogue under U.S. 108. The
shape of the ting (U.S. 108) is similar to that in the Ontario
Museum (Lo-yang; 233) The latter piece is not inlaid.   There
are three other ting in the Ontario Museum (Lo-yang 232A, B, and
234), the last two showing inscriptions in a late Chan Kuo script.
The style of these two types of ting was popular on the dated
Han ting, plain and without any decoration. The two inscribed
ting in the ROMA recorded their volumes on the vessel, a practice
frequently found on Han vessels. The tou in the Ontario Museum
(Lo-yang; 109, 11-13) are also similar to the Han vessels. The
silver objects and the human and animal figures(Chin ts'un ,

revised: plates 37-57) also belong to that period. All of the objects mentioned above, inlaid or plain, can be dated after 314 B.C. and before 222 B.C., because we do not find a single object of the Ch'in dynasty. Therefore they must be pre-Ch'in.

As I have mentioned before, this locality was once occupied by Lü Pu-wei who died in the year 235 B.C., twelve years before the unification of China. It might be that some of the tombs were of that period. Bishop White obtained two bone rulers and one bronze ruler (Lo-yang: 101), the latter piece was later in the Ferguson collection. They are all 23.1 cm. long, the same length as found in Shang-yang liang   (Chou chin: 6.123b-124a) made in 344 B.C. It was the official measurement of the Ch'in State.

It is obvious that there is a close similarity between the Chin-ts'un style and the Shou-hsien style. Take the ting for example. In Yen k'u: 10, there is a ting which was said to have been found at Shou Hsien in 1942. Its design is the same as that on the ting of Lo-yang: 233, and its general shape is similar to those of Lo-yang: 232 and 234. In both Chin-ts'un and Shou-hsien finds, we have the geometric designs and the inlaid technique.

V. Ma-p'o Finds

In 1929 a great many bronzes were unearthed in a place called Ma-p'o   in the Mang-shan foothills, five li northeast of present Lo-yang. There were from fifty to a hundred bronzes in the find. They are now scattered all over the world. From their inscriptions they may be divided into two groups:

(1) Ling set, Ming Pao set and the Tso-ts'e tien yu.

(2) Ch'en-ch'en set.

All of the first group bear the name of Ming Pao and all
of the second group bear the name of Ch'en-ch'en. All of these
pieces have been listed in the different sets. To my knowledge
there is one tsun of the Ch'en-ch'en which was found before 1892
and is thirty-six years earlier than the Ma-p'o finds. Therefore
these tombs were robbed before 1929. The date of these finds,
which has been discussed in the sets, is Early Western Chou.

Bishop White told me that the Shou Kung set, the buffalo
now in the Pillsbury Collection (36.521) and a yu and a tsun
were found together at Ma-p'o. The latter two are similar to
the Shih shang tsun and yu of the Ch'en-ch'en set.

VI. Hsin-cheng Finds

On August 25, 1923, a retired military officer, Mr. Li
Jui   (K'un-shan   ) found some thirty bronzes when he
dug a well in his back yard, outside the south gate of Hsin-
cheng   city in Honan province, about ten meters deep. He
sold three ting to Chang Ch'ing-lin   and hid the others.
On the first of September, General Ching Yün-p'eng   of
the 14th Army came to Hsin-cheng and hearing about this ordered
Mr. Li to deliver the remaining bronzes to the government. They
were as follows:

Lei (?)	1
Square hsien	1
Fragments	53
Jades	2
Large ting	6
Small ting	3
Kuei	4

Li	6
Fu	2

On the fifth of the same month the government bought the three ting at the original price from Mr. Chang. On the orders of General Ching, excavations were carried out from the third to the fifth of that month and the following articles were recovered:

Ting	6
Cheng	1
Po	4
Chung	17
Square hu	4
Round hu	2
Tan	2
Kuei	4
Fu	4
Yi	1
Oval vessels	2
Lu	1
P'an	1
Fragments	540

On the 7th and 8th the following pieces were recovered from the excavations:

Li	3
Yi	2
Animal tsun	1
Oval vessels	2
P'an	1
Small ting	1
Lid of ting	1

Support	1
Fragments	44

The totals for these excavations are:

Vessels	87
Fragments	637, of which 2 were ornaments to the square _hu._
Jades	2

These pieces were listed in the first volume of Ching's catalogue (Chapter III, no. 5). Further excavations were made from the 12th to the end of the month recovering the following on the dates indicated:

On the 12th

P'an	1
Oval vessel	1
Yi	1
Tun	2

On the 14th

Rings	4
Horse bells	1
Ornament	1
Fragments	5
Jades	4
Cowries	11

On the 18th

Mao	1
Kê	1
Fragments	17
Jades	2
Cowries	329

On the 19th

Chung	1
Pole fitting	1
Ch'ing tile	1
Pottery tou	1
Pottery vessel	1
Sung porcelain	2

On the 23rd

Han tomb tiles	1

Sometimes between the 12th and the close of the month an undated excavation turned up the following pieces:

Pole fitting	1
Chariot fittings	1
Fragments	13
Kê	1
Human bones	3
Jades	3
Cowries	1
Sung porcelain	1
Pottery tou	3
Tiles	6
Animal teeth	23

The totals for these excavations are:

Bronzes	18
Fragments	35
Jades	9
Pottery	5
Tiles	8
Porcelains	3

Cowries	341
Human bones	3
Animal teeth	23

A252

These pieces were listed in the second volume of Ch'ing's catalogue.

Later, Mr. Li presented to the government one animal tooth, one human jaw and three fragments of a human calavaria. There was a Mr. Wang who hid some bronzes which came from this site. In February of 1925 the governor, Hu Chin-yi sent an officer to search Mr. Wang's house in K'ai-feng. He recovered two ting, one with an ear lost, and two covered ting, one with the cover missing. Mr. Wang still had a large chung hidden. It was delivered to the government in 1927 when Mr. Wang got into some legal difficulties.

These bronzes and the other objects are now in the Honan Provincial Museum at K'ai-feng. From a map drawn by Mr. Yen Hsiang-ch'uan   , an officer under General Ching, we learn that the excavation was made in a pit 13 meters, east to west, by 11 meters, north to south. They found the tomb at the depth of 9.5 meters. It was said that the tomb formed an oval covered with vermillion. In it was a skelton and the jades. The bronzes were supposed to surround this forming an oval. A flight of stairs are reported to have been placed at the north-west leading down into the tomb. The head of the body faced the earth. Near this tomb were found bronzes in three places: one at the west, 2.5 meters from the surface; one at the east of the tomb, 5 meters deep and one at the south, 6 meters deep. This statement, though inaccurate, at least gives a hint that all of the bronzes did not come from the same level. They were even mixed with tiles of the Han and Ch'ing dynasties and the porcelains of Sung. It should also be noticed that the important sacrificial vessels were found by Mr. Li and all of the musical instruments were found after the fifth of September and excavated by General Ching. Therefore the musical instruments must have been arranged in some special order.

Date of Hsin-cheng Finds: It is difficult to date the Hsin-cheng finds because they cover a long period and because most of the bronzes have no inscriptions. There are only two vessels with inscriptions; one on a ting is not legible, and the other mentions the prince named Ying-ch'i   , which was a very popular name during that time. Many scholars hold different opinions as to the date of these finds depending on the date given the Ying-ch'i vessel which is not correct because Ying-ch'i can not be identified and even if he could be identified the whole group could not be dated by this, the latest vessel.

Roughly speaking, this group covered the whole of the Ch'un Ch'iu period. Here I take Hsin-cheng i ch'i (the numbers after the names of the vessels are the page numbers) as reference and divide the decorated vessels into three groups:

Group I

Chung: 7-27

Kuei: 69-78

Round hu: 109-113

P'an: 114-115

Animal-form tsun: 91-92

Li: 55-65

Group II

Po: 1-6

Ting: 40-46

Square hu: 95-99

Square hsien: 66-68 (or Group I)

Square hu: 100-108 (or Group III)

Tan: 88-90

   Group III

Large ting: 28-39

Covered ting: 47-54

Tan: 86-87

Cheng: 122

Vessels: 79-81

Fu: 82-85

The shape and decoration of Group I is a continuation of the Late Western Chou style. This group may be placed under the Early Ch'un Ch'iu period. It is quite obvious that Group III is different from Group I and that Group II is intermediate between I and III. Of the two sets of square hu the first is quite near I and the second set with the crane standing on top, is quite near III. I tentatively place Group II as Middle, and Group III as Middle or Late Ch'un Ch'iu period.

The cheng on p. 122 is similar in shape to another vessel which was found in Hsin-yang   , northeast of Lo-yang and not very far from Hsin-cheng (K'ao ku: 5.21). The inscription records the vessel as being a cheng and it was made by the Chiang State which was wiped out by Ch'u in 623 B.C. There is another vessel whose inscription records it as a cheng (Chou chin: 4.35) which was made by Chin Kung Wu   of Chin State. Chin Kung Wu is Ting Kung of Chin (511-475 B.C.). The decoration of that piece is later than Group III.

Thus I suggest that Group III covered Middle Ch'un Ch'iu and Group I was earlier than this, probably early Ch'un Ch'iu.

Group III is later than II but not as late as the close of Ch'un Ch'iu.

VII. I-hsien Finds

It was said that in the year 1892 four vessels with the same inscriptions, mentioning Ch'i Hou, were found in I   Hsien (formerly I-chou   ) of Hopei province. These four pieces formerly belonged to Shen Yüeh and are now in the Metropolitan Museum. The pieces are one _ting_ (13.220.40), one _yi_, one _tun_, and a _p'an_ (13.100.2-4). The _ting_ is a forgery. In _San tai piao_ the _yi_ was catalogued under _ting_, it noted, "In 1892, unearthed in Hopei province." Besides this group there were many military instruments of the late Yen State unearthed in recent years. With very few exceptions, which were found in Shantung, all of the Yen State weapons were unearthed between 1862 and the close of the 19th century, and in recent years.

VIII. Lai-shui Finds

Lo chen-yü said, "In 1890, in the place called Chang-chia wa   of Lai-shui   district in Hopei province, there were unearthed more than ten vessels, all of which had the inscription Pei Po." (_I wen_: 2.22) Some of these are as follows:

Ting	San tai: 2.41.8
Li-ting	San tai: 5.14.8 and Chui i: 4.14
Ting	Hsiao chiao: 2.46.4
Tsun	San tai: 11.26.2
Yu	San tai: 13.26b (Boston 14.84)

The first two vessels form a group and the last three form a group.

IX. Shou-chang Finds

Shou-chang   Hsien is located to the west of Chinan and Ch'ü-fü Hsien in Shantung province. A group of vessels all mentioning T'ai Pao were found in the Liang-shan foothills. There is some confusion as to the number of vessels and the date when they were unearthed. The Chui i: 4.2 says, "They were unearthed between 1851 and 1861." Jung Keng in his Shang chou: 1.46 says, "They were unearthed between 1821 and 1850." They were collected by Mr. Chung Yang-t'ien 鍾養田. They are:

(1) Ting Kai   (Tsun ku: 2.7) Chün ku: 12.5.3.

(2) Hsien   Sumitomo I: 11; Chün ku: 21.42.1.

(3) Ho   Sung chai II: 56; Chün ku: 21.55.1-2.

(4) Ting   Chün ku: 23.50.1

(5) Kuei   Chün ku: 23.82b.

(6) Yu (bird-shape)   Anyang Treasures: 36.

(7) Lu Kung ting   ?

From (1) to (5) were catalogued in Chün ku. There are other bronzes which have the same name of T'ai Pao. Their provenance is unknown. All of the above vessels were found in Shou-chang and belong to the Early Western Chou of the Yen State.

X. Ch'ang-ch'ing Finds

In 1919 there was a group of seven bronzes with the same inscription found in Ke-shan yeh 菌山驛 in the Ch'ang-ch'ing Hsien of Shantung province. Four vessels went to a private Japanese collection (Saito) and appear in Umehara's Shapes: plates, 43. 1-4. The seven pieces are as follows:

Square ting	San tai: 2.27.7.
Lei	San tai: 11.40.5-6.
Chia	San tai: 13.50.7-8.
Chüeh	San tai: 16.3.8
Yu	San tai: 12.47.5-6
Kuei	San tai: 6.11.3
Ku	No inscription

The four vessels before the ku are in the Japanese collection. Judging from the design and the shape of these four
vessels they are all Shang bronzes. (cf. I wen: 4.30 and Shan
tung: 2.2).

XI. Huan-t'ai Finds

Huan-t'ai   sometimes called Hsin-ch'eng   ,
is located to the west of Lin-tzu in Shan tung province. Sometimes after 1875 there was a group of bronzes uncovered in this
area. They were all from the same donor, Chu[4] Tzu. They are:

Ting	San tai: 3.40.1
Fu	San tai: 10.13b
Fu	San tai: 10.14a
Hsü	San tai: 10.36.1
Yi	San tai: 17.30.2

There is another fu, made by Chu[4] Kung (San tai: 10. 17.2-3),
which was found in Ch'i Tung   Hsien, the neighboring district to the west of Huan-t'ai. All of these bronzes belong to
the Ch'un Ch'iu period.

XII. Lin-tzu Finds

Lin-tzu   is located west of Huan-t'ai, north of

I-tou and west of Shou-kuang. It was the capital of Ch'i. The Chin shih lu : 13.2 says, "In the fifth year of Hsuan-ho (1123 A.D.) a farmer of Lin-tzu in the old city of Ch'i, while working in the fields unearthed many antiquities. There were ten bells with inscriptions. The longest inscription had 500 characters. The last mentioned piece was catalogued in Po ku: 22.5-10. It was made between 581 and 554 B.C., by Sung descendants who served under Ch'i Lin Kung. The Chin shih lu: 12.4 says, "In the year 1116 A.D. a farmer of An-ch'iu when ploughing the land got one p'an and one yi. I examined the inscriptions and they were made by Ch'i Hou for a daughter of Ch'u." An-ch'iu is located southeast of Lin-tzu. In the same work (12.2) it says, "During 1086 to 1093 A.D. the people of Lin-tzu at the old city of Ch'i found several vessels. One of them was a p'an which was made by Sung Mu Kung-sun for his daughter."

XIII. I-tou Finds

I-tou Hsien is located southeast of Lin-tzu in Shantung province. In September of 1930 a group of bronzes were found at a place called Su-p'u t'un 蘇阜屯 . Nine pieces are now in the I-tou Public Library. The whole find is as follows:

(1) P'an	San tai: 17.2.5	
(2) Ting	Shantung: 2.61.1	
(3) Ho	Seven characters	
(4) Chüeh	One character	
(5) Chio	Three characters	
(6) Chio	Three characters	
(7) Chih	Four characters	
(8) Ku	Four characters	

(9) Mao   San tai: 20.29b

(10) - (14) Mao   Shantung: 2.50b

      (1), (2) and (3) have the same inscription. The six mao have the same inscription, a single clan-name. All of these pieces are probably Late Shang or Early Western Chou.

XIV. Shou-kuang Finds

      Shou-kuang   Hsien is located east of Lin-tzu. It was the capital of Chi   State. Between 1736 and 1785 a bell of Chi Hou was unearthed at Chi-hou-t'ai   (Chi ku: 3.1-2) by a farmer. It belongs to the Late Western Chou period.

XV. Yi-shui Finds

      Yi-shui   Hsien is located some hundred kilometers south of Lin-tzu. In the Chin so i it says, "I met Hu Shih-ch'i   (1775-1829 A.D.) who told me that in the spring when he was magistrate of I-shui there was a farmer in the fields who unearthed twelve bells.... A dealer got one of them and sold it in Soochow. It was known as Ch'i Hou Po." The Ch'i Hou Po was catalogued in P'an ku: 2.1-13 in P'an Tsu-yin's collection and it says, "In 1870, in the 4th month, it was unearthed from the river bank near Ho-t'u-tzu   in Yang-ho   Hsien of Shansi province." This information is not correct because it was confused with the Lü chung which was unearthed in Yung-ho at that time. Therefore, I prefer Hu's information because I-shui was within the Ch'i boundary and the vessel was made by the descendants of Ch'i Hou.

XVI. Huang-hsien Finds

Huang　　　Hsien is located at the northern end of Shantung peninsula.　In 1896 a group of Early Western Chou bronzes
were found at Lai-yin　　　of this district.　They are:

(1) Ting　　　Meng yi II: 6　*寂疬*

(2) Hsien　　　Sumitomo I: 12　*曾遲鈄*

(3) Ting　　*尤白鼎*　San tai: 2.49.2　*古籥中擀鼎*

(4) Ting　　　Chün ku: 23.80a　*San tai: 4 16.1*

(5) Yu　　　San tai: 13.30.4-5.　*東自*

These finds illustrate the significant point that this
location was probably the point farthest east reached by the
Chou in attacking the rebelling barbarians.　From the inscriptions of (1) and (2) we learn that the Chou army had a camp
there.　This peninsula most probably was occupied by the Lai
barbarians.

XVII. Chiao Hsien Finds

Chiao　　　Hsien is located northwest of Ch'ing-tao in
Shantung province.　In 1857 there were three vessels unearthed
somewhere near an old city in Ling-shan-wei　　　of Chiao
Hsien.　All were in Ch'en Chieh-ch'i's collection (Chia chai:
24.6).　They are:

San tai: 18.17.1

San tai: 18.23a

San tai: 18.23b

They are all measures for the T'ien Ch'i period.

XVIII. Hsin-t'ai Finds

Hsin-t'ai　　　　Hsien is located to the east of T'ai-an

and Ch'ü-fu Hsien in Shantung. From about 1821 to 1850 a group
of bronzes of Ch'i[3] State were found. They are:

Kuei	San tai: 7.41.2-3
Kuei	San tai: 7.42.3
Kuei	San tai: 7.43a
Kuei	San tai: 7. 43b
Kuei	San tai: 7.44a
Ting	San tai: 3.33b
Ting	San tai: 3.34a
Yi	San tai: 17.30.1
Hu	San tai: 12.19
Chao	San tai: 18.18b

All of the inscriptions are similar and the vessels can be dated
in the Ch'un Ch'iu period.

XIX. Ch'ü-fu Finds

Ch'ü-fu   was the capital of Lu State and was located
between T'ai-an and T'eng Hsien. In 1932 a group of Lu State
bronzes was unearthed in a village near K'ung-lin   They
are:

    (1) Yi   Shantung chin: 1.15a (now in Ch'i Lu University)
    (2) - (5) P'u San tai: 10.48-50

        (1) is in the form of a water vessel Yi, but the inscrip-
tion refers to it as yü 盂 . The p'u are in the form of tou
but were called p'u on their inscriptions.   In 1830 a group of
Lu State vessels with the same inscriptions were unearthed by a
farmer of T'eng Hsien in Fung-huan-lin   . They are:

    (1) Yi   Chin so: 1.71; San tai: 17.32a
    (2)-(6) Li   San tai: 5.31b-33b

(7)-(9) Fu   San tai: 10.11.1-3. Same inscription

(10) P'an   San tai: 17.7b

(11)-(12) P'an   Shantung: 1.12b-13

(13) Ting

    (1), (10), (11)-(12) have the same inscriptions and together with the five Li (2) to (6) they formed part of a daughter's dowry in a marriage between the Lu and Chu[1] States. They were all from the same donor and the vessels can be dated in the Ch'un Ch'iu period.

XX. T'eng Hsien Finds

    T'eng   Hsien is located south of Ch'ü-fu. On March 12, 1933, the landlords, the Ch'en Shih-fa   brothers, unearthed twenty-two bronzes at a place one li north of An-shang ts'un   . These finds were afterwards returned to the Shantung Provincial Library. It was said that when the bronzes were unearthed the vessels contained both fish bones and animal teeth. In the same year, from the 24th of October to the 30th of November, the Academia Sinica and the Shantung Provincial Library cooperated on an excavation of the same site. They got a few bronze fragments and a knife. They also found grey pottery and black pottery, bones and stone objects. The bronzes are as follows:

(1) P'an   San tai: 17.17a

(2) Yi   San tai: 17.40b

(3) Ting   San tai: 3.52b

(4) Ting   San tai: 3.53a

(5) Kuei   San tai: 7.49.2-3

(6) Kuei   San tai: 7.50a

(7)	Kuei	San tai: 7.34.3
(8)	Kuei	San tai: 7.34.4-5
(9)	P'an	San tai: 17.4.4
(10)	Yi	San tai: 17.25.4
(11)	Li	San tai: 5.20a
(12)	Li	San tai: 5.20b
(13)	Li	San tai: 5.21a
(14)	Li	Inscription illegible
(15)	Lei	No inscription
(16)	Hu	No inscription

(1) and (2) have the same inscription. When unearthed
(2) and another piece, *a tui* without an inscription, were nested
in the p'an. (3) and (4) have the same inscription and were
made by Chu[1] State. (5) and (6) have the same inscription.
(7) and (8) have the same inscription. The four kuei were
from the same donor, and (9) and (10) were made for the same
person. (11) to (14) have the same inscription and were made
by the Shih   State. These sixteen pieces are now in the
Shantung Provincial Library. They were made by Chu[1], Shih and
other states. They can be dated in the Ch'un Ch'iu period.

XXI. Wu-kung Finds

Wu-kung   Hsien is located east of Fu-fung
Hsien. There is a ting made by the Teng State catalogued in
T'ao chai I: 1.29. Shensi chin shih chih says, "It was found
during Kuang-hsü (1875-1908) in Wu-kung."   It also says that
a lid of a hu made by the Teng State (T'ao chai I: 3.3; Meng
yi I: 1.25) was found in Chou-shih 忠庶 which is south of
Wu-kung. They were all of the Late Western Chou period.

XXII. Mei Hsien Finds

Mei   Hsien is located south of Fu-fung. During the
early days of Tao-kuang (ca. 1821) two very important ting were
unearthed in Li-ts'un   of Mei Hsien. Mei is the neighboring
district of both Fu-fung and Ch'i-shan, and these vessels are
sometimes referred to as coming from Ch'i-shan. They are:

    Large Yü ting   Shang chou: 2.45; San tai: 4.42.43

                       (P'an Tsu-yin's Collection)

    Small Yü ting   San tai: 4.44-45a

                   (Li Wen-jui   Collection)

Chui i: 3.25a says, "During 1821-1850 the river bank of
Ch'i-shan collapsed and three large ting were discovered. All
were in the possession of a Mr. Kuo of this district. When
Chou Yu-ch'iao   was made magistrate of Ch'i-shan he got
one of them (the large Yü ting). In 1874 it came into the
possession of General Tso Chung-t'ang   and he gave it
as a gift to P'an Tsu-yin. I studied it several times in P'an's
house in Peking. In all of my life this ting is the largest I
have ever seen." In Ch'i ku: 2.35-41, Pao K'ang's   notes
also say that it was found in Ch'i-shan and was first in the
possession of a Mr. Sung and then went to Chou. Ch'i ku further says, "During the early years of Kuang-hsü (1875) P'an
asked for a rubbing from Tso and Tso gave the vessel to P'an
as a gift."

The small Yü ting has a longer inscription than the
large Yü ting, but the characters are not so legible. Chün ku
says, "It was unearthed in Ch'i-shan when Li Wen-han
was the magistrate of that district and he got it." The vessel was lost during the period 1851-1861 and for this reason

illustrations of this ting are not available. The two vessels
belong to the Early Western Chou period.

XXIII. Ch'i-shan Finds

Ch'i-shan   Hsien is located southeast of Fung-
hsiang. Before the conquest of Shang it was the old capital
of Chou. Although during the early Chou the old capital was
further east than Ch'i-shan, Ch'i-shan held an important place.
During the late Ch'ing dynasty many important bronzes were
found in this area.

A. K'e set

The problem of the provenance of this group shows some
confusion. Lo Chen-yü wrote, "My friend Wang Kuo-wei, based on
information given by Wang Wen-t'ao   said, 'The K'e vessels were unearthed in the south of Pao-chi   Hsien (Shensi
province) on the southern bank of the Wei   River (Kuan t'ang
chi lin: 18.3).' Recently, I asked the curio-dealer, Chao Hsin-
ch'en   , and he said, 'This vessel really was unearthed
by Mr. Jen's   family in Jen ts'un near Fa-men-shih   of
the Ch'i-shan district (Shensi province).' Mr. Chao had been on
a visit to the Jen village, for P'an Tsu-yin, to buy these vessels
and he said that at that time there were more than 120 vessels
unearthed. The K'e chung, the K'e ting and the Chung I Fu ting
were in the same pit. That was in 1890." (I wen: 3.34-35). But
the notes to the second volume of Chou chin say, "According to
the chronological biography of P'an Tsu-yin, he got the ting in
1899." Jung Keng wrote, "In the year 1890 a group of K'e vessels was unearthed at the Jen village near Fa-men-shih of the
Ch'i-shan district. They are: one large ting, seven small ting
and two hsü." (Shang chou: I.297) However, Lo Fu-yi in his San
tai piao listed only six K'e chung and seven small K'e ting as

being unearthed in Jem village.

The other vessels in San tai piao which were unearthed
at Fa-men-shih are listed as follows:

Kuei	Heng hsien: 1.23
Kuei	San tai: 7.1.3 (lid only)
Kuei	San tai: 7.1.4

The inscription is a picture of a tiger. The design on these
kuei is the same as those on the K'e set. Therefore I believe
that they were unearthed at the same place as the K'e vessels.

    B. Chung I Fu set

        Lo Chen-yü believed, according to information received
from a dealer, that the ting were found with the K'e set in one
pit (I wen: 2-32), but according to Han Ku-ch'in's   note
on a rubbing of a li, "In 1888 there were two kuei (this should
read hsü as recorded on the inscription) and four li found at
the border between Fu-fung and Ch'i-shan." (Chin wen fen yü pien:
12.10b). This was two years before the K'e set was unearthed.

    C. Han Wang Fu set

        In Chün ku: 31.4.2 and 22.10.3   a kuei and a yi made by
Han-wang-fu are catalogued.   Chin wen fen yü pien:
12.10b says, "In 1933 a group of vessels were found in the
Ch'ing-hua chen   of Ch'i-shan." A ting and a p'an
with the same inscription as the kuei were catalogued in Chün ku.
There were two fu (eight characters) that were made by the same
family. The Shensi chin shih chih says, "During the Tao Kuang
(1821-1850) a hsien   was found in Hsien-yang   " which is
northwest of Ch'ang-an. It is catalogued in San tai: 5.7.3 and
was made by the same family.

D. T'ien Wu kuei	Shang chou: II. 298; San tai: 9.13b
Mao Kung ting	Shang chou: II.69; San tai: 4.46b-49a.

According to Chia chai sheng kao, "These two vessels were unearthed at the same time." They were in Ch'en Chieh-ch'i's collection. On one of his rubbings of the Mao Kung ting Ch'en says, "It was unearthed in the late years of Tao-kuang in Ch'i-shan." These two vessels are very important. The kuei is the only vessel which can be dated to Wu Wang's period and the ting has the longest inscription of all known bronzes.

All of the above four groups, except for the T'ien Wu kuei, are within the Late Western Chou period.

E. San tai piao lists two vessels as being unearthed at the same time in the same place in Ch'i-shan. They are two kuei without handles:

> (1) San tai: 6.8.1
>
> (2) San tai: 6.8.4 (Loo 81585, U. S. 456)

These two pieces are Shang bronzes. (1) has the clan name Ho, a man shouldering a kê. It also appears in the Kuo-chia wan finds and in the Ta-ssu-kung finds, both of the An-yang area, all now in the Ontario Museum. In Sung chai II: 34, a kuei is catalogued which was unearthed in Lo-yang with a ting, a lei, a chih, a yu, two tsun and two ku, all with the same inscription of Ho. The character for Ho is more like the An-yang vessels. It seems to me there is little doubt that the An-yang and the Lo-yang finds belong to the same family. If the Ch'i-shan find also belongs to the same family it gives a significant clue that some of the bronzes found in the western territory came from Shang.

F. Shensi chin shih chih says, "In 1899 two li were found in Ch'i-shan." They are:

Sung chai II: 20

T'ao chai I: 2.54

Both have the same inscription and both belong to the Late Western Chou period.

XXIV. Fung-hsiang Finds

Fung-hsiang   Hsien is located west of Ch'i-shan. During the Ch'ing dynasty many groups of vessels were found in this area. They are:

A. San Po set

The Chou chin wen ts'un says that four kuei with the same inscription and a yi with a shorter inscription were found in Fung-hsiang. These vessels were made by San Po for his daughter who married into the Tsê family. There is a San p'an now in the Palace Museum (San tai: 17.21b-22b). The Shensi chin shih chih says, "According to dealer Su's information it was unearthed at Fung-hsiang in the early days of Ch'ien Lung (1736)." San and King Tsê are mentioned on this p'an. There are three bronzes which mention the King of Tsê. The references are as follows:

Yu	San tai: 13.39a
Chih	San tai: 11.19.3-4; Chou chin: 5. 18-19a
Ting	Shih er: Chü 4-5 (11d only)

These three vessels are of Early Western Chou. For the chih, Chou chin wen ts'un says, "It was found in Fung-hsiang in 1917." The other San vessels are of Late Western Chou.

B. Kuo set

(1) P'an   Chou chin: 4.8

      (2) P'an   Shang chou: II. 841; San tai: 17.19

      (3) Kuei   Heng hsien: 1.37

For (1) the Chou chin wen ts'un says, "It was found in Fung-
hsiang in the late years of the Ch'ing dynasty."   There are a
hu (Shuang yü: 17) and a kuei (T'ao chai II: 1.35) with the same
inscription. It was said that (2) was found in the eastern suburb of Pao-chi. The Ch'i ku: 8.15-19 says, During Tao-kuang,
Hsu Hsieh-chün 徐變鈞 was the magistrate of Mei-hsien and he
got this piece at Kuo-ch'uan-shih 擴川司 of Pao-chi. But Liu
Hsi-hai says that it was found in the field of Li ts'un   of
Mei Hsien."   It must have been found somewhere between Fung-
hsiang and Pao-chi. San tai piao says that (3) "was found in the
east suburb of Pao-chi and Fung-hsiang." This group can be dated
to the Late Western Chou period.

    C. Chia set

        Ting   Heng hsien: 1.3; Chia chai: 4.20

        Kuei   Chia chai: 12.11

It was said that the above were found during the Kuang-hsu period.
of the Ch'ing dynasty. This group belongs to the Early Western
Chou period.

    D. Ting   Chin wen li su su chen: 1.10b
This is one of the important Early Western Chou bronzes. It records Chou Kung's attack on the Eastern Barbarians. It was unearthed recently somewhere near Fung-hsiang and Pao-chi. There
is no illustration for it, but it was said that the vessel was
with t'ao-t'ieh and a gold gilt.

              XXV. Pao-chi Finds

   Pao-chi   Hsien is located west of Fung-hsiang. Two

sets of vessels, both with a bronze rectangular stand, were found
in this area. Tuan Fang, in his catalogue, said, "One set was
found at Tou-chi-t'ai 30 li from Pao-chi-hsien, Shensi province,
in the autumn of 1901." (T'ao chai I; 1.1).   I have listed these
finds and discussed them under the Ting set in our catalogue. In
1929 another set of vessels was found at Tou-chi-t'ai   .
The whereabouts and references are not available. A long list of
vessels from this area is given in Chin wen fen yü pien; 12.11.
It is said that the stand, which has sixteen panels, is twice
the length of that belonging to the Tuan Fang set. Beginning in
1932 the Archaeological Department of the Peiping Research Institute made several excavations at Tou-chi-t'ai. The report has
not yet been published. They got a whole chariot and other
bronzes.

XXVI. Han-ch'eng Finds

        Han-ch'eng   Hsien is located northeast of Ch'ang-an
near the Yellow River.   In 1894 four hsü with the same inscriptions were found somewhere on the border between Han-ch'eng and
Ch'en-ch'eng   near P'u chou   . The references are as
follows:

            Tsun ku; 2.17

            San tai; 10.40a (lid lost)

            San tai; 10.41a

            San tai; 10.42b-43a (Yi Lin-kuan's collection)

All of these vessels belong to the Late Western Chou period.

        In 1059 A.D. a ting of Chin State was found in Han-ch'eng.
It is catalogued in K'ao ku; 1.6-8. This vessel is of the Early
Ch'un Ch'iu period.

XXVII. Li-yü Finds

cf Freer. p.58
至理克級表
③Revue des Arts
Asiatiques Tone VIII
Num. III

On the evening of February 28, 1923, a farmer, Mr. Kao
Fung-shan 馬鳳山 , of Li-yü   village, 15 li southwest of
Hun-yüan   Hsien in Shansi province, went to Miao-p'o 廟坡
to dig some earth and discovered some bronzes. These bronzes
were bought by a Mr. Yü. The mayor, Mr. Hsieh En-ch'en 謝思录 ,
heard of it and sent a police official to Li-yu to recover the
bronzes in the name of the government. They were handed over
and stored first in the middle-school and later in the district
library. In 1926, a wealthy local landlord bought the bronzes
under a contract requiring that the full price be paid before
1929. He died in 1927 and his son could not afford to pay the
debt. In 1932 the district government took the bronzes and
planned to sell them for the benefit of an educational foundation. A dealer, Lu Fung-nien 盧丰年 , gave a high price and
then had them transferred secretly to Peiping. The bronzes
were, however, detained by the Committee for the Preservation
of Antiquities of the Central Government, and they have been
kept in the district government ever since then.

A list of the bronzes was presented to the above mentioned committee by the representative of the district. In
Shang Ch'eng-tso's Hun yüan yi ch'i there are only 17
vessels and in Umehara's Study on Chan Kuo Bronzes there are
only 18 of the 26 vessels. Shang got the photographs from Mr.
Shih Po-chai   . On 18 prints there are two views of
one vessel. Shang's photographs are from the same source as
Umehara's, except that Umehara has one more. Umehara's notes
under these photographs read, "Somewhere in T'ai-yüan fu of

Shansi province." The eighteen pieces appearing in Umehara's
book with the plate or figure numbers are as follows: (Shang's
nine vessels and Umehara's eight not listed are those which are
in pairs).

Tsun, in the form of an animal	Plate 20 (1)
Decorated hu (pair)	Plate 6 (1) & fig. 6
Fou (pair)	Plate 16 (2)
Rabbit (pair)	Plate 20 (2)
Ting (pair, upper part decorated, lower part plain)	Plate 3 (1)
Covered ting (pair)	Plate 19 (1)
Covered ting (pair, with three birds on lid)	Plate 3 (2)
Ting (pair, cover lost)	Plate 4 (2)
Covered vessel with three legs	Plate 6 (2)
Tun (pair, two halves)	Plate 9 (1)
Tou (with four animal ears)	Plate 9 (2)
Tou (with ring ears)	Plate 19 (4)
Elliptical vessel (pair)	Plate 19 (3)
P'an	Plate 15
Plain hu	Plate 19 (2)
Hsien (lower part)	Plate 4 (1)
Chariot fitting	Figure 9

Many of the Li-yü bronzes went abroad. Umehara lists,
in his book, nine collections which had Li-yü vessels:

1. L. Wannieck (Paris)

14 vessels

1 weapon

12 chariot fittings and misc.

4 objects of horn

7 pottery fragments and jades

2. Freer Gallery (Washington, D. C.)

    1 vessel

    1 weapon

3. Metropolitan Museum (New York)

    1 <u>tou</u>

4. H. J. Oppenheim (London)

    1 rabbit

5. C. L. Rutherson (London)   *Charles Lambert*

    1 spoon

6. M.F.E.A. (Stockholm)

    1 lid fragment

7. C. T. Loo (Paris)

    3 fragments of a vessel

8. Cologne Museum (Germany)

    1 <u>ting</u>

9. Fujii Collection (Kyoto)

    1 <u>yi</u>

    1 rabbit

Jean Sauphar
及
Musée Cernuschi

All of these pieces are illustrated in Umehara's book
(plates 1-28). Of these 47 pieces many are similar to the 26
pieces of the original list and some of them are mates with
the pieces of that list. In the preface to his book Shang
wrote, "Those [bronzes] sold by the peasants were: two bronze
helmets, one yellow and one white, diameters of seven to
eight inches with a depth of half that; three covered <u>ting</u> with
three birds on the cover, height eight to nine inches; two <u>hu</u>
decorated with a three-legged animal, height 13 inches; one bronze
gourd, height 12 inches, with stand; inlaid swords and broken
swords, a pair each; one jade; a number of arrowheads, about one

inch in length and some gold leaves. Two small <u>tsun</u> in the form
of animals, a vessel with a round and a flat bottom   and a
rectangular vessel were damaged during the excavation." From his
description we know that the two inlaid swords were those two
weapons listed before in the Wannieck and Freer Collections, and
the covered <u>ting</u> with the three birds is also in the Wannieck
Collection. To my own knowledge, in the Spring of 1934 at a
place called Liu-lang-ch'eng 六郎城 of the Hun-yüan district,
the peasants unearthed two swords, one <u>ting</u>, one helmet, and
one which was probably a <u>hsien</u>. There are many other bronzes
from this district which have the same typical Li-yü decoration.
Therefore we may classify these bronzes under the 'Li-yü style.'

<u>Date</u> <u>of</u> <u>the</u> <u>Li-yü</u> <u>Finds</u>:   The date of the Li-yü finds is very
difficult to ascertain because the shape and decoration of the
Li-yü vessels are not conventional. All of the bronzes, with
the exception of two swords and one <u>pi</u> (<u>San</u> <u>tai</u>: 18.30a), are
without inscriptions. The script of the three exceptions is of
the Ch'un Ch'iu style. The decoration not only has its typical
style but there are also some new shapes. There are three
characteristics of the Li-yü bronzes: (1) a typical Li-yü
pattern which appears on most of the bronzes found in Li-yü
and also on the bronzes from P'ing-ting and T'ai-yüan, all of
Northern Shansi province; (2) it has a braided-cord band and
(3) it shows realistic animals on top of the lid or serving
as ears.

        It is fortunate that a pair of <u>hu</u> was found in 1935
near Chi-hsien in Northern Honan. Both of these are now in
the Cull Collection (<u>Cull</u>: 12). They were formerly in the

Worch Collection in Paris. It is also said that a set of _chung_
was found together with the _hu_. They are:

(1) Vereeniging van Vrienden der Aziatische Kunst in
    Amsterdam (cf. A Datable Pair of Chinese Bronzes
    by W. P. Yetts. _Burlington_ _Magazine_ LXX (1937)
    8-12, fig. 1, plate 1).

(2) M. A. Stoclet Collection. _London_ _Exhibition_: #181.

(3) Berlin State Museum. Kummel: _Chinesische_ _Bronzen_:
    Plate, 17.

(4) Winthrop Collection (now in the Fogg Museum: 43.52.180
    Chan _Kuo_: 99).

(5) Winthrop Collection (now in the Fogg Museum: 43.52.178).

Yetts listed (1) to (4), but (3) was published in 1928 and the
_hu_ were said to have been found in 1935.

The decoration of the _chung_ is similar to that of the
pair of _hu_. The inscription on the _hu_ told of the important
historical meeting between Chin and Wu recorded in the thirteenth year of Ai Kung in the _Ch'un_ _ch'iu_ (482 B.C.) (Cf. my
article, "A Study of the _hu_ of King Yu Han " _Yenching_ _Hsüeh_ _Pao_,
no. 21, pp. 207-299 and Yetts, W. P. _The_ _Cull_ _Bronzes_, pp. 45-75).
Therefore the _hu_ was made after 482 B.C.

The area around Chi-hsien was occupied by the Chin State
during the Ch'un Ch'iu period. The _Tso_ _chuan_ (Hsiang 23) says
that in 550 B.C. "Ch'i Hou attacked Chin and captured Ch'ao-kê."
In the thirteenth year of Ting Kung (497) it says, " [Ch'i
attacked Ho-nei   " which is now Chi Hsien of Honan. The
decoration of the _hu_ fits the three characteristics of the Li-yu
style mentioned above. The pattern in the middle part, one
zone from the bottom, also appeared on the animal-shaped _tsun_

found at Li-yü (Chan Kuo: 20.1).   Therefore the Li-yü finds must
be contemporary with the hu.   In Chan Kuo: plates 3.2 and 4.3
two ting are shown that were found in Li-yü which have a pattern
other than the typical Li-yü style.   They are similar to a ting
in the Ontario Museum: NB 3229, found in Chi Hsien of Honan.
Most of the Chi-hsien finds of this period were of the Li-yü
style.   Therefore, I date the Li-yü finds as Late Ch'un Ch'iu
or Early Chan Kuo. All of the bronzes found in Li-yü are contemporaneous with each other.

We may call the bronzes that were found at Li-yü the
'Li-yü style.'   They were made under the Chin State and to this
day the same term 'Chin' is used as an abbreviation for Shansi
province, so that they may be called the 'Chin style' as well.
The northern part of Shansi was the territory of Chao before
and after the extermination of Chin in 369 B.C.   Therefore
they may also be called the 'Chao style.'

XXVIII. P'ing-ting Finds

P'ing-ting   Hsien is located in middle Shansi near
the Hopei border.   In April of 1923 Dr. George Crofts bought
some bronzes for the Ontario Museum which were unearthed in this
district.   They are:

Hsien	NB 5297
Ting	NB 5292
Ting	NB 5304

The hsien in design and shape is quite near the Li-yü
style, and the ting is near the Chi Hsien style of Honan.   It
is interesting to note that Hun-yüan, P'ing-ting of Shensi
and Chi Hsien of Honan are nearly in the same straight line
north and south, with P'ing-ting midway.

XXIX. T'ai-yuan Finds

T'ai-yuan is the capital of Shansi province. A tsun in the form of a bird in Mrs. Meyer's Collection is shown in Shina kodo: 193. This piece is also shown in I shu lei cheng which says that it was found in T'ai-yuan. Since the decoration of this piece is of the Li-yü style and the inscription is similar to those on the bronzes made by Chih   of Chin State, this ascription of provenance is correct.

XXX. Yung-ho Finds

Yung-ho   Hsien is located south of Chi-hsien in Shansi province. A group of about fifteen bells, made by Lü X, was found near Hou-t'u-tz'u   of Yung-ho Hsien. P'an Tsu-yin got four of them and noted "They were found on a bank of the Yellow River during 1851-1861." (P'an ku: 1.9) Wu Ta-cheng says, "They were found near the river bank of Hou-t'u-tz'u of Yung-ho Hsien. In the early years of T'ung-chih (ca. 1862) the river bank collapsed and uncovered many vessels. A dealer from Ch'ang-an, Mr. Lei, got twelve bells of this set. P'an got nine and I got one." (Chia chai: 1.7.11) These are of the Ch'un Ch'iu period.

XXXI. T'ien-shui Finds

T'ien-shui   Hsien is located in Kansu province near the Shensi border. It was formerly called Ch'in chou In the early days of the Republic a kuei made by Ch'in Kung

was found there. The reference is <u>Shang</u> <u>chou</u>: II.344 and <u>Ta</u> <u>hsi</u>:
fig. 127. It was most probably made by Ch'in Ching Kung(576-
537 B.C.). A bell found during the Sung dynasty, catalogued in
<u>K'ao</u> <u>ku</u>: 7.9, has the same inscription. According to <u>Kuang</u>
<u>ch'üan</u> <u>shu</u> <u>pa</u>   a <u>kuei</u> of Ch'in Kung was found at
Shang   Hsien southeast of Ch'ang-an which may have the same
inscription as the above two pieces.

XXXII. <u>Shou-hsien</u> <u>Finds</u>

     Shou   Hsien was called Shou chou   during the
old days. Before the large excavation made in 1933 many bronzes
were unearthed in the previous decade. At that time a Swedish
engineer, Ovar Karlbeck, stationed at Peng-pu   in Anhui
province, got many chariot fittings, buckles, mirrors, and a few
vessels. Some of these pieces are now in the collection of
H.R.H., the Crown Prince of Sweden. From then on the so-called
Huai style was well known. In 1931 there was a flood in this
area and in the following year there was a drought so the local
people decided to make an excavation. They selected Li-san-ku-
tui   , three <u>li</u> south of Chu-chia chi   and
about thirty <u>li</u> southeast of Shou Hsien city in Anhui province.
This locality was selected because in 1909 a great flood
caused the ground to sink revealing the presence of tombs below
the surface of the ground. The Chu-chia chi families, all sur-
named Chu, and the P'ang family excavated this site together.
The excavation began with one hundred and twenty-four workmen
under twelve heads on the 11th of April and lasted into the
summer, a total of ninety-two days in 1933. In the first month
nothing was discovered, so they invited three experts with long

experience in tomb robbing from Honan province as advisers. On
the 14th of June they began to unearth bronzes and until the 12th
of July when the worked stopped they had uncovered more than
800 pieces. The excavation was halted by the government and the
bronzes were taken from the local people and transferred to the
Anhui Provincial Library in An-ch'ing   . Nevertheless,
some of the bronzes had already been given over to dealers and so
were scattered.

In November, 1934, the Academia Sinica sent Li Ching-
tan   to this site to investigate the Chu-chia chi and
twelve pre-Ch'in and eight post-Ch'in sites. He published his
findings under the title, "Report on the Preliminary Investigation
of the Ch'u Tombs at Shou-hsien, Anhui." (T'ien yeh k'ao ku pao
kao: #1, 1936). The finds were scattered in the following places:

Institutions

Anhui Provincial Library	712 (22 vessels inscribed)
Shou Hsien Public Library	30
Shou Hsien Educational Office	11
Shou Hsien Financial Committee	23
National Library, Peiping	10 (Cf. Ch'u ch'i t'u shih)
Committee for the Preservation of Antiquities of the Central Government	2
Ch'i Lu University	7

Private Persons

Fang Jo	10 (Shih er: Pao 1-16)
Liu T'i-chih	4 (Shan chai (d): 3.54-5; 12.2-3; Shan chai: 104-105)
Yeh Kung-ts'o	1 (Shih er: Hsia 10)
Yü Sheng-wu	1 (Shuang chieh II: 1.45)

Chu (Shanghai)   1

Chang   1

Anonymous   1

Local Persons

Chu Wen-han   15

Chu Jung-kan   2

Yü Sheng-wu had another piece which later went to Jung Keng. Jung Keng added it to the National Library of Peiping. These ten pieces were originally in Tsun ku chai's Collection (Shih er: Tsun 17-19). The two hu of Shan chai (d) were later in the collection of the National Central Museum.

Shou Hsien was called Shou-ch'un   in Late Eastern Chou. According to the Ch'u shih chia of the Shih chi, in the twenty-second year of Ch'u K'ao Li Wang "Ch'u moved its capital eastward to Shou-ch'un, and called it Ying." In the fifth year of Fu Ch'u the state was exterminated by the Ch'in. According to the Liu kuo piao of the Shih chi, the last year of Ch'u was the twenty-fourth year of Ch'in Shih Huang Ti, but according to the Ch'in shih huang pen chi, Ch'u was conquered in the twenty-third year of Ch'in Shih Huang Ti. Therefore the Ch'u made their capital in Shou-ch'un for only eighteen or nineteen years, from 241 to 224/3 B.C. The sacrificial vessels found on this site belonged to the last two kings, Yu Wang and Fu Ch'u, but there were many weapons of an earlier period.

XXXIII. Lin-chiang Finds

Lin-chiang   Hsien is located in central Chiangsi

province. The <u>Hsi</u> <u>ch'ing</u> <u>chia</u>: 17.2 says, "In 1761 a farmer
of Lin-chiang ploughing the land got 11 ancient bells. The
governor presented them to the court." Nine bells are catalogued
in <u>Hsi</u> <u>ch'ing</u> <u>chia</u>: 17.2-18. There are now in the Palace Museum
two bells which are the only ones known remaining. The other
nine were probably burned during the Boxer Rebellion in ~~1859~~.*1900*.
There is another bell, formerly in Liu T'i-chih's Collection
(<u>Shan</u> <u>chai</u>: 14), now in the National Central Museum, which also
belongs to this set. This set of bells was made by the king of
Wu named P'i Kao   , sometimes between 700 and 655 B.C.

In <u>Shan</u> <u>chai</u>: 16, there is a bell with an inscription
of about 60 characters of which only half are legible, which was
said to have been found during the Ch'ing dynasty in this district.

XXXIV. <u>Kao-an</u> Finds

Kao-an   Hsien is located north of Lin-chiang. The
<u>Chou</u> <u>chin</u>: 5.137 says, "In 1888, 4th month, when a farmer, Mr.
Hsiung, was digging in the field 45 <u>li</u> west of Kao-an, called
Ch'ing-chuan shih   , he got nine <u>to</u> and three <u>chih</u>,
(two) <u>to</u> were presented to P'an Tsu-yin." They are as follows:

<u>Chih</u>	<u>Chou</u> <u>chin</u>: 5.136a
<u>Chih</u>	<u>Chou</u> <u>chin</u>: 5.136b
<u>Chih</u>	<u>Chou</u> <u>chin</u>: 5.137-8
<u>To</u>	P'an Tsu-yin's Collection
<u>To</u>	<u>San</u> <u>tai</u>: 18.3-4, in P'an Tsu-yin's Collection.

Two of the <u>chih</u> mentioned Yi Ch'u   , the king of

Hsü[2], who was also mentioned in the sixth year of Chao Kung in the Tso chuan. Therefore this group probably belongs to 536 B.C.

XXXV. Chia-yü Finds

Chia-yü   Hsien is located southwest of Hankow. The Chin shih lu: 11.5 says, "In 1113 A.D. a bell was found in Chia-yü hsien." It was catalogued in Hsüeh shih: 6.68. It was made by the king of Ch'u, probably between 799 and 791 B.C.

XXXVI. Hsiao-kan Finds

Hsiao-kan   Hsien is located northwest of Hankow. The Chin shih lu: 13.1 says, "In the year 1118 A.D. a farmer of the Hsiao-kan district while ploughing the land got three square ting, two round ting and one hsien. The farmer reported it to the provincial governor and they presented them to the court. The casting was excellent and the inscriptions were archaic." These are the so-called 'six vessels from An-chou   . The Po ku t'u gives similar information. The vessels are:

Square ting	Po ku: 2.19
Square ting	Po ku: 2.20
Square ting	Po ku: 2.21
Round ting	Po ku: 2.16
Round ting	No reference
Hsien	Hsüeh shih: 16.172

In the Po ku the three square ting are plain. The second round ting was not catalogued in the Sung works and therefore Kuo Mo-jo thought that it might be the chih catalogued in

Po ku: 6.32. The Hupei chin shih chih   says, "In 1574 when building a moat a case was found which contained a ting." The inscription was said to be similar to that of the square ting. All of these vessels belong to the Early Western Chou period.

XXXVII. An-lu Finds

An-lu   Hsien is located northwest of Hsiao-kan. The Hsüeh shih: 6.7 says, "This bell was found in An-lu." The bell was made in the fifty-sixth year of Ch'u Hui Wang, 433 B.C.

XXXVIII. Ch'ang-sha Finds

Ch'ang-sha   Hsien is the capital of Hunan province. In 1936 and 1937 a great many antiquities were uncovered near the city. Mr. John H. Cox of New Haven, Conn., who was teaching in the middle school, Yale-in-China, brought home some of the finds and exhibited them at the Gallery of Fine Arts in Yale University. In 1937 when I was in Ch'ang-sha I told Shang Ch'eng-tso to begin to collect these finds. He got all the information and bought some of the finds for the Institute of Chinese Cultural Studies of the University of Nanking. In 1939 Shang published his results in a work called Ch'ang-sha ku wu wen chien chi in a woodblock edition by the above institution. In this book I wrote a preface discussing the dates of the finds.

There are many finds which belong to the post-Han period which I shall not discuss. For the pre-Han period the most interesting finds are not the bronzes but rather the wooden figures of humans and animals, lacquers and pottery, in-

deed they are so wonderful that they have not been equalled
elsewhere. In the Cleveland Museum a pair of lacquered cranes
standing on a serpent and a wooden sculpture owned by Mr. Cox
are two excellent examples of the lacquer and woodwork. Mr. Cox
found small bronze fittings, bronze mirrors, weapons and weights,
and Shang found weapons, a lid of a vessel and mirrors. A sword
made for the king of Yüeh was found there also. One of the
Ch'ang-sha mirrors formerly in the Cox Collection is now in the
Freer Gallery (Freer Catalogue: plate 36)

If the pottery ting found by Cox is compared with the
bronze ting in the Ontario Museum (NB 6213) and in Stockholm
the likeness is at once clear. There is no doubt but that the
pre-Han finds of Ch'ang-sha belong to the Ch'u State. In my
preface to Shang's book I adopted the terms used by Yang
Hsiung   in his Fang yen   , to divide the Ch'u bronzes
into three periods.

(1) Ching-ch'u   : Before the twenty-second year of
K'ao Li Wang of Ch'u, 241 B.C., when the capitals of Ch'u were
in the Ching area, now Hupei province.

(2) Nan-ch'u   : About the years of Ch'u Huai
Wang (328-299-278 B.C.). Ch'ang-sha was located in the
southern Ch'u area.

(3) Huai-ch'u   : After 241 B.C., the Ch'u capital was located at Shou-ch'un near the Huai River. It is now
called Shou Hsien, in Anhui province. The Shou-hsien finds are
of this period.

IV (appendix)

Notes on Chapter 4

a. For An-yang excavations, see

    1. <u>An-yang Fa Chüeh Pao Kao</u>

       Preliminary Reports of Excavations, Parts 1-4,

       pp. 1-733. Edited by Li Chi, Academia Sinica, 1929-1933.

    2. <u>Lu t'ung pieh lu</u>   , Academia Sinica, 1945.

       Li Ch'uang. Three articles by Shih Chang-ju

    3. <u>Yenching Hsüeh Pao</u>

          No. 17, pp. 199-204

          No. 19, pp. 228-229

          No. 20, pp. 594-595

          No. 21, pp. 282-292

    4. W. P. Yetts, <u>An-yang: A Restrospect</u>, London, 1942

    5. Chapter III, no. 109

b. For An-yang Finds, see

    1. <u>An-yang Fa Chüeh Pao Kao</u>, Part III, p. 480, pls. 5, 7,

       9, 11, 15.

    2. "Important Discoveries in the Last Five Excavations

       made at Hsiao-t'un," <u>Liu t'ung pieh lu</u>, part 1, pls. 3,

       4, 10-13.

    3. Chapter III, no. 109, fig. 4-14

    4. Chapter III, nos 106-108

    5. Chapter III, nos 15, 22, 31

    6. <u>Studies Presented to Ts'ai Yüan-p'ei</u>

       Part 1, pp. 73-104

    7. Chapter III, nos. 94, 96

8. Sueji Umehara, <u>Etude sur la Poterie Blanche Fouillee dans la Ruine de L'ancienne Capitale des Yin</u> 殷虛白

色土器之研究 Kyoto, 1932.

9. Chapter III, no. 97, pp. 326-390

c. For Chün Hsien excavations, see

1. Kuo Pao-chün, "Preliminary Report on the Excavations of the Ancient Cemetery at Hsin Ts'un, Hsün, Honan." <u>T'ien yeh k'ao ku pao kao</u>, no. 1, pp. 167-200, pls. 1-12. Academia Sinica, 1936.

2. <u>Yenching Hsüeh Pao</u>, no. 17, pp. 196-199

∂ ←——— For Chün Hsien finds, see

Chapter III, no. 25

d. For Chi Hsien excavations, see

<u>Yenching Hsüeh Pao</u>, no. 18, pp. 200-202

e. For Chin-ts'un finds, see

Chapter III, no. 93, 143.

f. For Hsin-cheng finds, see

Chapter III, nos. 5, 7, 9, 23, 53

g. For finds in Shantung province, see

Chapter III, no. 76

h. For Ch'ang-sha finds, see

<u>Ch'ang-sha ku wu wen chien chi</u> by Shang Ch'eng-tso. Preface by Ch'eng Meng-chia. Series A of the Institute of Chinese Culture Studies, University of Nanking, 1939.

<u>An Exhibition of Chinese Antiquities from Ch'ang-sha</u> Lent by John Hadley Cox. Gallery of Fine Arts, Yale University, 1939.

j ←—— For general information on finds in China, see K'ê Ch'ang-chi, <u>Chin wen fen yü pien</u> , 4 <u>ts'e</u> in 21 vols. 1930.

L 137

CHAPTER V

Geographical Distribution

I. The Geographical Distribution of States

II. Family Relationships among the States

III. Cultural Relations and Influences

Tables:

1. Names of States

2. ~~Names of States on Bronzes and in Literature~~

3. Duration of States (under Chronology Chapter)

CHAPTER V

Geographical Distribution

In studying the geographical distribution of the
bronzes it is necessary to give a short survey of the various
states during the Shang-chou period. As to the Shang dynasty
there are a few records of the feudal lords which bear little
relation with the bronzes. Ssu-ma Ch'ien in his Shih chi
listed the twelve most important feudal lords, beginning from
Late Western Chou, in his Shih er chu hou nien piao. He
also made another table, Liu kuo nien piao, for the six major
states after 476 B. C. to succeed the previous one. During
the Ch'un Ch'iu period (770-481 B.C.) there were some one hundred and twenty states, both large and small. Still there
were many other small states seldom mentioned in written
documents. Here we shall confine ourselves to those states
which were mentioned on the bronzes, and we shall exclude those
which represent only a family, a clan or those which can not
be determined to be a state.

The boundaries of most of the states were uncertain
and for a long period they were subjected to much shifting and
change. Some of the historical maps attempted to plot the area
of certain states at certain times. They are quite helpful, but
hardly accurate. For instance, the area of Ch'i during the
Chan Kuo period can not be given for the reason that it changed
too frequently on a single map. Usually, the capital represents

rigidly the focus of the state and the removal or establishment of new capitals due to political, economic and military situations, resulting in the migration of its people and its culture. Thus in order to trace the geographical distribution of the bronzes it is necessary to follow closely the history, and the changing of the capitals of the different states during different periods. Consequently, I shall present the geographical distribution under headings of states which were grouped together according to their location in different areas.

The bronzes of Shang and Chou were found in the provinces of Honan, Hopei, Shantung, Shensi, Shansi, Kansu, Chiangsu, Chechiang, Anhui, Chiangsi, Hupei and Hunan. Take Lo-yang, longitude $112\frac{1}{2}°$ latitude $34\frac{3}{4}°$, as a center the sphere of the important activities of states were within the area of longitude 105-123, latitude 30-40, which forms a clearly defined unit. Likewise, the whole territory can be divided into eight areas as follows:

A. **Shensi area**   (Wei River Valley)

B. **Shansi area**   (Fen River Valley)

C. Northern Honan area

D. Central Honan area   (on both banks of the
                                Yellow River)

E. Southern Honan area   (near the Huai River)

F. Hopei area   (I River Valley)

G. Shantung area

H. Chiang Huai area   (covering Hupei, Hunan,
            Chiangsi, Chiangsu, Anhui and
            Chechiang provinces)

These eight areas can be reduced into five main groups:

Western group   A.

Central group   C, D, E.

Northern group   B, F.

Eastern group   G

Southern group   H

The study of location, extermination and the family relations of each state are thus treated below.

I. The Geographical Distribution of States

A. Shensi area

All of the names of the places are in Shensi province except as otherwise indicated.

1. Ch'in: The Ch'in has a family name, the same as the Huai tribes, which was a branch of the Eastern barbarians. In the Ch'in pen chi of Shih chi the same legend of the first ancestor as being born from a bird's egg is told of the Ch'in. Therefore, although the Ch'in lived in the westernmost part of China, they may have come from the east. At the time when Chou moved the capital to Lo-yang in 770 B.C., Ch'in occupied the Chou territory in the western land. According to the Ch'in pen chi the capitals were as follows:

Wen Kung (765 B.C.)   Hsi-ch'ui

Ning Kung (714 B.C.)   P'ing-yang

Tê Kung (677 B.C.)   Yung

Hsien Kung (383 B.C.)   Li-yang

Hsiao Kung (350 B.C.)   Hsien-yang

Hsi Ch'ui is somewhere near T'ien Shui in Kansu province. It seems to me that before Wen Kung the Ch'in lived in
that area. In the second year of Ning Kung, who was the grandson of Wen Kung and succeeded him, he moved to P'ing-yang, west
of the present Ch'i-shan   Hsien. Yung was near present the
Feng-hsiang   Hsien. In the second year of Hsien Kung, he
made Li-yang his capital, which is near the present Ling-t'ung
Hsien. In the twelfth year of Hsiao Kung, Hsien-yang
near Ch'ang-an   was made his capital. Therefore, after
Wen Kung, the Ch'in State occupied the Wei Valley which formerly
belonged to Chou. One of the Ch'in bronzes was found in T'ien
Shui, their old territory. According to the Ch'in pen chi, from
the time of Wen Kung they began to keep records of their history. It seems to me that the Ch'in became important during
the Late Western Chou. At the beginning of the Eastern Chou period
they occupied most of the Western Chou territory and had adopted
the Chou culture. That is why, from that time to the unification under Ch'in in 221 B.C., the Ch'in script was more conven-
tionalized and so preserved more of the Chou style than did the
other states.

Hsien-yang was Ch'in's capital until the extermination
by the descendants of six states in 206 B.C.

2. Western Kuo: There were three Kuo: Ti li chih of
Han shu says, "The Northern Kuo was at T'ai-yang   (present
P'ing-lu   Hsien in Shansi); the Eastern Kuo was at Jung-
yang   (present Jung-yang   Hsien in Honan); and the
Western Kuo was at Yung   (present Feng-hsiang   Hsien,
in Shensi)."· The Northern Kuo was located at the old site of

YU   so in Cheng yü of Kuo yü, it was called Yü-Kuo and was
exterminated by Ch'in in 655 B.C.   The Western Kuo may be identified with the Small Kuo   which was exterminated by Ch'in
in 687 B.C.   The Eastern Kuo was taken over by Cheng during the
end of Western Chou.

3. Chou: The northern part of Shansi province is called
Ta Hsia   , the ancient site of the Hsia. It was within
the curve of the great bend of the Yellow River which turns
eastward here as it flows down from the north. Here many barbarians called the Jung   lived. Among them were two Tribes,
the Chou and the Chiang   , which intermarried. The first ancestor of the Chou was called Hou Chi   meaning "The God of
the Millet." This shows that the Chou, in its early days, was
an agricultural community. According to Chou pen chi of Shih
chi the capital was moved as follows:

Ch'ing Chieh:	Pin
Ku Kung:	Foothill of Ch'i mountain
Wen Wang:	Feng
Wu Wang:	Hao Ching
P'ing Wang:	Ch'eng Chou

It is my belief that Pin was in Shansi province and that
before Kung Liu the Chou tribe lived in Shansi in the valley of
the Fen River   . Ku Kung moved to the Wei   Valley of
Shensi. Ch'i is somewhere near present day Ch'i-shan   Hsien.
Feng is east of present Hu   Hsien, and Hao Ching is somewhere
near present Ch'ang-an. During Western Chou the western capitals were in the Wei Valley and the eastern capital was at
Ch'eng Chou about 30 li northeast of present Lo-yang   of

Honan province.   On the Western Chou bronzes we find the following capitals:

      (1) Tsung Chou

      (2) Chou

      (3) Ch'eng Chou

      (4) P'ang Ching

    In several cases more than one of the above capitals
were mentioned on a single bronze:

      (a) Mentioned both Tsung Chou, P'ang Ching
          and Ch'eng Chou (cf. Ch'en Ch'en H̲o̲
          catalogue, U.S.   )

      (b) Mentioned both Tsung Chou and Ch'eng
          Chou (cf. Shih Sung t̲i̲n̲g̲, Heng Hsien:
          1. 14; Ke t̲i̲n̲g̲; T̲'̲a̲o̲ chai: 1.36).

      (c) Mentioned both Tsung Chou and P'ang
          Ching (cf. Mai t̲s̲u̲n̲, H̲a̲i̲ C̲h̲i̲n̲g̲: 8.33).

      (d) Mentioned both P'ang Ching and Ch'eng
          Chou (cf. Ch'uan y̲u̲, S̲a̲n̲ t̲a̲i̲: 8.52a).

      (e) Mentioned both Ch'eng Chou and Chou
          (cf. Sung K̲u̲e̲i̲ catalogue, U.S.).

From these we know:

    Tsung Chou was not Ch'eng Chou (a) (b)

    Tsung Chou was not P'ang Ching (a) (c)

    Ch'eng Chou was not P'ang Ching (a) (d)

    Ch'eng Chou was not Chou   (e)

    Tsung Chou may or may not have been Chou .

    There is no doubt that (1) (2) (3) (4) are four dif-
ferent locations, but we can not make sure whether Tsung Chou

and Chou are one or different places. Since the name Tsung Chou
was used throughout the Western Chou bronzes and Chou was used
from Middle Western Chou to Late Western Chou, it is possible
that Chou was used as a substitute for Tsung Chou in later times.

The location of Tsung Chou is uncertain, but I am inclined to think it was in Ch'i-shan because the K'e ting set
was found there and mentioned that the king was at Tsung Chou.
Also, the large Yü ting (San tai: 4.42-43) found at Mei Hsien
near Ch'i-shan mentioned the king's being at Tsung Chou. This
ting is sometimes referred to as having been found in Ch'i-shan
also. The reading of P'ang Ching is not correct, it might be
Hao Ching.

There are two Western Chou vessels which mention that
the king was at Cheng   (San tai: 8.44b and 11.36.2) This
Cheng should be the western Cheng near Ch'ang-an. The commentary to the Ti li chih of the Han shu quoted Ch'en Tsan
as saying "Chou, from Mu Wang on, made its capital at western
Cheng." Shih pen says,"I Wang moved to Ch'üan Ch'iu   ."
It is somewhere in present Fu-feng   Hsien. Ti li chih of
Han shu under the district of Kuei-li   says, "Chou called
it Ch'üan Ch'iu, I Wang made it his capital." We can not prove
the validity of these two sources.

During the Western Chou period, Chou made the capitals
both in Western Land, the Wei Valley, and in Central Honan. We
may call them Western Capitals as Tsung Chou, P'ang Ching and
Hao Ching, and Eastern Capitals as Ch'eng Chou in Lo-yang respectively. The latter being a second capital during the
Western Chou period, and it became the only capital after

770 B.C. until the termination by Ch'in in 256 B.C.

It is quite safe to say that those bronzes which mentioned the above capitals, both western and eastern, were of the Western Chou period. It is possible for an Eastern Chou bronze to mention Ch'eng Chou, yet it is very strange that there is not a single Eastern Chou bronze which bears the name of Ch'eng Chou in its inscriptions.

4. Tu: Ti li chih of Han shu says, "Tu-ling was the old state of Tu" which is 50 li south of present Ch'ang-an Hsien. The story of Tu Po was recorded in both Chou yü of Kuo yü and Ming Kuei of Mo Tzu.

According to Ch'in pen chi of Shih chi, Tu probably was exterminated by Ch'in before 687 B.C. After that year, Tu became a district of Ch'in.

                              B. Shansi area

All of the names of the places are in Shansi province except as otherwise indicated.

5. Liang: According to Ch'un Ch'iu (Hsi 19) Liang was exterminated by Ch'in in 641 B.C. Chang's commentary quoted Kua ti chih   saying, "that 22 li south of Han's Ch'eng   Hsien (Shensi province) is the old city of Shao Liang   , where the state Shao Liang was located." After the extermination of Liang it became a name of a place as mentioned in Tso Chuan (Hsi 11), "Chin took the place called Shao-liang." There is only one bronze weapon made by this Liang (San tai: 19.53a). The history of both Ta Liang and

Shao Liang . is obscure.

6. Jui: According to Ch'in ~~shih chia~~ _pen chi_ of Shih chi, Jui
was exterminated by Ch'in in the same year as Liang. There
are two sites of Jui. One is in Shansi, the capital of Wei
which is the present Jui-ch'eng   Hsien. Tso chuan (Huan 3)
says in 709 B.C. "Jui Po went to live in Wei." The other one
is in Shensi province, Chang's commentary to Ch'in pen chi
quoted Kua ti chih saying that the old city of Jui was 30 li
south of Ch'ao-i   , of T'ung Chou   . It is now
Ch'ao-i Hsien of Shensi. There is a Fu made by Jui Po, which
was unearthed during 998-1003 A.D. at the Yellow River bank of
T'ung Chou. It was catalogued in K'ao ku: 3.40. This proved
that the capital of Jui was first in Ch'ao-i, and in 709 B.C.
it moved to Wei, the present Jui-ch'eng Hsien.

According to Tso chuan (Hsi 19) Jui was exterminated
by Ch'in in 640 B.C. _or 640 as recorded in Chin pen chi_.

7. Chih: According to Wei shih chia of Shih chi, Chih
was exterminated by Han, Chao and Wei in 453 B.C. Chang's
commentary says, "Kua ti chih said that the old Chih city was
40 li northwest of Yü-hsiang   Hsien. Ku chin ti ming
        said that Chih city was in Chieh   Hsien." There-
fore Chih must be somewhere between Chieh and Yü-hsiang, ~~on~~
~~the~~ west of the Salt Lake.

8. Northern Kuo: See under Western Kuo.

9. Yü: According to Wu shih chia of Shih chi, Yü
Chung was given fief at Hsia Hsü   , the old site of Hsia.
It was located at the present P'ing-lu   Hsien. Yü was
called Northern Yü   . According to Tso chuan (Hsi 5)
Yü was exterminated by Chin in 655 B.C.

10. Chin: Both Chin shih chia of Shih chi and Tso chuan
(Chao 1) say that Shu Yü of Chin got his fief at T'ang   .
Shih pen says,"Shu Yü lived in Ê   ."   T'ang was also called
Ta Hsia   (Tso chuan Chao 1), Hsia Hsü   (Tso chuan
Ting 4), and Chi Fang   (Tso chuan Ai 6). All of these are
different names of the same place, somewhere in the low land at
the curve of the Yellow River in the southern part of Shansi
province, the Ho Tung Commentary   of the Han dynasty. The
Salt Lake was within this area from which the name of T'ai
Yüan   is derived. (cf. Kung Yang chuan, Chao 1) Thus
T'ai Yüan is also Ta Hsia, etc. It is not the present T'ai-
yüan which is further north and is situated in the central part
of Shansi. Furthermore, according to Chin shih chia in 745 B.C.
Chao Hou of Chin had already made I   his capital and in
678 B.C. "Wu Kung began to make Chin Kuo   the capital,"
and in 669 B.C. the eighth year of Hsien Kung, "Hsien Kung
began to make Chiang   the capital." There has been
much confusion about the locations of I and Chiang and also
about whether they are one or two places. Chang's commentary
to Chin shih chia quoted Kua ti chih "The old I city was also
called old Chiang, located 15 li southeast of I city." Again
Chang quoted Chu hou p'u   "Mu Kung of Chin (811-785 B.C.)
moved his capital to Chiang, whose great grandson Hsiao Kung
(738-724 B.C.) changed the name Chiang to I, then during Hsien
Kung's (676-652 B.C.) time it was called Chiang again." Therefore, I may be identified as Chiang. If this is true then both
Chao Hou and Wu Kung had their capital at the same place as
Hsien Kung. According to Tso chuan (Ch'eng 6) in 585 B.C.
"Chin moved to Hsin-t'ien   ." It was called new Chiang .

which is the present Hsin-chiang   Hsien. From Chu Shu we
know that in 369 B.C. Chao and Han moved Huan Kung of Chin to
Tun-liu   , the present Tun-liu Hsien. According to Chao
shih chia, in 359 B.C. Han and Wei divided the Chin territory
and moved Chin to Tuan-shih   , the present Hsin-shui
Hsien, and in 349 B.C. Chao took Tuan-shih from Chin and moved
Chin back to Tun-liu. We may thus list Chin's capitals as
follows:

    Shu Yü (1027 B.C.)   T'ang = Ê = Ta Hsia = Hsia
                                    Hsu = Chi Fang = T'ai
                                    Yuan.

    Mu Hou (811 B.C.)   Chiang = I
    Chao Hou (745 B.C.)   I
    Hsiao Hou (738 B.C.)   I
    Wu Kung (678 B.C.)   Chin Kuo (may be I)
    Hsien Kung (669 B.C.)   Chiang
    Ching Kung (585 B.C.)   Hsin-t'ien
    Huan Kung (369 B.C.)   Tun-liu
    _____ (359 B.C.)   Tuan-shih
    _____ (349 B.C.)   Tun-liu

After 369 B.C. although Chin still occupied a small
territory, it can not be considered as a state. Both Chin shih
chia and Chu Shu ended the recordings of Chin in this year. We
therefore made 369 B.C. as the year of Chin's extermination.

    11. Han: According to Han shih chia of Shih Chi, Han
Wu Tzu was given fief by Chin at Han-yüan   , present Han-
ch'eng   Hsien in Shensi province. It was during the Ch'un
Ch'iu   period. After the year 563 B.C. "Hsüan Tzu moved to

Chou   ." Commentaries say that it was in Hsin-yang   of
Honan province. This is not correct. It should be somewhere in
southern Shansi province. After 497 B.C. Chen Tzu moved to
P'ing-yang   the present Lin-fen   Hsien. Chu shu says
"Han Wu Tzu made P'ing-yang the capital." Shih pen says,"Ching
Tzu (408-400 B.C.) lived in P'ing-yang." Both Han shih chia
and Chu shu agree that in 375 B.C. Han Ai Hou exterminated Cheng
and made Cheng (Hsin-cheng) the capital and changed the name of
the Han State to Cheng. We may therefore list the capitals of
Han as follows:

          Wu Tzu   Han-yüan

          Hsüan Tzu (after 563 B.C.) Chou

          Chen Tzu (after 497 B.C.) P'ing-yang

          Wu Tzu (424-409 B.C.)   P'ing-yang

          Ching Tzu (408-400 B.C.)   P'ing-yang

          Ai Hou (375 B.C.)   Cheng

All of these places are in southern Shansi province except Cheng,
which is in Honan province. Cheng was Han's capital until the
extermination by Ch'in in 230 B.C.

        12. Chao: According to Chao shih chia of Shih chi,
Chao Fu was first given fief at Chao   , the present Chao-
ch'eng   Hsien. In 661 B.C. Chao Su was given Keng   ,
the present Ho-chin   Hsien. Ch'eng Chi, who died in the
year 622 B.C. lived at Yüan   , the present Yuan-p'ing chen
          , south of Kuo   Hsien. Before 517 B.C. Chao Chien
Tzu was already the ruler of Chao. He lived at Chin-yang   ,
the present Yang-ch'ü   Hsien, in central Shansi province.
In 423 B.C. Hsien Hou made Chung-mou   his capital.
Chang's commentary says, "Chung-mou is the present T'ang-yin

Hsien of Honan." Han-tan   became Chao's territory in
491 B.C. (Tso chuan: Ai 4), but it was Chao's capital only after
386 B.C., the first year of Ching Hou. Han-tan is now located
in the southern Hopei province. During this time, Chao was
called Han-tan in Chu shu.   We may thus list Chao's capitals as
follows:

Chao Fu	Chao
Chao Su (661 B.C.)	Keng
Ch'eng Chi (before 622 B.C.)	Yüan
Chien Tzu (before 517 B.C.)	Chin-yang
Hsien Hou (423 B.C.)	Chung-mou
Ching Hou (386 B.C.)	Han-tan

Han-tan was Chao's capital until the extermination by
Ch'in in 222 B.C.

13. Wei (Liang): According to Wei shih chia of Shih chi,
in 661 B.C. Pi Wan was given fief by Chin at Wei   , which is
the present Jui-ch'eng   Hsien, and thus made Wei the name
of the state. Shih pen says, "Wei Wu Tzu (Pi Wan's son about
635-628 B.C.) lived at Wei, and Tao Tzu (about 627-572 B.C.)
moved to Hê   ." Wei shih chia also says, "Wei Tao Tzu
moved to Hê, the present Hê   Hsien. Both Wei shih chia and
Shih pen say that Chao Tzu made An-i   his capital. Chao
Tzu was contemporary with Chin Tao Kung (572-558 B.C.). An-i
is near the present An-i Hsien and Hsia   Hsien. According
to Chu shu, Hui Wang of Wei made Ta-liang   his capital
in 364 B.C. Ta-liang was originally the state of Liang, which
is the present K'ai-feng   Hsien of Honan province. Here
Shih chi made a mistake on the date of Wei's moving from An-i
to Ta-liang. From that time on, Wei changed its name to Liang.

We may thus list the capitals of Wei as follows:

     Pi Wan (661 B.C.)   Wei

     Tao Tzu (ca. 627-572 B.C.)   Hê

     Chao Tzu (ca. 572-558 B.C.) An-i

     Hui Wang (364 B.C.)   Ta-liang

     Wei's capital was Ta-liang until the extermination by Ch'in in 225 B.C. All of these places except Ta-liang are in Shansi province.

C. Northern Honan area

     All of the names of the places are in northern Honan province except as otherwise indicated.

     14. Shang: The origin of Shang is uncertain. I accept the theory that the Shang people came from the north-eastern part of China. There is a legend that the first Shang ancestor was born from a bird's egg. It was recorded in the Shang sung of the Shih ching and in the Yin pen chi of the Shih chi. This legend was popularly believed in the Korean area. The Shang people used the scapula in divination, and it was also used by the Eastern barbarians (cf. Tung i chuan of Hou Han shu and T'ai p'ing yü lan, vol. 726). The Eastern barbarians called the I   were an ally of the Shang people and probably came from the northeast also. It is likely that the Shang people themselves were also of the I. Keeping this notion in mind, let us examine the following table abstracted from the Chu shu:

          T'ang: Lived at Po

Chung Ting:	Moved from Po to Ao
Ho T'an Chia:	Moved from Ao to Hsiang
Tsu I:	Lived at Pi
Nan Keng:	Moved from Pi to Yen[3]
P'an Keng:	Moved from Yen[3] to Yin

Yin is in An-yang of Honan province and Yen[3] is Ch'ü Fu   of
Shantung province. Both are mentioned in Tso chuan (Chao 9)
as Shang Yen   . We can not locate Pi and Ao; most probably
they were in Shantung. Hsiang probably was the place mentioned
in Tso chuan (Ting 4) as the Eastern capital of Hsiang T'u
. With regard to Po there are many different opinions.
I believe that this Po is Yen[1] Po   as mentioned in the Tso
chuan (Chao 9). Because there were many Po in different areas,
Yen Po means "Po of the Yen State" of Hopei province. We shall
discuss below the place of I   which was in Yen's territory.
According to Chu shu, one of the earliest prince's of Shang was
a guest of I state, and it is possible that Shang was at one
time located near I. If this conjecture is correct, the Shang
people lived in Tung San Sheng   before T'ang's reign.
During the period of T'ang they moved southward to Po in Hopei
province and afterward moved to Shantung where they remained
for quite a long time. At last, P'an Keng made his capital at
An-yang and it stayed there until the extermination by Chou in
1027 B.C. This explains why more Shang bronzes are found in
Hopei and Shantung than elsewhere.

Yin pen chi of Shih chi made a little different
statement:

T'ang:	Began to live at Po
Chung Ting:	Moved to Ao
Ho T'an Chia:	Lived at Hsiang

Tsu I: Moved to Hsing

P'an Keng: At the time of P'an Keng,
                          Yin had already established
                          its capital at Hopei (on
                          the north side of the Yellow
                          River), and then crossed the
                          river southward to Po.

Wu I: Yin again left Po for Hopei

The location of Hsing is uncertain. It might be

Hsing Ch'iu   of Honan province. If this is true, then

Yin moved to Honan before P'an Keng's time. According to Shih

chi, Hopei (place not province) was located north of the Yel-

low River and Po was on the south. Po in Ssu-ma Ch'ien's

mind, might be the Po of Honan province, south of the present

Shang Ch'iu   city. The old Yellow River channel was north

of Shang Ch'iu. I suggest that Hopei might possibly be Shang

Ch'iu, where Shang's descendants, Sung, made it their capital.

If this is the case then the Yellow River at that time was

between Shang Ch'iu and Po. However, there is another possibi-

lity that Hopei might be Yin, the An-yang city. For the Shang

capitals, I think that Chu shu's statement is more reliable.

15. Wei: Wei might be the same name as Yin. In both

Shen ta chapter and Shen shih chapter of Lü shih ch'un ch'iu,

the character I   was used as a substitute for Yin   . The

former has the same phonetic element   as Wei. Wei had its

capital at Ch'ao Kê   . Wei shih chia of Shih chi says, that

Wei had the fief at old Shang Hsü   , between the Yellow River

and the Ch'i River   . Tso chuan (Ting 4) says, "K'ang

Shu took his fief at Yin Hsü." Yin Hsü is Shang Hsü. It is
somewhere between the present Chun   Hsien, Chi   Hsien, and
Ch'i   Hsien. According to Tso chuan (Min 2), in 660 B.C. Wei
was defeated by Ti   and Tai Kung moved to Ts'ao   , the pre-
sent Hua   Hsien. Shih pen also says, "Tai Kung lived at
Ts'ao." Again Tso chuan (Hsi 2) says that in 658 B. C. Ch'i
and other feudal lords established a capital for Wei at Ch'u-
ch'iu   near present Hua Hsien. In 629 B.C. (Tso chuan :
Hsi 31), the barbarian Ti again attacked Wei and Ch'eng Kung of
Wei moved to Ti-ch'iu   , the present P'u-yang   Hsien.
Ti Ch'iu may be identified as P'u-yang. Shih pen says, "Ch'eng
Kung moved to P'u-yang." According to Wei shih chia in 320 B.C.
Wei occupied only P'u-yang, and in the fourteenth year of Yüan
Chün (238 B.C.) Wei moved to Yieh-wang   , the present
Hsin-yang   Hsien, until the extermination by Ch'in in
209 B.C. We may thus list Wei's capitals as follows:

      K'ang Shu (1027 B.C.)   Ch'ao Kê

      Tai Kung (660 B.C.)   Ts'ao

      Wen Kung (658 B.C.)   Ch'u-ch'iu

      Ch'eng Kung (629 B.C.)   Ti-ch'iu

      Yüan Chün (238 B.C.)   Yieh-wang

D. Central Honan area

All of the names of the places are in Central Honan province except as otherwise indicated.

16. Tung Chou: Tung Chou can literally be translated
as Eastern Chou, but the term "Eastern Chou" was used by later

historians to indicate a period between 770-256 B. C., when Chou
made its capital at Lo-yang. Throughout this whole work,
Western Chou and Eastern Chou indicate the name of two periods,
and Tung Chou and Hsi Chou indicate the name of two feudal lords.
In the early Chou, Chou Kung Tan first held the title of Chou
Kung, the duke of Chou. After his death, one of his son's inherited the title and duty to serve the royal family, thus the
So yin to Lu shih chia says, "The first son of Chou Kung (Tan)
took his fief at Lu; the second son remained and assisted the
royal house to be the successor of Chou Kung (title) from generation to generation." There might be some interruption of
the succession of this title. In Chou pen chi of Shih chi it
is recorded that "K'ao Wang (440-426 B.C.) made his brother a
fief in Honan   (a district name, about 5 li northwest of
present Lo-yang). Huan Kung was supposed to continue the
title and duty of Chou Kung (title). Huan Kung died. His son,
Wei Kung, succeeded. Wei Kung died. His son, Hui Kung succeeded. Then he made his younger son a fief in Kung   (a district) to serve the king. It was called Tung-chou Hui Kung."
There were two Chou Kung at that time, the one in Kung district
located east of Lo-yang was Tung Chou Kung (The Eastern Duke of
Chou), and the one in Honan was Hsi Chou Kung (The Western Duke
of Chou). Ssu-ma Ch'ien inserted this paragraph in the Wei
Li Wang period, but he did not mention the exact year in which
the Tung Chou Kung was established. In Chao shih chia it is
recorded that "In the eighth year of (Chao) Ch'en Hou, Han and
Chao divided Chou into two parts." Pei's commentary quoted
Kua ti chih saying, "Shih chi says, 'In the second year of Chou
Hsien (Wang), Hsi Chou Hui Kung made his younger son, Tzu Pan,

a fief at Kung. It was called Tung Chou.'" In Chou pen chi
Chang's commentary quotes Shu cheng chi saying, "Shih chi says,
'In the second year of Chou Hsien Wang, Hsi Chou Hui Kung made
his younger son, Pan, a fief at Kung to serve the royal family.
It was called Tung Chou Hui Kung.'" Neither of these quotations
can be found in the text of the present day Shih chi, but if we
compare these two quotations with the statement from Chou pen
chi it seems that the present edition of Shih chi has lost some
sentences. According to Liu kuo piao of Shih chi, the second
year of Chou Hsien Wang was the eighth year of Chao Ch'en
Hou (367 B.C.), and therefore the establishment of Tung Chou
Kung was in that year. According to Chu shu, Tung Chou Hui
Kung died in the ninth year of Chou Hsien Wang (360 B.C.). In
Shih chi and Chan kuo ts'e, these two Chou Kung were mentioned
as Tung Chou Chün   and Hsi Chou Chün   and sometimes as Tung-Hsi Chou or as Tung Chou and Hsi Chou. The last
king of the Chou dynasty was Nan Wang, who died in the fifty-
ninth year of his reign (256 B.C.). According to Chou pen chi
"After the death of Chou Nan Wang, the Chou in the east was
terminated. The Ch'in took the nine ting and the precious vessels and moved Hsi Chou Kung to Ti-hu. Seven years later
Ch'in Ch'uang Hsiang Wang terminated Tung Hsi Chou." Ch'in
pen chi dates the termination of Tung Chou Chün as the first
year of Ch'in Ch'uang Hsiang Wang. This was in the year 249 B.C.,
just seven years after 256 B.C., the year of the death of Nan
Wang.

17. Hsi Chou: See under Tung Chou.

18. Su: Ch'un ch'iu (Hsi 10) recorded that when Ti

exterminated Wen   , Wen Tzu fled to Wei   . Tso chuan called
Wen Tzu, Su Tzu. It was recorded in Tso chuan (Yin 11), that
Wen was one of the lands of Su state, hence Su may be called Wen.
Wen is the present Wen   Hsien. After 646 B.C., Su still existed
as it appeared in Ch'un ch'iu (Wen 10, 617 B.C.), thus Su was
exterminated after 617 B.C.

19. Hsing: Hsing first made its capital at Hsing
Ch'iu   , between the present Wen Hsien and Hsin-yang Hsien.
According to Tso chuan (Hsi 1), in 659 B.C. Ti attacked Hsing
and Hsing was compelled to move to I-i   , which was located
at the present Hsing-t'ai   Hsien of Hopei province. According to Ch'un ch'iu (Hsi 25) Hsing was exterminated by Wei
in 635 B.C.

20. Eastern Kuo: See under Western Kuo.

21. Cheng: According to Cheng shih chia of Shih chi,
in the twenty-second year of Chou Hsüan Wang (806 B.C.), Huan
Kung of Cheng got his fief at Cheng   near the present Hua
Hsien in Shensi province. Shih pen says, "Huan Kung lived at
Yü-lin   , then moved to Shih   ." Yü-lin was also mentioned in Tso chuan (Hsiang 14 and 16). Cheng Hsüan's Shih
p'u   says, "Hsüan Wang gave a fief to his brother Yu at
Hsien-lin   , in the imperial domains of Tsung Chou. This
is Cheng Huan Kung. It is now Cheng Hsien (of Shensi in Han
times)." Yü-lin could be identified as Cheng, and Hsien-lin
might be the misprint of Yu-lin or vice versa, because the
characters Yu   and Hsien   are so similar. Cheng shih chia
again says, that during the end of Chou Yu Wang, Cheng moved
eastward to make the present Hsin-cheng   or New Cheng
his capital. During 697-680, Li Kung of Cheng was forced to

flee to Li   , the present Yü   Hsien, and he returned to
Hsin-cheng in 680 B.C. Shih pen says, "Wen Kung (672-628 B.C.,
the successor to Li Kung), moved to Cheng," which means that
Wen Kung again made Hsin-cheng his capital. In the year 375 B.C.,
Cheng was exterminated by Han, and from that time on Han called
itself Cheng.

22. Hsü[3]: Ch'un ch'iu (Yin 11) recorded that in 712 B.C.
Lu, Ch'i and Cheng entered Hsü. This Hsü was located at the
present Hsu-ch'ang   Hsien. Hsü was uneasy about the aggression of Cheng and tried to move to the southern part of Honan
province. Tso chuan recorded the moving of Hsü's capitals as
follows:

Ch'en 15 (576 B.C.)   Moved to Yeh

Chao 9 (533 B.C.)   Moved to I

Chao 11 (531 B.C.)   Moved to Ching

Chao 18 (524 B.C.)   Moved to Hsi-shih

                             and Pai-yü

Ting 4 (506 B.C.)   Moved to Jung-ch'eng

Yeh was located at the present Yeh   Hsien, and was also
called Hsü. Since that year (576 B. C.), the old Hsü was
occupied by Cheng and was called Chiu Hsü   , the old Hsü,
as mentioned in Tso chuan (Hsiang 11). I   was 70 11
southeast of the present Po   Hsien of Anhui province. Ch'un
ch'iu (Chao 11) recorded that in 531 B.C. Ch'u exterminated
Ts'ai. Tso chuan made a detailed report of that event under the thirteenth year of Chao Kung, saying that when Ch'u exterminated
Ts'ai, Ch'u Ling Wang moved six small states including Hsü to
Ching   , the location of which is uncertain. Hsi-shih

and Pai-yü were in the east of the present Nei-hsiang   Hsien.

Jung-ch'eng was located east of Yeh Hsien.

Ch'un ch'iu (Ting 6) recorded that in 504 B.C. "Cheng

exterminated Hsü," but Ch'un ch'iu (Ai 1) still recorded Hsü's

affairs in 494 B.C., thus Hsü was exterminated after 494 B.C.

23. Ying: According to Tu's commentary to Tso chuan

(Hsi 24), Ying was located at Pao-feng   Hsien. There is

no record of its extermination, but judging from Ying's bronzes,

it did exist from Early to Late Western Chou.

24. Ch'en: According to Ch'en ch'i shih chia of Shih

chi, and Tso chuan (Hsiang 25), Ch'en was given fief

in the beginning of Chou. It was called Ch'en-ch'iu   or

Wan-ch'iu   , the present Huai-yang   Hsien. According

to Tso chuan (Ai 17) Ch'en was exterminated by Ch'u in 478 B.C.

25. Sung: Sung made its capital at the present Shang

Ch'iu   Hsien in the eastern part of Honan near the Shan-

tung-Chiangsu border. The capital was never moved, but accord-

ing to Ch'ien Mu's   opinion, Sung moved its capital before

385 B.C. to P'eng Ch'eng   which is the present T'ung-chan

Hsien of northern Chiangsu province. He gave some evidence for

his opinion, but the histories do not state the fact explicitly.

According to Liu Kuo piao, Sung was exterminated by Ch'i[2] in

286 B.C.

26. Tai: Ti li chih of Han shu says, "Tsai   is the

ancient site of Tai state." It is near the present K'ao-ch'eng

Hsien. Tsai and Tai have the same phonetic element   , the

place was called Tsai because it was the ancient Tai state.

Tso chuan (Yin 10) recorded that in the year 713 B.C. Tai was

attacked by some states and the capital was occupied by Cheng.

The extermination of Tai may tentatively be put in this year.

27. Yung: Chou pen chi of Shih chi says, "Wu Wang was anxious about the unorganized Yin, and so ordered his brother Kuan-shu Hsien and Ts'ai-shu Tu to assist Lu-fu (son of the last king of Shang) to govern Yin." This 'Yin' should be interpreted as 'Yin people' since in Kuan ts'ai shih chia of Shih chi it is related that Kuan and Ts'ai were ordered to govern the remaining Yin people." There was then the so-called 'San Chien' or 'three surveillances' and the three states of Shang under the surveillance of Chou. The three states were Pei , Yung , and Wei . There was confusion about the location of the three states and the relation between surveillances and states. According to Ti li chih of Han shu, the three states were within the imperial domains of the Shang. Lu-fu was the master of Pei, Kuan-shu was the master of Yung, and Ts'ai-shu was the master of Wei. Ti wang shih chi held another theory that the east of Yin capital was Wei under the surveillance of Kuan-shu, the west of it was Yung under the surveillance of Ts'ai-shu, and north of it was Pei under the surveillance of Hê-shu. Tso lo of Yi chou shu says that Kuan-shu was stationed in the East, Ts'ai-shu and Hê-shu were stationed at Yin to keep the Yin people under surveillance. I shall leave out Hê-shu since he was not mentioned in the participation of the surveillance in Shih chi. Through the discovery of the Pei state bronzes in Lai-shui of Hopei province, we can locate Pei as being near Yen state. Tsê chuan (Chao 21) says, "Sung built the old Yung," thus Yung was near the Sung capital.

We have thus far the location of the three states:

Pei near Yen[1], Wei at Shang's capital, and Yung near Sung. 尻
li chih says, "In Chung-mou   there was Kuan-shu's fief."
Chung-mou was located between An-yang and Ch'ao-kê. Therefore,
it is possible that Lu-fu was made a feudal lord at Ch'ao-kê
under the surveillance of Kuan; Yung was under the surveillance
of Ts'ai since Ts'ai was not far away from Sung; and Pei was
probably under the surveillance of Yen[1]. The history did not
mention Yen[1] as one of the surveillances, probably because Yen[1]
did not join Kuan and Ts'ai in the rebellion against Chou during Ch'eng Wang's time. The rebellion was recorded in Shih chi.
Shang and Kuan Ts'ai and other old Shang allies in the East
united to attack Ch'eng Chou. They were defeated by Chou Kung,
and Lu-fu and Kuan-shu were executed for being the leaders of
the rebellion. Then K'ang Shu, Wu Wang's brother, was ordered
to be the master of Wei state, and another descendant of Shang
was ordered to be the master of Sung, to substitute for Yung.
It seems to me that Pei still existed after that event, since
the bronzes of Pei were later than that time.

E. Southern Honan area

All of the names of the places are in southern Honan
province except as otherwise indicated.

28. Ts'ai: Kuan ts'ai shih chia of Shih chi says that
at the beginning of Chou, Shu Tu was given fief at Ts'ai.
Shih pen says, "Shu Tu lived at Shang Ts'ai   ," the
upper Ts'ai, the present Shang-ts'ai Hsien. Shu Tu was exiled
after the rebellion in Chou Ch'eng Wang's time. Later, his
son Hu   was given back the fief from Chou Kung. Here

Chang's commentary quoted Sung Chung　　　　(who made the commentary to Shih pen) saying, "Hu moved to Hsin Ts'ai　　　　　　,
the new Ts'ai, the present Hsin-ts'ai Hsien. Most likely Sung
Chung got his information from the lost Shih pen. But Ti li
chih of Han shu says that Ts'ai P'ing Hou (528-522 B.C.) moved
to Hsin-ts'ai. I believe that the latter one is more reliable.
Both Kuan ts'ai shih chia and Ch'un ch'iu (Ai 2) say that in
the twenty-sixth year of Chao Hou (493 B.C.) Ts'ai moved to
Chou-lai　　　　by Wu.　Chou Lai was called Hsia-ts'ai　　　　　　,
the lower Ts'ai, somewhere near Feng-t'ai　　　　Hsien of Anhui
province. We may thus list the capitals of Ts'ai as follows:

　　　　Shu Tu (1027 B.C.)　　　　　Ts'ai or upper Ts'ai

　　　　P'ing Hou (528 B.C.)　　　　Hsin-ts'ai or new Ts'ai

　　　　Chao Hou (493 B.C.)　　　　Chou-lai or lower Ts'ai

According to Ch'u shih chia, Ts'ai was exterminated by
Ch'u in 447 B.C.

29. Shen: According to Tu's commentary to Tso chuan
(Wen 3) Shen was located near present Ju-nan　　　Hsien. Tso
chuan (Ting 4) recorded its extermination by Ts'ai in 506 B.C.

30. Chiang: According to Tu's commentary to Tso chuan
(Hsi 2), Chiang was located near present Hsi　　　Hsien. Ch'un
ch'iu (Wen 4) recorded its extermination by Ch'u in 623 B.C.

31. Huang: According to Tu's commentary to Tso chuan
(Huan 8), Huang was located near present Huang-chüan
Hsien. Ch'un ch'iu (Hsi 12) recorded its extermination by
Ch'u in 648 B.C.

32. Teng: The bronze vessels of Teng were found in
Shensi province. It is likely that Teng moved to the southern
part of Honan during the Ch'un Ch'iu period. Ti li chih of
Han shu says, "Teng　　　Hsien (of Honan) is the old site of

Teng." According to Tso chuan (Ch'uang 6) Teng was exterminated by Ch'u in 678 B.C.

33. Jo: According to Tso chuan (Hsi 25) in 635 B.C. Ch'in and Chin attacked Jo. Tu's commentary says, "After then Jo moved to Jo   Hsien," which is near present I-ch'eng Hsien of Hupei province. The old Jo was located at Hsi-ch'üan Hsien of Honan province.

According to Tso chuan (Ting 6) in 504 B.C., Ch'u made Jo Hsien the capital, therefore the extermination of Jo may be before 504 B.C.

On the bronzes there were Shang Jo (upper Jo) and Hsia Jo (lower Jo). It is not clear how to divide the boundaries of these two Jo.

F. Hopei area

All of the names of the places are in Hopei province except as otherwise indicated.

34. Yen[1]: According to the Yen shih chia of Shih chi, Yen made its capital at Pei Yen[1]   , somewhere near present Ta-hsiang   Hsien. Shih pen says, "Huan Hou (697-691 B.C.) moved to Lin-i   ," which is the present I Hsien, where both Yen[1] and Ch'i[2] bronzes have been found. Ch'i[2] and Yen[1] were neighbors and during the Chan Kuo period fought many wars against each other. About 284 B.C. Yen[1] attacked Ch'i[2], entered the capital, captured seventy cities, and took away the Ch'i[2] treasures. This explains why Ch'i[2] vessels were found in the Yen[1] territory.

According to Ch'in shih huang pen chi, Yen[1] was exterminated by Ch'in in 222 B.C.

35. Pei: See under Yung.

G. Shantung area

All of the names of the places are in Shantung province except as otherwise indicated.

36. Ch'i^3: According to Ch'en ch'i shih chia of Shih chi, Tung Lou Kung was given fief at Ch'i^3 in Chou Wu Wang's time. The location of Ch'i^3 was said to be at Ch'i^3 Hsien of Honan province. However, Ch'i^3 moved to Shantung before the Ch'un Ch'iu period.   For Ch'i^3 bronzes were found at Hsing-t'ai   Hsien of Shantung, and Ti li chih of Han shu says, "Ch'i^3 moved to the northeastern part of Lu before Ch'un Ch'iu." Hsin-t'ai is located northeast of Ch'ü-fu, the capital of Lu. According to Tso chuan (Huan 5) in 707 B.C., "Ch'un Yü Kung went to Ts'ao   and for fear of the danger in his state, he never came back." It is generally believed that the aggression of Ch'i^3 was the cause of Ch'un Yü Kung's fear, and it is presumed that in the next year (706 B.C.), Ch'i^3 made Ch'un-yü   , the present An-ch'iu   Hsien, the capital. According to Tso chuan (Hsi 14) in 646 B.C. "Ch'i^3 moved to Yüan-ling   ," which is the present Ch'ang-lo   Hsien. Tso chuan says that (Hsiang 29) in 544 B.C. feudal lords made a city for the location of Ch'i^3. This was also recorded in Tso chuan (Chao 1) as a city at Ch'un-yü. Therefore, Ch'i^3 moved back to Ch'un-yü in 544 B.C. We may thus list the capitals of Ch'i^3 as follows:

Tung Lou Kung (1027 B.C.)	Ch'i^3
Before 770 B.C.	Hsin-t'ai
Wu Kung (706 B.C.)	Ch'un-yü
Ch'eng Kung (646 B.C.)	Yüan-ling
Wen Kung (544 B.C.)	Ch'un-yü

According to Ch'u shih chia, Ch'i^3 was exterminated by

Ch'u in 445 B.C.

37. Chi: According to Ch'en ch'i shih chia of Shih chi,
"In the eighth year of Ch'i^2 Hsiang Kung (690 B.C.), Ch'i^2
attacked Chi, and Chi moved away from its capital." Chang's
commentary quoted Kua ti chih as saying "The old Chü   city
was 30 li north of Shou-kuang   Hsien. It was the old Chi
city." Chang's commentary quoted Chu shu as saying "Ch'i^2
Hsiang Kung exterminated Chi and moved Chi away." Chi's capital after 690 B.C. was uncertain, it should have been somewhere i
Shantung province.

Several of Chi's bronzes were found in Shou-kuang. Its
extermination was uncertain, probably after 690 B.C.

38. Ch'i^2: According to Chi shih chia of Shih chi,
Ch'i^2 was given the fief at Ying Ch'iu   at the beginning
of Western Chou, now Lin-tzu   Hsien. During Chou Yi
Wang's time, Hu Kung of Ch'i^2 moved his capital to Po-ku   ,
northeast of present Po-hsing   Hsien, northeast of Lin-
tzu. The capital was not long at Po-ku. When Hsien Kung
attacked Hu Kung and became ruler of Ch'i^2 he moved the capital
back to Lin-tzu.

Many Ch'i^2 bronzes were found in Ch'i^2's territory,
and also in Yen^1's territory.

According to Ch'i shih chia, in 379 B.C., the T'ien
family, formerly the chief of staff, usurped the throne and
became the ruler of Ch'i^2. Since the Ch'i^2 was the Chiang
family, we call the Ch'i^2 before 397 B.C. the Ch'i^2 of Chiang,
and after that , Ch'i^2 of T'ien, which was exterminated by
Ch'in in 221 B.C. On the bronzes Ch'i^2 of Chiang was called
Ch'i Hou while the Ch'i^2 of T'ien was called Ch'en Hou. The
T'ien family came from Ch'en. In ancient times the pronunciation

of Ch'en and T'ien was the same.

39. Chu[4]: There is some confusion about the location
of Chu[4]'s capital. Chu[4]'s bronzes were found at Huan-t'ai
and Ch'i-tung   Hsien, but we have no record of its capital being there. Tu's commentary to Tso chuan (Hsiang 23) says
that Chu[4] was in Shê-ch'iu   Hsien, the present Fei-ch'eng

Hsien, which is quite far away from Huan-t'ai. Tso
chuan (Hsiang 23) mentions Chu[4]; its extermination must have
been after 550 B.C.

40. Lu: According to Lu shih chia of Shih chi, Lu was
given fief at Ch'ü-fu   and he made it the capital. It is
the present Ch'ü-fu Hsien, and it was the old territory of
Shang Yen, which will be discussed below. Lu was exterminated
by Ch'u about 250 B.C.

41. Shang Yen[3]: Tso chuan (Chao 9 and Ting 4), recorded that the people of Shang Yen[3] were under the reign of Lu
when Lu was given the fief at Ch'ü-fu. Tso chuan (Chao 1) also
says, "Chou had Hsü[2] and Yen[3]." During Ch'eng Wang's time,
Yen[3] participated in the rebellion against Chou, and was defeated
by Chou Kung. This important event was recorded in history.
Keng chu chapter of Mo tzu and Shuo lin chapter of Han fei tzu
called Shang Yen[3], Shang Kai   , since in ancient times the
pronunciation of yen[3] and kai was the same.

This Yen[3] was originally the old site of Shang (discussed before under Shang), so it was called Shang Yen.

42. Po Ku: Tso chuan (Chao 9) says, "After the conquest of Shang by Wu Wang, Po Ku and Shang Yen were our
(Chou's) eastern territory." The location of Po Ku has been
discussed under Ch'i[2]. Po Ku participated in the rebellion

against Chou during Ch'eng Wang's time. On one of the important

bronzes, the inscription says that Chou Kung attacked Eastern I

and Po Ku (Chin wen li so su cheng: 1.11).

43. Chu[1]:   Shih pen says, "Chu Yen lived at Chu[1]   ,

Fei moved to Ni   ." Sung Chung's commentary says, "Fei was

given fief at Ni and was called Hsiao Chu Tzu (Small Chu)."

Chu[1] is the present Tsou   Hsien, and Ni is southeast of pre-

sent T'eng   Hsien. Tso chuan (Wen 13) says that in 614 B.C.

"Chu moved to I   ." It is the present I   Hsien, southeast

of present Tsou Hsien. Chu[1]'s bronzes were found in T'eng Hsien.

The extermination of Chu[1] is uncertain. Ch'u shih chia

recorded that in the year of 281 B.C. Chu[1] still existed.

44. Ni: It was a branch of Chu[1], so it was also called

Hsiao Chu (Small Chu).

45. Shih: According to Ch'un ch'iu (Hsiang 13) in the

year 560 B.C., Shih was taken by Lu. Ti li chih of Han shu

says that the old site of Shih was at Han's K'ang-fu

Hsien, southeast of present Chi-ning   Hsien. There was

another place called Shih, mentioned in Tso chuan (Hsiang 18),

near P'ing-yin   Hsien which might be the original site

of Shih. Shih's bronzes were found at T'eng Hsien.

46. Ts'ao: According to Kuan ts'ai shih chia of Shih

chi, after the conquest of Shang, Shu Cheng To was given the

fief of Ts'ao. It is located at the present Ting-t'ao

Hsien.

According to Tso chuan (Ai 8), Ts'ao was exterminated

by Sung in 487 B.C.

47. Tseng: Tseng, in Tso chuan, was in Shantung area.

Tu's commentary to Tso chuan (Ai 7) says, "Tseng is present

Tseng   Hsien of Lang-ya   ," which is eighty li east of
I Hsien. Although Ch'un ch'iu (Hsiang 6) says that the state
was exterminated by Ch'ü in 567 B.C.; on the bronzes there is
the name of a Tseng recorded on a Chung which was made by the
Ch'u state in 433 B.C. (Hsiao T'ang 90) and a Hu made by the
Ch'u state in 344 B.C. (San chai: 104-105). From these two vessels, it seems to me that Tseng had very intimate relations with
Ch'u. It might not be the same Tseng as   the one recorded in
the Tso chuan.

     48. Chü; Ti li chih of Han shu says, "Chü Tzu was first
established in Chi-chin   , and later moved to Chü."   Chi-
chin could be identified as Chieh-keng   , the present
Kao-mi   Hsien. Tso chuan (Hsiang 29) says that in 544 B.C.,
Ch'i[2] attacked Chü and took Chieh-keng. Therefore, the moving
of Chü from Chieh-keng to Chü, the present Chü   Hsien should
be after 544 B.C.

     According to Ch'u shih chia, Chü was exterminated by
Ch'u in 431 B.C.

     49. T'eng: Shih pen says, "Tsou Shu Hsiu
was the son of Chou Wen Wang who lived at T'eng," which is present T'eng   Hsien. Chu shu recorded that in 415 B.C. T'eng
was exterminated by Yüeh. But until the time of Meng Tzu (ca.
390-305) T'eng still existed. Sung ts'e of Chan kuo ts'e
says, "K'ang Wang (of Sung) exterminated T'eng." This K'ang
Wang may be identified as Chün Yen   in Sung shih chia,
whose reign according to Chu shu was about 337-286 B.C. Therefore, T'eng's extermination should be about that period.

     50. T'an: Ch'i shih chia of Shih chi says, "In the
second year of Huan Kung, T'an was exterminated by Ch'i[2], and

T'an fled to Chü."   Ch'un ch'iu (Ch'uang 10) recorded,"Ch'i[2]'s
army exterminated T'an   ." This was in the year 684 B.C.
In these two sources, the characters for T'an were written differently, but they could be identified as one. After that year
T'an established its new state in the present T'an   Hsien, and
Ch'un ch'iu continued the recording of T'an's affairs. Chu shu
says that in 414 B.C. T'an was exterminated again by Yüeh, but
Ch'u shih chia recorded that in the year 281 B.C. T'an still
existed.

In David-Weill's collection there are a pair of kuei
(San tai: 9.26b) which recorded that Chou Kung attacked Ch'u
at T'an   in early Western Chou. This T'an was located near
P'ing-yin Hsien. Tu's commentary to Tso chuan (Ch'uang 10)
says, "T'an state was located southwest of P'ing-yin Hsien,"
which is near the present Chi-nan, the capital of Shantung province. During 1930-1932, Academia Sinica made an excavation
at Ch'eng Tzu Yai, which was the old site of T'an, and got
relics of the Shang and pre-Shang period. The T'an culture
can be considered as the Shang culture.

51. Hsüeh: According to Tso chuan (Ting 1) one of the
descendants of Hsüeh says that "Ch'i Chung   , the ancestor
of Hsüeh lived at Hsüeh, to be the master of the Chariot of
the Hsia Kingdom. Ch'i Chung moved to Pei   ."   The old site
of Hsüeh   was located southeast of the present T'eng
Hsien, and Pei was near the present I Hsien.

52. Hsü[2]: Hsü[2] had the same family name as Ch'in. In
Chang's commentary to Chao shih chia and Ch'in pen chi he
quoted Pu wu chih   as saying that the king of Hsü[2]
was born from a bird's egg. Although Hsü[2] played an important
part among the Eastern States in both the Western and the

Eastern Chou period, there were few records about its capital.
It was probably first located somewhere in the Shantung area,
and then moved to northern Chiangsu province.

According to Ch'un ch'iu (Chao 30) in 512 B.C. Hsu[2]
was exterminated by Wu and Hsü[2] Tzu fled to Ch'u. It existed
under Ch'u's protection for some time.

H. Chiang Huai area

53. Ch'u: In Tso chuan (Chao 12), the ruler of Ch'u says,
"Formerly our deceased king, Hsiung I   (during Chou Wen
Wang's time), lived far in the mountain of Ching   .... For-
merly the uncle of our great grandfather K'un Wu   lived at
old Hsü   ." The location of the latter is the present
Hsü-ch'ang   Hsien, the old capital of Hsü[3]. Northwest of
Hsu-ch'ang at Yu   Hsien is the Ching mountain. It seems to
me that the Ch'u tribe lived in this area in the early days.
According to Ch'u shih chia of Shih chi, "Hsiung I lived at
Tan-yang   ," somewhere near the Tan River   of southern
Honan. But Shih pen says, "Yü Hsiung   lived at Tan-yang."
He was several generations before Hsiung I. Further, Shih chia
says, "Wen Wang (689-675 B.C.) lived at Ying   ," which is
the present Chiang-ling   Hsien of Hupei province. But Shih
pen says, "Wu Wang (740-690 B.C.) moved to Ying." Both Ch'u
shih chia and Tso chuan (Ting 6) say that in the twelfth year of
Chao Wang (504 B.C.) Ch'u moved northward to Jo   which is located at present I-ch'eng   Hsien of Hupei province, the
second capital of Jo. Ch'u shih chia says, in 278 B.C. the
twenty-first year of Hsiang Wang (278 B.C.), Ch'u moved north-

eastward to Ch'en   city, the present Huai-yang   Hsien in
Honan, the old capital of Ch'en. This Ch'en was also called
Ying according to the coins of that period with the inscriptions
"Ch'en-Ying." Liu kuo piao of Shih chi says that in the tenth
year of K'ao Li Wang (253 B.C.) Ch'u moved to Chü Yang, the location of which is unknown. Ch'u shih chia says, "In the
twenty-second year of K'ao Li Wang (241 B.C.), Ch'u moved eastward to Shou-ch'un   and called it Ying." It is the present
Shou_ Hsien of Anhui province. It seems to me that Chü-yang
should be west of Shou Hsien. We may thus list Ch'u's capitals as follows:

Yü Hsiung	Tan-yang
Hsiung I	Hsu
Hsiung I	Tan-yang
Wu Wang(740 B.C.)	Ying
Wen Wang (689 B.C.)	Ying
Chao Wang (504 B.C.)	Jo, also called Ying
Hsiang Wang (278 B.C.)	Ch'en, also called Ying
K'ao Li Wang (253 B. C.)	Chü-yang
K'ao Li Wang (241 B. C.)	Shou-ch'un, also
	called Ying

It seems to me that Tan-yang of Yü Hsiung and Hsiung I
should be the same place in southern Honan. After Hsiung I and
before Wu and Wen, Ch'u may have been established in I-ch'ang
Hsien and Chih-chiang   Hsien, west of Chiang-ling, where
both districts had a place named Tan-yang. After Wu Wang,
whereever they moved they called their capital Ying. Ying is
a common name for the capital of a city in the Ch'u dialect.
Even at the present time the people around Shou Hsien still

call the village Ying.

Ch'u was the strongest state in the southern part of
China occupying the vast area of Hupei, Anhui, and part of
Chiangsu, all on the northern side of the Yangtzu River. Most
of the territory on the southern side, except for Wu and Yueh
which came to power for a short while in the Late Ch'un Ch'iu
period, also belonged to Ch'u. Ch'u was exterminated by Ch'in
in 223 B.C.

54. Wu: Wu claimed to be a descendant of Chou. Shih
pen says, "Shu Tsai   lived at Fan-li   , Shu Ku
lived at Kou-wu   ." Fan-li could be identified as Mei-li
        , somewhere near present Wu-hsi   Hsien of Chiangsu
province. The location of Kou-wu is uncertain. Shih pen says
again, "Chu Fan   moved southward to Wu" which should be
the present Wu   Hsien, formerly called Su Chou or Soochow
        . According to Ch'un ch'iu (Ai 22), Wu was exterminated
by Yueh in 473 B.C.

55. Yueh: According to Yueh shih chia of Shih chi,
Yueh first made its capital at K'uai-chi   the present
Shao-hsing   Hsien of Chechiang province. According to
Chu shu, in 379 B. C. Yueh moved to Wu, the present Wu Hsien.

According to Chu shu, in 415 B.C. and 414 B.C. Yueh
exterminated T'eng and T'an, and its territory extended to
southern Shantung and northern Chiangsu. Ti li chih of Han shu
says "Lang-ya   was once the capital of Yueh Wang Kou-chien."
Both Wu yueh ch'un ch'iu, vol. 10 and Yueh chueh shu, vol. 8
say that "Kou-chien moved to Lang-ya." If this is true, then
Yueh made Lang-ya its capital earlier than 414 B.C., that is,
in Kou-chien's time (496-465 B.C.).

According to Chu shu, Yüeh was exterminated by Ch'u in 333 B.C.

We have just made a short study of the different states, their capitals and their extermination. It should be noticed that the present location for the ancient site is not very accurate because many cities remained to be called by the same old name, although the original site of the city had moved during the several dynasties. Thus, the present name only refers to the vicinity of the original site. In many cases, the name of the capital was the name of the state, hence the history recording a certain state exterminated by another state would refer to the capturing of the capital of the exterminated state only. Moreover, the name of the occupied capital is sometimes adopted by the conqueror as the name of his state, such as Han, Chao and Wei were called Cheng, Han Tan and Liang respectively after the occupation of these capitals. When the states moved from one place to another, the name of the place adopted as their capital usually remained unchanged, as in the case of Ts'ai, Jo, Hsing, Jui and Hsu[3]. In short, by tracing the names of mountains, rivers and cities, the migration of the states are made clearer for our understanding of the moving of the culture.

A table of states listing their names, their duration , their extermination, and the source of such information may be found under the chapter on Chronology. This chart gives us the general view of the interstate relationships and the duration of each state.

Another table, giving the various writings of the same names of the states found in books and on bronzes, is listed at the end of this chapter.

II. Family Relationships among States

Among the fifty-five states, with few exceptions, the
family name of each state was recorded in various books. Often
the states that were derived from the same family were widely
separated, but through the study of the family names, their
origin, migration and history could be clearly understood. There
is no suitable English translation for hsing   . It is somewhat similar to the surname, but it should not be confused with
shih   . The former is of maternal origin and the latter is
usually of paternal origin. In studying ancient history, hsing
is much more important than shih for certain well known reasons. Following, twelve family names are listed (Numbers in
parenthesis are the same as those used above):

A. Chi   family - Chou descendants.   Chou pen chi

    1. Chou (3), Tung Chou (16) Hsi Chou (17)   Chou pen chi

    2. Lu (40)   Tso chuan (Hsi 24); Shih pen

    3. Wei (15)   Tso chuan (Hsi 24); Shih pen

    4. T'eng (49)   Tso chuan (Hsi 24); Shih pen

    5. Ts'ao (46)   Tso chuan (Hsi 24; Ting 4);

                              Shih pen.

    6. Ts'ai (28)   Tso chuan (Hsi 24)

    7. Wei (Liang) (13)   Tso chuan (Hsi 24; Hsiang 29)

    8. Chin (10)   Tso chuan (Hsi 24; Hsiang 29;

                              Ting 4)

    9. Han (11)   Tso chuan (Hsi 24; Hsiang 29)

    10. Ying (23)   Tso chuan (Hsi 24)

    11. Hsing (19)   Tso chuan (Hsi 24)

    12. Shen (29)   Shih pen

    13. Jui (6)   Shih pen

    14. Cheng (21)   Shih pen

15. Yen[1] (34)   Shih pen

16. Yu (9)   Tso chuan (Hsiang 29)

17. Kuo (2, 8, 20)   Tso chuan (Hsiang 29)

According to Tso chuan (Hsi 24), 2 to 7 were the descendants of Wen Wang, 8 to 10 were the descendants of Wu Wang, and 11 was the descendant of Chou Kung.

    B. Ssu   family - Hsia descendants   Hsia pen chi, Tso chuan (Hsiang 29).

18. Ch'i[3] (36)   Tso chuan (Hsiang 29); Chou yü II; Shih pen; Hsia pen chi.

19. Tseng (47)   Chou yu II; Shih pen; Hsia pen chi.

It is known that the site of Hsia was in the northern part of Shansi province (discussed under the Chin State), yet the Hsia descendants in Chou's time were mostly in the eastern areas.

    C. Chiang   family - T'ai Yüeh   descendants Tso chuan (Yin 11, Ch'uang 23).

20. Ch'i[2] (38)   Chou yü II, III; Shih pen; Ch'i shih chia.

21. Hsü[3] (22)   Chou yu II, III; Shih pen.

22. Chi (37)   K'ung's commentary to Tso chuan (Yin 1) quoted in Tu Yü's Shih chu p'u.

We know that the Chiang family was originally located at Shansi province.

    D. Kuei   family - Shun   descendants   Ch'en ch'i shih c｜
      or Huang Ti   descendants   Bronze

23. Ch'en (24)   Ch'en ch'i shih chia

24. T'ien (38)   T'ien shih chia

E. Jen   family - Huang Ti descendants   Chin yu IV

or T'ai Kao descendants   Tso chuan (Hsi 21)

25. Chu[4] (39)   Shih pen

26. Hsüeh (51)   Shih pen

According to Tso chuan (Hsi 21) Jen and the other three
states which were located in Shantung province were of the
feng   family who served the sacrifase of T'ai Kao   .
According to Chin yu IV of Kao yu there were twelve family names
including jen, which belonged to Huang Ti's descendants. Therefore, jen was derived from the feng group. It seems to me that
the kuei family is somehow related to the jen family, for the
Tso chuan (Chao 17) says, "Ch'en was the old site of T'ai Kao,"
which is the ancestor of jen, and also the T'ien bronze (Shan
chai 88) claimed that Huang Ti was T'ien's ancestor. Here we
should notice that Huang Ti, T'ai Kao, Shao Kao   and other
names which were claimed by different states as their ancestors
were merely legendary ancestors in the tribal mythology.
Moreover, during the later period some states adopted legendary
ancestors other than their own, and thus the confusion increases.
Scholars of the late Chan Kuo period tried to build up an ideal
ancient world under the influence of "Taoism" which made different sources into one single origin. There, we find Huang Ti
as a mystic figure and he became the common ancestor to all
states.

F. Tzu   family - Shang descendants   Yin pen chi

27. Shang (14)   Yin pen chi

28. Sung (25)   Yin pen chi; Shih pen

29. Tai (26)   Ch'ien fu lun

30. Shih (45)   Shih pen

31. Hsü[2] (52)   Tso chuan (Ting 4)

32. Pei (35)

33. Yung (27)

34. Chih (7)   Chang's commentary to
                         Chao shih chia

G. Ying   family - Shao Kao descendants   Tso chuan (Chao 17)
                                              Feng shan shu of
                                              Shih chi

35. Ch'in (1)   Ch'in pen chi

36. Chao (12)   Ch'in pen chi;
                         Chao shih chia

37. T'an (50)   Ch'in pen chi; Ch'ien fu lun

38. Chü (48)   Ch'in pen chi; Shih pen

39. Chiang (30)   Ch'in pen chi; Shih pen

40. Huang (31)   Ch'in pen chi; Shih pen

41. Liang (5)   Tso chuan (Hsi 17)

30. Shih (45)   Ch'ien fu lun

31. Hsü[2] (52)   Ch'in pen chi; Shih pen

42. Yen[3] (41)   Shih pen

H. Mien   family - Lu Chung   descendants Ch'u shih chia

43. Ch'u (53)   Cheng yü; Shih pen

44. Yüeh (55)   Cheng yü; Shih pen

I. Ts'ao   family - Lu Chung descendants Ch'u shih chia

45. Chu[1] (43)   Cheng yü; Shih pen

46. Ni   (44)   Shih pen

38. Chü (48)   Cheng yü

J. Chi³ 己   family - Lu Chung descendants   Ch'u shih chia

        or Shao Kao descendants   Shih pen

    47. Su (18)   Cheng yu; Chin yü I.

    38. Chü (48)   Shih pen; Tso chuan (Wen 7, 8).

K. Man   family

    48. Teng (32)   Shih pen

L. Yün   family

    49. Jo (33)   Shih pen

The close relationships between Tzu and Ying are:

(1) Hsü² and Shih, each has both Tzu and Ying as

       his name.

(2) Hsü², Ch'in and Shang had the same legend claiming

       that their ancestor was born from a bird's egg.

(3) Shao Kao was the ancestor of the Ying family,

       which can be identified as Ku   , the first

       ancestor of Shang. (cf. my article "Myths and

       Witchcraft during the Shang Period, " Yenching

       Hsueh Pao, no 20, pp. 490 ff.; and "The Names

       of the King of Shang," ibid., no. 27, pp. 117ff).

(4) According to Tso chuan (Chao 29), one of the four

       uncles of Shao Kao named Kai   can be identified

       as the prince of Ying named Hai (cf. above men-

       tioned articles).

The close relations between Chi[3] and Ying are:

(1) Both claimed to be the descendants of Shao Kao.

(2) Chü had both family names Chi[3] and Ying

(3) Yen[3] of Ying originally occupied the old site of Shao Kao.

The close relations between Chi[3], Ts'ao and Mien are:

(1) All three of the families were the descendants of Chu Jung   according to Cheng Yü's statement. Also these three names were the three sons of Lu Chung according to Ch'u shih chia, Shih pen, and Ti hsi of Ta tai li.

(2) Chü had both of the names of Ts'ao and Chi[3].

(3) Both Cheng yü and Shih pen say that K'un Wu is of the Chi family.

In Tso chuan (Chao 12), Ch'u claimed that Kun Wu was the uncle of their great grandfather, who lived at old Hsü[3]. Therefore, Kun Wu of the Chi family had the same ancestors as Ch'u of the Mien family.

(4) According to Tso chuan (Chao 29), one of the four uncles of Shao Kao named Chung   can be identified as Chung, in Ch'u shih chia, who was the ancestor of Ch'u.

From the above, we reach the conclusion that Tzu, Ying, Chi[3], Ts'ao and Mien were probably derived from the same origin. During Ch'eng Wang's time, when the Shang descendants and Kuan and Ts'ai of the Chou family rebelled against Chou, many of the five families joined the rebelling side.

As we have mentioned before, T'ai Kao and Shao Kao are legendary ancestors. The general distribution of their old sites could be traced according to the records in Tso chuan

Ting 4:   Lu - the old site of Shao Kao, now Ch'ü-fu.

Ai 17:   Wei - the old site of Kun Wu, now P'u-yang.

Chao 17:   Ch'en - the old site of T'ai Kao, now Huai-yang.

Chao 17:   Cheng - the old site of Chu Jung, now Hsin-cheng.

According to Tso chuan (Chao 12), Kun Wu also lived at
old Hsu^3, now Hsu-ch'ang Hsien. The fief of Ts'ao State and the
one time capital of Wei in 660 B.C. possibly occupied the
original area of the Ts'ao family.

The general distribution of the above mentioned families
can be summarized as follows: The Chi of Chou were derived from
the southern part of Shensi, during the Chou dynasty it covered
all of the areas except Chiang Huai. I doubt that Wu was of the
Chou family as he claimed himself to be. During the Chou
dynasty, the Ssu family was in the Shantung area and the Chiang
family was in central Honan and Shantung areas, although both were
originally from Shansi province. The Kuei family was in central Honan. One of its branches moved to the Shantung area. The
Jen family was in Shantung. The five families Chi^3, Ying, Tzu,
Ts'ao and Mien occupied the vast area of Honan, Shantung, Hopei,
and Chiang Huai. These also extended to southern Shensi province
in the early days. There was a branch of the Shang people who
lived in southern Shansi province that was called northern Yin   .
It was exterminated by Ch'in and the king fled to Jung   in
714 B.C. (recorded in Ch'in pen chi). Although Ch'in stayed in
Kansu and Shensi, we have little doubt that Ch'in originally
came from the East. In Ch'in pen chi, Fei-lien   was one
of Ch'in's ancestors, and later the name became the name of a
tribe. T'eng wen kung II of Meng tzu in recording the attack of
Chou in the East said, "He forced Fei-lien   to the corner

of the sea and killed him." This Fei-lien should be considered
as a tribe in Shantung.

The Man may be the same as the Mien. The Yün must have
had close relations with the other five tribes.   It may be the
Yün 允 family mentioned in Cheng yü, one of the eight names derived from Chu Jung.

III. Cultural Relations and Influences

We are now in the position to discuss further the cultural relations and influences between the states. In ancient
times, the Yellow River Valley was the cradle of Chinese culture.
Hsia, Shang and Chou, the so-called 'Three Dynasties'
were situated along the banks of the river from West to East.
In the North, the Great Wall, an artificial line, was the northern boundary of Chinese culture. This culture was extended
north of the Great Wall during the Ch'in and Han periods. In
the south, the Yang Tzu River was the natural boundary which
separated the South from the North. During the Three Dynasties,
the Hsia in the west was conquered by Shang of the east. The
latter moved westward to occupy the territory in Honan, the so-
called "central plain"   , thus Shang probably adopted a
great deal of Hsia's culture. Later, Chou of the west with her
overwhelming military power invaded eastward and conquered Shang,
which had already attained the height of her culture and aesthetic
achievements. The successive dynasties did not interupt the
continuous development of the essential traditional Chinese culture. That is, the conquerors adopted the culture of the defeated.

There are many evidences from the bronzes to show that Chou, as
a whole, adopted Shang culture. Here we quote Confucius, "Yin
taking advantage from Hsia's rites, of which the omitted or the
added parts could be known; Chou taking advantage of Yin's rites,
of which the omitted or the added parts could be known." (Wei
cheng of Lun yü).

The direction of the contact made among these three
kingdoms was East and West. Shang went westward as far as the
central plain. Chou came from the West, took the central plain,
established the Eastern capital there and then moved further east
to Shantung. Thus Chou, under one sovereignty, occupied the
Western, Central and Eastern part of China along the Yellow River.
During the Western Chou period the culture of this vast area was
represented by one unified type as reflected in the uniform
styles, decorations, inscriptions, etc. on the Western Chou
bronzes. The earlier group of the Hsin Cheng bronzes, which can
be dated as Early Ch'un Ch'iu, preserved the Western Chou style
in some ways, but after that time the style of the later group
changed. During the Ch'un Ch'iu period Chin and her three chiefs,
who later found three states, viz., Han, Chao and Wei, began to
expand their power from North to South. At the end of that
period, Wu and Yüeh of the southern area came in contact with the
central and eastern states, and thus brought in new cultural
patterns. About the same time, Ch'u from the South and Yen[1]
from the Northeast became powers. Thus Yen[1] and Chin of the North
together with Wu, Yüeh and Ch'u from the South had greatly modi-
fied and enlivened the old culture of the Yellow River Valley.
These Southern and Northern states were in turn possibly influenced by the boundary culture of the neighboring tribes who
made possible the introduction of culture from the remote areas.

Table 1, part I

I. Names of States

A. Shensi area

    1. Ch'in

    2. Western Kuo

    3. Chou

    4. Tu

B. Shansi area

    5. Liang

    6. Jui

    7. Chih

    8. Northern Kuo

    9. Yu

    10. Chin

    11. Han

    12. Chao

    13. Wei (Liang)

C. Northern Honan area

    14. Shang

    15. Wei

D. Central Hoana area

    16. Tung Chou

17. Hsi Chou

18. Su

19. Hsing

20. Eastern Kuo

21. Cheng

22. Hsü[3]

23. Ying

24. Ch'en

25. Sung

26. Tai

27. Yung

E. Southern Honan area

28. Ts'ai

29. Shen

30. Chiang

31. Huang

32. Teng

33. Jo

F. Hopei area

34. Yen[1]

35. Pei

G. Shantung area

36. Ch'i^3

37. Chi

38. Ch'i^2

39. Chu^4

40. Lu

41. Shang Yen^3

42. Po Ku

43. Chu^1

44. Ni

45. Shih

46. Ts'ao

47. Tseng

48. Chü

49. T'eng

50. T'an

51. Hsüeh

52. Hsü^2

E. Chiang Huai area

    53. Ch'u

    54. Wu

    55. Yüeh

取府

Names of States on Bronzes and in Literature

Shih chi	Bronzes	Other Literature
1. 秦	森	
2, 8. 虢	虢	
3. 周	周 周	
4. 杜	杜	
5. 梁	汋	
6. 芮	内	
7. 知	智	智 (说文)
9. 虞	吴, 虞	
10. 晉	晉	晉 (说文)
11. 韓	荀	
12. 趙		邯鄲 (紀年)
13. 魏	鄴, 梁	梁 (紀年, 孟子)
14. 商	商	
15. 衛	衛	
16. 東周	東周	
17. 西周		
18. 蘇	魷, 蘇	

	Shih chi	Bronzes	Other Literature
19.		井	郉 (说文)
21.	鄭	奠	
22.	许	鄦, [illegible]	鄦 (说文)
23.	應	雁	
24.	陳	敶	
25.	宋	宋	
26.	戴	𢦏	戴 (左傳) 載 (公羊) [illegible] (说文)
27.	鄘		
28.	蔡	[illegible]	
29.	沈	沈	邥 (廣韻)
30.	江	邛, 〃	
31.	黄	黄	
32.	鄧	[illegible]	
33.	鄀	鄀, [illegible], [illegible]	鄀 (左傳) 若 (漢志)
34.	燕	匽, 郾	
35.	邶	北	
36.	杞	杏, [illegible], 杞	

<u>Shih chi</u>	Bronzes	Other Literature
37. 紀	己	
38. a. 齊 b. 田	𨫼,坴 陳,陸	
39. 祝	鑄	祝（周本紀,樂元） 鑄（呂氏慎大,左傳,潛夫論
40. 魯	魯	
41. 奄	芸	商蓋（韓非子説林,墨子耕柱
42. 薄姑	專古	
43. 邾	鼄,邾	邾子（左傳,敳果伯） 邾婁子（春秋,公羊傳） ~~小邾~~ 鄒（説文） 騶（陳世家,漢志）
44. '	奠邑	小邾子（左傳） 郳（説文）
45. 郭	寺,郭	郭（春秋,説文） 詩（公羊,漢志） 時（潛夫論）
46. 曹		
47.	鄶	鄶（左傳,國語,説文） 繪（夏本紀,敳果,鈔策）

Shih chi	Bronzes	Other Literature
48. 莒	簹, 鷺	
49. 滕	朕	
50. 郯	炎	郯 (紀年, 齊世家) 譚 (春秋) 鄲 (說文)
51. 薛	辥	
52. 徐	郐	邻 (說文) 俆 (詩, 周化鐘氏)
53. 楚	楚, 荆楚, 查, 邑楚	荆 (郭沫)
54. 吳	工盧, 攻敔, 吳, 邗, 攻吳	
55. 越	戉, 姑	於粵 (紀年)

1. name of States

A. Shensi area

   1. Ch'in 秦

   2. Western Kuo 西虢

   3. Chou 周

   4. Tu 杜

B. Shansi area

   5. Liang 梁

   6. Jui 芮

   7. Chih 知

   8. Northern Kuo 北虢

   9. Yu 虞

   10. Chin 晉

   11. Han 韓

   12. Chao 趙

   13. Wei (Liang) 魏

C. Northern Honan area

   14. Shang 商

   15. Wei 衛

D. Central Honan area

   16. Tung Chou 東周

   17. Hsi Chou 西周

   18. Su 蘇

   19. Hsing 邢

   20. Eastern Kuo 東虢

   21. Cheng 鄭

   22. Hsu[3] 許

   23. Ying 應

   24. Ch'en 陳

   25. Sung 宋

26. Tai 戴

27. Yung 鄘

E. Southern Honan area

     28. Ts'ai 蔡

     29. Shen 沈

     30. Chiang 江

     31. Huang 黃

     32. Teng 鄧

     33. Jo 鄀

F. Hopei area

     34. Yen[1] 燕

     35. Pei 邶

G. Shantung area

     36. Ch'i[3] 杞

     37. Chi 紀

     38. Ch'i[2] 齊

     39. Chu[4] 鑄

     40. Lu 魯

     41. Shang Yen[3] 商奄

     42. Po Ku 薄姑

     43. Chu[1] 邾

     44. Ni 郳

     45. Shih 郭

     46. Ts'ao 曹

     47. Tseng 曾

     48. Chü 莒

     49. T'eng 滕

     50. T'an 郯

     51. Hsüeh 薛

52. Hsü² 徐

H. Chiang Huai area

53. Ch'u 楚

54. Wu 吳

55. Yüeh 越

L 187

CHAPTER VI

TERMINOLOGY

The names of the parts of a whole vessel were freely
used by scholars without definitions. It is not easy to give
each part an adequate name, and yet it is necessary to have
terms in discussing typology so I have tried to make out the
following tentative definitions and classifications. Some of
the names were adopted from the old Chinese terms such as ears,
mouth, shoulder, legs, belly, neck, etc. Definitions were
given to restrict each term into a more definite sense and this
method will be followed throughout this work.

Before discussing each part of a vessel, first we should
be clear about the meaning of the different 'pieces' of a vessel.
A vessel may be divided into the following parts:

1. Vessel with only main body: It has no lid or other
   separate pieces attached to it. The vessel was made
   as a whole piece and could function by itself, such
   as ku.

2. Vessel with body and lid: This can be subdivided into
   three groups:

   a) Lid has no other function than to cover the mouth
      or the opening of the body, such as the lid of
      kuang. Here the lid is only a subordinate piece.

   b) Lid serving as an independent function, more than
      to cover the mouth of the main body. Such as the
      lid of hsü, which is a dish at the same time. The

lid is smaller than the main body. It is itself
a vessel as well as a part of the main body.

c) Lid serving as an independent function, more than
to cover the mouth of the main body and is identical with the body. Such as in <u>tun</u> and <u>fu</u>, the lid
can be separately used as the body. I call this
'part'. Therefore the <u>tun</u> and <u>fu</u> ~~were~~ each composed of
two identical 'parts'.

3. Vessel composed of two compartments, such as <u>hsien</u>:
The upper part is <u>tseng</u> and the lower part is <u>li</u> or
<u>ch'i</u>. It can not be considered as two individual
vessels because it was often made in one piece, that
is, the two compartments were usually cast together
as one vessel.

Some vessels were used together with other vessels, such
as the water vessel <u>i</u> with the <u>p'an</u> and the <u>shao</u> with wine vessels. They should be considered as independent vessels because
they were made in separate pieces, and they do not belong to a
particular vessel, that is, the <u>i</u> may ladle water for any <u>p'an</u>
or the <u>shao</u> may ladle wine for any wine vessels.

All descriptions are based on a vessel standing in its
normal position, that is, a vessel standing on its base or feet
with the lid in position; the handles or spout to left and right
om a plane facing the observer at eye-level. If the vessel's
cross section is circular or square, the front view is determined
by its decoration. If the vessel's cross section is other than
circular or square, the long side of a vessel is considered the
front. If the vessels have handles from front to rear, the front
is determined by the decoration and the larger side.

I. Height and width: The height of a regular vessel
is measured along a vertical axis taken through the
center, and the width of the vessel is measured on
a horizontal axis taken along the line of maximum
width. The height of irregular vessels is measured
along a perpendicular dropped from its highest
point to the plane of its base.

II. Proportion of the vessel

A. "High": Axis of greatest length in the vertical.
Height greater than width.

B. "Medium": Equidimensional, height equals appro-
ximately the width.

"Low": Axis of the greatest length in the horizontal. Width greater than height.

The terms 'long,' 'tall' and 'short' are also used in
the same sense. For instance, the ratio of the height and width
of a certain vessel is 2 to 1, then this vessel is high or long,
if the reverse is true then the vessel is low or short.

III. Proportions of the parts within a vessel (or type):
For instance, take a certain vessel A (or a type A),
the proportion of the height of its body and the
base is 4 to 1, and another vessel B (or type B),
the proportion of such is 6 to 1, then in comparison, the base of A is higher or taller than that
of B and is thus called 'tall base' as in the description of vessel A.

IV. Size of the vessel: The terms 'large' and 'small'
are used to indicate the volume or size of a certain
vessel or type. Such as when we say the chia is

larger than the <u>chüeh</u> we mean that the general size
or volume of the <u>chüeh</u> is smaller than that of the
<u>chia</u>.

Terminology for Food, Wine and Water Vessels

A. Lid

I. Component parts of the lid

   A. Tops: The function of the top is to hold the lid or to
support the lid when it is inverted such as under 7 in
the following.

     1. Knob

       a) Spherical   as in <u>yu</u> I

       b) Mushroom-shaped   as in <u>chih</u> I

       c) Gable-roof-shaped   as in <u>Fang-i</u> I

     2. In the form of a bird   as in <u>Yu</u> VI

     3. In the form of an animal as in <u>ho</u> IV (<u>Ku kung</u>: 27.2)

     4. Circular ring   as in <u>ho</u> III, IV (<u>Sumitomo</u> I:100)

     5. Semi-circular ring or loop as in <u>ho</u> II-IV

     6. Cup-shaped

       a) Circular   as in <u>hu</u> III

       b) Elliptical   as in <u>yu</u> VII

       c) Oblong   as in <u>hsü</u>

       d) Trumpet   as in <u>tou</u>

     7. Small feet

       a) Rings   as in <u>tun</u> I

       b) hooked rings   as in <u>tun</u> I

       c) Semi-circular rings   as in <u>ting</u> VII

       d) Vertical right angle plates as in <u>hsü</u>

One to six are always one in number on the center of the lid. Seven is usually in groups of three or four symmetrically arranged on the lid.

B. Beaks: Two in number situated on both sides between the domed part and the lower part of the lid, as in <u>yu</u> IV, X.

C. Links: a series of links connecting the lid to the body. The links were fastened to a ring on the lid and to a ring on the neck (sometimes on the top of the handle), as in <u>ho</u>.

D. Collar: That part of the lid extended downward from the domed part of the lid forming a surrounding wall which directly rests on the mouth of the body, as in <u>yu</u> I.

E. Inserted lip: An extending and curving inside edge underneath the lid to be inserted to fit over the mouth of the body, as in <u>chih</u>.

F. Teeth: Several small plates projected from the rim of the lid or the body to overlap the rim of the other part in order to hold the two parts (the lid and the body) firmly, as in <u>fu</u>.

II. The shape of the lid

A. Flat

1. Plate   as in <u>ting</u> III

2. Plate with a collar   as in <u>ting</u> VII

B. Domed

1. Domed as in <u>lei</u> I

2. Domed with collar as in <u>yu</u> I

C. Corona: Crown shaped blades, spreading out petal-like

on the collar without a top, as in hu VI.

D. Truncated pyramid: Rectangular as in hsü, square as
   in hu VII.

E. Gable-roof: As in fang-i.

F. Eccentric domed shape: The center of the dome is
   offset to one side.

   1. Saddle-shaped: The edge of the two sides of the
      lid makes a monoclinal curve above the spout and
      inclines towards the other direction above the
      single handle, as in kuang.

   2. Like the saddle-shaped as in kuang, but flattened
      at the center, as in i (Siren: 22). *u.s.836*

G. Warped: symmetrical, convex lid like a saddle that is
   slightly depressed at the center where the top rests,
   as in chiao.

B. Body

The body is the main part of the vessel used to receive
or hold various materials.

I. Depth of the body

   A. "Deep": The vertical axis of the body is greater than
      its width, as in lei.

   B. "Medium depth": The vertical axis of the body is
      nearly equal to its width, as in kuei I.

   C. "Shallow": The vertical axis of the body is smaller
      than its width, as in p'an.

II. Bulged parts of the body

   A. "Upper bulge": Maximum diameter of the body above the
      center, as in lei

B. "Middle bulge": Maximum diameter of the body at
the center, as in _ying_ I.

C. "Lower bulge": Maximum diameter of the body is below the center, as in _yu_ X.

III. Mouth: The mouth is the opening of the body. The shape
of the mouth generally determined the shape of the lid
and the body in its transverse section.

A. The shape of the mouth

1. Circular

2. Elliptical

3. Oblong

4. Square

5. Rectangular

6. Rectangular polygon other than square

7. Irregular

B. Proportion of mouth with the belly

1. Wide mouth: Width of the mouth is greater or equal
to the width of the belly, as in _tsun_ and _ting_.

2. Trumpet mouth: Wide mouth with a spreading rim like
a trumpet, as in _ku_.

3. Medium mouth: Width of the mouth is smaller than
the width of the belly, as in _kuei_ V.

4. Small mouth: Width of the mouth is much smaller
than the width of the belly, with a short neck,
as in _lei_.

5. Bottle mouth: Small mouth with a high neck, as in
_hu_ X.

IV. Rim: The edge of the mouth is called the 'rim'.

A. Spreading rim: The rim turns outward, spreads widely,

as in <u>ku</u>.

    B. Limited spreading rim: Not as wide as above, as in <u>chih</u>.
All vessels with constricted necks are bound to have
limited spreading rims.

 V. Neck: The section under the rim and above the shoulder or
belly that has a smaller diameter than either the mouth
or the belly. Vessels may or may not have a sharp line
of demarcation between the neck and the belly.

    A. Height of the neck

      1. High, as in <u>hu</u> I.

      2. Low, as in <u>min</u>.

    B. Curvature of the neck

      1. Straight: Extends upward from the shoulder, as in
<u>lei</u> II.

      2. Constricted: Usually low

 VI. Belly: That part of the body below the neck and above the
base.

 VII. Shoulder: The upper bulged part of the belly is the shoulder.

    A. Curved, as in <u>lei</u> I.

    B. Angular, as in <u>tsun</u> I.

VIII. Bottom: The lowest part of the belly sitting on the legs
or feet or the base.

    A. Hemispheric, as in <u>ting</u> VI.

    B. Slightly concave upward, as in <u>ting</u> I.

    C. Flat, as in <u>ting</u> III.

    D. Tripartite: divided into three equal parts, as in <u>ting</u> II.

    E. Tetrapartite: divided into four equal parts, as in
<u>ho</u> IV.

IX. Spout: A projection of the body for pouring the liquid.

    A. Tube-shaped: Inserted in the body at the shoulder, as
in ho.

    B. Channel-spout: Projecting and turning outward from
the rim of the mouth in the form of a channel, the
edge of which remaines open, as in i I.

    C. Animal-head spout: As in B, but the end is closed
and the whole spout is in the form of an animal-head
with the opening through the mouth of the animal, as
in i II.

X. Tails: The salient part of the rim that turns upward,
outward and forms a triangular shape, as in chiao.

C. Handling Parts

I. Ears: Placed on or under the rim of the mouth, originally
used for moving with hooks when the vessel's hot as in wine vessels;
sometimes for holding by hands as in water vessels.

    A. Vertical ears: Usually two in number placed on each
side of the rim, as in ting I.

    B. Bent ears: Placed under the rim and bent upward, as
in yü I.

    C. Pillars: Usually two in number with various knobs on
them, as the following:

        1. Bottle-shaped

        2. Mushroom-shaped

        3. Gable-roof-shaped

        4. In the form of a bird, as in chia (Sumitomo: 88).

D. Bent pillars: The position on the vessel is the same
　　as the bent ears, as in chia (Hakkaku: 17).

II. Handles: Used to carry or move the vessel by hand.　Placed
　　at one or more sides of the vessel.

A. Semi-circular: Generally attached under the rim of the
　　mouth.

　　1. Single handle, as in ho.

　　2. Two handles, as in kuei II.

　　3. Four handles, as in kuei III.

　　4. Movable single handle, as in hu VIII.

B. Swing-handles: Generally attached to two rings, loops
　　or pegs on both sides under the rim of the mouth.

　　1. Solid

　　　　a) Rope, as in yu Ia

　　　　b) Flat, as in yu Ib

　　2. Chain, as in hu VI

　　3. Bridge, as in ho VII

C. Loose rings: Two or more large rings hung on animal-
　　heads, rings or loops on different sides under the
　　rim of the mouth. *as on hu VI and chien*

D. Rings: Two or more circular (annular) rings attached
　　to different sides of the vessel, as in tou.

E. Loops: Two or more small semi-circular rings attached
　　to different sides of the vessel, as in ~~chien~~. *lei II*

F. Lugs: Usually two in number, appear between the rim
　　and the shoulder of the body.　The lugs are hollow
　　in the center in order to let the handle (other than
　　bronze materials) go through, as in hu II, III.

G. Handles in the form of birds or animals, as in hu (Cull

(Cull: 12)

III. Stem: The cylindrical part under the body and above the
     base used for holding, as in tou.

IV. Rod: A long rod attached to the body.

   A. Flat, as in shao

   B. Other than flat

V. Nose: A semi-circualr holder located at the lower part
    of the body above the base, as in lei.

D. Supports

Generally placed under the bottom of the body.   A heating vessel is one which is placed under another vessel in such
manner as to allow the fire to go up without interruption.   The
function of containers is to bear up its weight and hold it
firmly in place.

I. Legs: Attached to the bottom of the body.   The function
    is for heating, or setting the vessel on the fire.

   A. Solid

      1. Cylindrical, as in ting I

      2. Three-facet, as in chia I, II, III

      3. Hoof-shaped, as in ting Vb, VI, VII

      4. Pointed as in ting   (Wu ying: 79)

      5. In the form of animals, as in ting IV

   B. Hollow: Usually hollow in the upper part and solid in
       the lower part.   The upper part is extended from the
       tripartite or tetrapartite bottom of the body.

   Relation of legs with bottom--   Hollow legs usually
   support tripartite (if three legs) or tetrapartite (if
   four legs) bottom .   Three solid legs usually support a

concave or hemispheric bottom . Four solid legs usually support a flat bottom.

Relation of legs with mouth.-- Three-legged vessels usually have a circular mouth. Four-legged vessels usually have a rectangular or oblong mouth, except the ho which sometimes has four legs and a circular mouth.

C. Parts of the legs

Knee and hoof: The top part of the leg attached to the bottom of the body is called the 'knee' and the 'hoof' is a foot-like terminus to the leg, as in ting V, VI, VII. 'Decorated knee' is a knee with decor, as in ting I.

II. Feet: Legs under the base, or small feet under the bottom used to support the vessel.

A. Legs under the base as in kuei. (Fogg: 44.57.8)

B. Small feet under the bottom

   1. Rings, as in tun I

   2. Hooked ring, as in tun I

   3. Solid, as in tun, i, kuang

III. Base: A surrounding wall under the bottom functioning as feet, always hollow inside. Varieties of base:

A. Shape of transverse section

   1. Circualr

   2. Elliptical

   3. Oblong

   4. Square

   5. Rectangular

   6. Regular polygon

   7. Irregular

B. Height of wall

   1. Low

   2. High

C. Curvature of the wall

   1. Curved: The high wall curved from the upper part
downward to the spreading brim.

   2. Straight: Vertical or slightly diverged downward

   3. Brimmed: The lowest continuation of the upper portion of the base which abruptly spreads outward
and forms a brim with certain height and width.

   4. Pedestal, as in hu (Pillsbury: 36.42)

D. Other shapes

   1. Quadruped: A rectangular base divided into four
symmetrical portions (or slotted in the center of
each side), as in fang-i.

   2. Truncated cone-shaped: for circular high base only,
as in ying.

   3. Truncated pyramid-shaped: for rectangular and square
high base only. Rectangular as in kuang (Yu and
Kuang: 46); square as in hu VII.

E. Socle: A square or rectangular stand with a flat top.
The vessel which the socle supports is either attached
or placed on top of the socle.

   A. Connected, as in kuei II, tsun (Burhcard Catalogue:
pl. 24, no. 273).

   B. Detached, as in yu (Metropolitan: 24.72.3).

The above mentioned parts can be classified under two

headings: (1) The determinative part, and (2) the non-determina-

tive part. The determinative part shows the main function of
the vessel. Thus it can be seen that all heating vessels have
legs, ears or pillars, while all containers, usually with lids,
have feet or base, but no legs. Water vessels have wide mouths
without lids, while wine containers have narrow mouths and,
usually, lids, although some wine containers as ku and tsun have
wide mouths and are without lids. These vessels were probably
used not to store wine but for drinking wine during the performance of the ceremony. The swing-handle or the spout is the
determinative part of a yu or ho, while without this it is a hu
or chia respectively.

The non-determinative part *is a minor addition of the part
which was added to a vessel and which was not the characteristic
of the type of the vessel in question*. Such as tsun which are usually
without handles, ~~but sometimes a tsun~~ may appear with a handle.
Despite the appearance of the handle, we shall still call it a
tsun because the original function of the tsun has not been
changed. Yu may have spouts, but they can not have legs at the
same time. Ting or p'an may have small channel spouts as the
water vessel i, but if the vessel is still in the shape of the
ting or p'an it is a ting or p'an.

The size of a vessel is not very significant in the study
of typology. Some of the types are always small in size, such as
chüeh and chih. Usually yü and lei are large in size. The vessels made for burial purposes are sometimes so very small in
size that they could not have actually been used.

I have distinguished legs from feet to make it clear that
legs were used on heating vessels and feet were used for supports.

And I deliberately call the part for the hook on heating vessels
the ears, and not handles, because the handles are actually to
be held by hands.   It should be borne in mind that sometimes
the feet on containers may be as high as the legs of heating vessels. They are called feet despite their length because of the
defined function. The water vessel <u>p'an</u> quite often has ears,
but in comparison with the quantity of the heating vessels they
are not great enough to change the heating function of ears to
a supporting function. And furthermore, the water vessel has
bent ears but not vertical ears. Therefore vertical and bent
ears are still the characteristics of heating vessels.

It should be noticed also that a vessel of a certain
class must require more than one characteristic of its own class.
This means that it must have at least more than one determinative
part which is common to its own class. For instance, a <u>ting</u> must
have both ears and legs. If it has no ears it should not be
considered as a <u>ting</u> unless it was so proved by other evidence
such as being referred to in its inscription as <u>ting</u>, etc.

E. Ornamental Appendages

I. Protuberances: Usually on lid, three or four in number,
in the form of birds or animals, as in <u>ting</u> VII.

II. Animal-heads

A. At the end of swing-handles, as in <u>yu</u>

B. On the top of handles, as in <u>kuei</u>

C. On the shoulder, as in <u>tsun</u> I

D. On the neck, as in <u>kuei</u> X

E. On the knee, as in ting

III. Pendants: Hang from the underside of the handles

    A. Rectangular, as in kuei

    B. Hooked, as in kuei II

    C. Filled-hook, as in kuei II

IV. Flanges: Run up and down on the edges or between the edges of the lid and the body, four or eight rows in number.

    A. Solid, as in ting I

    B. Hooked, as in yu III

V. Projecting beams: Both on the lid and on the body, as in fang-i (Fogg: 44.57.37).

Except for the projecting beams, which serve as supports on the lids and as handles of the body, the rest have no function. They are plastic figures projecting from the decorated or undecorated surfaces. Their presence can only be explained in terms of their ornamental uses.

CHAPTER VII

CLASSIFICATION

The different purposes for which bronzes were made may be listed under three categories: (1) for general purposes, (2) for ceremonial purposes, and (3) for funeral or mortuary purposes. Among the pre-Shang pottery we found many cooking vessels and containers which were the forerunners of the bronze vessels and which were used in every day life and for mortuary purposes. In fact there is no great difference between these three categories. Bronze vessels used every day that were made for general use could also be used for ceremonies and burials. The ancient people treated their deceased ancestors as though they were alive. Therefore the descendants made the ceremonial vessels in the form of daily used vessels. For burial purposes they may bury their dead with the daily used vessels, the ceremonial vessels or the vessels specially made for funeral purposes. The mortuary type was called <u>ming-ch'i</u> . <u>T'an Kung</u> of <u>Li chi</u> says, "Ming-ch'i was made for the deceased man (to be used in another world), and the sacrificial vessel was made for the living man (to be used when presenting offerings to their ancestors.")

The materials and the decorations found on the vessels of the three catagories are sometimes different because of the different purposes for which they were used. The burial objects were often made in a practical way. They have less decoration and are more coarse in grain. The weapons used for burial could not be actually used in fighting. Other materials were sub-

stituted, such as pottery, pewter, or probably wood and bamboo.
It should be noticed that those things found in a tomb were not
necessarily made for burial purposes, for often the vessels of
daily use or the ceremonial vessels were buried. The ceremonial
vessels were often made in a more ornate decoration.

It is difficult, though not impossible, to establish a
completely acceptable classification of Chinese bronzes for the
shapes and forms of certain types of vessels changed according
to their times, their place of origin and their uses. Furthermore,
the uses of certain vessels are still obscure. Below I try to
divide all of the bronzes into three groups according to their
uses and functions:

    I. Ceremonial Objects

        A. Food vessels

           a. Heating vessels　煮食器

           b. Containers　　盛食器

           c. Spoons

        B. Wine vessels

           a. Heating vessels　溫酒器

           b. Containers　　盛酒器

           c. Spoons

沃盥器具

        C. Water vessels　盥器

        D. . Supports　　承器

        E. Musical instruments

    II. Military Objects

        A. Weapons　　兵器

        B. Chariots and harness fittings　車馬器

    III. Domestic Objects

        A. Daily use articles

        B. Agricultural and hand tools

B. Agricultural and hand tools

C. Measurements

I have called the first group 'Ceremonial' rather than 'Sacrificial' vessels because they were not only made for and used in sacrifice, but also in burials, dowries and other ceremonies and great events. Chariots are classed as military objects although they were used both in ceremonies and in warfare. Military objects may be called 'Semi-ceremonial' because of the ceremonial use with the ceremonial objects proper and because they were also buried in tombs and were sometimes made in the mortuary type. Supports were used for the wine and food vessels, and occasionally for the musical instruments.

The wine containers may be subdivided into smaller groups as follows:

1. For storage -- large vessels with fitting lids, as <u>lei</u>

2. For drinking -- small vessels, as <u>chih</u>

3. For containing wine for a short time -- medium vessels with a wide mouth, as <u>tsun</u>.

The spoons in both food and wine vessels were used to transfer dry materials (as meat and rice) or liquid (as wine) respectively. I have used the word "wine" to include those liquids made from grain panicled millet, black millet or wheat, and the mixing of grain wine and fragrant herbs.

The musical instruments may be subdivided into smaller groups as:

1. For ceremonial purposes

A. Forming a set, as Shang bells, <u>chung</u>, <u>kou-ti</u>

B. Single, as <u>chung</u>, <u>po</u>.

2. For military purposes, as <u>to</u>, <u>cheng-ch'eng</u>.

Since the present catalogue will publish the ceremonial
vessels first, more details will be given to this group. The
names of the vessels of this group were, for the most part, first
given in the Sung catalogues. After that, scholars tried to
correct some of their mistakes and supplemented new names. Since
the bronzes after Early Chou often record the name of the vessel
in the inscription, it is easy for us to determine the proper
names. There are vessels, especially the wine vessels, which only
appeared during Shang and Early Chou and disappeared afterwards.
During that period the names were usually not given. Therefore
it is quite difficult to find out the original name. In this
case we can not but adopt the convential names already given by
the Sung scholars which have been generally accepted.

In table I, I have listed the important names of the
ceremonial vessels, and in table II, different writings of the
names on the bronzes are listed. These names are derived from
five sources:

1. The name is referred to in its inscription on the vessel.

2. The name is taken from the pictographic character cur-
   rently used to describe or name this type of vessel.

3. The name is given by the Sung catalogue which was so
   named only because it appeared in the Classics or Ritual
   books and was assumed to be the name of this type of
   vessel without strong evidence.

4. The name is simply given to the vessel without any
   source, being only a vague description of the vessel.

5. The name is given according to the description in some
   other books.

It is obvious that the first two sources are more reliable.

In the following, when the origins of the bronze vessels are discussed, it will be apparent that many are derived from pottery
forms and it is understood that the pottery, the pre-historic
pottery, under discussion is earlier than the bronzes. The pre-
historic pottery mentioned in the following pages was found in
the following sites:

     Honan province

       Mien-ch'ih Hsien

         Yang-shao Ts'un

         Pu-chao Chai

         Wan-shou Ssu

         Kou-pu Ts'un

         Yang-ho Ts'un

         Ma-k'o Ts'un

         Hsi-chung Ts'un

       An-yang Hsien

         Hou Kang

       Kuang-wu Hsien   (formerly Ho Yin   )

         Ch'in-wang Chai

     Shantung province

       Chi-nan Hsien

         Lung-shan Chen

       Jih-chao Hsien

         Liang-ch'eng

     Shansi province

       Wan-ch'üan Hsien

         Ching Ts'un

       Hsia Hsien

         Hsi-yin Ts'un

Kansu province

  Ning-ting Hsien

    Ch'i-chia P'ing

  Lin-t'ao Hsien   (formerly Ti Tao   )

    Ssu-wa

  T'ao-sha Hsien

    Hsin-tien

    Hui-tui

  Lo-tu Hsien   (formerly Nien Po   )

    Ma-ch'ang

  T'ao-ho Hsien

    Ssu-shih-ting

  Lan-chou Hsien   (or Lan Chou)

Tungsan province

  Kuan Tung Chou

  Kao-li Chai

The materials were taken from the following works with their abbreviations listed:

  E.C.C. - J. G. Anderson, "An Early Chinese Culture," _Bul-letin of the Geological Survey of China_. No. 5, part 1.

  P.O.C. - J. G. Anderson, "Prehistory of the Chinese," _BMFEA_. No. 15.

  C.T.Y. - S. Y. Liang _et al. Ch'eng Tsu Yai_. Published by Academia Sinica.

  P.P.C. - G. D. Wu, _Prehistorical Pottery in China_.

The scholars in the field give different dates for the sites. Here I list the chronology made by Anderson and Liang Ssu Yung. Anderson changed his opinion quite often in his recent work. I believe that Ssu Wa should be pre-Shang. All of the dates are tentative and uncertain.

1. Anderson I	2. Liang	3. Anderson II	
Ch'i-chia 3500-3200	3500-3200	2500-2200	
Hou Kang	2900-2600		*Late*
Yang-shao 3200-2900	2600-2300	2200-1700	*Stone age*
Ma-ch'ang 2900-2600	2300-2000	1700-1300	
Lung-shan	2300-2000		
Hsin-tien 2600-2300	2000-1700	1300-1000	
Ssu-wa 2300-2000	1400-1100	1000-700	*Bronze age*
Sha-ching 2000-1700	800-	700-500	

1. J. G. Anderson, "Preliminary Report on Archaeological Research
                 in Kansu," Memoirs of the Geological Survey
                 of China. Series A, no. 5.

2. S. Y. Liang, "Hsiao-t'un, Lung-shan and Yang-shao," article
                 Studies Presented to Ts'ai Yuan P'ei. Part II,
                 pp. 555-565.

3. J. G. Anderson, Prehistory of the Chinese.

        Besides the gray and black pottery, the Academia Sinica
found many ting, hu, lei and tou white pottery fragments in Hou-
chia Chuang and Hsiao-t'un of An-yang. They also found kuei,
p'an and fou, but illustrations of them are not available.
However, in An-yang Finds, pls. 1-22, some of the white pottery
in the Japanese collections have been reconstructed into their
original shapes. Judging from their shape, decorations and inscriptions, they are of the Shang period but earlier than the
Shang bronzes. I have often compared the marble and bronze ves-
els. They also come from An-yang and are generally contempory
with the Shang bronzes but sometimes they are a little bit earlier.

        The gray and black pottery, the white pottery, and the

marble or stone vessels are earlier than the Shang bronzes.
There is a lot of Shang pottery which is contemporaneous with or
later than the Shang bronzes. They will not be treated here because their shapes are copied from bronzes.

I. Ting

Ting is a vessel with solid legs underneath the bottom,
and two vertical ears on the rim. The character for ting on both
oracle bones (Chia ku wen pien: 7.11a) and bronzes (Chin wen
pien: 7.13) is a pictograph of the vessel. All of the heating
vessels for food and wine must have solid or hollow legs connected
immediately underneath the bottom. The function of the two vertical ears is the same as the pillars on the wine-heating vessels,
to move the vessel with hooks called hsüan 鉉 or yü 鋊 .

It seems to me that the bronze ting were derived from
the pottery which was earlier than Shang:

  Examples:

   1. E.C.C. pl. 7.5 from Yang-shao

   2. C.T.Y. pl. 26.2 from Ch'eng-tzu-ya

   3. P.O.C. pl. 179.1 from Pu-chao Chai

   4. C.T.Y. pl. 26.1 from Ch'eng-tzu-ya

   5. P.P.C. fig. 36g from Liang-ch'eng

   6. C.T.Y. pl. 21.5 from Ch'eng-tzu-ya

   7. P.P.C. fig. 4 from Hou-kang

   8. P.O.C. p. 258, fig. 106 a2 from Ch'in-wang Chai

   9. C.T.Y. pl. 21.6 from Ch'eng-tzu-ya

   10. C.T.Y. pl. 24.3 from Ch'eng-tzu-ya

   11. E.C.C. pl. 16.2 from Yang-shao

The pottery ting from Ch'eng-tzu-ya were found in the

lower strata (cf. C.T.Y. pl. 18 figs 6-10). The marble or stone
ting in An-yang Treasures; pl. 61 has very short legs. It probably came from An-yang and is older than the bronze ting. A
pottery ting, in P.O.C. pl. 141 (K 5685), found in Ssu-wa has the
shortest legs. In the same book p. 184 fig. 61, there are three
small pottery ting, bought in Ssu-wa, which have longer legs than
the one in P.O.C. pl. 141 (K 5685). All of these examples are
the forerunners of the bronze ting, Type I, except the last
example which has a shallow body and a wide mouth and is similar
to Type IV bronze ting.

There is a kind of vessel which can rest on the rim of
the ting that is used to cut meat. It was called tsu   . One
is illustrated in Sumitomo II: 192. It is a Shang bronze. Another
one, found at Shou Hsien, is illustrated in International Exhibition: 106. Both look like a small table, but the second one has
four crosses on its surface to let the meat juice come down.

In the inscription of the bronze ting sometimes a special
name is mentioned according to their volume. In San tai: 4.45b
the inscription calls itself ox-ting. In Hsiao chiao: 2.74+the
inscription calls itself sheep-ting. In Shan chai: 28 the inscription mentioned the gift of a pig-ting. In San tai: 8.40b-
41b there are two kuei with the same inscription which also mentioned a pig-ting. The illustrations and sizes are not available
for the ting called ox-ting, sheep-ting and pig-ting. Cheng
Hsuan's commentary to Shan fu of Chou li quoted Chiu chia i saying, that the ox-ting has the largest volume, the sheep-ting
is next and the pig-ting has the smallest. It seems to me that
the names were given according to the volume, that is, the ox-
ting was used to boil the ox, the sheep-ting to boil the sheep
and the pig-ting to boil the pig. The three huge ting found in

Hsin-cheng were large enough to contain a whole sheep or pig, and they may have either of the three names.

The different names, other than _ting_, in the inscriptions for the different types of _ting_ are:

a. _Ch'i_: The rectangular _ting_ were called _fang-ting_ by some scholars. Since '_fang_' means 'square' or 'rectangular' in Chinese, it is better to translate it as 'rectangular _ting_' in English. These rectangular _ting_ were called _ch'i_ in their inscriptions.

Examples are:

_Po ku_: 2.12; _Hsü k'ao ku_: 4.17; _Chen sung_: 1.25;
Shan chai (d): 2.7 (U. S. 67); _Shan chai_ (d): 2.6;
Ch'ang-an: 1.3.

The character _ch'i_ for the first three is a combination of _ch'i_ and ting; for the last three it is a combination of _ch'i_ and _ming_. . They are the same characters in different writings. This is the special name for the rectangular _ting_.

b. _Li-ting_: In the Sung catalogue _Hsüeh shih_: 9.10-11 (_Chün ku_: 22.68a) there is an inscription on a _ting_ which calls itself _li-ting_. No illustration is available. The inscription may be read as "made precious _li-ting_" or "made precious _li_ (and) ting." If the second reading is right, then the term _li-ting_ did not exist in Early Western Chou, or on any bronze. In _Chui i_: 4.14, the author called the tripartite _ting_ the _li-ting_.

c. _Shih-t'o_: During the Ch'un Ch'iu period there were _ting_ which called themselves _shih-t'o_ as shown in _Shang chou_: II, 90 and _Sung chai_ II: 15. The latter was found in Shensi. The body of this is very deep and it has bent ears. _Shih-t'o_ may be the dialect in the western part of China for special type <u>ting</u>.

d. <u>Yü</u>: During the Ch'un Ch'iu period there were <u>ting</u> which called themselves <u>yü</u> as in <u>K'ao ku</u>: 1.19 and <u>Chen sung</u>: 1.17. The shape is like the <u>shih-t'o</u>-- a very deep body, bent ears, and very short legs. In <u>Shang chou</u>: II, 78 the inscription on a <u>ting</u> calls itself <u>yü-ting</u>. The shape is similar to the above two vessels, but this one is earlier

e. <u>Fan</u>: During the Ch'un Ch'iu period there were <u>ting</u> which called themselves <u>fan</u> in their inscriptions as shown in <u>Shan chai</u>: 37-38 (two vessels). Another vessel's inscription is cata-logued in <u>San tai</u>: 4.18b. The shapes of these vessels are similar to the <u>shih-t'o</u> or <u>yü</u>.

f. <u>Tzu</u>: Both <u>Shih ch'i</u> of <u>Er ya</u> and <u>Shuo wen</u> say, "Those <u>ting</u> with a round shape and covered (with a lid) on the top are called <u>tzu</u>." It is a combination of ts'ai 才 (as phonetic element) and <u>ting</u>. <u>Shuo wen</u> also recorded a current writing of <u>tzu</u> 鎡 which had <u>tzu</u> 兹 as its phonetic element. This shows that during the Han dynasty it was pronounced as <u>tzu</u>. According to the above description the <u>tzu</u> is a vessel with its lid form-ing a global or geoid shape. The following <u>ting</u>, in their in-scriptions, called themselves <u>tzu</u>:

1. <u>Sung chai</u> II: 11-12;   2. <u>Po ku</u>: 3.22;

3. <u>Pao yün</u>: 23;   4. <u>T'ao chai</u> I: 1.29

5. <u>Po ku</u>: 3.20   6. <u>Po ku</u>: 3.27

7. <u>Pao yün</u>: 25   8. <u>Yen k'u</u>: 9

9. Yale 40.3.318 (U. S. 92   )   10. <u>Shan chai</u> (d): 1.51

11. <u>Ch'eng ch'iu</u>: 5   12. <u>Po ku</u>: 3.3

13. Po ku: 3.9   14. Hsu k'ao ku: 5.16

15. Ch'ang an: 1.12   16. Shih er: Chiu 1

17. K'ao ku: 1.21   18. Ta hsi: fig. 44

19. Pao yün: 32   20. Shang chou: II, 98

21. Shih er: Pao 1   22. T'ao chai I: 5.6

Numbers 1-2 are ordinary Middle Western Chou ting, and
3-6 are ordinary Late Western Chou ting. In these cases the
name tzu was used as a substitute for ting. Numbers 7-8 are of
the Late Western Chou period, but the vertical ears had changed to
bent ears. The ears were so arranged that a lid could rest on
them without interference from *the vertical ears.*   9-14 are
vessels of the Ch'un Ch'iu period with very deep bodies, bent
ears and lids. In shape they are very much like the shih-t'o and
yü. There is another ting in Shan chai: 39 with the same shape
which was called tzu 𦥑 in its inscription. This character
tzu and the tzu in the inscriptions of the above twenty-two vessels were derived from the same phonetic element ts'ai   .
This proves that this class of ting (1-22) should be called tzu.
15 is similar to 9-14, only the body is flatter and it is of the
Chan Kuo period. 16-17 are only lids; the bodies of the vessels
were lost. 18 has no ears and is of the Ch'un Ch'iu period.
19 has long legs similar to those on the ting found in Shou Hsien
of the Chan Kuo period. 20-21, which will be discussed below,
are also Ch'u vessels. 22 is a Han vessel. A ting made by the
Cheng state (Ch'u ch'i: fig. 9), in its inscription (Ta hsi lu:
200b) called itself tzu, which is the combination of the phonetic
element tzu 𦥯 and ting. This vessel is similar to 21, which
has a spout and bent ears. Again, this proves that the pronunciation of tzu is correct. Shuo wen recorded the current writing

of tzu as tzu   which has the same phonetic element   as the

Cheng bronzes.

From the above we know that the name tzu for ting was not

used until Late Western Chou, so in 17 it was called yü-tzu as

some vessels were called yü-ting (cf. section d). From Late

Western Chou on, those ting which bear the name tzu generally

have lids, bent ears and geoid formed bodies. From the phonetic

element, we know that it was first pronounced as ts'ai and in the

Han dynasty it was pronounced as tzu. Thus tzu after Late Western

Chou became a special type of ting.

g. Ch'iao-tzu: The 21 under f., which was found at Shou Hsien,

called itself Ch'iao-tzu in its inscription. Shuo wen says,

"Ch'iao is like ting but with long legs." The ting, found at

Shou Hsien, which often have long legs is a special type of the

Late Chan Kuo period.

h. I-tzu: The 20 under f., found at Shou Hsien, called it-

self I-tzu in its inscription. The vessel has a rather shallow

body with a channel spout like the water vessel I on one side.

In I shu lei cheng: 10 a ting is illustrated with the same in-

scription as the 7 under f. The illustrated one has a channel

spout. In Pao yun: 27 there is a ting with bent ears a short

channel spout and a small handle on the opposite side of the

spout. In Ch'u ch'i: fig. 9 there is a ting of the Cheng State

with a channel spout and vertical ears. These three are of Late

Western Chou.

II. Li

The li is similar to the ting except that it has hollow

legs. Shih ch'i of Er ya says, "The ting with hollow legs is called li." The character for li in the bronzes (Chin wen pien: 3.15b-16a) is the pictograph of the vessel. The bottom of the vessel forms a tripod, that is tripartite. This makes the heating surface larger than the one for the ting. It was used to hold boiling water to steam something through the perforated bottom of another vessel which rested on the li.

There is no doubt that the li was derived from the pottery tripods which were of different types:

I

1. P.P.C. fig. 31 from Pu-chao Chai

2. E.C.C. pl. 7.6 from Pu-chao Chai

3. E.C.C. pl. 7.7 from Pu-chao Chai

4. P.O.C. pl. 167.2 from Pu-chao Chai

5. P.O.C. pl. 200.1 from Yang-shao

6. P.O.C. pl. 200.4 from Yang-shao

7. P.O.C. pl. 167.1 from Hsi-chung Ts'un

8. P.O.C. pl. 167.3 from Ma-k'o Ts'un

9. P.O.C. pl. 167.4 from Yang-ho Ts'un

All of these came from Mien-chih Hsien of Honan province. The vessels are tall with a rather high neck and one handle.

II

1. P.O.C. pl. 173.1 from Ma-ch'ang

2. P.O.C. pl. 173.2 from Ssu-wa

3. P.O.C. pl. 174.1 from Ssu-wa

4. P.O.C. pl. 174.2 from Hui-tui

All of these are from Kansu province. The first two vessels have two handles, and the last two have one. This type is shorter than group I.

III

1. P.O.C. pl. 172.1 bought in Ssu-wa

2. P.O.C. pl. 172.2. bought in Ssu-wa

3. P.O.C. pl. 172.3 from Ssu-shih-ting

These are from Kansu province. The vessels are shorter than group II and have no handles.

IV

1. C.T.Y. pl. 30.6 from the upper strata of Lung-shan

2. P.O.C. pl. 170.2 from Kuang-wu Hsien in Honan

3. Ontario: NB 1090

The last two show rudimentary legs and the body is low.

V

1. P.O.C. pl. 169.1

2. P.C.C. pl. 169.2

3. P.C.C. pl. 169.3

4. An-yang pao kao: pt. I, pl. 10

5. An-yang pao kao: pt. I, pl. 11

6. An-yang pao kao: pt. III, pl. 17

Numbers 1-2 were bought in Kou-pu Ts'un and 3 was bought in Wan-shou Ssu, both in Mien-chih Hsien. Numbers 4-6 were excavated from Hsiao-t'un in An-yang. The legs are not very high. They are a little bit later than group IV and are of the Shang period. It is very strange that the bronze li of the Shang period look very much like group I, but they are quite different from the An-yang pottery and those found in Shantung and Honan in Group IV. In proportion to their shape, the bronze li of Late Western Chou are quite similar to the Shang pottery.

There is another kind of vessel also called li in its

inscription. The body is oblong and the upper part is like a
rectangular _ting_. Underneath it there is a kind of closet with
two doors at the front for charcoal. There are three pieces:

    1. Fogg: 44.57.18 with inscription _(U.S. 136)_

    2. _Shih_ _er_: Ch'i 24-27

    3. _Tsun_ _ku_: 2.22; _Burchard_: vol. I, pl. 23, no. 270.

III. _Hsien_

     Sometimes _hsien_ is pronounced _yen_. The _Shuo_ _wen_ says,
"_Hsien_ is a kind of _li_." It is a combination of two compartments: the upper one has a perforated bottom called _pei_   and
rests on the lower part which has hollow legs like the _li_. The
pei is either a detachable piece or it is made with the bottom.
The vessel was made either in a single piece or the upper and
lower halves were made separate. The character for _hsien_ on
both the oracle bones (_Chia_ _ku_ _wen_ _pien_: 12.19b) and the bronzes
(_Chin_ _wen_ _pien_: 16a) is the pictograph of the vessel. Sometimes
on the bronzes it was written as _hsien_   , originally the name
of a dog. It was used to steam rice or other food in the upper
compartment. In P.P.C. fig. 53, there is a pottery _hsien_, found
at Kao-li-chai, which was made in one piece. Other pottery found
which are earlier than Shang are:

    1. P.O.C. p. 260, fig. 108a (E.C.C. pl. 15.1 and 6) from
       Pu-chao Chai

    2. C.T.Y. pl. 22.1-3 from lower strata of Lung-shan

    3. _Ts'ai_ _Yuan_ _P'ei_: Pt. II, p. 555, pl. 26a, b from Hou
       Kang of Lung-shan strata.

     In Pu-chao Chai, the lower part (E.C.C. pl. 15.6) was

not found with the upper part (E.C.C. pl. 15.1), but because the
lower part had a ring-shaped platform inside the neck Anderson
combined these two parts into one as shown in P.O.C. fig. 108a.
In Lung-shan, there are separate perforated bottoms which were
found in lower strata as shown in C.T.Y. pl. 32.13.

The upper part is called tseng. Shuo wen under the
classifier   says, "Tseng is hsien   ." And "Hsien is tseng,
read yen." The Fang yen: vol. 5 says, "Tseng from the east of
Han-ku-kuan   was called hsien." It seems that tseng is
another name for hsien. We shall use tseng for the upper part
only and hsien for the whole vessel. At first the lower part of
hsien was called li. Later the mouth became small, and it seems
to me that it should be called ch'i 鑄 . The commentary to
Ts'ai p'ing of Shih ching says, "Ch'i is a kind of fu^3 釜 , with
legs it is called ch'i, without legs it is called fu^3." Tu's commentary to Tso chuan (Ying 3) also says the same thing. Kuo's
commentary to Fang yen, vol. 5 says, "Ch'i is the three legged
fu^3." Shuo wen says, "Ch'i 敲 is the three legged fu^4 鍑 ."
As we know fu^4 is the same as fu^3 , which is used for
steaming, but is without legs. The following vessels should be
called ch'i:

> Lo-yang: 222a, b, c (NB 4313, 4312, 4327) found in
>   Chin Ts'un
> Ch'u ch'i: fig. 11 found in Shou Hsien
> Chan kuo: pl. 4.1 found in Li-yü
> Kogei: 8

All of these should be the lower parts of the hsien. I
have seen only one complete hsien with the lower part like these.
That is the piece in Ontario NB 5927 which was found in P'ing-ting

of Shansi province. Anderson listed a piece of pottery which is a oh'i in his P.C.C. pl. 177.2. It was found in Yang-ch'u Hsien, Shansi province, and is contemporary with the P'ing-ting bronze hsien of the Early Ch'un Ch'iu period. I should be inclined to say that this type of oh'i was popular first in Shansi province as seen from the finds in Li-yü, P'ing-ting, and Yang-ch'ü during the Ch'un Ch'iu period. Later ch'i were found in Chin Ts'un in central Honan. In the Late Chan Kuo period it was used in the southern area as it was found in Shou Hsien. Shuo wen says, "Between the Chiang and the Huai Rivers fu^3 was called ch'i." Fang yen: vol. V says, "Between Chiang, Huai and Ch'en Ch'u fu^4 was called oh'i." It seems that ch'i is the name in the southern dialect used during the Han period. Ch'i, in this book, is used as the special name for the lower part of a hsien of the Eastern Chou period, and tseng is used for the upper part.

IV. Kuei

There was much confusion about the name of kuei. In the Sung catalogues like K'ao ku and Po ku, the kuei were divided into two classes. The earlier kuei of Shang and Early Chou, which did not mention the name kuei in their inscriptions, were called I   . The kuei after Early Chou, which mentioned the name kuei in their inscriptions, were called tun   , also pronounced as tui. The hsü, the name that was mentioned in its inscription, was also wrongly called kuei. Chien Tien   in his catalogue Shih liu: 2.7 first pointed out that the character kuei 殷 in the inscription is not tun, but should read kuei. Yen K'o Chün   in Ch'uan shang ku san tai wen: 13.8 also corrected

tun to kuei   . Other scholars have also discussed this problem. The character for kuei   in the bronze inscriptions was
listed in Shuo wen under the classifier   but was interpreted as 'twist' and pronounced as chiu. In the same work under
the classifier   , kuei was interpreted as a square vessel
which was a container for cereals. Chiu and kuei are the same
character. Shuo wen's interpretation of kuei is wrong. Cheng
Hsüan in his commentary to Shê jen of Chou li says, "The vessel
was a container for cereals. If square it was called fu   , if
round, kuei." Cheng is correct.

        In bronze inscriptions, the character for kuei is a com-
bination of two parts. The right part is a pictograph of the
vessel with lid, round body and base. It looks very much like
the white pottery kuei found in An-yang, illustrated in An-yang
Finds: pls 6-7. They are earlier than the bronzes with lids and
without handles. In An-yang Finds: pl. 31 and An-yang Treasures:
pl. 63 there are two marble or stone kuei which are contemporaneous with the Late Shang bronze kuei. Among the Shang bronzes
we have two types of vessels which are similar to kuei but are
without lids and handles. I can not decide whether they should
be considered kuei or yü, or whether the one with a middle bulge
should be considered kuei. However, for the time being, I shall
follow the conventional way and list them under Type I kuei in
the next chapter.

        The lids of the kuei and the tun were called hui   .
In Kung shih tai fu li of I li it says, "Open the hui of the
kuei." Cheng's commentary says, "Hui is the lid of the kuei."
In Shih shang li of I li it says, "For tun, open the hui."
Cheng's commentary says, "Hui is the lid." In the Shih yü li of

I li it says, "Open the hui." Cheng's commentary says, "Hui is
the lid of the tun." In Chen sung: 2.39 there is a lid which
is called hui in its inscription. In Shan chai: 87 there is a
lid of a kuei which has a long inscription ending with two
characters "kuei hui." The name hui, which is now so pronounced,
had the same pronunciation as kai   which means lid or cover.

Often, there were eight kuei in one set, as shown from
the inscriptions on three kuei (San tai: 7.49.2-3; 8.40b-41b;
8.43a). In the Hsin-cheng finds eight kuei formed a set. Li chi
and I li also recorded that eight kuei were used in ceremonies.

V. Hsü

There is no doubt about the origin of the hsu. It was
derived from the kuei during the Late Western Chou period. Shuo
wen says, "Hsü, kan-hsü is the vessel to be carried (when travelling)." And again, under the classifier ⊏ it says, "Kan 醢
is a small cup." Both Yü p'ien and Kuang yün noted that "Kan is
a vessel to be carried [when travelling]." We found in the inscriptions on the hsü that they were often referred to as 'travelling hsü'. The difference between the hsü and the kuei is that
the hsü developed the lid into a separate vessel for use as a
dish when removed and inverted. Also, when the kuei changed to
hsü the mouth changed from a circualr to an oblong shape. It is
in fact a combination of kuei and fu, the latter being rectangular
and with a lid identical to the body. Because hsü were derived
from kuei some of the hsü are referred to, in their inscriptions,
as kuei:

    1. Pillsbury: 39.107.1-2 (U. S. 262-263)

    2. Wu ying: 83

　　　3. **Shan** chai (d): 8.15

　　　4. **Chün ku**: 22.86b

Occasionally, the inscription refers to the vessel as
hsü-kuei:

　　　1. **Meng yi** I: 1.18

　　　2. **San tai**: 10.28.2-3

　　　3. Ontario: NB 2599

In the Sung dynasty, the K'ao ku: 3.32-38 listed four
hsü and called them kuei. Po ku made the same mistake. Even in
the catalogues of Wang Kuo-wei and Lo Chen-yü the old classification
is still used. But because they were a new type and refer to themselves as hsü in their inscriptions it is proper to classify these
vessels under a new class.

The hsü appeared only in Late Western Chou and were used
for travelling. From the provenances, which have been recorded
and which can be determined, it may be suggested that hsu was the
name in the dialect in the area of Shensi province. When the
Chou capital moved to the East, after 771 B.C. the technique for
making such vessels was lost. We seldom found a hsü of the
Eastern Chou period.

In Tsun ku: 2.18-19, a vessel of the Shang dynasty was
catalogued. The lid is like the hsu's and the body is oblong
with four feet which are similar to the kuei's in Sung chai I: 10
of the Middle Western Chou period. The latter was referred to as
kuei in its inscription. If this is true, then we can trace the
hsu to Early Shang. However, Yung Keng in his commentary to
Shan chai: 14 says that the Tsun ku vessel was found in Lo-yang
in several broken pieces. The pieces were put together to make
a whole vessel. The lid appeared later. It is possible that
such a type existed during the early days. At least there were

kuei with oblong mouths during the Middle Western Chou.

VI. Fu

Fu is a vessel combined from two parts, a lid and a body.
Both the mouth and the base are rectangular in shape, but the
base is smaller than the mouth. There is a base and handles on
both parts. In K'ao ku: 3.40 there is a fu which was wrongly
called fou 缶 . But the author did suggest that it may be called fu. The name fu was first established in Po ku: 18.7. Like
the kuei and the hsu, the fu was used to hold cereals. In the inscriptions, the fu is sometimes referred to as k'uang. Shuo wen
says, "K'uang 匡 is a rice vessel." The character for fu in
the inscriptions on the vessels is different from Shuo wen's. It
has at least four different forms. The origin of the fu will be
discussed under p'u.

Chang kê of Chou li says, "Fu ten." From this we know
that in the ceremonies a set, which consisted of ten fu, was used.

VII. Tou

The character for tou both on the oracle bones (Chia ku
wen pien: 5.7a) and on the bronzes (Chin wen pien: 5.14a) is a
pictograph of the vessel. Shuo wen says, "Tou is an ancient
vessel to contain meat." In the archaic characters we have seen
a tou containing cereals. The bronze tou was derived from the
pottery form. A pottery tou from Yang/Shao is shown in E.C.C.
pl. 15.2. Two pottery tou from the lower and upper part of the
Lung-shan site respectively are shown in C.T.Y. pls. 23.9 and 30.5.

VIII. <u>Tun</u>

<u>Tun</u> may be read as <u>tui</u>. It is a combined form of two
identical parts. Each part forms a hemisphere and the whole vessel forms a shpere. In <u>Shao lao k'uei shih li</u> of <u>I li</u>, K'ung's
commentary quoted <u>Hsiao ching kou ming chüeh</u>   saying "Tun has a round shape. The upper and lower parts are round
and connected together." In <u>Shih ch'iu</u> of <u>Er ya</u> Hsing's commentary quoted Hsiao ching wei   saying, "<u>Tun</u>, <u>fu</u> and <u>kuei</u>
have the same volumes, but the <u>tun</u> is different in shape. Its
upper and lower parts, its inside and outside are round [that is,
spherical]." These two quotations came from the <u>Wei shu</u>   of
the Han dynasty. References earlier than this have not been located. There are six vessels with inscriptions which are referred
to therein as tun:

1. Metropolitan 13.100.3 (U. S. 296)

2. <u>San tai</u>: 7.23.5

3. <u>San tai</u>: 7.24.1-2

4. <u>Shih er</u>: Chü 12

5. <u>Wu ying</u>: 97

6. <u>Shan chai</u>:88

The first three pieces were made by the Marquis of Ch'i^2
of the Chiang family. The other three were made by the Marquis
of Ch'en of the T'ien family who succeeded Ch'i^2 of Chiang as
the ruler of that state. Almost all of the <u>tun</u> with inscriptions were made in the Ch'i^2 state. The Metropolitan piece is
very flat and the lid is smaller than the body. The body has
neither base nor feet. It is the so-called <u>fei-tun</u>   .
Cheng's commentary to <u>Shih shang li</u> of <u>I li</u> says, "Fei-tun is

the tun without feet used to hold rice." If the lid is taken off
it looks very much like the yu in K'ao ku: 6.9. This is why Kuo's
commentary to Shih chiu of Er ya and Shih ch'i of Kuang ya say,
"Tun is yü."

   According to the Ritual Books, there were three kinds of
tun: (1) pottery tun as mentioned in Shih shang li of I li;
(2) jade tun as mentioned in Yü fu and Jung yu of Chou li; (3)
bronze tun as mentioned in Shao lao k'uei shih li of I li. There
were two or four vessels to a set for the ceremony.

IX. Pi

   A pi is very much like a spoon. It is used to transfer
meat or cereal from a vessel. Shuo wen says, "Pi is used to
transfer rice." Cheng's commentary to the Shih hun li of I li
says, "Pi is used to take a piece of meat from the whole body."
The same commentary to the Shao lao k'uei shih li of I li says,
"Pi is used to transfer the cereals." The bowl of the spoon is
shallower than that of the shao.

X. Chia

   Chia is a vessel with two pillars on the rim of the
mouth, a single handle, called pan   , and three or four solid
or hollow legs. It is larger and taller than the li. The
character for chia on both the oracle bones (Chia ku wen pien:
14.3a) and on the bronzes (San tai: 6.2.5) is a pictograph of
the vessel. Chia and chueh were used to heat wine. The phenomena
about the chueh is that pillars were added to the bronze vessels
which appeared on neither pottery chia nor chueh earlier than the
bronze vessels.

In this catalogue the Ruben's <u>chia</u> (U. S. 330   ) has no pillars.
For this reason I believe that the bronze <u>chia</u> were derived from
the pottery <u>chia</u>;

    1. P.P.C. fig. 39L from Ching Ts'un

    2. P.O.C. p. 259, fig. 107a from Pu-chao Chai

    3. P.O.C. p. 258, fig. 106al (Mueller Collection), probably
       from Ma-ch'ang

    4. P.O.C. pl. 179.2 from Pu-chao Chai

    5. C.T.Y. pl. 22.5 (pl. 19.8) from Lung-shan (lower strata)

    Numbers 1 and 2 are quite similar in shape; 2 and 4
were found in the same site and have similar shapes, except that
2 has solid legs like 1 and 4 has hollow legs like the <u>li</u>. But 4
can not be called <u>li-ting</u> because (a) bronze <u>ting</u> always have
solid legs and this is hollow; (b) bronze <u>li</u> always have tripartite bottoms and this has not; (c) bronze <u>chia</u> usually have
rather high necks and deep bodies and no. 4 is similar to the
bronze <u>chia</u> of this description. Therefore, this pottery should
be called <u>chia</u> although it has no pillars. We can see from the
pottery <u>chueh</u> that pillars were added in the bronzes. So there
were some vessels without pillars in both bronze <u>chia</u> and <u>chueh</u>,
yet judging from their general shape they are <u>chia</u> or <u>chueh</u> respectively. Number 5 has a single handle and is almost like a
bronze <u>chia</u>. The rim of the mouth was broken off. It might have
had a spout, but I do not think that there were pillars on it.
In C.T.Y. pl. 22.6 there is a similar piece of pottery which
may also be called <u>chia</u> that has a deeper body and shorter legs
than no. 5. Both of these pieces have traces of fire-marks.

    The name of <u>chia</u> was given by <u>Po ku</u> in vol. XV.

XI. Ho

The ho is similar to a chia except that it has a spout
and no pillars. In Shuo wen the character ho is used as a verb
meaning 'to savor'. The name of ho was given by K'ao ku: 5.20.
Ho were used for the heating of wine and other flavouring
materials. It seems to me that they were derived from the pottery found in the lower strata of Lung-shan. (cf. C.T.Y. pl. 28)
This piece still has traces of fire-marks showing that it was
really used. It has a channel spiut turned up at about 45
degree angle and three hollow legs. Several archaic bronze ho are
listed in the next chapter under Types Ia and Ib ho. These
examples have hollow legs. The tubed spout is placed on top of
the lid in the same angle as on the pottery piece. The treatment of the lid with the spout and the hole is so similar to
a pair of pottery vessels illustrated in P.O.C. pls 37.4 and
38 bought from Lan Chou of Kansu province that Anderson calls
it the Ch'i Chia P'ing stage.

Among
In wine heating-vessels only the chia, chueh and chiao
have three facet legs exclusively. These kinds of legs may
be derived from the pointed hollow legs like the ones on the
pottery and early bronzes.

XII. Chueh

Chueh is a vessel with two pillars placed on the rim,
a single handle, three three-facet legs and a spout with a tail
opposite the spout. It is smaller in size than the chia and ho
and, with no exceptions, the legs are always solid.   In the

An-yang pao kao: pt. 3, pp. 447-480; Li chi: fu shen tsang: pls.
10, 13 (1, 2, 4), four pottery vessels like the chueh, lacking
the pillars and the tail, are listed. The first was excavated
in An-yang by Academia Sinica. Li chi says that this is the forerunner of the chueh . I have seen other examples of this type in
America and Canada. Lo Chen-yu, in his Ku ming ch'i t'u lu: 2.1,
first catalogued this type of chueh and called it chia.   In
E.C.C. pl. 16.6 there is a chueh from Yang-shao. It seems to me
that the pillars were added to the bronze vessels because the
metal had a higher rate of heat conductance and retained the heat
longer. The pillars were also added to facilitate handling with
hooks.

        In the Chin wen pien; sup. 2.26a there are two characters,
pictographs of chueh without pillars and one of the two appeared
inscribed on a chueh. In Chin wen pien: 5.23a two characters
for chueh are listed and in Chia ku wen pien: 5.11b, fifteen
characters for chueh from the oracle bones are listed. All of
them are different from the Shuo wen's. Thus the name for chueh
is quite uncertain. The chueh was first so named in Po ku
with no evidence except that the name appeared in the Classics
and in the Ritual Book. All of the wine vessels that did not
have the name of the vessels in their inscriptions were named
by early scholars in this way.

                        XIII. Chiao

                or chio
            The chiao is similar in size and shape to the chueh
except in the following ways: (1) it has two tails; (2)it has
no spout; (3) it has no pillars and (4)it often has a lid.
The chiao was first named in Po ku without any evidence.

XIV. Tsun

The name tsun, without any evidence for its use, was given to this type of vessel in both K'ao ku and Po ku. P.P.C. fig. 1c, 36b, 54 (≠ E.C.C. pl. 7.4)listed three vessels from Hou Kang, Liang-ch'eng and Yang-shao. C.T.Y. pl. 17 (1-3) listed the pottery tsun from the lower strata of Lung-shan. This pottery looks very much like the bronze tsun especially the piece from Yang-shao which is similar in shape to the tsun in Cleveland: 38:13 (U. S. 436). None of this pottery is of greater height than 15 cm., but the bronze tsun always exceed this height.

In bronze inscriptions, both tsun and i were used as common names for vessels. Here the name tsun is used only to indicate a special class of vessels as defined in the chapter on typology.

The character for tsun on both the oracle bones(Chia ku wen pien: 14.28b-29a) and the bronzes (Chin wen pien: 14.34-37a) is a pictograph of the vessel with two hands under the bottom. However, the vessel shown in the character has a hemispheric bottom without a base. The example of the tsun in Loo Catalogue (1924): 16, except for the fact that it has a base, looks very much like the vessel in the inscription.

XV. Ku

Ku is similar to tsun except that they are much slenderer. The ku was named in K'ao ku and Po ku with no evidence. No origin for this vessel can be found in the pre-historic pottery.

XVI. Chih

The chih is similar to a tsun except that in size it is
smaller and often has a lid, which the tsun proper never had.
The "Pottery tsun" from Liang-ch'eng may be considered chih.   The
name chih was first given to this type of vessel in Po ku without
any evidence for its use.   Three chih which were made during the
Ch'un Ch'iu period (cf. Chen sung: 2.12-13) are called tuan
in their inscriptions.   Wang Kuo-wei identified them as chih (cf.
Kuan t'ang chi lin: 6.12-13).

There is a marble or stone chih which is similar to
the bronzes in An-yang Finds: pl. 29. I saw another one with a
lid in Mayell's Collection which is also from An-yang.

XVII. Yu

The name for yu was first used during the Sung dynasty.
In the fourth volume of K'ao ku the author listed i, yu, tsun,
hu, and lei as one great category.   He called some of the vessels in the shape of a yu, 'yu', but at the same time he called
the same type 'i'   , which merely means vessel.   He also called
some of the vessels in the form of ts'ung, chih, and lei, 'yu'.
This shows that the author could not clearly distinguish the yu
from other types.   Later, in Po ku: vols. IX-XI, the classification
was much improved.   The vessels under the classification 'yu'
were actually of that single type.   This classification was followed by later scholars.   Until the present day we have lacked
direct evidence that these vessels should be called 'yu', because
none of these vessels mentioned the name 'yu' in their inscriptions.   Yet I believe that the name 'yu' is correct.

There is only one yu (Shuang chien I: 1.32) with a long
inscription on the body and a short inscription on the lid. The
latter reads, "Made travelling fu   ." The character for fu
may have been pronounced as hu or ku in ancient times. There
is a close relationship between the hu and the yu, for two of the
hu (Shan chai (d): 3.52; Tsun ku: 2.33) among the Eastern Chou
bronzes are called 'yu' in their inscriptions. Although these
are later vessels, the construction of the character for yu is
similar to that appearing on the oracle bones (Chia ku wen pien:
7.10b). Based on this evidence, I believe that the name 'yu' is
correct. Furthermore, the yu vessel was used for pouring wine,
hence the yu had a swing-handle used for this purpose. There are
two characters for 'yu' in Shuo wen: concerning the first, in
the first part of volume five, Hsü Shen said, "Yu 卣 is the
appearance of moving clouds, pronounced as yu 攸 ." Chin wen
pien: 5.10 listed all the characters for 'yu' on the bronzes
under this character. The second, in the first part of volume
seven, reads, "Yu 卣 is a pictograph of the hanging fruit of
trees, pronounced as t'iao   ." Chin wen pien: 7.12 listed
two characters for 'yu' on the bronzes under this character.
Chia ku wen pien: 7.10b lists the character for 'yu' on the
oracle bones under this character, which should be listed under
the character in the first part of volume five of the Shuo wen
given above.

          Both on the oracle bones and on the bronzes, in Shang
shu and Shih ching, the character for yu 卣 was used only as a
standard of measurement as shown in the Chiang Han of Shih ching,
Wen hou chih ming of Shang shu and on the Mao kung ting (San tai:
4.46b-49a) "One yu of mixed wine." Because of this use as a unit

we have reason to believe that the container of the mixed-wine was also called 'yu'.

The yu was used to contain the mixed-wine called 'ch'ang'   . Shuo wen's commentary on this character says that ch'ang was a fermented wine mixed from a grain wine and fragrant herbs which had been boiled in water. It was used to call up the spirits desired. As we have indicated before, the swing handle was used in pouring the mixed-wine from the vessel during the ceremony.

XVIII. Fang-i

The name, fang-i, for this class was first used during the Sung dynasty. There is a vessel of this class in Po ku: 8.15 which is called fang-i, however, the lid to this piece was lost. In the same catalogue (27.26-27) there are two vessels of this class, with lids, which were listed among the vessels of the Han dynasty and were called lien   , 'toilet boxes'. Before Po ku, K'ao ku: 4.28 called a rectangular ting, fang-i. This is wrong. This class disappeared after Middle Western Chou, and even on the Middle Western Chou bronzes the name of the vessels of this class is never given. Thus we can not help but accept the name fang-i given by the Po ku. It is only a vague description of the vessel, meaning 'a square vessel'.

The inscriptions on the fang-i mentioned 'the precious sacrificial vessels' and we know from this that they were used in sacrifice. The lid is very close fitting, and the vessel itself is without legs thus indicating that it was used as some

kind of container. They were probably wine-containers. The
reasons for this are as follows:

1. The inscriptions on the fang-i show it to be part of
   a set of wine vessels, and therefore most probably a
   wine-container itself. The examples are:

   a. Ling fang-i and tsun (U. S. 652)

   b. Ch'uan fang-i and tsun and kuang (U. S. 653)

   c. Tzu Fu fang-i and ho, ku and chüeh (U. S. 695)

   d. Yung Tzu fang-i and tsun and ho (U. S. 654)

   e. Hsiang fang-i and tsun, chia, ku, hu and chueh
      (U. S. 643)

   f. Yu fang-i and hu and chiao (U. S.   )

   g. Fang-i (Eumo: A19) and kuang (Hsi ch'ing: 32.13)

   h. Fang-i (Sumitomo I: 27) and Kuang (San tai: 17.26.
      3-4, P'an Tzu Ying's Collection)

   i. Fang-i (Yeh II: 1.11) and Shao (Sung chai II: 96)

   j. Fang-i (Yeh II: 1.12) and shao (Shuang chien I: 50)

The ho, hu, chüeh, chiao, chia and tsun are all wine
vessels, and the shao is a dipper used to transfer wine from
one vessel to another. Of the last example the author of the
Shuang chien I says, "The dealer said, 'This shao was originally
within a lei.'"

2. The lid of the fang-i is similar to the lid of a certain type of lei. Lei was also a wine-container.

3. The lid of the fang-i in Shang chou: II, 604 shows a
pair of square slots in the rim resting on the mouth. From the
Shou kung kuang (Burlington Magazine, June, 1934) slotted in a
like manner, we know that these slots were used to permit the
handle of the shao to project when the shao was placed in the

covered vessel. Shao is the spoon to ladle wine.

XIX. Kuang

The type of vessel which we now call kuang was classified under the same class as the water vessel i in K'ao ku. In
Hsu k'ao ku: 2.8 and 3.21 two vessels are listed which the
author called kuang. In the same book, 3.27, a water vessel i
was again called kuang. In the Imperial Collection of the Ch'ing
dynasty the name kuang appeared only once in Hsi ch'ing chia:
12.17 on a bronze vessel in the shape of a buffalo-horn. This
vessel is similar to the one excavated by the Academia Sinica in
An-yang. The name for this piece is still undecided. In Wang
Kuo-wei's article On kuang (Kuan t'ang chi lin: 3.12-13) he
divided the so-called i, catalogued from the Sung to the present,
into two classes. In the first class, the vessel was shallow
and large, with feet and without lid. The channel spout was
narrow and long. In the second class, the vessel was smaller
and deeper, with or without feet but always with a lid which was
in the form of a bull. The channel spout was broad and short.
He called the first class water-vessel i and the second class
wine-vessel kuang. Wang is perfectly right in separating the
kuang from the i because i is the water vessel and its name is
mentioned in the inscriptions. We know that the kuang appeared
only in Shang and Early Western Chou and the i appeared in Late
Western Chou. Although the two types of vessels are similar in
shape they do not belong to the same period and their functions
were quite different. It is also true that kuang is a wine-vessel, but the evidence for calling this class of vessel kuang is

very weak. It is quite obvious that the _i_ was derived from a
half-gourd used to ladle water. It seems to me that since the
kuang is similar to it, it is possible that it was originally
a kind of ladle used to ladle wine from a larger container.
Therefore, I think that this class should be called _tou_ 斗 .
In the _Hsin wei_ of _Shih ching_ it says, "To ladle the wine with a
large _tou_." This shows that the _tou_ was used to ladle wine.
In _San tai_: 14.5.10 there is an inscription from a _ho_ which has
the character for _ho_ that is a combination of two parts: the
phonetic element _ho_ and the form element which is a picture of
the vessel of the _kuang_ type. This form element can not be read.

XX. Niao Shou Tsun

The name for these vessels is only a vague description
of this class. The _Ssu tsun i_ of _Chou li_ gives six kinds of
tsun and six kinds of _i_ (meaning 'vessel') in various forms of
birds and animals. _Chou li_ was compiled in a late period and
we are not going to adopt all of the names mentioned in that
book.   In _Po ku_ (vols 6-7), the bronze vessels in the form of a
bird, an elephant, etc. were called bird _tsun_, elephant _tsun_, etc.
I can not help but accept this name and call them _Niao shou tsun_,
meaning the _tsun_ in the form of birds and animals.

XXI. Hu

Both the oracle bones (_Chia ku wen pien_: 10.14a) and
the bronzes (_Chin wen pien_: 10.9) give a pictographic character
for this vessel. The name _hu_ is referred to in its inscription.

It was used as a wine-container; sometimes as a water-container.
There is no known single piece similar to the early bronze hu in
prehistoric pottery.

Hu and yu are closely related, so sometimes, as mentioned
under the yu section, hu were called yu in their inscriptions.
In Kogei: 12 there is a hu with domed lid and lugs. It looks
very much like a yu except that it has no permanent swing handle.

The flat hu was sometimes referred to as yu^4 in its inscription as shown in Tsun ku: 2.39.   The character is a combination of the phonetic element 㪅 and the form element 皿 .   It
can be identified as 㿻 in Shuo wen meaning "small ou 甌 ."
In Hsi ch'ing: 34.5 there is a flat hu of the Han dynasty which
called itself ou in the inscription. This proves that yu is a
large ou which is also a flat hu.

During Han times the hu was called chung   in its inscription and the new name of fang   appeared for the square
hu. Shuo wen says, "Chung is a wine vessel and Fang is a square
chung." The square hu appeared in the Chan Kuo period but bore
no name in its inscription. The Yen li of I li mentioned both
square hu and round hu. They were used in pairs during the
ceremony as mentioned in the inscriptions of hu, "two hu and
eight ting." (San tai: 12.34a-35a).

                          XXII. Lei

Only one lei, which can be dated as Late Western Chou,
is referred to as lei in its inscription. It is illustrated in
T'ao chai I: 3.7 and in Shang chou: II, 794. Evidently this
lei is derived from earlier lei but is without a nose. The

absence of a nose on this lei makes it similar to the fou of a
later period. However, the general shapes of the lei and the
fou are ~~quite~~ *somewhat* different. Many commentaries say that the lei was
a container for wine. In size it is larger than the hu so the
Liao wo of Shih ching says, "If the p'ing   is empty it is the
shame of the lei." The commentary adds: "P'ing is small and lei
is large." The p'ing was a kind of hu. It is probable that
the lei was derived from the pottery. There is a white pottery
lei of the Shang dynasty which is similar to but older than the
Shang bronze lei in Freer Gallery: 39.42. It has no base. A
similar shaped clay pottery lei was excavated by the Academia
Sinica at An-yang. (cf. An-yang pao kao: pt. III, pl. 18).

The lei without bases, mostly of Shang, were probably
the so-called chu-tsun 著尊 . Shih ch'i of Kuang ya says,
"T'ai, shan-lei, chu are tsun." Chu-tsun was mentioned in Ssu
tsun i of Chou li. Ch'eng's commentary says, "Chu-tsun stood
on the ground without feet (or base)." Ming t'ang wei of Li
chi says, "Chu was the tsun of the Yin dynasty." Ch'eng's
commentary says, "Chu stood on the ground without feet (or base)."

XXIII. Fou

Fou is in reality another name for lei. Fang yen: vol. V
says, "The small fou was called p'ing." We stated above that
the p'ing was small and the lei was large. If the small fou was
called p'ing, the large fou is the same as the lei. A fou,
which is so named in the inscription, is illustrated in Shang
chou: II, 803. This vessel was made by the family of Chin in
the Ch'un Ch'iu period. The shape is similar to the one in
Boston: 11.1447 (U. S. 786).

Shuo wen says, "Fou is a pottery vessel used to hold
wine and liquor. The people of the Ch'in territory struck it
while singing songs." The twenty-one characters under this
classifier show that fou was a common name. The characters
for ts'ung ling and tan on the bronzes were written with fou
as the form element. The character for ling in Shuo wen is also
under the classifier fou. This proves that fou was a common
name for all of these vessels.

XXIV. Ling

Ling is another name for lei and fou. Shuo wen says,
"Ling is an earthen ware vessel." Both Yü p'ien and Kuang yün
say, "Ling is similar to p'ing with ears." A ling of Late
Western Chou, referred to as ling in the inscription, is illus-
trated in Chou chin: 5.27. In shape it is similar to the lei
and the fou. This vessel was found in Ch'i-shan Hsien of
Shensi province. It seems to me that ling is the name in the
Western area dialect.

XXV. Ts'ung

Fang yen, vol. V says, "Between the rivers Chiang and
Hsiang, ying was called ts'ung 甇 ." Shih ch'i of Kuang ya
says, "Ts'ung is p'ing 瓶 ." Shuo wen, under the classifier
fou, says, "Ying is fou." Therefore, we know that the ts'ung
is a vessel similar to the lei and the fou. It is the name in
the dialect of the Chiang Hsiang area of Hunan province even to
this day. There are three vessels which, in their inscriptions,
are called ts'ung, but scholars misinterpreted this character.

The three vessels are:

     1. Po ku: 10.37 同从

     2. Shang chou: II, 801 (Palace Museum) 岳从

     3. Shang chou: II, 800 (Rubbing) 金从

These three vessels look alike, and they have no bases. From
their inscriptions we know that they were used only for travelling.

XXVI. Ying

Shuo wen says, "Ying is fou." These vessels, sometimes
quite huge, have a low body, a mouth wider than the lei, and a
very low neck. Sometimes they have lids. If we compare these
vessels with the character for fou, on both the oracle bones
and the bronzes, they look very similar especially when the lids
are on. Jung Keng in his Shang chou followed Po ku in calling
this type p'ei 缶告 . According to Shuo wen and other commentaries p'ei is a small fou. Therefore I prefer to use the new
name as a substitute and leave fou to indicate the Eastern Chou
type of lei.

There are three pottery vessels in Ontario NA 2142-2143,
2146 that were unearthed with the one shown in London (no. 15,
Yetts Collection). They look very much like the ying and belong to the Shang period. The Academia Sinica excavated
similar specimen at An-yang.

XXVII. Tan

Fang yen, vol. V says, "To the northeast of Ch'i[2], between the sea and T'ai Shan, ying 罌 was called tan 僋 ." In

the <u>Ho</u> <u>chih</u> <u>li</u> <u>chüan</u> of <u>Shih</u> <u>chi</u>, Chang's commentary quoted <u>Hsü</u>
<u>Kuang</u>   as saying, "<u>Tan</u> is a large <u>ying</u>." The commentary to
the <u>K'uai</u> <u>t'ung</u> <u>chüan</u> of <u>Han</u> <u>shu</u> quoted Ying Shao 應劭 as saying
"The Ch'i² people called the small <u>ying</u> 罌 , <u>tan</u>." Ying's interpretation is correct. A vessel illustrated in <u>Pao</u> <u>yun</u>: 91,
which was made by a statesman of Ch'i² during the Ch'un Ch'iu
period, is called <u>tan.</u> The shape of this vessel is similar to
the <u>lei</u> and the <u>fou</u> except that it is low.

                          XXVIII. <u>Min</u>

     There is only one vessel which is called <u>min</u> in its
inscription (<u>Pao</u> <u>yun</u>: 95). It is similar to Pillsbury 43.1082
(U. S. 799). <u>Min</u>, according to <u>Shuo</u> <u>wen</u>, means a food vessel.
Here it seems to me to be a kind of wine-container like the <u>tan</u>.
The name is probably from one of the dialects, but no records
are available.

                          XXIX. Cheng

     <u>Fang</u> <u>yen</u>, vol. V says, "In the old capital of Ch'in,
<u>ying</u> 罌 was called <u>cheng</u>." Both <u>Yü</u> <u>p'ien</u> and <u>Kuang</u> <u>yun</u> say,
"<u>Cheng</u> is <u>ying</u>." There are three vessels with inscriptions
that refer to them as <u>cheng</u>:
                1. <u>Chou</u> <u>chin</u>: 4.35
                2. <u>Chou</u> <u>chin</u>: 4.38
                3. <u>K'ao</u> <u>ku</u>: 5.21
     The first one was made by the ruler of the Chin State
during the Ch'un Ch'iu period. From <u>Fang</u> <u>yen</u> we know that Ch'in
and Chin spoke a similar dialect, therefore we know that the

name <u>cheng</u> is a dialect. This vessel, without the lid, looks
like the late <u>yü</u> which will be discussed under <u>yü</u>. It also
looks like the <u>p'en</u> illustrated in <u>Sung chai</u> II: 48. It was called <u>p'en</u> in the inscription, but I have some doubt about the
authenticity of the inscription. <u>Fang yen</u>, vol. V says, "From
the west of Han-ku-kuan the <u>ying</u> was called <u>p'en</u>."

  This class of vessel was called <u>an</u> in <u>K'ao ku</u>: 5.21.
This is wrong. Jung Keng corrected it in his commentary to
<u>Sung chai</u> I: p. 8. The <u>cheng</u> in <u>K'ao ku</u> was found in Hsin-yang
Hsien in Honan province and was made by the Chiang State.
Chiang was located in southern Honan. The vessel found in Hsin-
cheng (cf. <u>Hsin Cheng</u>: 120) with the same shape as the Chiang
vessel may be called <u>cheng</u> or flat <u>tun</u>.

XXX. P'i

  The <u>Shih ch'i</u> of <u>Kuang ya</u> says, "The flat <u>kai</u> 榼 was
called <u>p'i</u> 椑 ."   <u>Shuo wen</u> says, "<u>Kai</u> is a wine vessel and
<u>p'i</u> is a round <u>kai</u>."   In <u>Shuo wen</u> 'round' sometimes means
'elliptical'. Cheng's commentary to <u>K'ao kung ch'i</u> of <u>Chou li</u>
says, "<u>P'i</u> is elliptical (in shape)." Therefore the vessel was
called <u>p'i</u> because of its shape. The description of Pillsbury's 37.1797 corresponds to this and so should be called <u>p'i</u>.
The phonetic element for <u>p'i</u> may be pronounced as <u>pei</u> or <u>pi</u>. In
Hsü <u>k'ao ku</u>: 5.3 a vessel of this type was illustrated and was
called <u>pei</u> 杯 , meaning 'cup'. May be both <u>pei</u> and <u>p'i</u> are derived from the same source, only the <u>p'i</u> has a cover, because
the <u>kai</u> was originally derived from <u>kai</u> 蓋 meaning 'lid' or
'cover'. Since <u>p'i</u> is a flat <u>kai</u> it must have a lid. As a matter
of fact the <u>cheng</u> should also be considered under this type.

XXXI. Pei

The Ch'i su of Huai nan tzu says, "If you look at your
face in the water in a p'an it is round. If you look at your
face in the water in a pei it is elliptical. The shape of your
face never changes and the reason why your face sometimes looks
round and sometimes looks elliptical is because the vessels into
which you look at the water are different in shape."   This
proves that the pei was elliptical in shape. Under Hsü we discussed the fact that the lid was a cup called kan, and since
the hsü was oblong in shape the cup on it was also oblong.
Yen's commentary to Chi ch'iu pien says, "Pei is a drinking cup,
it is also called kan." An elliptical shaped pei of the Han
dynasty, which is called pei in the inscription, is illustrated
in T'ao chai: 6.23.   Wines, and sometimes soup, were served in
the pei.

XXXII. Shao

Shao is a ladle or dipper with a long rod handle. It
was used to ladle wine. The character for shao is a pictograph
of it (cf. my article, "The Sacrificial Systems as Found in
Ancient Inscriptions of Shang and Chou," Yenching Hsüeh Pao, no.
19, p. 137).

XXXIII. Yü

The yü is similar to the kuei, but usually it has two
bent handles underneath the rim. Shuo wen says, "Yü is a rice (?)

vessel." It also says, "Wan is a small yü." A yü, which had a
lid and was called yü in its inscription, was found with a p'an
and a shao in the excavation from Hou-chia Chuang. These three
pieces formed a set of water vessels. A yü, called yü in its inscription (San tai: 18.12.3), in Hsi ch'ing chia: 16.1 is similar
in shape to the yü in Freer: 37.1 and Toledo: 35.47 (U.S.   ).
All of these pieces belong to the Shang or Early Chou period. In
K'ao ku: 6.9 there is a vessel of the Late Western or Early
Eastern Chou period which is also called yü in its inscription.
It has no base and it has ring ears instead of bent ears. It
looks like a vessel (Shan chai: 99) found in T'eng Hsien with a
water vessel i (Shan chai: 99b) and a p'an (Chen sung: 2.35).
(and U.S.829)
(cf. I wen: 10.42). Since this i was apart of the water vessel,
it and the yü of K'ao ku should be treated as a water vessel.

XXXIV. P'an

The p'an is shallow with a wide mouth. Inscriptions on
this type of vessel often refer to it as 'p'an', or 'washing p'an'.
It was no doubt a water vessel. It is understood that during the
ceremony someone held a p'an, the guest held his hands over the
p'an and a third used an i to pour water on the guest's hands,
which drained off into the p'an below.

The character for p'an was derived from min 血 , which
is a picture of the p'an.

XXXV. I

I, the shape of which has been discussed under kuang,
was used to ladle water. No i have been found earlier than Late

Western Chou, although there are p'an of Shang and Early Chou.

XXXVI. Chien

The chien is larger in size and deeper than the p'an.
The largest chien were sometimes used for bath tubs. The Tze
yang of Chuang tzu says, "To bathe together in a chien." This
shows that the chien was used for the bath.

Shuo wen says, "Chien is a large p'en 盆 [and] chüan 絹
is a small p'en." Therefore the chüan is smaller than the chien,
but all belonged to the p'en class. Several chüan of the Han
dynasty were called chüan in their inscriptions. They are also
similar in shape to the chien.

XXXVII. P'u

There is a kind of vessel in the Holmes' Collection
(Shina kodo: 157) [handwritten: U.S. 847] which looks like the tou. The name, p'u
first appeared in K'ao ku: 3.46. This work noted, "Its shape
looks like the tou. It is not in the same class as fu. If it
is a tou, it should not be referred to as p'u in its inscription." The handle stem is low, and the upper part does not
form a bowl but has a flat bottom with low surrounding walls.
There are three similar vessels which are listed below. The
first two examples are called p'u in their inscriptions;the
third example is called fu in its inscription.

    1. K'ao ku: 3.46   鋪

    2. Hsi ch'ing: 29.44   鋪甫

    3. Shang chou: II, 399   西

The p'u is not used to hold food, but rather it is used
as a support for other vessels.   It should be called feng
as described in Cheng Hsüan's commentary to I li. In Hsiang she
li he says, "Feng is used to support a chüeh. Its shape is like
a tou, but low." In Kung shih ta fu li he says, "Feng is used to
support a chih, it is like a tou, but lower." In Ta she li he
says, "Feng is used to support a tsun." Therefore the feng was
used to support wine vessels, and it is like a tou but lower.
From this evidence it seems clear that the p'u in Holmes' Collection is really a feng, and the bronzes specially named p'u are
also feng. Sometimes it was referred to as tou in its inscription as in Po ku: 18.16.

The vessel shown in Shang chou was made by the Lu State
and was unearthed with two other pieces (cf. Ch'ü-fu Finds).
These vessels have lids and were called fu in their inscriptions.
The character for this fu is the same as the one for the food-
container fu. Both p'u and fu have the same phonetic element
and in ancient times they were both pronounced alike. It seems
to me that the support, p'u or fu, was derived from the same
origin as the food-container fu.

During the Shang period there were two kinds of supports.
One was rectangular in shape with a flat bottom and low walls
surrounding it as shown in An-yang pao kao: pt. I, pl. 14;
An-yang Finds: pl. 28; and in the Ontario Museum. The first
piece is pottery and the other two are marble or stone. Judging
from the shallow bodies they must have been used to support
vessels. The food-container fu was derived from this kind of
vessel, but it differed from it in that it had a deep body and
duplicated the lower half for the upper part. It was called fu.

The other kind of support has a round and shallow body with a
low handle or base as shown in An-yang pao kao: pt. III, pl. 16
and Ontario: NB 4070. The first is pottery and the second is
marble or stone. The support p'u, fu or feng is derived from
this type. In both the oracle bones and the bronzes the character for feng is a picture of a tou. The round support may also
be called fu because both the rectangular and the round supports
had similar functions. In order to distinguish them it is
better to call the tou-shaped support p'u or feng.

XXXVIII. Chin

Chin is a kind of socle, rectangular or square, used as
a support for vessels. It was described in Cheng Hsüan's commentary to I li. In Shih kuan li he says, "Chin is the vessel
to support the tsun." In Hsiang yin chiu li and Hsiang she li
he says, "Ssu-chin   is the chin resting on the floor without feet." The Li ch'i of Li chi mentioned that fei-chin
was used by the emperor and yü-chin   was used by the
officials. The fei-chin should be like the fei-tun, meaning
"without feet." Cheng's commentary to Li ch'i says, "Yü is
ssu-chin. It is called yü because it has no feet." It seems
to me that both the yü-chin and the ssu-chin were without feet.
There is a rectangular chin from the Tuan Fang set in the
Metropolitan: 2472.1. In this set the yu (Metropolitan: 2472.2)
with a detached square socle is also a chin. During the Early
Western Chou period many kuei had square socles made with them.
They were derived from the square chin. I have seen a picture
of a tsun with a square socle made with it. (Burchard's Catalogue: pl. 24, no. 273).

XXXIX. Chü

Shuo wen says, "Chü is the stand for Chung and Ku. (musical instruments) Ornamented with fierce beasts."

XL. Shang Bell

Shuo wen says, "Cheng   is nao   , it is like a ling, the handle is hollow and opens at either end." It also says, "Nao is cheng." Cheng's commentary to Ku Jen of Chou li says, "Nao is like a ling   with a handle but without a tongue (clapper), hold (in hand) when making the sound." From this description from the above sources, the small bell found exclusively at An-yang is very similar to the cheng or nao. But cheng and nao, according to Shuo wen and other references, were used for military purposes. The small bells found at An-yang often had three to a set with different volumes and tones. They are probably musical instruments that were used in the ceremony rather than for military purposes.

Judging from the decoration and the inscription, we know that the mouth of the barrel should be upward. The handle is a hollow stem, and both the end attached to the barrel and the other end are open. The mouth is convex inward towards the barrel. They are of the Shang dynasty.

XLI. Chung

The Shang bell is smaller in size than the chung. We found bells similar to but larger than the Shang bells. There is a new type of bell after the Shang bell and before the chung that is larger in size than the Shang bell. The examples are:

Po ku: 26.36, 37, 39, 41-46; Holmes Collection

(Shina kodo: 158); Ontario: NB 2825; Wacker Collection

The last four examples have hollow handles like the Shang bells
that are open at both ends. From the drawings of Po ku, it seems
to me that all of them have hollow handles, but the author only
mentioned 26.46 as the one that is open at both ends. These
bells are similar to each other and all have the t'ao-t'ieh decoration that is more ornate than that on the Shang bells. Po
Ku called them cheng. The part of the handle near the barrel
has a bulged surrounding. Except for the one in the Wacker Collection which has no curve in the mouth and can be rested on a
plane, the rest have a mouth that is convexed inward towards the
barrel. These can be dated Late Shang and Early Western Chou.

Later another kind of bell appeared with a barrel that
is higher than that of the above type. It has a yoke or high
loop on the top of the barrel instead of a handle or stem. The
mouth has no curve. The examples are:

Po ku: 25.13; Loo Catalogue (1924): 7; Sumitomo I:

123; Shapes: 36.7.

All of these have flanges (or animals) on both sides and the
last two have two rows of spikes. Usually there are three rows
on the chung of Late Western Chou.

Probably the chung was derived from the above two types
in the Late Western Chou period. Some are very large. The
mouth is an inverted curve and the handle is larger and more
solid with a ring on it. A hook was placed in the ring so that
it could be hung on a frame. In its inscription it was called
chung. According to the K'ao kung chi of Chou li the handle was

yung   and the lower part near the mouth was called ku

meaning 'strike' the area in which the bell was struck on the
outside with a stick. The main part of the barrel, under the
yung and on the ku, where the three rows of spikes were arranged
was called cheng . Sometimes the chung were called ling-
chung in their inscriptions, such as the one illustrated in
Chen sung: 1.2. It is small like a ling. In the Provincial
Honan Museum at K'ai Feng there is a set of three bells, found
at Hui Hsien of Honan, with everything just like a chung except
that they had clappers. It proves that the ling-chung is derived from that. These pieces are not earlier than the Late
Ch'un Ch'iu period.

A hook was used to connect the chung with the frame.
Two hooks of chung are illustrated in Shih er: Chiu 5-6. The
first one has an inscription which reads, "Hook of chung." It
has a ring on one side and a hook on the other.

The chung is either single or forms a set in different
sizes which was called pien-chung . Their inscriptions
were continued from one to another. Pien-chung were mentioned
in the Ch'ing shih of Chou li.

XLII. Po

Shuo wen says, "Po is a large chung, a kind of Ch'un-yü."
The three bells that were called po in their inscriptions are:

Po ku: 22.5; P'an ku: 2.1 and San tai: 1.35a.
All three were made by the Ch'i[2] State. The first two have illustrations with the mouth resting on a plane without the inverted
curve. It seems to me that they were derived from the bells with
yokes described under chung. Although the name po is in the dia-

lect of the Ch'i[2] State and in other states, the po were called chung in their inscriptions. I shall use the name po to indicate this particular type.

XLIII. Ling

Shuo wen says, "To is a large ling and ling is ling-ting   ." There is only one ling which is so called in its inscription. It is illustrated in Sung chai I: 25. The very small ling should be attached to banners, but the ling illustrated in Sung chai and the low-Beer piece are a little larger than usual. They were probably used as musical instruments in the great ceremony as mentioned in the Ching ch'ê of Chou li.

XLIV. To

Both Shuo wen and the Ta ssu ma of Chou li indicated that the to were used for military purposes. This is also indicated by the inscription on the to. I have seen only three to which were referred to as to in their inscriptions. They are:

Sung chai I: 24; Sung chai II: 122; Yau Collection. The last two, from the inscriptions, have the mouth downward, but Yau's to has a decoration facing in the other direction. The Pillsbury to has a solid handle and according to the decoration the mouth should be upward. The to has a tongue. Li i of Yen t'i lun says, "The to of Wu State was broken by its own tongue." The second example has a ring that is supposed to be the original clapper.

The earliest to was the one in Eumofopoulos Collection, Yetts in Eumo II: B4 describes the clapper of it as follows:

The handle is hollow, but closed at either end.
The clapper is 4.8 inches long. Its ring moves
freely on a bar running across the shorter diameter of the barrel. The clapper stem is roughly
five-sided and measures .3 inches in diameter;
it ends in an enlargement, .6 inches in diameter
which just is visible below the lip of the mouth.

This piece can be dated probably as Shang. Its decoration shows
that the mouth should be held upward. The handle is closed like
those to with a solid handle.

XLV. Kou-ti

Two sets of kou-ti are known to us. The first set was
found in Wu K'ang of Chechiang province during the early years
of Tao Kuang (1821-1850 A.D.). It is a set of more than ten,
two of which had inscriptions (San tai: 18.1b-2a) and Shang chou:
II, 936 illustrate the rubbing of the instrument. In 1788
another kou-ti was found in Ch'ang-shu   of Chiangsu province
(San tai: 18.2a-3b). These kou-ti belonged to the Wu or Yueh
State. From the inscription we know that the mouth should be
upward and it was used on ceremonial and feasting occasions. It
was called kou-ti in its inscription. The character for ti can
not be found in any dictionary. It is probably the southern
dialect for to. Kou should be read as k'ou. Shuo wen says,
"K'ou means to strike." Since to has a tongue or clapper for
striking, the kou-ti has no clapper in it but was struck from the
outside, and for this reason was called kou-ti.

In the notes of Chou chin wen ts'un, vol. I, the author
                              the same
said he saw a third kou-ti w th an inscription as the one on
the first set. In size it was between the two. It indicates
that this set was found in different sizes as the Shang bell
and the chung.

XLVI. Cheng-ch'eng

There are two vessels which are called cheng-ch'eng in
their inscriptions. One is illustrated in Shang chou: II, 933
and the inscription is in San tai: 18.4b-5a. It was said to
have been found in Hunan procince, and was probably made by the
Ch'u State. Another one is catalogued in San tai: 18.3b-4a.
This was made by the Hsü[2] State. From the inscription we know
that the first one has the mouth downward and the second one
upward. The first one has a handle and looks very much like the
one illustrated in the Loo Catalogue (1924): 26. From the inscription of the second we know that the cheng-ch'eng was a
military instrument.   The cheng as discussed under the Shang
bell is the abbreviation for cheng-ch'eng. Both Tu's commentary
to Tso chuan (Hsuan 4) and Wei's commentary to Chin yü V and
Wu yü of Kuo yü say, "Ting-ling is cheng."   Ting-ling was struck
outside the barrel as described in Wu yu.

Kou-ti and cheng-ch'eng were similar in shape but were
different in the following ways:

1. Kou-ti may be formed into a set and were used
   in ceremony while cheng-ch'eng is single and
   was used on military occasions.

2. Kou-ti were made in the Wu and Yueh States, and
   cheng-ch'eng were made in the Hsü[2] and Ch'u States.

3. The names are different.

Both were made during the Ch'un Ch'iu period. The cheng-
ch'eng with the mouth upward should be earlier than those with
the mouth downward.

XLVII. Ch'un-yü

Ch'un-yu was sometimes called ch'un   as mentioned in the ku jen of Chou li. Wu yü of Kuo yü described the meeting in Huang-shih of Chin and Wu, and at that time Wu Wang himself held the drum-stick to sound the chung, to strike the ting-ling (cheng), and ch'un-yü, and to ring the to. This indicates that the ch'un-yü was struck with a stick from the outside, and was used by the military men. From the records we know that the ch'un-yü was found in Southern China. It must have been an instrument used by the people of Wu, Yüeh and Ch'u.

XLVIII. Ku

Only one example of the early bronze drum has ever been found. In Sumitomo I: 130 a ku is illustrated which can be dated Shang. We found drums of later periods (after the Han dynasty) in various places in Southern China, but they bear no relation to the ancient ku.

In the foregoing sections the forty-eight classes have been listed and discussed. The name of the class was either referred to in its inscription or not mentioned at all as in the following list:

IA Names given on Western Chou bronzes:

1-7, 11, 21-22, 24, 33-35, 37, 41, 43.

B Names given on Eastern Chou bronzes:

8, 16, 23, 25, 27-29, 36, 42. 44-46.

C Names given on Han bronzes:

31.

II Names not given on bronzes:

9, 10, 12-20, 26, 30, 32, 38-40, 47, 48.

The names of the wine containers 10-20, except 11, were never mentioned in the inscriptions. Since these classes disappeared after Early Western Chou and at that period the name of the vessel was seldom mentioned, it is impossible to have a correct name. Among them 10 was named chia based on the pictographic character of this vessel. We may follow the same method to discover the unknown names, but unfortunately, some of the pictograph characters for certain vessels can not be read because both the type of the vessels and the characters were discontinued in their use in the earlier days. Therefore we can not help but accept those names given in the Sung catalogues without any strong evidence. They were mostly names that appeared in the Classics or Ritual books and some of them were merely vague descriptions of the vessels as 18 and 20. I have tentatively given names for 26, 30, 39 and 40. Thirty-eight was named by the original owner, Tuan Fang, and 9 and 10 were named by Lo chen-yü. Wang Kuo Wei saved much discussion on 19, although the name kuang was first used by Hsü k'ao ku t'u. Twenty-nine was determined by Jung Keng.

Among those names which were referred to in their inscriptions, the names in Western Chou bronzes were of the unified official language and the names on Eastern Chou bronzes were mostly in the dialects of different the states. In the latter, some of the names are really different names for the same class or type of vessel. Therefore for those bronzes which have no inscriptions or the names of the vessels were not mentioned in their inscriptions, will be named in two ways: (1) by the name given in the same type of other vessels that have names mentioned

and belong to the proper period, that is, either Western Chou
or Eastern Chou; and (2) by the name we have given to those
vessels which never had names mentioned in any period, but were
so named by Sung catalogues and recent scholars only because
these names appeared in books. Thus we consider the names on
Eastern Chou bronzes the names for the special types during their
period despite their being dialects. So if we classified those
vessels under any class of IB they should be Eastern Chou bronzes,
and those under IA may be either Shang, Western Chou or Eastern
Chou.

Since most of the names were established in the Sung
catalogues, let us now make a short review of them. Po ku followed K'ao ku in the following names: 1, 2, 3, 7, 11, 12, 14, 15,
17, 21, 22, 33, 34, 35, 37, 41, 44, 47, altogether eighteen
classes. Po ku also made the same mistakes as K'ao ku: (1) hsü
were called kuei; (2) early kuei were called i   ; (3) late
kuei were called tun (or tui); (4) ts'ung were called yu; (5)
cheng were called an; (6) made no differences between water i
and wine kuang. But if we compare Po ku with K'ao ku we will
find that the former made many improvements. K'ao ku was confused about many terms, such as besides having tun, tsun, lei,
hsien, ho and ku as separate classes, the author at the same
time called them i in Vol. 4. Furthermore, hu were sometimes
called tsun, square ting were sometimes called fang-i, yu and
lei were sometimes called hu; ting and ho were sometimes called li;
lei were sometimes called yu; ku were sometimes called chü   ,
etc. These indicate that the author of K'ao ku did not have a

clear idea of each class. Po ku, in Vol. 6-7a, made the same
mistake in calling chih, hu ku, etc. tsun, but as a whole it
had a more distinct definition for each class. Po ku also
added new classes like fu, chia, chih, fang-i and tsun in the
form of animals. For food vessels, it listed fu, kuei (should
be hsü), tun together in Vol. 18. For water vessels, it listed
p'an, i, yu together in Vol. 20b. For wine vessels, it listed
chia, ku, chüeh, chiao together in Vol. 15. These indicate that
the author began to have a vague idea of 'group', that is, to
make food, water, and wine vessels into different groups.

The three main purposes of making vessels, discussed at
the beginning of the chapter, were: for general use, for ceremonial and for funeral purposes. However, by studying the inscriptions, we find four important purposes, namely, for sacrificial use, for travelling use, for daily use, and for dowries.
These were indicated in the inscriptions by (1) calling the vessel by a general term, such as "made this sacrificial vessel;"
and (2) by putting a modifier like "travelling" before the
general term "vessel" or the special class name like "hu" such
as "made this travelling vessel" or "made this travelling hu."
These terms and modifiers are listed in four groups:

    I. Sacrificial vessel

       A. General terms

          tsun   , meaning vessel in sacrificial use

          i   , same as above

          tsun-i , same as above

          pao-ch'i   ,precious vessel   鼓彤 鬵舟 仲戉父塱

          nien-ch'i   , memorial vessel   臺彤

          chi-ch'i   , sacrificial vessel   簫辰彤

ssu-tsun 祠尊 , same as above   小臣艅尊

ssu-ch'i 示 , same as above   邦王盉

tsun-ch'i , same as above   商王文饮

B. Modifiers

pao , to be treasured

ssu , to sacrifice

tsung , family temple

hsiu , to present or offer

chien , to present or offer

tsun , to sacrifice

meng , name of sacrifice

chiang , name of sacrifice

ch'ang , name of sacrifice

II. Travelling vessel

A. General term

hsin-ch'i 行器 , travelling vessel   窦子匿

B. Modifiers

hsin 行 , to travel

lü 旅 , to travel

tsai 戴 , to carry

III. Dowry

A. General term

Sheng-ch'i , vessel for dowry   叔姬匿

B. Modifier

sheng , dowry

IV. Daily use-vessel

Modifiers

yu , to feast

shih , to eat

ssu   , to feed or to feast (cf. Chin wen pien: 5.24)

shu   , to cook

shan   , to cook, or meal

pen   , meals (cf. Chin wen pien: 5.23b)

yung   , to use

yin   , to drink

lung   , amusing, to be appreciated, to entertain,
          or to play with.

kuan   , to wash (hands)

mei   , to wash (face) (6f. Chin wen pien: 11.4a)

By using the above as criteria and adding them to the
military purposes, which were also mentioned in the inscriptions,
we got the following results:

1. Vessels that were made for sacrificial, travelling,
   dowry and daily use:
   ting, li, hsien, fu, hu, i.

2. Vessels that were made for sacrificial, travelling and
   daily use:
   hsü, tou

3. Vessels that were made for sacrificial and travelling:
   chia, ho, chüeh, tsun, ku, chih, yu, ling, yü, p'u.

4. Vessels that were made for sacrificial and daily use:
   tun, niao-shou-tsun, chung .

5. Vessels that were made for sacrificial use:
   chiao, fang-i, kuang, lei, fou, po.

6. Vessels that were made for sacrificial, dowry and daily
   use:
   p'an.

7. Vessels that were made for dowry and daily use:
   cheng.

8. Vessels that were made for daily use:
   tan.

9. Vessels that were made for travelling:
   tsung, kou-ti.

10. Vessels that were made for military use:
    to, cheng-ch'eng.

It should be noticed here that "daily use" included feasts and ceremonies other than sacrifices. The quantity of the wine vessels of the early period, sometimes mentioned in their inscriptions to be used while travelling, is comparatively small. The vessels made for dowry were mentioned in their inscriptions as not being earlier than Late Western Chou. The hsü were sometimes for sacrificial and daily use, but the majority of hsü were made to be used while travelling.

So far, I have discussed the different classes of vessels of the pre-Han period. Two categories are left to be cleared up. There are not many specimen of pre-Han vessels that remain to be put in a new class, and their names are hard to determine. I shall list them as miscellaneous vessels. Vessels of the Han dynasty will be discussed below.

Generally speaking, Han bronzes continued the latest type of the Late Chan Kuo period. The vessels are mostly plain without any decoration.

I. Food vessels, being all heating vessels

    A. Ting. The following is a selection of datable ting of Western Han:

        Illustrated ting

Tsun ku: 4.6 dated 68 B.C.

Tsun ku: 4.1 dated 53 B.C.

Shuang chien I: 2.53 dated 24 B.C.

Liang lei: 9.3 dated 15 B.C.

Tsun ku: 4.3 dated 11 B.C.

Non-illustrated ting

Hsiao chiao: 11.57.2 dated 126 B.C.

Hsiao chiao: 11.63.2 dated 122 B.C.

Hsiao chiao: 11.56.1 dated 65 B.C.

Hsiao chiao: 11.57.4 dated 52 B.C.

Hsiao chiao: 11.55.4 dated 39 B.C.

Hsiao chiao: 11.62.2 dated 23 B.C.

Hsiao chiao:11.62.3 dated 23 B.C.

I wen: 13.13 dated 19 B.C.

Hsiao chiao: 11.67.1 dated 15 B.C.

Hsiao chiao: 11.67.2 dated 15 B.C.

Hsiao chiao: 11.66.3 dated 10 B.C.

Hsiao chiao: 11.66.4 dated 10 B.C.

T'ao chai I: 5.27 dated 4 B.C.

These ting are similar in form, and they undoubtedly came from the Type VII ting.

2. Li. There is only one known li of the Han dynasty. The inscription is catalogued in Ts'ung ku: 5.18. No illustration is available.

3. Hsien, Hsien-fu[4], Fu[3]. A tseng, illustrated in Heng hsien: 116, is called hsien in its inscription. This is why in Shuo wen, hsien and tseng are synonymous. During the

Han dynasty, the upper part of the hsien was called hsien and the
lower part was called hsien-fu[4] as in the inscriptions of K'ao
ku: 9.27 and Hsiao chiao: 13.50.1. The former has an illustration showing the vessel without legs but with a small mouth and
two ring handles. The lower part was also called fu[3] in its inscription as shown in Hsü k'ao ku: 1.14. The hsien-fu[4] or fu[3]
are set on the mouth of a stove as shown in Sung chai: 31 and
Hsü k'ao ku: 1.11. The fire goes directly through the bottom of
the fu[3].

    4. Chiao-tou. There are three vessels of this type
which are called chiao-tou in their inscriptions and of which
illustrations are available.

      Chin so: 3.24, 25 dated 65 B.C.

      T'ao chai I: 6.61 dated 31 B.C.

    The vessel has a wide and shallow mouth with three legs
and a single long handle. Shuo wen says, "Chiao is chiao-tou."
There is no available illustration for one vessel which calls
itself "Chiao, to warm wine." It is catalogued in Hsiao chiao:
13.61.3, dated 10 B.C.

  II. Wine vessels

    A. Heating vessels

    5. Ho   see Type VIII ho under Typology

    6. Chiao-tsun. There are two vessels of this type,
catalogued in K'ao ku: 10.3a and 10.3b, which were wrongly called
ting. In Chin so: 1.90, a similar vessel is illustrated which
is called chiao-tsun in its inscription. It was found in Ch'ü-fu
in Shantung province. The vessel has a chain handle, three legs
under the bottom and the lid could be used as a drinking cup when

inverted.   In my book, Chinese Bronzes in Foreign Collections,
Vol. I, p. 22, I stated that both chia and chiao were used to
boil the ch'ang, a kind of mixed wine from a grain wine and
fragrant herbs which had been boiled in water.   Therefore, it is
possible that chiao-tsun are a late type of chia.   In typology,
it looks very similar to two Shang vessels; one is shown in
London: No. 195 (David Weill's Collection), and the other is in
An-yang Treasures: 40 (Fujii's Collection). Both have three low
legs and a domed lid.

        7. Wu.   Shuo wen says, "Wu is a kind of fu." A wu
in Ch'ang an: 2.13 (Chen sung: 3.20) was called wu in its inscription.   It looks like a ho of the Chan Kuo or the Han period,
(Tsun ku: 3.14).

        8. Hou-lou.   There is only one vessel which is called
hou-lou in its inscription (Tsun ku: 4.14; T'ao chai I: 7.2).
Another similar vessel is catalogued in Hsiao chiao: 13.51.4
(inscription only).   It looks like the Type VIII ho, but it has
no spout.

    B. Containers
        9. Hu.   The following vessels were called hu in their
inscriptions:

        1. Shina kodo: 222 (David Weill's Collection).
            Gilded.

        2. T'ao chai I: 6.20

        3. Po ku: 12.35 (Hsü k'ao ku: 1.21). Gilded,
            dated 8 B.C.

        4. Loo Catalogue (1924): 32

        5. Hsiao chiao: 11.78a. Dated 16 B.C. (no illus-
            tration).

The first three examples are similar in shape to the
Type VI pre-Han hu. Example 4 has a long neck and was called
"wen hu" in its inscription, meaning a hu to warm wine. It
seems to me that it should be called hsing 鉶 as described in
both Shuo wen and Kuang yün "Hsing is a kind of wine vessel
which looks like chung 鍾 but has a long neck." There is no
illustration for the last example. However, there is a similar
inscription in Heng hsien: 109 which calls it chung. If this
chung is an authentic one, then there must be some difference
between the hu and the chung in the Han dynasty. First, the
volume of the chung is much larger than that of the hu. Second,
the chung is also a measure. Third, the chung always has a
middle bulged belly.

There is a hu, which is a copy of the fifth example,
in Walters Gallery (54.1262). I wrongly included it in Chinese
Bronzes in Foreign Collections, pl. 61. It has a long neck.
Perhaps, the original one is like that one.

10. Chung. The following, which have illustrations,
were called chung in their inscriptions:

     1. Heng hsien: 109   dated 16 B.C.

     2. T'ao chai I: 6.4 (Meng yi: 2.5) dated 3 B.C.

     3. Tsun ku: 4.17 dated 13 A.D.

     4. K'ao ku: 9.26 dated 44 A.D.

     5. Hsi ch'ing: 34.11 dated 126 A.D.

     6. Shih er: Shih 14 dated 128 A.D.

     7. Tsun ku: 4.18 dated 139 A.D.

     8. T'ao chai I: 6.9 dated 158 A.D.

9. T'ao chai I: 6.6

10. T'ao chai I: 6.2

11. Pao yün: 117

12. Wu ying: 156

13. Chen sung: 2.40

14. Huai mi: 2.31

There are three inscriptions without illustrations (Hsiao chiao: 12.4.2; 12.4.4; 12.16.1) which can be dated 110 A.D., 134 A.D. and 139 A.D. respectively. All of the chung except the last four (5-8) are similar in shape to the Type VI pre-Han hu. The last four have high truncated cone-shaped bases which are of a later period. Cleveland 13.15 (U.S.   ) is similar to these.

11. Fang. Shuo wen says, "Fang is a square chung." It is similar in shape to Type VII pre-Han hu. The fang in Heng hsien: 110 can be dated 5 B.C. and the fang in T'ao chai I: 6.11 can be dated 4 A.D.

12. Ou. A flat hu in Hsi ch'ing: 34.5 was called ou in its inscription. Ou is a measure. In the Chicago Natural History Museum there is a set of pottery ou with different volumes.

13. Fou. A fou, illustrated in Wu ying: 163, is called fou in its inscription. The ornate decoration on this vessel was added later, since it covers eight characters of the inscription. This vessel is lower than the pre-Han fou and has no base.

III. Water vessels

14. P'an. A p'an, illustrated in Shuang chien I: 2.55,

can be dated, by its inscription, 57 A.D. It is similar to
Type XV pre-Han p'an which are without bases and very shallow.

15. P'en. A p'en, illustrated in Ch'ang an: 2.16,
is called p'en in its inscription. It looks like the chien
with two ring handles, but it has a middle bulged belly.

16. Chüan, Tiao, P̲i̲e̲n̲ (Hsi). Both chien and chüan belong
to the p'en class, but the chien is larger. However, in the
Shih ch'i of Kuang ya, it says, "Chuan 銷 is called tiao 金兆 "
and Shuo wen says, "Tiao is a warming vessel." There is one
vessel (I wen: 15.6), without an illustration, that is called
tiao in its inscription. Chün ku: 22.51 describes a vessel like
the p'en but it is larger and is called tiao 盉 in its inscription.
In that case, chüan may also have been a heating vessel.

The following are datable chüan, with illustrations,
which are called chüan in their inscriptions:

    1. Ch'ang an: 2.14 dated 65 B.C.

    2. Po ku: 21.27 dated 65 B.C.

    3. Hsiao chiao: 13.54 dated 12 B.C.

    4. T'ao chai I: 6 dated 8 B.C.

All of the above vessels belong to the Western Han period.

Here, we must discuss the problem of a vessel which
was called hsi 洗 for a long time. Among all the vessels which
were named hsi in different catalogues, not a single one called
itself hsi in its inscription. I have checked more than thirty
datable hsi and found that they were made between 76 A.D. and
194 A.D., that is, in the Eastern Han period. Many of them have
a fish decoration which indicates that they are water vessels.
Their shape is similar to that of the chüan.

17. I. An I, illustrated in Ch'eng ch'iu: 58, is called I in its inscription. Its shape is similar to Type IIb pre-Han I. The Metropolitan 13.220.47 is of this type.

With the gilded hu as the only exception, all Han vessels are without any decoration. The gilded hu, such as David Weill's (Shina kodo: 222) and Chicago 27.315 (U.S.   ) were incised after the vessels were made.

VII
appendix

TABLE I

Names of the Ceremonial Vessels

I. Food Vessels

  A. Heating vessels

    1. Ting 鼎, 礉艐, 石沱, 釪, 鼎霥, 鎬, 盂鼒, 鉰. 鼒
                                     簹, 錥鼎, 釶艂

    2. Li 鬲, 鎘

    3. Hsien 鬳, 甗瓦, 甗犬, 甑, 錥鬳, 鼎攴

  B. Containers

    4. Kuei 毁, 簋

    5. Hsü 盨, 須, 盨瓦, 錥鈃, 錥盨, 拋頪

    6. Fu 盙, 匡, 匡, 盙瓦, 甅, 盦, 簋, 盙攵

    7. Tou 豆

    8. Tun 敦, 犀, 錥犀

  C. Spoons

    9. Pi 匕

II. Wine Vessels

  A. Heating vessels

    10. Chia 斝

    11. Ho 盉, 盉禾, 盉禾, 鬶, 錥鬶, 和

    12. Chüeh

    13. Chiao

  B. Containers

    14. Tsun

    15. Ku

    16. Chih 觶, 觶瓦, 鎬

    17. Yu

    18. Fang-i

19. <u>Kuang</u>

20. <u>Niao-shou-tsun</u>

21. <u>Hu</u> 壺, 皷, 鍾, 壼, 畢

22. <u>Lei</u> 罍, 罌, 㼈

23. <u>Fou</u>

24. <u>Ling</u> 瓴甀

25. <u>Ts'ung</u> 瓽, 甌, 㼽, 金瓮

26. <u>Ying</u>

27. <u>Tan</u> 儋, 甔, 甀(史記)

28. <u>Min</u> 鈤

29. <u>Cheng</u> 甑, 畚

30. <u>P'i</u> 柈

31. <u>Pei</u> 桮

C. Spoons

32. <u>Shao</u>

III. Water Vessels

33. <u>Yü</u>

34. <u>P'an</u> 槃, 般, 鎜

35. <u>I</u> （設）匜, 也, 卺, 鈕, 鑑

36. <u>Chien</u> 金監, 鑑

IV. Supports

37. <u>P'u</u> 鋪

38. <u>Chin</u>

39. <u>Chü</u>

V. Musical Instruments

40. <u>Shang bell</u>

41. <u>Chung</u>

42. <u>Po</u>

43. <u>Ling</u>

44. <u>To</u>

45. <u>Kou-ti</u>

46. <u>Cheng-ch'eng</u> 鉦重塑, 征城

47. <u>Ch'un-yü</u>

48. <u>Ku</u>

CHAPTER VIII
TYPOLOGY

I shall now follow the terminology and the classification discussed in the previous chapters in order to study the different types of each of the forty-eight classes. The establishment of the forty-eight classes was based mostly on the names of the proper class mentioned in their inscriptions. They were grouped according to their functions. In this chapter we shall analyze the shapes or forms within each class during the long period of evolution and show how they differ from each other. Under each class a general characteristic is first given and this is followed by the qualifications of the different types under that class. Some of the types may be divided into sub-types. The differences between these sub-types are listed. Type I, Type II, etc. show the different types under one class, and Ia, Ib, etc. show the sub-types. The order I, II, III, etc. was arranged not only according to chronology, but also according to the shapes or forms as well. Thus the types I, II, etc. do not necessarily show the chronological sequence, but rather they are adopted here as a convenient arrangement for discussing typology.

It is obvious that the shapes of each type changed during the long evolution, and they can not be studied as still objects. The types were more or less made in an artificial way. The dating given to each type is certainly relative and flexible. The overlapping of more than one type which extends over a rather long period is quite often.   We know that this was due to the inheritance of the craftsmanship and the admiration

of the old forms that prevented them from fading away in a
nurry. But there were always conservative and progressive
members among the craftsmen and donors, and so the new type
was born while the old type was still in use. The change
from the old type to the new was a long gradual process.
However, in spite of this, a certain class of vessels might
have several different shapes during the same period. The
existance of the four types of ting (I-IV) at the same time
was due to the different tastes of the people and the slightly
different functions of the ting.

        The criteria for distinguishing the types of vessels
are as follows:

    I. Criteria for Types

        A. Shape of the vessel

This includes the shape of the mouth, rim, neck,
shoulder, belly and bottom, and the relation between these parts. It only describes the body
which is the main containing part, excluding
the covering, the handling and the supporting
parts of the vessel.

        B. Subordinate parts

These include the covering, handling and the supporting parts of the vessel such as the lid,
handles, base, legs, etc.

        C. Ornamental appendages

These are appendages such as flanges which have
no function on the vessel. Decoration of the
vessel is not considered the criterion for the
types, unless the decoration was influenced by
the position of the subordinate parts such as
on the yu, where the shifting of the handles
has a definite influence on the decoration. No
matter whether it is ornate, moderate, or simple
such features have no significance in distinguishing the types.

    II. Criteria for Sub-types

These are based on minor differences within one
type which are not significant enough to exclude

them from their own type. Such a difference is
certainly not significant enough to serve as a
criterion for distinguishing types.

The study of typology in bronzes emphasizes the historical evolution of types. Therefore in a certain period
there might be two different types similar in general shape,
although they were derived from different sources and trends
and have different functions. The reasons for this are: (1)
parallel evolution of two entirely different classes toward a
similar type; (2) during the process of evolution, one type is
usually apt to be influenced by the other, so that towards the
later period no important difference remained between the
features of the two classes. The difficulties of distinguishing types are due to the missing links that relate one to the
other, and to the fact that a lot of the vessels were not
named in their inscriptions, hence the function of the vessel
was obscure. Under such circumstances, similar shapes of the
vessels were classified under different types solely on the
basis of the importance of the difference in trend of evolution
and function.

I. _Ting_

1. Mouth: circular or rectangular, wide.

2. Ears: vertical or bent.

3. Bottom: slightly concave for Types I, IV, V;
   tripartite for Types II, VIII;
   flat for Type III;
   hemispheric for Types VI, VII, IX.

4. Legs: solid, but not three-facet
   hollow to the end for Type VIII.

5. Lid: seldom on Early types
   flat for Type IV;
   low domed (or flat) for Types VI, VII, VIII, IX.

Type I - Round Ting

      1. Mouth: circular

      2. Ears: vertical

      3. Bottom: slightly concave

      4. Legs: cylindrical

      5. Lid: seldom present

      6. Flanges: often present

Examples of this type found at An-yang are:

K'ao ku: 1.21, 1.23; Yeh II: 1.5 (now in Kahn Collection),
1.6, 1.7; Yeh III: 1.5, 1.6, 1.7, 1.10, 1.11, 1.16;
Trautmann: 3, 4; Yen k'u: 6, 7, 8; Tsun ku: 1.3; Shuang
chien I: 1.5; Shih er: Chü 3, 7; Ontario: NB 4022, 3217,
2633, with constricted neck; Yeh I: 1.9, 1.10, 1.14;
Yeh III: 1.8; Trautmann: 2; Ontario NB 3230. *proway tselsmes: sc*

Examples of this type with decorated knee and with hoof are:

University:41.25.1; Hakkaku: 2; Shapes: 23.5; Ku kung:
24.1, 27.6, 28.7; Tsun ku: 1.23; Shang chou: II, 45.

Type II - Tripartite Ting

      Similar to I except that it has a tripartite bottom
and it rarely has flanges. *the legs are smaller at the ends.*

Examples of this type found at An-yang are:

Yeh I: 1.11, 1.12; Yeh III: 1.9 (now in Falk Collection), 1.12; *ct.S.38*
Yen k'u: 1.5; Lochow: 3.

      There are vessels in this type with constricted necks *U.S.43*
such as Loo 87029, Shu kan: 13 and Kodo-ki: 2. It should be
noticed that though they look similar to the early types of li,
they can not be called li. The difference is that the solid
part of the legs is longer than that of the li. In other words,
the tripartite part of the li is much deeper than that of the

ting of this type.

Type III - Rectangular **Ting**

Similar to I except in the following ways:

1. Mouth: rectangular

2. Bottom: flat

3. Legs: four in number

Examples of this type found at An-yang are:

Yeh II: 1.3; Yeh III: 1.3, 1.4; Yen k'u: 1.4; Illustrated London News (April 14, 1936), fig. 10 (Academia
Sinica).

The area of the mouth is always slightly larger than
that of the bottom. Sometimes it has a flat lid and a broad
loop in the center as shown in Tsun ku: 1.25 and Shih er:
Chü 4. Both vessels still have vertical ears, so that both
sides of the lid were cut in rectangular slots to let the
ears through. *Flanges were often appeared*

Type IV - Animal Leg **Ting**

Similar to I except that it has a shallow body and
three or four legs in the shape of an animal or a
bird. If it has four legs, the mouth is rectangular.

Examples of this type found at An-yang are:

Yeh I: 1.13; Yeh II: 1.4; Yeh IV: 1.15, 1.17; Trautmann: 5;
Ontario NB 4089 (all have three legs).

The above four types are contemporaneous, by their provenance, and can be dated in the Shang. These types also
extend to Early Western Chou, but they disappeared completely after
that period. We found in many instances that at least three of
the types were made in one set. There must have been some

functional differences between the round, tripartite and rectangular ting.

All of the pottery ting found at Yang Shao, Lung-shan,
and Hou Kang, under classification (in ting section) have constricted necks. This shows that the ting with a constricted
neck is slightly earlier, i.e., in the Shang.

All ting that were unearthed at An-yang had cylindrical
legs, sometimes with decorated knee, and belong to the Shang
period. ~~The examples above have legs~~ with decorated knee and
with hoof. The last example (Shang chou: II, 45) can be dated
by its inscription in the Early Western Chou period. Therefore
I am inclined to think that a ting with this type of legs belongs
to a later period than Shang, i. e., to Early Western Chou.
By further evolution, as shown in the bronzes after Middle Western
Chou, the knee and hoof look more or less like a horse's leg.

The presence of a lid on Type I of University 41.25.1
and Shapes: 23.1 are the only examples of this type.

Type V - Lower Bulge Ting

1. Bottom: slightly concave
   Ears: Vertical
2. Neck: slightly constricted

3. Body: lower bulge

4. Lid: seldom had

a. Legs: cylindrical without hoof

   Decoration: usually moderate style

b. Legs: with knee and hoof

   Decoration: ornate, mostly of kê ting style

This type covered the whole Late Western Chou period,
and extended to the Early Ch'un Ch'iu period. Subtype Va from
second half
its inscription, first appeared in the ~~middle~~ of Early Western

Chou. Until the latter part of Middle Western Chou it was over-
shadowed by Vb and other types. Subtype Vb is later than Va.
The kê ting of Vb can be dated in Yi Wang's period, the latter
part of Middle Western Chou.

Late

Type VI - Hemispherical Ting

    1. Body: shallow

    2. Bottom: usually hemispherical

    3. Legs: with knee and hoof

    4. Lid: seldom had

This type, from the inscriptions thereon, covers the
whole Late Western Chou period. When this type was extended
to the Ch'un Ch'iu period the vertical earsbecame bent outward.

Type VII - Geoid Shaped Ting

    1. Body: deep

    2. Ears: bent

    3. Bottom: usually hemispherical

    4. Legs: with knee and hoof

    5. Lid: always present with the body forming a
       global shape or geoid

This type began after the Early Ch'un Ch'iu period and
extended to the end of the Chan Kuo period. During the Ch'un
Ch'iu period the vessels that were called shih-t'o, yü or fan,
which have been discussed under classification, usually had
deeper bodies. Later, the legs became shorter and stouter and
the body became somewhat flatter.

Type VIII - Hollow Leg **Ting**

    1. Body: deep

    2. Ears: bent (or circular rings)

    3. Bottom: tripartite

    4. Legs: hollow to the end

    5. Lid: low domed

This type can be dated in the Chan Kuo period. It is possible that it came from Northern Shensi.

Type IX - Han **Ting**

    Similar to the late form of VII, but is plain, without any decoration.

    Types V to VII are the continuation of Type I with the addition of the lid, the development of the knee and hoof on the legs, and changes in the shape of the body. Only a few examples of Type VIII show the revival of the tripartite bottom. Types I to IV always have vertical ears. They ~~even~~ _do not always_ have lids. Sometimes Types V and VI have bent ears, but Type VII always has a lid and is exclusively with bent ears. At the end of the _Late_ Western Chou and the Early Eastern Chou periods some vessels still ~~had~~ _have_ vertical ears, but they were turned outward.

II. **Li**

    1. Mouth: circular (except Type V is oblong), wide

    2. Ears: vertical or bent for Types I, III; absent for Types II, IV

    3. Neck: constricted

    4. Bottom: tripartite

    5. Legs: hollow, always three in number except

for Type V

    6. Lid: always none

Type I

    1. Ears: vertical

    2. Body: tall

Examples: <u>Siren</u>: 11; <u>Shina kodo</u>: 95; <u>Sung chai</u> II: 18;
<u>Sung chai</u> I: 6; <u>Chen sung</u>: 1.26; <u>Shih er</u>: Shih 9;
<u>Wu ying</u>: 35; <u>Shan chai</u>: 46; <u>Hai wai</u>: 4; <u>London</u>: No. 198.

According to the inscriptions and the decorations, this
type can be dated in the Shang. In <u>London</u>: No. 258, a <u>li</u> of
this type without ears is an exception.

Type II

    1. Ears: absent

    2. Handle: single

    3. Body: low

There is only one vessel of this type, Moore 1023 in
our catalogue. The shape and the single handle may have been
patterned after the pottery <u>li</u> found in Shih-wa and Hui-tui
as listed under the classification <u>li</u>, Type II. This belongs
to Shang.

Type III

    1. Ears: vertical or bent

    2. Body: low

Examples: <u>Meng yi</u> II: 1.7 ; <u>Sung chai</u> II: 19 (found in
Shensi province.)

From the provenance and inscriptions, this type can be
dated in the Middle Western Chou period or later.

Type IV

    1. Ears: never appeared

    2. Body: low

    3. Flanges: sometimes present

Examples: Sung chai II: 23 (found in Shensi); Pao yün: 36;
Sumitomo I: 7, 8; Shan chai: 47 (found at Ch'i-shan);
Tsun ku: 2.20, 2.21; Shih er: Hsüeh 5, Chiu 2; Hsia 7;
Meng yi II: 8; Yen k'u: 15(found at Lin-tzu).

From the inscriptions and the decorations, they belong
to the Late Western Chou and Early Ch'un Ch'iu periods.

Type V

    1. Mouth: oblong

    2. Ears: bent

    3. Compartments: The upper part looks like a

        rectangular ting, and the lower part is a closet.

This type has been discussed under the classification.
Judging from the inscription and decoration, it is of the Late
Western Chou period. The shape of this type is quite different
from the above types. Since, in its inscription, it was referred
to as li it is listed here.

All of the li have three legs except a square li in the
Palace Museum (Hsi ch'ing: 31.11; Ku kung: 20.18; London: 7;
International Exhibition: 2) which has four legs and which can
be dated according to its decoration in the Early Western Chou
period. This is the only exception. There is another one in
Hsi ch'ing: 31.9 with two handles on each side but the inscription is spurious.

III. Hsien

1. Mouth: circular (or rectangular), wide

2. Ears: vertical or bent

3. Legs: hollow, three (or four) in number

4. Compartments: upper and lower, connected (or
     detached for Type II)

5. Bottom of upper compartment: perforated, con-
     nected or detached

6. Bottom of lower compartment: tripartite or
     tetrapartite

7. Ears of lower compartment: sometimes with bent
     ears, or loose ring handles for late types

8. Lid: always none

Type I - Round Hsien

1. Mouth: circular

2. Ears: vertical

3. Bottom: tripartite

4. Legs: hollow

a. Compartments: connected

   Perforated bottom: detachable

   Examples of this type found at An-yang are:

   Shuang chien I: 1.10; Liu t'ung pieh lu: art. 4, p.7.

b. Compartments: detachable

   Perforated bottom: connected with the upper

   compartment

   Examples are:

   K'ao ku: 2.19; Sumitomo II: 179; Ontario: NB 5297

   (found at P'ing-ting).

Judging from the provenance and inscription, Type Ia can
be dated in the Shang and Early Western Chou periods; Type Ib
can be dated in the Late Western Chou period and it may have
extended to Early Ch'un Ch'iu. *Eastern Chou*

Type II - Rectangular Hsien

1. Mouth: rectangular

2. Ears: vertical or bent

a. Ears: bent on both upper and lower compartments

   Bottom: slightly concave

   Compartments: detachable

   Legs: cylindrical

   Examples: Shina kodo: 100 (Sheng kao: 8-9).

b. Ears: vertical or bent on upper compartment, bent

   on lower compartment if present

   Bottom: tetrapartite

   Compartments: detachable

   Legs: hollow

   Examples: Ku kung: 35.7; Hsin cheng: 66;

   Tsun ku: 2.26 (found at Chi Hsien of Shansi).

From the inscriptions and the decorations, Type IIa can
be dated in the Early Western Chou period, and IIb in the Late
Western Chou and Early Ch'un Ch'iu periods.

In bronzes, the two compartments were connected during
the Shang and Early Western Chou periods. (Sometimes) during the
Early Western Chou period the two compartments were cast in
separate molds. The two examples under Type II show that the
lower compartment is just a rectangular ting. In Burchard's
catalogue, 1935, no. 278, there is a hsien similar to these *this* two
except that the mouth is circular. The lower compartment is so

similar to the _ting_ that we are inclined to think that a _ting_
was sometimes used to serve such purposes.

In _Hsi_ _ch'ing_: 31.10; _Nin_ _shou_: 12.35 and _Chin_ _so_: p. 11
(one of the ten vessels in Confucius' temple in Chu-fu) the
three vessels are the lower parts of Type II.

IV. _Kuei_

1. Mouth: circular, wide (medium for Type V)
2. Handles: paired semicircular with pendants;
                none for Type I, four for Type III
3. Bottom: slightly concave or flat
4. Body: usually with slightly lower bulge
5. Base: circular, low, usually brimmed
6. Socle: appeared after Shang
7. Lid: low domed with cup-shaped top, seldom on
   Type I

62 Type I Handleless _Kuei_

1. Handles: none
2. Base: seldom brimmed
a. Is smaller in size than b, with lower bulge
   Examples of this type found at An-yang are:
   An-yang _Treasures_: 31; _Shuang_ _chien_ I: 1.18;
   Sung _chai_ I: 1.7; _Shih_ _er_: Chü 8; Ontario NB 3214,
   3195.
b. The belly is not bulged. The diameter of its
   mouth is greater than the lower part of the belly.
   The outline of it comes down in a rather straight
   line. It is larger in size than a.

Examples of this type found at An-yang are:

Yeh III: 1.25; Yen k'u: 1.16.

From the provenance, this type can be dated as Shang exclusively. There is not a single vessel which bears the name kuei in its inscription.

Type II - Early Kuei

a. Without pendants

Examples of this type found at An-yang are:

Yeh I: 1.16; Yeh III: 1.27, 1.28; Shuang chien I: 1.19; pottery, Ontario: NA 2123, 2157; marble, An-yang Einds: 31.

b. Handles: usually have the animal-heads with horns and ears laid back; with hooked pendants

Example of this type found at An-yang is:

Yeh III: 1.26 (with lid).

c. Handles: like b, but with rectangular pendants

d. Handles: have raised horns on both sides of the animal's head which are level with the rim; with pendants like c.

Examples of this type found at An-yang are:

Sheng kao: 10; marble, An-yang Treasures: 63.

e. Handles: have upright horns on the top of the animal's head which stand erect over the rim; with pendants like b and c.

The five sub-types under Type II form one type, but the relationship between these sub-types is not the same as the relationship between the ting types I-IV. We seldom found identical inscriptions which belonged to more than one of these

subtypes. Therefore, these subtypes might be the result of
different decades or different provenance. From the provenance,
we definitely know that a, b and d first appeared during the
Shang. There is a very good example in our catalogue of a kuei
(U.S.   ) that belongs under the c classification which has
an inscription that is certainly Shang; whereas e is mostly
Early Chou. A very good example is the K'ang Hou kuei in Malcolm's Collection. The inscription on this kuei is historical
evidence that there was a Ch'eng Wang period.

Type III - Four Handles Kuei

        In this type, the handles have various styles just
as those under Type II. I have given this type a special classification because the pair of kuei in the Fogg Museum (44.57.8-9)
was found with kuei of Type II and bear the same inscription.
Many vessels of this type, from their inscriptions, belong to
the Early Western Chou period. The examples of this type are
listed below:

        a. Like Type II but with four handles
           Shang chou: II, 248; Tsun ku: 1.44; Tsun ku: 2-7
           (T'ai pao kuei); Eumo: A18 (Hsing Hou kuei).
        b. With socle
           Shang chou: II, 298 (T'ien wu kuei).
        c. Very long pendants used as legs
           Shang chou: II, 303; Shu kan: 18 (Shiobara Col-
           lection); Hsi ch'ing: 14.7.

        With the exception of the first two examples in a,
which could be Shang, the rest of the examples are of the Early
Chou period. But none of them, in their inscriptions, referred

to themselves as <u>kuei</u>

    Type IV - Bent Handles <u>Kuei</u>

       The handles are bent ears similar to those of the <u>yü</u>.
The examples are as follows:

          a. With small feet under the base

             <u>Shan chai</u>: 70-71 (<u>Shiao Ch'en Lai kuei</u>); <u>Sung chai</u> I:

             11; <u>Shan chai</u>: 73, 77; <u>P'an ku</u>: II, 36 (<u>Heng hsien</u>:34).

          b. Without feet and lower bulge like <u>a</u>

             <u>Tsun ku</u>: 1.49, 2.6; <u>Shang chou</u>: II, 286 (<u>Hsi ch'ing</u> I:

             6.34); <u>Trautmann</u>: 18.

          c. With socle

             <u>Hsi ch'ing</u>: 27.13.

             This type covered the whole Western Chou period.

    Type V

          1. Mouth: medium

          2. Handles: sometimes with spiral horns or flaring ears

             on the top and with filled hooked pendants.

          3. Body: the body and the lid form a flat globe with

             the long diameter horizontal.

          4. Support: small feet under the base

          5. Lid: always present with cup-shaped top

       This type, according to the inscriptions, began during
the Middle Western Chou period, was popular during Late Western
Chou and extended to Ch'un Ch'iu. The horizontal grooves are
the dominant motifs. The small feet, which appeared occasionally
during the Middle Western Chou, were common during the Late
Western Chou period. Sometimes the handles have loose-rings and
sometimes they are without-pendants like the Ch'un Ch'iu vessels.
There

Type VI

    1. Handles; animal shape, only the lower end attached
        to the body

    2. Socle; usually present

    3. Lid; usually present with corona top

    Examples are:

    Eumo; A48; Chen sung; 1.36 (Lü Hou kuei);

    Pao yün; 74 (Ch'en Hou Wu kuei)

According to the inscriptions, this type belongs to the
Ch'un Ch'iu period. There is one kuei in Shan chai (d); 7.49
without a socle which was made during the Early Western Chou
period. There is another kuei with a lid, but without a socle,
in Hsi ch'ing; 27.11 which is also dated Early Western Chou.
The handles are in the form of the trunk of an elephant. Both
could be listed as the exceptional examples of Type II.

There are three kuei which were made by the Ch'u State.
One is in Shih er; Hsia 4, dated 515-489; two are in Shih er;
Pao 7-8, found in Shou Hsien, dated Late Chan Kuo. The latter
pairs have lids, but are without handles. All of these vessels
have socles. In all of the specimen that we found, none of
them could be dated as Shang. Therefore, it might be true that
the socle was attached to the vessel at the very beginning of
Western Chou.

V. Hsü

    1. Mouth; oblong, wide

    2. Handles; semicircular without pendants (or bent ears)

    3. Bottom; slightly concave

    4. Base; rectangular, low, brimmed, quadruped, or
        oblong

     5. Lid: shallow with vertical right angle plates in
          two parallel rows on the top; or oblong cup-
          shaped top

Since _hsü_ were used only in Late Western Chou and disappeared afterwards they have only a few variety of types. The differences between them are so inconsistent that it renders division into types very difficult if not impossible. Here the exceptional parts are listed:

     1. Rectangular mouth: example, _K'ao ku_: 3.36

     2. With four legs: example, _Po ku_: 18.12

     3. With bent ears: example, Pillsbury 39.107.1-2;
        Roberts.

VI. _Fu_

1. Mouth: rectangular, wide

2. Teeth: present in the later period

3. Handles: paired semicircular without pendants
   (sometimes with loose-rings)

4. Bottom: flat, rectangular in shape

5. Base: rectangular, low, brimmed quadruped

6. Parts: the lid is identical with the body. If
   the lid is inverted it looks like the body

7. Lid: truncated pyramid, rectangular

The earliest _fu_ appeared during the Late Western Chou period, and were more popular during the Eastern Chou period. Although they persisted through such a long period, the shapes have little variation.

VII. Tou

1. Mouth: circular, wide

2. Handles: rings(sometimes animal-shaped)

3. Bottom: concave

4. Stem: solid (sometimes hollow)

5. Base: pedestal

6. Lid: usually present with trumpet-shaped top

San tai: 10.46.1-5 listed three tou with Shang inscriptions. The illustrations of these three are not available, and in the inscription the name tou is not mentioned. So far, the tou that I have seen mostly belong to the Eastern Chou period. Although some vessels, whose illustrations are also not available, can be dated from their inscriptions as Late Western Chou. Among the Eastern Chou tou there is only one type, except the following variations:

        Handles: a. animal-shaped; b. rings; c. without handles

        Lid: a. cup-shaped; top   b. three rings

The mouth of the tou is generally circular. There are, however, two specimen that have a square mouth and body. One is in the Ontario Museum (Lo-yang: no. 220), and one is in the Stockholm Museum (BMFEA: no. 6, plate 30 (2))

VIII. Tun

1. Mouth: circular, wide

2. Handles: rings or loose-rings

3. Bottom: hemispheric or concave

4. Supports: three small feet (sometimes none, or with base)

5. Parts: In Type I the lid is identical with the body

Type I - Spherical Tun

    1. Parts: identical to each other

    2. Support: three small rings or hooked rings

       Examples are:

       Shih er: Chü 12; Wu ying: 97; Shan chai: 88;

       Sumitomo I: 116; Ku kung: 16.12; Chan kuo: 45;

       Pao yün: 76.

Type II - Flat Tun

    1. Maximum diameter: horizontal

    2. Support: three small feet, base or without

    3. Upper part: smaller than the lower part with

       rings or shallow cup-shaped top

       Examples are:

       Chan kuo: 8(2) (found at Li-yü); Chan kuo: 9(1)

       (found at Li-yü); Eumo: A5; Shang chou: II, 388;

       Sung chai I: 4.

Pillsbury: 39.433 and Metropolitan: 13.100.7, with three
feet, belong to this type. These vessels can not be considered ting.
They must be considered tun because they do not have ears.

Type III - Ovaloid Tun

    1. Maximum diameter: vertical

    2. Support: three small feet

    3. Upper part: much smaller than the lower part

       and the lid and mouth are proportionally

       rather small. Three small rings on top.

Examples are:

Chin ts'un: 14; Shina kodo: 211.

This type can not be called ting because the mouth is small and it has no ears.   The feet are small and low.   Type I, from ~~its inscriptions~~, *from Late Chun Ch'iu t* can be dated ~~in~~ the Chan Kuo period.   In the inscriptions of Types I and II, the vessels were referred to as tun.

IX. Pi

1. Handle: long flat rod

2. Bowl: shallow

> Type I - Early pi, with spindle-shaped bowl
> > Examples: Yeh I: 1.33; Louvre: AA119
> > (all from An-yang); Chen sung: 2.41
> > (Late Western Chou)

> Type II - Late pi, with oval-shaped bowl
> > Examples: Sung chai II: 101 (from
> > Lo-yang); Chen sung: 2.41; Sung chai II:
> > 102 (from Hui-an of Hopei); Chen sung:
> > 2.42; Chan kuo: 26(3)(Musée Louvre, ex-
> > collection of Wannick); Chan kuo: 26(4)
> > (ex-collection of Rutherston, open work;
> > all from Li-yu).

Type I can be dated from Shang to Late Western Chou, and Type II belongs mostly to Eastern Chou.

X. Chia

1. Mouth: circular, wide

2. Pillars: two in number, with various types of

knob on top

3. Handle: single

4. Bottom: slightly concave or tripartite

5. Body: deep

6. Legs: three facet or hollow

7. Lid: flat when present

Type I - Round Chia

1. Mouth: circular, wide

2. Neck: constricted

3. Body: lower bulge

4. Bottom: slightly concave

5. Legs: three facet

6. Lid: flat with animal top if present

   Example of this type found at An-yang is:

   Yeh IIIb 1.37a (Loo 87041)

Type II - Goblet Chia

1. Mouth: circular, wide, *with spreading rim* trumpet-shaped

2. Body: deep

3. Bottom: slightly concave, almost flat

4. Legs: three-facet

   Examples of this type found at An-yang are:

   Yeh III: 1.35; Yen k'u: 1.24; An-yang Treasures:

   48, 49; Ontario NB 4206, 1515.

Type III - Rectangular Chia

1. Mouth: rectangular(nearly oblong), wide

2. Neck: constricted

3. Body: lower bulge

4. Bottom: oblong, slightly concave

5. Legs: four in number and three-facet in shape

6. Lid: flat with animal top if present

Examples of this type found at An-yang are:

Yeh I: 1.21; Yeh II: 1.19-21 (Nelson 34.66);

Yeh III: 1.37b.

Type IV - Tripartite Chia

1. Mouth: circular, wide, trumpet-shaped *with operating rim*

2. Neck: high

3. Body: deep

4. Bottom: tripartite

5. Legs: hollow

Examples of this type found at An-yang are:

Yeh III: 1.36; Sheng kao: 44; Ontario: NB3213, 3193.

Other examples of the Shang period are:

Shih erh Ch'u 11 (definitely Shang inscription);

Shapes: 43.1 (found at Ch'ang ch'ing of Shantung);

Shih er: Chü 28 (with others forming a set);

Shih er: Ch'i 12 (with others forming a set).

By studying the provenance and inscriptions, most of
the chia, with very few exceptions, belong to the Shang dynasty.
They may extend to Early Western Chou. The lid appeared only
in Types I and III. Rubens' chia of Type IV lacks the pillars
(cf. under chüeh in the classification).

XI. Ho

1. Mouth: circular, medium or small

2. Neck: constricted or clearly demarcated

3. Spout: tube, usually under the neck, except in Type I

4. Handles: single, except bridge for Type VII

5. Bottom: tripartite, tetrapartite, hemispheric or
   concave

6. Legs: cylindrical or hollow (small feet for
   Types VI, VII, VIII)

7. Lid: domed with various styled tops
   shapes of

Type I - Archaic Ho

1. Mouth: small, and on the side of the handle

2. Spout: opposite the mouth, on top of the vessel

3. Legs: hollow

4. Upper part of the body: above the handle it is
   hemispherical with the opening of the mouth and
   the spout on both sides

a. Cross section: square

Legs: four in number with solid ends

Bottom: tetrapartite

Examples of this type found at An-yang are:

An-yang Treasures: 44-46

b. Cross section: circular

Legs: three in number, hollow throughout

Bottom: tripartite

Example of this type found at An-yang is:

Sheng kao: 23

Other examples are:

Foreign Collections: 27; Shina kodo: 142;

Hsü k'ao ku: 4.22. *(Ro ku : 12.21)*

博 12.21
was called
chia

From the provenance, there is no doubt that the above
are of the Shang dynasty.

Type II - Round Bottom Ho

 1. Mouth: circular, medium

 2. Spout: under the neck

 3. Neck: constricted

 4. Body: deep

 5. Bottom: concave

 6. Legs: cylindrical, three in number

 Examples:

 Sumitomo I: 98, 99; Shina kodo: 109, 140.

Type III - Tripartite Ho

 1. Mouth: circular, medium

 2. Spout: under the neck

 3. Bottom: tripartite

 4. Legs: hollow, three in number

 a. Neck: constricted

  Belly: deep

  Example: Pao yün: 88, 89.

 b. Neck: clearly demarcated

  Belly: shallow or deep

  Examples:

  Tsun ku: 3.13; Sung chai II: 54, 55; Shu kan: 14;

  Shuang chien I: 1.29 (found at I Hsien of Hopei).

Type IV - Tetrapartite Ho

 1. Mouth: nearly square *or oblong*

 2. Neck: clearly demarcated

 3. Bottom: tetrapartite or nearly flat

 4. Belly: shallow and squat

    5. Legs: cylindrical, four in number

    a. With tetrapartite bottom

       Examples:

       Sumitomo I: 100; Shan chai: 108; Shina kodo: 141;

       Ku kung: 4.13.

    b. With nearly flat bottom

       Examples:

       Sumitomo I: 101; Ku kung: 35.14; 27.2; Ch'ih an: 17.

Types II-IV can be dated, from their inscription and
provenance, as Early Western Chou. Some of them extended to the
early part of Middle Western Chou. No ho of these three types
was found at An-yang. This naturally leads us to think that
these three types may be of the Chou period. Yet, there is
still a possibility that some of them might belong to the Late
Shang period.

    It seems to me that the tall ho (II and IIIa) might be
earlier than the others. Pao yün: 89; Loo 87131 of IIIa, and
Boston 12.1051 have a knob; and Sumitomo I: 88, 89 have a cup-
shaped top. Ku kung: 4.13; Sumitomo I: 100; Shu kan: 14 have
a circular ring top. Others have a ring top. It seems to me
that those with knobs are earlier. (cf. yu section below).
The shallow and squat belly ho appeared in the Early Western
Chou period. Therefore, Type II might be earlier than Type III.

    Type V - Low Ho

       1. Mouth: small

       2. Support: circular low brimmed base, or three very

          low small feet

       Examples:

Hsi ch'ing: 31.35 (Heng hsien: 93); Sumitomo I: 102.

From the inscriptions and the decoration, this type can be dated as Late Western Chou or Early Eastern Chou. It is referred to as ho in its inscriptions.

Type VI - Flat Ho

    1. Mouth: small

    2. Support: four small feet or truncated pyramidal base

    3. Body: flat, like flat hu

       Example: Po ku: 17.29

These do not bear any inscriptions, but from their shape and typology they are listed here as a special type of ho. They are of the Ch'un Ch'iu period.

Type VII - Bridge-handle Ho

    1. Mouth: small

    2. Handle: bridge-handle, usually stationary

    3. Feet: three in number

    4. Bottom: concave

       Examples:

       Po ku: 19.36, 40, 41, 42, 43, 44, 45, 47, 49;

       Cull: 17.

This type can be dated in the Chan Kuo period.

Type VIII - Han Ho

    Similar to Type VII except that the handle is projected horizontally from the middle part of the belly. It is hollow and has a receiver for a wooden rod to be attached thereon.

       Examples:

       T'ao chai II: 2.36; Shan chai (d): Jen ch'i 30 (dated 31 B.C.).

there is a vessel of

In T'ao chai II: 2.36 this type was referred to, in its
~~which~~
inscriptions, as ho. Therefore we are quite sure that this is
the latest type of ho. It helped us to prove that Type VII,
although it seldom has any inscriptions, should also be a ho.
The author of T'ao chai: 3.6 called a ho of Type VII a chiao
hu   and Jung Keng called this type chiao. However, Jung
Keng's conclusion was based solely on memory, he thought he re-
membered seeing one of the Type VII ho with an inscription
calling it a chiao (the inscription is recorded in Hsiao chiao:
13.61, but the illustration is not available). There is a ho
of Type VII in Po ku: 19.36 which has an inscription. The
character for ho is not clear, but the author transliterated it
as ho. In Kodoki: 27, a ho of this type has two characters
"made ho", this is also not very clear. But I think that Type VII
should be considered a ho. It might have been called a chiao
during the Han dynasty.

There are exceptions to Types VII and VIII. In Shina
kodo: 192 there is a ho similar to Type VII, except that it
has a small handle in the shape of an animal on one side of the
shoulder instead of a bridge-handle. In Tsun ku 3.14 (also
Loohow: 20) there is a ho, that has a shape like a hu, a base
and a single animal-shaped handle, which has an inscription
that calls it a ho. Both belong to the Chan Kuo or Western Han
periods.

~~From the decoration, Type VII can be dated in the Ch'un
Ch'iu period. It covered the Eastern Chou period and extended
to the Han.~~ Type VIII is exclusively of the Han period.

The use of the ho covered a very long period from the
Shang to the Han dynasty. Its shape changed greatly during

this time. During the early period, the tripartite and the tetrapartite bottom were the dominating characteristics. After that,
the bottom became concave. The hollow or cylindrical legs were
quite long during the early period, then they became short and
sometimes were substituted by a base. The single handle was
substituted by a bridge-handle during the Chan Kuo period. The
medium mouth became small and the spout became short on the later
types. The body was deep and tall in the early types and became
squat in the later types.

XII. Chüeh

1. Mouth: wide, extends outward on both sides to form
      spout and tail
2. Pillars: two in number, with top of various shapes
3. Spout: channel
4. Tail: on the opposite side of the spout
5. Handle: single
6. Bottom: hemispheric
7. Body: deep
8. Legs: three-facet, always three in number
9. Lid: always none

There is only one type of chüeh, but it can be subdivided into four subtypes according to the treatment of the
decoration:

   a. Flanges and decoration on belly and under rim,
       but no decoration on the bottom
   b. Without flanges and decoration only on the belly
   c. Without flanges and decoration on the narrow
       frieze

d. Exceptional pieces and pewter ones

Most of the chüeh were of the Shang and Early Western [some were of]
Chou periods, and there was no great change of style during this
time. They disappeared after the latter period. [Early Chou] Some of the
exceptional pieces are:

1. Square body

   Examples: Shina kodo: 63 (Ford Collection);
   T'ao chai II: 2.11.

2. Flat bottom

   Example: Sumitomo I: 85.

3. Single pillar

   Examples: Pao yün: 105; Tsun ku: 3.7; Ontario:
   NB 1191, 3236 (found at An-yang).

4. Without handle

   Examples: Ontario: NB 2720, 2721 (found at Lo-yang)
   Yen k'u: 66 (found at Lo-yang).

5. With lid

   Example: Shang chou II: 430

6. Without pillars but with lid

   Examples: Tsun ku: 3.1; Kogei: 18; Shang chou II: 442
   (lid lost).

I am not quite sure of the authenticity of the two examples
of the square chüeh. I was told that a square chüeh was excavated
from An-yang by the Academia Sinica. Both 5 and 6 have lids.
Number 5 is a chüeh because all of its characteristics are the
same as those of a chüeh, but it has the addition of a lid. Number 6 is similar to a chüeh, except that occasionally it does
not have pillars. This is analogous to the case of a chia. There
is no pillar on the pottery chüeh, therefore we believe that it
should be classified as a chüeh.

The many chüeh, said to have been found at An-yang, are listed
below under the headings a, b, c, d according to their sub-
types:

a. Yeh I: 1.26; Yeh II: 1.28; Yeh III: 1.46, 47, 48, 49,
   50; Sheng kao: 41; Yen k'u: 1.30, 31, 36, 37, 38;
   An-yang Treasures: 50(1); Ontario: NB 4031, 4032,
   2809, 3196, 3224, 3225, 1507.

b. Yeh I: 1.27; Yeh II: 1.26, 27, 30, 32; Yeh III: 1.45;
   Yen k'u: 1.26, 27, 28, 32; Sung chai II: 82; Ontario:
   NB 4068.

c. Yeh II: 1.25, 29, 31; Yen k'u: 1.40, 42, 44, 45, 46,
   47, 48; An-yang Treasures: 50(2); Sung chai II: 92;
   Ontario: NB 3216; An-yang pao kao: pt. III, pl. 9.

d. One pillar, Ontario: NB 1191, 3236.

XIII. Chiao

1. Mouth: wide, extends outward on both sides to
   form two tails

2. Tails: two on both sides lined up with the handle

3. Handle: single

4. Bottom: hemispheric

5. Body: deep

6. Legs: three-facet, always three in number

7. Lid: warped, top at the center

There is only one type which can be dated as Shang. It
probably extended to Early Western Chou and disappeared thence.
There are some exceptional pieces:

1. With bent pillars and bulged body

   Example: Hakkaku: 17

2. Flat bottom

Example: Rubens (U.S.   ).

Examples of this type found at An-yang are:

Yeh II: 1.33 (Trautmann: 16)

XIV. Tsun

1. Mouth: circular (sometimes square), trumpet-shaped

2. Spreading rim: present

3. Bottom: concave or flat

4. Body: deep

5. Base: circular (or square), usually high, except
   for Type IV. Truncated cone-shaped or truncated pyramid-shaped

6. Sections: the whole vessel is usually divided
   into three sections (except Types II, V) with
   demarcations:
   Upper part: long neck with trumpet mouth
   Middle part: about belly, the bottom is located at
   the demarcation line between the belly and
   the base
   Lower part: the base

7. Lid: always none

Type I

1. Sections: clearly divided into three

2. Shoulder: present, angular, with three or four
   animal-heads on it

3. Flanges: usually present and entirely decorated

4. Base: high, usually truncated cone-shaped without
   brim
a. Circular cross section under the neck
   Examples of this type found at An-yang are:
   Yeh II: 1.8, 10a, 10b; An-yang Treasures: 37, 38;
   Lochow: 9, 10; Yeh III: 1.19 (plain without flanges);
   Academia Sinica (not published).
b. Square cross section under the neck
   Examples are:
   Sumitomo I: 28; Ku kung: 2.15.

Type II

The only example of this type is in our catalogue
(U.S.   ). It has no demarcation line between the upper
part and the belly. Several pottery tsun of this shape, said
to have been found at An-yang, are in the Ontario Museum and
in the Minneapolis Institute of Arts. Types I and II can be
dated as Shang exclusively. Ib, sometimes with a brimmed base,
seems to me to be a little bit later.

I have seen two photographs (in Gumps and Hellstrom's
Collection) with a similar shape, but they are small and may be
classified under chih.

Type III

This type has three demarcated sections but no shoulder.
Usually, the base has a brim.

      a. Circular cross section under the neck, with flanges
         and decoration on three sections
      b. Square cross section under the neck, with flanges
         and decoration on three sections

Examples are:

Hakkaku: 6; Shan chai: 132; Ku kung: 3.14;
Hsi ch'ing: 8.33.

c. Circular cross section with decoration on the
   middle (sometimes also lower) section, and
   without flanges
   Example of this type found at An-yang is:
   Yeh II: 1.9

In general, this type is later than Types I and II and
earlier than Type VI. It can be dated in the Shang and Early
Chou periods.

Type IV

   This type has a handle (or handles) and a slight de-
   marcation line between the upper and middle sections.
   a. With two semicircular handles
   Example of this type found at An-yang is:
   Yeh III: 1.20.
   b. With single semicircular handle
   Examples are:
   Shih er: Hsüeh 11; Shan chai: 133; London: 187.

From the provenance and inscriptions, IVa can be dated
as Shang and IVb as Shang and Early Chou.

Type V

   1. Demarcation: indistinct between the upper section
      and the middle section if not utterly absent
   2. Body: distinct   lower bulge
   3. Base: low, circular, brimmed
      a. with circular face
      b. with square

a. With single handle

Examples are:

Shih er; Hsüeh 11; Shan chai: 133.

b. Without handle

It seems to me that Va is slightly earlier than Vb. The latter existed in Early Western Chou as shown on their inscriptions. By studying the decorations, one is able to see that it existed until Middle Western Chou, and after that period tsun were rarely discovered.

The tsun and the yu were used during the same periods and for the same length of time. Tsun types did not change as much as the yu types during the period of existance. The high truncated cone-shaped base was lowered and brimmed during the Late Shang dynasty. The shoulder disappeared after that time. Consequently, in Type III the middle part does not bulge as much as those with the shoulder. The middle section was slightly middle-bulged. And during the Early Western Chou when Type Vb was dominant, the base was lowered and the belly or the middle section was strikingly bulged near the base. Thus the demarcation line between the upper and the middle section disappeared was dissolved and the height of the body was several times more than that of the base.

XV. Ku

Similar to the tsun, except in the following ways:

1. The middle part is slender within the degree of a
   grasp

2. The base, always circular, is more spreading than
   that of the tsun

3. The outline from the mouth to the base forms an
hyperbolic arc. The middle part does not bulge
like the tsun's

4. The proportion of the middle part to the upper
part is greater than the same proportions of
the tsun

There is only one type which can be dated as Shang, and
it extended to Early Western Chou and disappeared thereafter.
According to the decoration it can be divided into two subtypes:

a. Flanged and with decoration all over

b. Without flanges, and sometimes with moderate
decoration

The flanges, if present, are mostly limited to the
middle and lower parts of the vessel, only a few have flanges
which extend to the upper part.

There is one exceptional piece, in Wu ying: 133, with
a square-shaped mouth and cross section.

The many ku, said to have been found at An-yang, are
listed below under a and b according to their subtypes:

a. Yeh I: 1.22-24; Yeh II: 1.21, 22; Yeh III: 1.40,
43, 44; Yen k'u: 1.49; Sung chai II: 61; Royal
Tombs: fig. 9 (Academia Sinica); Ontario NB 4033,
3194, 3232, 3211, 3210, 3231, 4066, 4063, 2808.

b. K'ao ku: 5.12; Yeh II: 1.23; Yeh III: 1.38, 39, 41,
42; Yen k'u: 1.19, 50, 51, 54-56; An-yang pao kao:
Pt. III, pl. 11; Ontario: NB 4034, 3215, 4065,
2814, 4064.

XVI. Chih

1. Mouth: wide with limited spreading rim

2. Body: usually deep

3. Size: smaller than tsun

4. Lid: often present, with inserted lip

Type I - With Elliptical Mouth

    Examples of this type found at An-yang are:

    Yeh I: 1.25; Yeh II: 1.24; Yeh III: 2.1;

    Trautmann: 14, 13 (Tsun ku: 2.46); Ontario:

    NB 4028 (all have lids); Yeh II: 1.15 (Knapp

    Collection); Yen k'u: 1.59, 60; An-yang

    Treasures: 50.1 *Sung chai: II: 77, 78*

    Other examples are:

    Hakkaku: 19; Shang chou: II, 570; Shih er:

    Hsüeh 13, Ch'u 6; (all have lids). Wu ying: 139;

    Sung chai I: 15; Sung chai II: 80; Shan chai: 141;

    Ku kung: 36.14.

Type II - With Circular Mouth

    Examples of this type found at An-yang are:

    Yeh k'u: 1.58; Sung chai II: 71

    Other examples are:

    Shan chai: 140 (with lid), 142 (with small

    single handle).

Type III - With Circular Mouth and Tall Slender Body

    Examples are:

    Shapes: 108; London: 185.

rectangula

Type IV - With Square or Oblong Mouth

Example: <u>An-yang</u> <u>Treasures</u>: 50.2

There are not very many Type IV specimen. All of these types appeared during the Shang period. Type I, without a lid, extended to Western Chou. We found <u>chih</u> of Type III of the Ch'un Ch'iu period (cf. Kao-an Finds).

There is a <u>chih</u> in <u>Yeh</u> III: 2.2 which is an exceptional piece that is tall and without a neck.

XVII. <u>Yu</u>

1. Mouth: usually elliptical, medium wide for Type VIII, small and circular for Type VI, sometimes rectangular for Type V.

2. Beak: present on Types II, IV, X

3. Handle: swing handle

4. Base: usually elliptical, low, brimmed, feet for Type II.

5. Lid: domed with top

Type I - Knobed <u>Yu</u>

1. Mouth: elliptical, medium

2. Collar: concave, plain

3. Handle: left-right, decoration facing front-rear

4. Body: middle bulge

5. Lid: domed with spherical shape *knob*

6. Decoration: usually a frieze

a. Rope type handle

   Examples of this type found at An-yang are:

Yeh I: 1.19, 20; Yen k'u: 1.21, 22, 23;

Ontario: NB 3222, 3197.

Other examples are:

K'ao ku: 2.33; Po ku: 9.33, 10.3, 9, 16, 21,

11-14, 29, 31; Ku kung: 1.13, 4.9, 33.10;

Heng hsien: 56; Shan chai: 110, 111, 112;

Shuang chien II: 1.27; Tsun ku: 2.11, 12;

Shih er: Tsun 14; New Studies: pl. 44, no. 527;

Hsi ch'ing shih yi: 12.

b. Flat handle without animal-heads

Examples found at An-yang are:

Yeh III: 1.32; Sheng kao: 24.

Another example is:

Shan chai: 113, 114.

c. Flat handle with animal-heads

Examples are:

Eumo: A24; Shuang chien II: 1.30; Yu and Kuang:

30, 34; Sumitomo I: 61; T'ao chai I: 236;

Ku kung: 6.3; Hakkaku: 12 (definitely Shang

inscription).

I have come to the conclusion that Types a-c are Shang
because (1) Ia is, on the whole, found at An-yang and should be
dated Shang; (2) the rope type handle of Ia, which disappeared
entirely after the end of Shang, is the earliest type; whereas
Ic extended to Early Chou as shown in the inscription in
Fogg: 43.52.114; (3) the spherical knob was adopted from the
white pottery which is earlier than the Shang bronzes and it
was substituted by cup-shaped tops later; (4) the inscriptions

are mostly of the Shang dynasty; and (5) the body is seldom squat, while the later vessels tend to have a squat belly.

Thus Type I has three types of handles which are connected to each side with the loop. The rope type handle never has animal heads (except Yeh III: 1.31) and is the earliest, the flat type is next and the flat type with animal heads is last. So a is exclusively Shang, c is Shang and extended to Early Chou, and b is between a and c, i.e. between Shang and Early Chou.

This type has two transitional pieces:

Chen sung: 1.44   and   Shapes: 39.2

These two examples are similar to Ia except that they are tall and have cup-shaped tops. From the inscription on the first one, we know that it belonged to the same clan as that of a yu,illustrated in Kogei: 10, which was found at An-yang. Both yu were of the Shang period. The second piece was found, with other bronzes, in Ch'ang Ching Hsien of Shantung, and is probably Late Shang.

Type II - Owl Yu

   1. Mouth: elliptical, medium

   2. Beaks: on left-right sides of the lid

   3. Collar: none

   4. Handle: front-rear, attached to loops (or lugs),
         decoration facing left-right.

   5. Belly: lower bulge

   6. Form: in the form of an Owl with four small feet

   7. Lid: domed with knob of mushroom, spherical or
         gable-roof shaped.

   8. Decoration: usually all over the vessel

Examples of this type found at An-yang are:

Yeh II: 1.14, 18; Yeh III: 1.23, 34

Other examples are:

Sumitomo I: 69, 70, 71; Shapes: 26.7, 8;

Eumo: A22, 23: Po ku: 11.35, 36, 38.

I have come to the conclusion that this type is Shang and is contemporaneous with Type I because (1) the shape of the knob is in typical Shang style; (2) it also has a rope type handle, although other types of handles also existed; (3) the beaks which turn downward are evidently earlier than the beaks of the later ones which were turned upward and were stylized; (4) most of them were found at An-yang; and (5) the inscriptions are mostly of the Shang period.

The whole vessel is in the form of a double owl, divided by a cross-handle in the front and the rear. Therefore facing left or right there are two owls, each with one beak and two feet. The beak under the eyes of the bird was originally a beak of a bird in realistic form which pointed downward. Later it changed and became an upright beak as shown on the later types (Type X for example). The handle is so arranged that it does not interfere with the beaks. Therefore if we change the position with the ordinary position which made the handles left and right, then one of the owl's is facing toward the observer in a realistic owl form.

In this type those with lugs often had their handles missing. Originally, in all likelihood, no cast bronze handles were made and handles made of plaited bamboo or braided cord were used instead. The rope type handle in bronze is an imitation of such. The same phenomenon was found in the early hu with lugs, but without handles. It is quite a common phenomenon

in early pottery to find vessels with handles or ears on both
sides, but they never had any swing handles. The flanges are
not popularly used in this style.

Type III - Flanged Yu

   Similar to Type I except in the following ways:

   1. Flanges: solid or hooked, always present

   2. Handles: left-right, usually flat handle with
         animal heads, decoration facing front-rear.

   3. Decoration: usually all over the vessel
         Examples of this type found at An-yang are:
         Yeh I: 1.18; Yeh II: 1.17a.
         Other examples are:
         Eumo: A26; Pao yün: 98; Ku kung: 32.11;
         Sumitomo I: 59; Shina kodo: 75; Heng hsien: 57;
         Pe ku: 10.7, 23, 28; New Studies: pl. 15, no.487,
         pl. 16, no. 509.

From the inscriptions, they were a little bit later
than Type I and extended to Early Western Chou. Those with
hooked flanges are a little later than those with solid flanges, *namely,*
Early Chou.

Type IV - Beaked Yu

   Similar to Types I and III except in the following ways:

   1. Beaks: always present, turned upward, stylized

   2. Collar: almost straight

   3. Handle: front-rear, flat with animal heads con-
         nected on pegs, decoration facing left-right.

   4. Flanges: solid

   5. Decoration: usually all over the vessel

Examples of this type found at An-yang are:

An-yang Treasures: 32, 33.

Other examples are:

London: no. 246; Cull: 3; Sumitomo I: 58;

Shina kodo: 74; Yu and Kang: 10-12; Shuang

chien II: 1.29; T'ao chai I: 2.37; Po ku: 9.10,

20, 23; 10.29; 11.25.

It is obvious that this type is later than Type II,
because the beaks were adopted from Type II and because the
beaks have been stylized and the handles have animal-heads.
The handle of this type was also adopted from Type II, that is
front-rear. But this type belongs to the earlier type because
of the knob. Since the spherical knobs survived in the Early
Western Chou period, I am now inclined to say that this type
first appeared in the Late Shang period, and survived in Early
Western Chou. For example, the Worcester yu (U.S.   ) has
the same inscriptions as other vessels found at An-yang. The
Metropolitan yu (U.S.   ) were found in Pao-chi of Chou's
territory and their decoration is similar, but older, to the tsun's,
shown in Shang chou: II, 515, which has an inscription refer-
ring to the attack of the Eastern barbarians during the period
of Ch'eng Wang.

There is a transitional piece illustrated in Meng yi II:
26 which has no demarcation line between the domed part and
the collar of the lid. This is similar to Type Xb.

Type V - Tall Yu with Spherical Knob

    1. Mouth: rectangular or elliptical, medium

    2. Collar: almost straight

3. Handles: left-right, flat with animal-head, attached
      on pegs or loops, decoration facing front and
      rear.

4. Belly: rectangular or elliptical

5. Body: tall

6. Lid: like Type III

7. Flanges: solid, usually present

8. Decoration: usually all over the vessel

   Examples of this type found at An-yang are:

   Yeh II: 1.17b; Yeh III: 1.33a

   Other examples are:

   Ku kung: 7.4; Sumitomo I: 72; Sumitomo II: 182;

   Shapes: 17.3.

According to the provenance and the inscriptions they
are probably Shang. Sumitomo I: 72 has the same inscription as
the ting in Yeh III: 1.9 (now in Falk's Collection) which is
said to have been found at An-yang. Judging from the flanges,
the lid and the handles, this type was probably contemporary
with Type III but within the Shang period.

Type VI - Hu-shaped Yu

   1. Mouth: circular, small

   2. Neck: long slender hyperbolic curvature

   3. Collar: none

   4. Handle: left-right, long, flat, following the
         curvature of the neck, decoration usually
         facing front-rear.

   5. Links: sometimes present

   6. Body: lower bulge

   7. Lid: domed with knob on bird top (sometimes
         cup-shaped)

8. Decoration: usually on friezes

a. As above

Examples of this type found at An-yang are:

Illustrated London News (April 4, 1936), fig. 6;

Yeh III: 1.33b; An-yang Treasures: 34, 35.

Another example is:

Cull: 4.

b. Similar to a except that the body is low and the

neck is short, sometimes with cup-shaped top.

Examples are:

Sumitomo I: 60; Shina kodo: 76 (Yu and Kuang: 39);

New Studies: pl. 47, no. 621.

VIa were mostly found at An-yang. They are undoubtly
of the Shang period. Sometimes they have a rectangular belly
as in Pillsbury: 41.1328 and in An-yang Treasures: 34.

This type is called the hu-shaped yu because if the
handle is removed there is no distinct difference between it and
the earlier hu. The only difference between this type of yu
and the hu of similar shape lies in the fact that the yu has a
permanent bronze handle.

Type VII - Tall Yu with Cup-shaped Top

1. Mouth: elliptical, nearly circular, medium

2. Collar: none

3. Handles: left-right, flat attached to loops

4. Body: lower bulge

5. Lid: domed with cup-shaped top

Examples of this type found at An-yang are:

K'ao ku: 4.5; Ontario: NB 2811.

a. Flat handle without animal-heads

Examples are:

Po ku:10.10, 21, 22; Hsü k'ao ku: 5.10; Ku kung:
3.18; Ch'eng ch'iu: 49; Ch'iu ku: 2; Shih er:
Ch'i 11.

b. Flat handle with animal-heads

Examples are:

Tsun ku: 2.14; Trautmann: 12; Shina kodo: 82, 83;
Heng hsien: 59; Shan chai: 121; ch'eng ch'iu: 32,
33; Shuang chien II: 1.19; London: no. 196;
Chou chin: 5.105; New Studies: pl. 56, no. 596,
pl. 17, no. 591, pl. 45, no. 552; K'ao ku: 4.25.

I have already stated before that the flat handle
without animal heads is earlier than the ones with animal-heads.
Therefore VIIa should be earlier than VIIb, probably Shang.
Ku kung: 3.18 has a spout, and Ch'iu ku: 2 has both a spout
and a single handle. It can not be considered as a ho, because
the ho is a heating vessel for wine requiring legs. The
Brundage yu (U.S.   ) is of this type but the body is
shorter and stouter. The provenance of Shih er: ch'i 11 is unknown, but it was unearthed with a set of vessels illustrated in
the same reference 6-16, all with the same inscription and without decoration. Among them was a kuei without a pendant underneath the handle which I consider Shang, so this piece is most
probably of the Shang period.

VIIb is contemporary with VIIa but extended to Early
Western Chou. Among these vessels Tsun ku: 2.14 and Trautmann:
12 were a pair found at Chün Hsien. From their inscriptions,
they were made during Ch'eng Wang's period. In Shina kodo: 84

(U.S.   ) and in <u>Shih</u> er; Tsun 15 (U.S.   ) there is a pair
of <u>yu</u>, found at Ma-po of Loyang with other bronzes, of the Early
Western Chou period.   Therefore, VIIb might have existed from
the Late Shang dynasty and survived in the Early Western Chou
period.

A lid that is illustrated both in <u>Shang chou</u>: II, 912
and in <u>Chen</u> sung: 2.38 looks very much like the lid on this type
of <u>yu</u>. On that lid the inscription reads, "Chung made this
travelling <u>kuan</u>   ." It shows that this lid belongs to a vessel called <u>kuan</u> which may be of this type of <u>yu</u> or the tube-
shaped <u>yu</u>. If this is true <u>yu</u> might be called <u>kuan</u>, but unfortunately the body of this lid was lost and there is no other
evidence or example to support such a hypothesis.

Some vessels of Type VIIb have a cross hoop decoration
on the front and rear sides of the body which might be an imitation of the remainder of a net made of cords which was used to
hold the vessel.

The two examples of this type found at An-yang are
transitional specimen. The one in <u>K'ao ku</u> has a knob like Type I
and the one in the Ontario Museum is not as tall and has a
round belly with middle bulge.

Type VIII - Tube-shaped <u>Yu</u>
    1. Mouth: elliptical, wide
    2. Handles: left-right, flat with animal-heads
    3. Body: tall, cylindrical
    4. Lid: domed with cup-shaped top, without collar
       Examples are:
       <u>T'ao chai</u> I: 2.35; <u>Ch'eng ch'iu</u>: 34; <u>Sumitomo</u> I: 74;

New Studies: pl. 18, no. 621 (London: no. 203,
Oeder Collection).

The provenance is unknown to us. The vertical ribs
and the bird design are similar to some of the bronze yu of
Type IV, which have been dated from Late Shang to Early Western
Chou. ~~Judging from the inscription, they might be exclusively~~
~~Shang.~~

Type IX

This type is similar to Type Ic except for the cup-
shaped top, and it is also similar to Xa except that it has
no beaks. Therefore this is really a transitional type   linking
Ic and Xa.

Examples are:

Sumitomo I: 62; Shan chai: 119, 122 (found at Lo-yang);
Ku kung: 8.16; P'an ku: 2.19 (Heng hsien: 58); Pao yün:
97; Shapes: 39.4 below; Yu and Kung: 17a; Hui mi: 1.25.

Judging from the provenance and inscription, most of them
might be dated as Early Chou but some of them might be of the
Late Shang period. There is one specimen in our catalogue
(Loo 86428, U. S.   ) which has a domed lid without a demarcation line as in Xb.

Type X - Chou-type Yu

1. Mouth: elliptical (sometimes oblong), medium
2. Beaks: always present and turned upward, stylized,
    shorter than before.
3. Collar: usually concave

4. Handles; left-right, flat with animal-heads,

   parallel to the position of the beaks,

   decoration facing front-rear.

5. Body: lower bulge

a. There is a distinct demarcation line between

   the domed part of the lid and the collar which

   is usually undecorated.   The mouth is sometimes

   oblong.

   Examples are:

   Shuang chienI: 1.32; Hakkaku: 13; Shina kodo:

   78, 79; Hui mi: 1.27; Chou chin: 5.96; Tsun ku:

   2.13; Shang kao: 28; Sumitomo I: 63, 64, 65;

   Chün hsien: 15; Heng hsien: 66, 67; Chen sung:

   1.45; T'ao chai I: 2.33, 38, 39; Ku kung: 9.3;

   Wu ying: 130; Heng hsien: 68 and Ku kung: 24.12.

   Po ku: 10.19, 24, 33, 11.22.

b. There is no demarcation line between the domed

   part of the lid and the lower part of the lid,

   but the beaks are in the same position as those

   in a.

   Examples are:

   Shina kodo: 80; Sumitomo I: 66, 67; Eumo: A27;

   Chou chin: 110-111; Hsi ch'ing: 15.20; Po ku:

   11.3 (with rope type handles and animal-heads).

There are several transitional yu of Type Xa showing

that the new type was formed at the very beginning of Early Western

Chou, or it may have come down from the close of the Shang dynasty.

            Chicago: 27.602

            Shan chai: 118

            Chou chin: 5.85

The first example still has a spherical knob which is the characteristic of Type I. Likewise, the second example still has a handle without animal-heads, and the third example has flanges, straight collar and ornate decoration all over the vessel. The last two examples can be dated, by their inscription, as Early Chou.

By studying the inscriptions and provenance, Xa could be dated from the beginning of Early Western Chou to the first half of Middle Western Chou. In this group, the vessels with an oblong mouth are generally later than those with an elliptical mouth.

There are also several transitional yu of Xb which show that this type may have come down from the close of the Shang dynasty:

> Fogg: 43.52.95
>
> <u>Shapes</u>: 39.3 below
>
> <u>Shapes</u>: 45.5 and 6

The first two examples have flanges as the transitional piece under Xa. The third (both vessels) has a mushroom knob and flat handle without animal-heads. These two vessels are made of tin or pewter, and were found with other types of vessels (<u>Shapes</u>: 45.1-7). They are probably of the Late Shang or Early Chou periods.

By studying the inscriptions and provenance, Xb could be dated from the very beginning of Early Western Chou to the late part of Early Middle Western Chou. Some of the vessels are later than Xa. That means that this type survived longer than Xa. After that no yu have ever been found.

Type XI - Animal-form Yu

>   Sumitomo I: 58 (London: no. 238)
>
>   London: no. 243 (Musee Cernuschi)
>
>   An-yang Treasures: 36
>
>   Yeh III: 1.30 (Freer:42.1, U. S.   ).

The first two examples are nearly identical and both were exhibited in London's exhibition in 1935-36. The vessels show a beast swallowing the head of a human being . They are of the Shang period. The third piece is in the shape of a bird which was probably found with a set of vessels at Shou-chang as discussed under the Shou-chang finds. Its date is Early Western Chou, not Shang. The fourth piece was found at An-yang and it is no doubt of the Shang period. The lid has a human like face with two horns. The ears are right above the lugs. The handle is missing (which originally was probably not made of bronze), but if it is present it goes through the lugs and ears. It also has a spout, but it can not be considered as a ho for the same reasons that I stated before.

The chronological sequence of Types I-X may be listed as follows:

	Low yu	Owl yu	Tall yu
Shang (earlier part)	Ia, Ib	II	VI
Shang (later part)	I, III, IV, IX	II	V, VI, VII, VIII
Early Western Chou	Ic, III, IV, IX, X		VIIb
Middle Western Chou	Xb		

Among the types, Ia, Ib, II, V. VI, VIIa and VIII are
of the Shang period; Ic, III, IV, VIIb and IX are of the Late
Shang and Early Chou periods; only Xb extended to Middle Western
Chou.

Among the low yu both III and IV have the same shape as
I, except that IV adopted the beaks from II and both have flanges
IX and X retained the old shape of I, except that IX'sknob became cup-shaped and X adopted the beaks and its knobs also became cup-shaped. The handles of IX and X have almost crystallized in the type that is flat with animal-heads. X adopted the
beaks from II and IV and stylized them. Therefore X is a combination of the previous types, i. e., it has the shape of
Type I, the beaks of Types II and IV, and the cup-shaped tops
of Types VII and VIII. During the Shang many types of yu
existed about the same time, but by the time of Early Western
Chou they had at last crystallized into one type.

Thus from the above discussion one may see how the beaks
influenced the position of the handles. During Late Shang
when some yu adopted the beaks from II the position of the handle was changed from left-right to front-rear. And during Early
Western Chou, the handle and decoration returned to the old
style, i. e., the handle became left-right and the decoration
faced front-rear.

	Handles	Beaks	Decoration
Types I, III, V, VI, VII	left-right	none	front-rear
Types II, IV	front-rear	left-right	left-right
Types IX, X	left-right	left-right (if present)	front-rear

The above table shows that the shifting of the decoration follows the shifting of the handle. There are a few exceptions such as Boston 34.64,[3] where a yu of Type III has the usual position of the handle and the decoration of the body, but the decoration of the lid faces left and right, normal to that of the body.

The three types of handles, namely, rope type, flat type, and flat type with animal-heads have been fully discussed above.

The tall yu disappeared after Early Western Chou, while the low yu, in the later period, had a squat body, i. e., changing from middle bulge to lower bulge of the body.

During the Shang period both knobs and cup-shaped tops were used, but with few exceptions the cup-shaped tops usually appeared on tall yu. Cup-shaped tops dominated all yu in the Chou period.

It seems to me that the domed lid is earlier than the lid with a collar. Except for Type V, all tall yu and owl yu have domed lids.

The flanges were first a raised edge on the surface of the body, then came the solid ones and the hooked ones were the latest. After Early Western Chou the flanges disappeared.

There is only one speciman (Metropolitan: 24.72.3) of Type IV which has a detachable socle under the vessel.

The three styles of decoration, namely, ornate, moderate and simple were used at the same time in every period, but in Late Shang the ornate predominated, while in Early Western Chou the moderate was dominant and was followed by a resurgence of the ornate.

XVIII. Fang-i

1. Mouth: rectangular, wide

2. Flanges: usually present (except for Type Ia)

3. Base: rectangular, high, quadruped (except for
   Type III)

4. Body: deep

5. Lid: gable-roof shaped with gable-roof knob on
   top

Type I

1. The outline of the four edges came down verti-
   cally from the rim to the end of the base.

2. Body: comparatively higher than other types

3. Base: quadruped

a. There is a slight or no demarcation line between
   the belly and the base. It usually has no
   flanges, but when they are present they do
   not project.
   Examples of this type found at An-yang are:
   Yeh II: 1.12 (Trautmann: 8); Yen k'u: 20;
   Cull: 10 (Foreign Collections: 25).
   Other examples are:
   Po ku: 27.16, 17; Foreign Collections: 24; New
   Studies: pl. 56, no. 1277.

b. There is a slight demarcation line between the
   belly and the base. It usually has eight
   flanges.
   Examples of this type found at An-yang are:
   Yeh II: 1.11; Yeh III: 1.21, 22.
   Other examples are:
   Tsun ku: 1.43; London: no. 202; Hakkaku: 20;
   Shapes: 20.6.

Type II

    1. Clear demarcation; the flanges are discontinuous
       between the belly and the base.

    2. Body: lower than I

    3. Flanges: eight in number

       Examples of this type found at An-yang are:

       Yeh I: 1.15; Illustrated London News (April 4,
          1936); fig. 11 (Academia Sinica).

       Other examples are:

       Ku kung: 31.9; Eumo: A19; New Studies: pl. 27,
       no. 1268.

Type III

    Similar to Type II except in the following ways:

    1. Body: lower and bulged

    2. Base: truncated usually brimmed

       Examples are:

       Sumitomo I: 27; Shang chou: II, 604; Ch'ang an:
       1.14; Hsi ch'ing I: 6.25; Hsi ch'ing: 13.10.

From the provenance and inscriptions, I have no doubt
about placing Types I and II in the Shang dynasty. Ia is comparatively early in the Shang period. The chronological order
of these three types are: Ia, Ib, II, and III, each succeeding
the previous type. Type Ia in Cull: 10 has the same inscription
as Type II in Yeh I: 1.15, but the decoration is different.
Type III have long inscriptions related to Early and Middle Chou
history. Thus we may date them as Early Western Chou and Middle
Western Chou. Moore's Collection (U. S.   ) shows an ancient
decoration and script, therefore Type III might have come down

from the Late Shang period.

There are several vessels that are similar to the Type
III fang-i, but they are lower and have two handles like the kuei.

Shina kodo: 121

Ku kung: 14.13

Ning shou: 6.11

These three pieces have no lids, we do not know whether
they were made without lids or whether they are just missing. If
we should call them square kuei the shape is evidently taken
from fang-i since all have flanges, but flanges never appeared
on kuei except on the Type I kuei.

The fang-i in Fogg Museum (U. S.   ) has projecting
beams on the lid and on the body which are used to allow the
lid to stand up when removed, and the projecting beams on both
sides of the body serve as handles. The last two examples under
Type III also have two projected appendages which are vertical
and serve as handles. The latter two are much later, probably
they belonged to the Middle Western Chou period.

There are vessels (Po ku: 27.16-17; Trautmann: 8) in
Type Ia with four flanges that do not project. It seems to me
that they are later than those without flanges. In Ib all have
eight flanges except Yeh III: 1.21, which has four instead of
eight. Therefore those with eight flanges may be later than
those with four. The brimmed base became dominant in Type III,
and it is my belief that though it first appeared in the Late
Shang period it became popular in Early Western Chou. This is
also true for the kuei, tsun, hu and other classes. When the
lid is gabled-roof the knob is also always gabled-roof. Only
a few exceptions were found as on Ku kung: 31.9 which has a
spherical knob. In most cases when the lid is placed on the body

the decoration (mostly t'ao-t'ieh) of the lid is inverted. This
also happened on the lei. It seems to me that in the performance of the ceremony the lid was removed and held in the inverted
position, hence the fang-i of Moore's and Fogg's Collections are
two of the exceptions which do not invert the decoration of the
lid when the lid is placed on the body. It is obvious that the
body was at first high and rather straight, and then became low
and demarcation appeared between the belly and the base, and
finally the belly became bulged.

XIX. Kuang

1. Mouth: wide, one side extends outward to form a
    spout

2. Spout: channel

3. Handle: single

4. Belly: oblong or elliptical

5. Bottom: concave or flat

6. Base: elliptical or rectangular, high, sometimes
    brimmed

7. Flanges: frequently present

Type I No demarcation above the belly

a. Elliptical base with or without brim

    Examples of this type found at An-yang are:

    Yeh III: 2.5 (Metropolitan 43.25.4, U. S.   )

    Other examples are:

    Tsun ku: 3.19; Shina kodo: 147.

b. Three or four feet for support, without base

Examples of this type found at An-yang are:

Yeh III: 2.3 (Loo 86413, U. S.   ).

Another example is: Po ku: 20.40.

Type II With clear demarcation above the belly, usually
indicated by a groove, and the abrupt bulge of
the belly.

    a. With elliptical base

    Examples of this type found at An-yang are:

    Yeh III: 2.4 (Freer: 39.53, U. S.   ); An-yang
    Treasures: 43; Ontario: NB 4027.

    Other examples are:

    Cull: 9; Sumitomo I: 94; Ku kung: 39.7; T'ao chai I:
    3.36; Hsü k'ao ku: 3.21; London: no. 253, no. 259;
    New Studies: pl. 27, no. 1284.

    b. With rectangular (sometimes truncated pyramid) base,
    brimmed.

    Example: Hsü k'ao ku: 2.8. *Yu and Kuang. 46-50; Chun Chiu: 5. 74-75*

Both types have vessels that were unearthed at An-yang,
hence, we may easily date them as Shang. Some of them may extend to Early Western Chou, but after that period kuang disappeared entirely. Many kuang have a bull head-lid. The kuang
(London 253) in Raphael's Collection is the only one that has
a belly made up of two compartments separated by a partition
and a lid that has a slot so that the handle of a shao can pass
through when the shao is left in the kuang. The shao was found
with the vessel. This is shown in Burlington Magazine, June,
1934, pp. 253-254. Freer: 38.5 has a raised animal-head instead
of a more regularly defined handle. Loo: 86413 has almost a
circular cross section body. There is only one speciman which

has a detachable socle under the vessel. This is shown in Shina kodo: 147.

XX. Niao-shou Tsun

The whole vessel is either in the form of a bird or an animal, with lid on the back or head of the animal, and with feet. We can divide them into groups according to their form:

    a. Owl
       Example: Eumo: A14.

    b. Bird

    c. Elephant
       Examples: Shina kodo: 36; Shan chai: 136.

    d. Ram
       Examples: Eumo: A11-12; Ning shou: 5.30.

    e. Buffalo
       Example: Hsi ch'ing: 36.18.

    f. Bull

    g. Animal
       Examples: Ku kung: 15.11 (with bird's head);
       Hsin cheng: 91; Chan kuo: 20(1).

    h. Fowl

All tsun in the shapes of owls, elephants, and rams can be dated as Shang exclusively. Those in the form of bulls and buffaloes can be dated as Shang and Early Western Chou. Animals and fowls may be dated as Eastern Chou. Those in the form of birds covered a long period, from Shang to Ch'un Ch'iu.

XXI. Hu

1. Mouth: various types but not rectangular; small

or medium

2. Neck: usually high except for Type IX

3. Handles: two in number, except that Type VIII

    has a single handle

4. Links: only on Type VIII

5. Body: usually deep

6. Lid: usually present

Type I

1. Mouth: circular, small

2. Neck: bottle shaped

3. Body: lower bulge with round belly

4. Base: circular, low

    Example of this type found at An-yang is:

    Yeh II: 1.16

There are only a few vessels of this type, all belong

to the Shang dynasty.

Type II

1. Mouth: elliptical, medium

2. Handles: lugs

3. Body: lower bulge

4. Base: low, elliptical, without brim

5. Decoration: all over the vessel

    Examples of this type found at An-yang are:

    Yeh I: 1.17; Yeh III: 1.29; Trautmann: 10.

    Other examples are:

    Ku kung: 19.17; Shan chai: 101; Shang chou: II,

    716; Shina kodo: 131; Kogei: 12; New Studies:

    pl. 18, no. 624; pl. 48, no. 628.

From the inscription, provenance, and design, they all
belong to the Shang dynasty. The lid was usually not found for
this type, except for the one in Kogei: 12 which has a domed
lid with a knob. Shang chou: II, 716 mentioned the name hu in
its inscription. This piece is probably Early Western Chou.

    Type III

        1. Mouth: circular, small

        2. Handles: lugs

        3. Body: slender and tall, middle bulge

        4. Base: low, circular, brimmed

        5. Lid: domed, usually cup-shaped top

           Examples are: Sumo A:71;

           Shina kodo: 138; Sumitomo I: 43; Shih er: Shih 10;

           Foreign Collections: 49; Hsi ch'ing: 19.8;   Bur-

           chard Catalogue: Vol. I, pl. 25, no. 272; Liang

           lei: 2.20; Chen sung: 1.43; Shan chai (d): 3.44.

    The last three examples and Cleveland: 44.61 (U. S.   )
were referred to as hu in their inscriptions. The lid of the
Cleveland hu when inverted functions as a small cup. This type
can be dated as Early Western Chou, some of them might have
come down from Late Shang.

    Type IV

        1. Mouth: oblong, medium

        2. Handles: usually loose rings

        3. Body: lower bulge

        4. Base: oblong, low, brimmed

        5. Lid: various types

Examples are:

Wu ying: 87, 99, 102; Ch'eng ch'iu: 30, 31;

Shan chai: 103, 104-105; Ku kung: 7.17;

Shuang yü: 17; Chou chin: 5.3; Shan chai (d):

3.52; Shina kodo: 132; Hsin cheng: 95, 99, 100,

108.

This type is no doubt a descendant from Type II, although
it is much later. We could not find the transitional types between II and IV to show the continuous change of the mouth from
elliptical to oblong and the change of the handles from lugs to
loose rings. By studying the inscriptions we find that they
first appeared in Late Western Chou and extended to the Early
Ch'un Ch'iu period. The Hsin-cheng vessels were of the Middle
Ch'un Ch'iu period, and the pair in Shan chai: 104-105 was made
in 344 B.C. The cross hoop decorations and the waved broad
bands were popularly used during this time.

There are three kinds of lids on this type of hu: the
oblong cup-shaped tops were used during Late Western Chou and
Early Ch'un Ch'iu, and they were followed by the corona lid in
Middle Ch'un Ch'iu, and in the Chan Kuo period the lid was flat
with small feet. When the lid is on the vessel the inscription
is upside down, this proves that when exhibited the lid should
be inverted as the fang-i.

Type V

    1. Mouth: circular, small

    2. Handles: usually loose rings

    3. Body: lower bulge with round belly

    4. Base: low, circular, brimmed

    5. Lid: domed, cup-shaped top if present

Examples are:

Shuang chien II: 1.20; Tsun ku: 2.30; Ku kung:

13.2, 5.10, 36.17, 37.17; Wu ying: 105;

P'an ku: 2.21; K'ao ku: 4.40; Hsin cheng: 109,

113.

This type was derived from Type I although it is much later. We could not find transitional types between I and V. This type is similar in shape to Type IV because it is of the same period. The two dominant decorations as described in Type IV were also popularly used on this type. From the inscriptions, this type belongs to Late Western Chou and Early Ch'un Ch'iu. Hsin-cheng vessels were probably of Early Ch'un Ch'iu.

Type VI - Chung-type Hu

1. Mouth: circular, small

2. Handles: loose rings on loops

3. Body: middle bulge

4. Base: low, circular

5. Lid: flat or corona if present

6. Chain: sometimes present

Probably this type first appeared in the Ch'un Ch'iu period. Cull's hu (Cull: 12) of this type can be dated, by its inscription, about 482 B.C. It was popularly used during the Chan Kuo period and extended to the Han dynasty. The cup-shaped lid disappeared entirely and the corona type became more popular.

Examples of this type with chains are:

Shih er: Tsun 10; Shina kodo: 222 (David Weill

Collection); Foreign Collections: 56; Wu ying:

113; Shina kodo: 169.

In this type, sometimes there are four or more small loose rings on the neck and on the lid, the purpose of which is to allow the cords or strings to pass through that fasten the lid. Some of the vessel's designs were inlaid with lacquer, gold and other materials.

Type VII - Fang-type Hu

1. Mouth: square, small

2. Handles: loose rings, two or four in number

3. Body: middle bulge, square cross section throughout. Divided into four faces by four right-angle edges.

4. Base: square, truncated pyramid

5. Lid: truncated pyramid, square with small feet on it.

This type was called fang in the Han dynasty. Judging from their provenance and decoration, most of them were of the Chan Kuo period. University C 243 (U. S.   ) can be dated by its inscription as 315 B.C. The designs of many of the vessels were inlaid with lacquer, gold and other kinds. of material.

Type VIII - Gourd Hu

1. Mouth: circular, small

2. Neck: bent

3. Handles: movable single, attached to two loops

4. Body: egg-plant shape

5. Base: low, circular without brim.

6. Links: linking the handle and the lid

7. Lid: small domed or flat with bird or loop tops

8. Rim: flat or waved

Examples are:

Ku kung: 38.14; Sumitomo I: 46, 47; Kodoki: 36.

This type of hu is an imitation of the gourd which was used for water and wine.   It was particularly made for travelling.   It can be dated as Late Ch'un Ch'iu and Chan Kuo.

Type IX - Flat Hu - Ou Type Hu

1. Mouth: circular, small

2. Handles: loose rings on narrow sides

3. Body: flattened, front and rear view are elliptical, and the other two sides are narrow (flattened canteen-like, with right-angle edges).

4. Base: low, rectangular, brimmed

This type can be dated in the Chan Kuo period, and was probably used for travelling purposes.   Some of the vessels have rectangular bands arranged in a brick wall pattern.   This is an imitation of the net that was used to carry vessels of this kind made in all materials except bronze.

Type X - Hsing-type Hu   鈃

1. Mouth: circular, small

2. Neck: high, bottle shape

3. Belly: squat

4. Base: low, circular, without brim

Examples are:

Loo Catalogue (1924): pl. 32; Shuang chien I: 1.28.

This type appeared in Late Chan Kuo and extended to the Han dynasty.   The handles disappeared and the neck became very long and slender.   Loo's hu has the inscription of the Han dynasty, and was referred to as wen-hu, the heating hu.

The use of the hu   covered a very long period, from

Shang to the Han dynasty. Its style did not change very much during this time. Types I and II disappeared after Early Western Chou but were substituted by Types IV and V. Type III also disappeared after Early Western Chou. After the Middle Ch'un Ch'iu period, Types VI and VII became the dominant types, and about the same time the gourd _hu_ and the flat _hu_ appeared. They were used for special purposes. The lugs were used in the early types. Loose rings were the dominanting characteristics of the later types. Sometimes animal handles were used. The lid of the early types, i. e., Types II and III, were cup-shaped tops. The corona was sometimes used during the Late Ch'un Ch'iu period. During the Chan Kuo period the flat lid on a circular mouth and the truncated-pyramid on a square mouth were popular. At the same time small rings under the rim, on the lid, and the chain appeared.

The elliptical shaped mouth on the earlier types changed into oblong shape during the Late Western Chou period, afterwards the mouth was either rectangular or circular.

In Types I and II the base has no brim. In later types the brimmed base is more popular. But during the Chan Kuo period the base became very low without a brim. In Types I, II, IV and V the body, for the most part, has a lower bulge. In Types VI and VII the body has changed to middle bulge.

XXII. Lei

1. Mouth: circular or rectangular, small
2. Neck: low
3. Handles: loose rings or semi-circular rings
4. Nose: usually present

5. Body: deep, upper bulge

6. Base: circular or rectangular, low; none
    for Type Ia.

7. Lid: gable-roof shaped with knob on top
    for square mouth; domed for circular
    mouth.

Type I - Round Lei

1. Mouth: circular, small

2. Lid: domed with cup-shaped top or knob,
    without collar

a. Without base

    Examples of this type found at An-yang are:

    Yeh II: 1.37; Yeh III: 2.20 [2.10]; Lochow: 16

b. With base

    Examples of this type found at An-yang are:

    Ontario: NB 4029, 3218

    Other examples are:

    Hakkaku: 15; Shapes: 12.4; Tsun ku: 2.27;

    T'ao chai II: 2.7; Shan chai: 106; Sumitomo II: 172;

    Ch'ih an: 13; T'ao chai I: 3.7; Hsi ch'ing shih yi:14.

Type II - Rectangular Lei

1. Mouth: rectangular

2. Lid: gable-roof shaped with gable-roof knob

a. Without base

Examples of this type found at An-yang are:

An-yang Treasures: 42; Yeh II: 1.38.

Other examples are:

London: no. 240; Shina kodo: 48.

b. With base

Example of this type found at An-yang is:

An-yang Treasures: 41.

Other examples are:

Tsun ku: 2.28; Sumitomo I: 26; T'ao chai II: 2.5;

Shina kodo: 49; Kogei: 22.

From the provenance, we can date most of the lei as
Shang although some of them extended to Early Western Chou, and
a few of them were even as late as Late Western Chou as shown
in the inscription of T'ao chai I: 3.7 of Type Ib. This one
is the only specimen which was referred to as lei in its inscription. The body was low and the nose was omitted. Most of the
lei without bases were found at An-yang and the white pottery
lei of Freer: 39.42 without a base was also found at An-yang.
Since white pottery is earlier than the Shang bronzes it follows
that the lei without bases were earlier than those with bases.
It seems to me that the round lei are earlier than the
rectangular lei since most, if not all, of the bronzes were

copies of pottery. In the Ontārio Museum there are some gray
pottery lei of Type Ia which were found at An-yang, but no rectangular pottery was found there, probably because of the difficulty in making such shapes. Most of the earlier types of
bronzes are round rather than rectangular. This is due to the
same reason. Those with a base but without a brim are earlier
than those with a brim. Lei disappeared after Late Western
Chou and were substituted by fou which have no nose.

XXIII. Fou

Similar to lei except in the following ways:

1. Lower than lei
2. Four rings on the shoulder
3. Circular mouth
4. Flat lid with a collar, rings on it
5. Without nose
6. Low circular base without brim

   Examples are:

   Shang chou: II, 803; Shih er: Tsun 23; Sumitomo I:
   48.

All of the fou can be dated as Eastern Chou and they
belonged to one type until the end of the Chan Kuo period. The
first example can be dated in the Ch'un Ch'iu period and the
second can be dated in the Late Chan Kuo period. The ~~last~~ first example
was referred to as fou in the inscription, and it is similar to
Boston: 11.1447 (U. S. 786   ).

XXIV. Ling

Similar to _fou_ except in the following ways:

1. Mouth: with limited spreading rim
2. Handles: two rings
3. Base: none
4. Body: upper bulge

There are only three vessels which were referred to as _ling_ in their inscriptions. One is illustrated in _Chou chin_: 5.27 (rubbing of the vessel). The other two, with inscriptions on the lid and on the body, are illustrated in _San tai_: 18.15b and 18.16a. Since the first was found at Ch'i-shan of Shensi we can date it as Late Western Chou.

XXV. Ts'ung

Similar to _fou_ except in the following ways:

1. Mouth: circular or oblong
2. Handles: rings or loose rings, usually two in number
3. Base: always none
4. Body: middle bulge, tall

See chapter VII, section 25 for examples. The shape of this type is similar to the _hu_ of Type IV, but this type never has a base.

XXVI. Ying

1. Mouth: circular, small
2. Neck: very low

3. Shoulder: sometimes has animal-heads on it

4. Handles: always none

5. Body: low with middle or lower bulge

6. Base: truncated cone-shaped

7. Lid: sometimes present, domed with knob on top

Type I - With Upper or Middle Bulge

    a. Without flanges

       Examples of this type found at An-yang are:

       Yeh I: 1.30; Shuang chien I: 1.22 (all have no lid).

       Other examples are:

       Shina kodo: 124; Wu ying: 141, 143, 145;

       Sumitomo I: 50.

    b. With flanges

       Examples of this type found at An-yang are:

       K'ao ku: 4.44; An-yang Treasures: 39 (with lid).

       Other examples are:

       Sumitomo I: 51, 55; Ku kung: 22.16.

Type II - With Low Bulge

       Example: Shina kodo: 125 (Foreign Collections: 66).

    Judging from the provenance, decoration and inscription, many of this type could be dated as Shang. None of them ever mentioned the name of this class in their inscriptions. The two examples of Type Ia, which were found at An-yang, are plain without any decoration and are very similar to the pottery. I consider these the earliest. Type Ib, with flanges, is later than Ia. There are only a few specimen for Type II, all have fish and frog decorations which are the common motifs for water vessels. I am, therefore, inclined to believe that Type II might have been made for that purpose.

I can not find many specimen of this class in Western Chou bronzes. But I believe that the tan, which will be discussed in the next section, is the continuation of the ying.

XXVII. Tan

1. Mouth: circular, small with limited spreading
   rim
2. Neck: low
3. Handles: two semi-circular or four loose rings
4. Body: low, upper bulge
5. Base: none or very low

There is only one type in this class.

Examples are:

London: no. 145; Trautmann: 20; Ku kung: 16.16; Hsin cheng: 86; Loo Catalogue (1924): 29; Shina kodo: 185; Hsin cheng:88; Pao yün: 91.

The last example is the only one which was referred to as tan in its inscription. It was made by a chief of staff of the Ch'i^2 State, whose activity was recorded in Ch'un ch'iu and Tso chuan during the period 599 B.C. to 573 B.C. The other tan, judging from their inscriptions, can be dated in the Ch'un Ch'iu period.

There is a pair of bronzes in Chan kuo: 66-67 which is rather tall but similar in shape to the tan. This class of tan might have come down from the ying. The specimen in

Ku kung: 16.16 is very similar to Wu ying: 145 of the ying type.
The inscription of the former shows its date as Western Chou.   In
this inscription the name of that vessel was mentioned, but unfortunately the reading of the character can not be deciphered.

XXVIII. Min

    1. Mouth: circular, small

    2. Neck: low

    3. Handles: two loose rings

    4. Base: circular, low, straight

    5. Body: low, upper bulge

Only a few of the min are known to us. They belong to
the Chan Kuo period.

    Examples are: Hakkaku: 23; Pao yün: 95.

    The last one was referred to as min in its inscription.

XXIX. Cheng

    1. Mouth: circular, wide, with limited spreading rim

    2. Neck: constricted

    3. Handles: two rings, or loose rings

    4. Base: none

    5. Lid: domed

See chapter VII, section 29 for examples and date.

XXX. P'i

    1. Mouth: elliptical, wide

2. Handles: loops or loose rings

3. Support: base or small feet

4. Lid: low-domed, with elliptical open work of
    small feet

The specimen of this class are not earlier than
Eastern Chou.

XXXI. Pei

1. Mouth: elliptical, wide

2. Handles: two rings

3. Base: none or with small feet or elliptical
    low base

The specimen of this class are not earlier than Eastern Chou.

XXXII. Shao

1. Ladle: deep

2. Handle: long flat rod, sometimes connected with
    wooden rod

Type I - Long and Flat Handle with a Small Ladle

Examplesof this type found at An-yang are:

Yeh II: 1.41; Shuang chien I: 1.50, 52; Sung chai II:
99; Ontario NB 4024.

Other examples are:

Yu and Kuang: 68; Burlington Magazine: June, 1934,
pp. 253-254; Foreign Collections: 67, 68.

Type II - The Ladle with a Larger Volume than Type I

and a Short Hollow Handle usually Fitted

by a Wooden Rod

Examples of this type found at An-yang are:

Yeh I: 1.32 (Sung chai II: 96); Yen k'u: 65;

Ontario NB 4025, 4156.

Another example is:

Ku kung: 26.13.

Type III - With a Short Hollow Handle and a Hemispherical Ladle

Examples of this type found at Shou Hsien are:

Sung chai II: 97; Ch'u ch'i: 2.

From the provenance, there is no doubt that Types I and II can be dated in the Shang period, although there are specimen of the Western Chou period. Type III can be dated as Late Chan Kuo.

There is an exceptional specimen in Loohow: 15 which is somewhat like Type I, but the bottom of the laddle is added with a base so that it can rest on a plane. This piece was found at An-yang in recent years.

XXXIII. Yü

1. Mouth: circular, wide with limited spreading rim

2. Handles: bent ears for Type I; none for Type II;

   semi-circular for Type III.

3. Body: deep, not bulged

4. Lid: sometimes present

Only a few specimen of this class are known to us, so

I tentatively make the following divisions based on this scarce
material:

Type I

    1. Handles: bent

    2. Body: similar to kuei of Type Ib

    3. Base: truncated

    4. Lid: low domed with spherical knob

This description is based on a yü excavated by the
Academia Sinica at Hou-chia Chuang of An-yang in 1935.
It was called yü in its inscription. Hsi ch'ing chia: 16.1
and the two specimen in our catalogue also belong to this type.
They are either Shang or Early Chou.

Type II

    1. Handles: absent

    2. Body: similar to kuei of Type Ia

    3. Base: low, brimmed

    4. Lid: low domed with cup-shaped top

This description is based on a pair of travelling yü
made by Yen Hou of the Early Chou period. I saw this pair in
a New York dealer's place in 1946. It was called yü in its
inscription. The height and the diameter is 19cm. *(Of. R. 461-462)*

Type III

    1. Handles: semi-circular

    2. Body: low

    3. Base: none

This description is based on a yü in K'ao ku: 6.9 (Po ku:
21.34) of the Late Western Chou or Early Ch'un Ch'iu periods.

Other vessels which were called yǔ in their inscriptions
are:

   1. San tai: 18.12.1-2 with lid, Western Chou

   2. San tai: 18.12.4   Western Chou

   3. Chui i: 28.1b   Late Western Chou

   Numbers (1) and (2) were made for travelling purposes
according to their inscriptions.

                        XXXIV. P'an

   1. Mouth: circular, wide (rectangular 於 III)

   2. Handles: none for Type I, bent ears for Type II
        and loose rings for Type III

   3. Body: shallow

   4. Base: circular, truncated cone-shaped for Type I,
        low brimmed for Type II, quadruped for Type III
        and none for Type IV.

   Type I

      1. Handles none

      2. Base: truncated cone-shaped without brim
         Examples of this type found at An-yang are:
         Yeh I: 1.28; Yeh III: 2.6, 8, 9; Trautmann: 17
         (Yeh II: 1.34); Lochow: 18.
         Other examples are:
         Hakkaku: 21; Shan chai:91,93; Shang chou: II, 826;
         Sung chai II: 46 (found at Lo-yang).

   Type II

      1. Handles bent ears, semi-circular paired ones

2. Base: brimmed, except Early Western Chou ones

Examples are:

Kumo: A 64; Shang chou: II, 829; Sumitomo I: 110;

Yin and chou: pl. 25, B153; B155; pl. 44, B40;

Shina kodo: 151; Pao yün: 78, 97; Ku kung: 1.1;

Tsun ku: 3.20; Shina kodo: 153 (Ontario);

T'ao chai I: 3.38; Shuang chien II: 1.26.

Type III - Rectangular P'an

    1. Mouth: rectangular

    2. Handles: two loose rings on each side

    3. Base: quadruped

       Example: Shang chou: II, 841.

Type IV

    1. Ears: loops

    2. Base: very low

       Example: Chen sung: 2.35

Type V

    1. Without base

       Example: Shih er: Tsun 24 (found in Shou Hsien).

It is obvious that Type I can be dated Shang, although quite a few of them extended to Early Western Chou. The decoration on this type sometimes has fish, turtles, dragons or frogs. These are typical patterns for water vessels. With the exception of the Eumorfopoulos one (fig. 59 in our catalogue), which has no brim on the base and which can be dated as Early Western Chou, Type II covered the Western Chou period and extended to Ch'un Ch'iu. The vessel in Wu ying: 85 has a spout and a single handle which is an exception in Type II. The diameter of the base of Type II is larger than that of Type I, but in the Eastern Chou period some of the vessels of Type II had smaller bases and bent ears turned outward as shown in Ku kung:

36.7 and _Tsun ku_: 3.21. Type III is represented by only one specimen which is a rare type. Since it is referred to as _p'an_ in its inscription we have to list it under this class. Type IV can be dated as Eastern Chou and it extended to the Han dynasty. The evolution of the _p'an_ has convinced us that the vessels with a brimmed base are usually of a later date than the same type vessels without a brimmed base.

XXXV. _I_

1. Spout: various types
2. Handle: single
3. Support: four feet for Type I, three feet or a
   base for Type II
4. Lid: occasionally appears on Type II

Type I

1. Handles: like those on _kuei_ V
2. Spout: channel spout
3. Support: four feet
   Examples are:
   Shuang chien I: 1.21; _Sumitomo_ I: 96; _Burlington Magazine_, November, 1930; _Shan chai_: 96, 97, 98; _Ku kung_: 3.10, 35.17; _Shan chai_: 99, 95 (with animal-head spout).

The last two examples may be dated as Early Ch'un Ch'iu and the rest belong to the Late Western Chou period.

Type II

1. Handles: usually semi-circular or ring-shaped
2. Spout: usually animal-head type

3. Support: three feet or without

a. With three feet

Examples are:

Loo Catalogue (1924): 17 (with channel spout);

Sumitomo I: 97 (with channel spout); Shina kodo:

190; Chan kuo: 12 (found at Li-yü); Kogei: 27.

b. Without feet as support

Examples are: Hsi Ch'ing: 118-119

Shih er: Hsueh 16; (with channel spout); Chan kuo:

11 (found at Li-yü); Ku kung: 8.2; Shih er: Pao 15

(found at Shou Hsien).

There is a pair of inscriptions in San tai: 17.18a

classified under i which can be dated as Shang or Early Western

Chou. The illustration is not available and in the inscription

it did not mention the name of the vessel as i. So far as we

know the earliest type belongs to Late Western Chou.

Type I can be dated as Late Western Chou, although some

of them extended to Early Ch'un Ch'iu. The style of this type

is more or less consistent. Type II covered the Eastern Chou

period and had quite a variety of feet, spouts and handles with

the three-feet and animal-head spouts the dominating styles.

Those without feet and those with animal-head spouts are limited

to the Eastern Chou period. Types IIa and IIb are among the

Li-yü finds; thus a and b are contemporaneous.

XXXVI. Chien

1. Mouth: circular, wide

2. Neck: constricted

L351

3. Handles: two or four loose rings

4. Base: circular, low, without brim

   Examples are:

   Yin and chou: pl. 52 c 183 (found at Shansi);

   Hakkaku: 22; Sheng kao: 14 (found at Chi Hsien of

   Honan); Shina kodo: 156, 174; Chan kuo: 56.

All of the chien can be dated in the Chan Kuo period,

and there were no great changes in their style during that time.

L 352

CHAPTER IX

PALAEOGRAPHY

CHAPTER IX

Palaeography

I stated in Chapter II that from the Sung dynasty on
the study of bronzes was parallel to the study of palaeography.
During the Ch'ing dynasty the study of Shuo wen chieh tzu
reached its climax and some scholars began to feel that Shuo
wen could not satisfactorily solve all of the problems in
palaeography unless it was supplemented with other materials of
earlier scripts. At that time, numerous bronzes were unearthed
together with the Shang oracle bones which, at last, gave us
the earliest script that helped us to study the evolution of
Chinese characters. On the other hand, after the Han dynasty
Shuo wen became the authoritative work in the field of palaeography. Many important works have been written which have aided
us in deciphering the ancient character. During the Late Ch'ing
dynasty not only were bronzes and oracle bones, the records of
the aristocratic class, unearthed in great quantities, but also
inscriptions on other materials, which represent a certain amount
of provincial script and the writing of the common people, were
at our disposal. With the help of these inscriptions the date
and the provenance of vessels can be determined. Therefore it is
obvious that the study of inscriptions is exceedingly important.

During the Han dynasty the study of palaeography was a
branch of the Classics since palaeography functioned as a tool
or a key to the understanding of the Classics. And in the Sung

dynasty the study of the inscriptions on bronzes and stone monuments was a branch of palaeography. It was not until recent
years that the study of bronzes became a part of archaeology. The
relations between these three branches of study are still very
close.   Therefore it is necessary for me to write a chapter on
palaeography since it is one of the important means for solving
a lot of problems involved in the present comprehensive study of
Chinese bronzes.

I. The Origin of Chinese Characters

It is very difficult to make any answer to the question,
"When did Chinese characters begin?" First, because the records
of the writing in its earliest stages are not available. Second, the traditional stories concerning the origin of the characters are based on both legends and myths, and third, the chronology of the early states is obscure. If we believe Hsü Shen's
statements in his preface to the <u>Shuo</u> <u>wen</u> <u>chieh</u> <u>tzu</u> that the
characters were created by Ts'ang Chieh   , the historian of
          there were written characters
Huang Ti, then in Huang Ti's time .
Even if this is true, we are still unable to indicate at what
time they appeared. There have been those who believed that there
was writing during the Hsia dynasty because certain bronzes
listed in the Sung catalogues were considered to be of Hsia origin. Modern archaeology has however thus far revealed no bronzes
of the Hsia dynasty. Again, based on an ambiguous phrase in the
<u>Lun</u> <u>yü</u>, there have been scholars who held that there was writing
during the time of Yao   . Basing their contentions on a certain kind of painted pottery with human and animal figures on it

from the neolithic site at Hsin-t'ien in Kansu, there are scholars
who date writing back to that period; and other scholars, with no
evidence at all, believe that the Chinese pictographs date back
some ten thousand years. We can not accept all of these supposi-
tions and conjectures. The only certain thing now is based on
evidence found which shows that during the latter part of the
Shang dynasty writing had been in use for some time. Most of the
writing of this period is on the oracle bones and the bronzes.
Small scraps of writing of this time have been found on pottery,
jade and stone. From these inscriptions I list the following
facts:

1. The fundamental structure of the Chinese character,
   namely, pictographs, phonetic-compounds and phonetic
   borrowings, was already formed in the Shang dynasty.

2. The inscriptions of the Shang period show a high degree of flexibility. In later times the flexibility
   is not so great, there being a tendency to stabilize.

3. The use of pictography is more often in the Shang
   period while the phonetic-compound is more frequently
   used in later periods.

4. The clan names, personal names, place names, and names
   of states that were common in the Shang period disappeared later.

5. Since the inscriptions which we have are from the royal
   family only, we know very little of the writing of the
   common people.

6. The syntax is not sharply different from the later
   periods. In the Shang and Western Chou inscriptions
   certain personal pronouns are used with case and number;
   this usage disappeared in later times.

It may be concluded that the Shang writing was, in a
certain degree, advanced, but not very far advanced from its
original stage. It seems to me that the beginning of the writing of characters is not remote from this period, perhaps five
hundred to a thousand years.

Painted pottery with an occasional animal decor but no
writing has been found in Yang-shao in Honan, and in Hsin-tien,
Ma-ch'ang and Pan-shan in Kansu. J. D. Anderson wrote:

> In the sepulture furniture of some graves of this
> stage (the Chu Chia Chai site in Hsi Ning Hsien)
> were found some bone objects which deserve special
> mention. They are small rectangular bone plates,
> wither smooth as (a) or incised as (b) and (c).
> Sometimes these bone plates were found in small groups
> lying side by side as shown by (d). I am tempted to
> think that they represent some kind of primitive
> writing or otherwise record some abstract ideas con-
> nected with the dead.
> (Preliminary Report on Archaeological Research in
> Kan-su, p. 14).

And further he stated:

> In all our extensive excavations in the prehistoric
> sites of Kansu we never saw on any pottery vessel or
> other object the slightest indication of writing, in
> spite of the fact that our attention was constantly
> bent in that direction (the incised bone plates of
> the Yang Shao time described on p. 14 are at the most
> some kind of primitive record, in no way related to
> the archaic Chinese script).
> (Ibid., p. 30).

Nils Palmgren writes of the Kansu mortuary pottery:

> Both in the Pan Shan and the Ma Ch'ang pottery we
> find occasional instances of painted mortuary vessels
> having marks on them that are not directly associated
> with the otherwise quite coherent decor with which the
> vessels are ornamented. With a very few exceptions
> the same colours are used for these marks—black and
> reddish violet—as those in which the rest of the de-
> cor is painted. After the vessel had been built up
> and the ware dried, the marks were painted on prior
> to baking. Marks of this kind are placed either on
> the bases or on the bottoms of the vessels....
> (Kansu Mortuary Urns of the Pan Shan and Ma Ch'ang
> Groups, p. 174).

And later the same author wrote:

> In their construction all these marks are, with a
> few exceptions, extremely simple. I have dealt
> with the exceptions above. As compared with the
> other patterns on the vessels, the marks, regarded
> as drawings, are exceedingly primitive. Moreover,
> they are indifferently done, being often painted
> with extreme carelessness. They apparently repre-
> sent attempts at a record of words and figures,
> that is to say, a primitive form of writing.
> (Ibid., p. 179).

These points indicate, in a general way, that before
2000 B.C. there was no writing. The marks on the pottery were
only a kind of symbol and the later writing was not derived from
such marks. Both marks and characters were inscribed on the
pottery of Lung-shan. The Lung-shan culture is divided into two
parts: (1) Lower stratum, black pottery, and (2) Upper stratum,
grey pottery. Altogether there were eighty-eight pieces of
pottery with marks from Lung-shan, of which only three pieces
were from the lower level. The lot showed that the vessels of
the tou type were always incised on the support or the cup; jars
of the yung type were carved on the outside of the lip, and
basins of the p'an type were carved on the inside of the rim.
All of the inscribed pottery was from the upper stratum, and
about four pieces (cf. C.T.Y. pl. 16, nos.10, 12a, 14, 17) had
the same characters as those on the oracle bones found at An-yang.
Liang Ssu-yung dates the lower stratum of the Lung-shan culture
between 2300-2000 B.C. The white pottery of An-yang is, in my
opinion, earlier than the Shang bronzes. A few inscriptions
were occasionally found on it as shown in An-yang Finds, p. 15,
fig. 6. They are contemporaneous with the early oracle bones
which are after 1300 B.C. Thus, from the materials available it
would seem that the earliest attempts at writing were somewhere
between 2000 and 1300 B.C. This period then would also include

the Hsia. I may now venture to say that writing was used after
2000 B.C., but most probably not before this date. The earliest
inscriptions known are the An-yang oracle bones, but the inscriptions on the early bronzes may not always be of a date later than
the oracle bones.

In Hsü Shen's preface to Shuo wen chieh tzu he wrote
that the knotted strings were used before Ts'ang Chieh created
writing the Eight Trigrams. Later he recorded, "Ts'ang Chieh
made characters by imitating the forms according to the unit of
each class." This means that the early writing came from the
pictures of things. He also used the term shu ch'i
for 'writing' or 'characters', literally, shu means 'writing'
and ch'i means 'tally'; this gives the wrong impression that
the early writing was derived from tallies.

The Eight Trigrams, the Pa Kua   , were derived
from a system of divination by stalks of the milfoil. This was
first used by the Chou people. We find no evidence in the oracle
bone inscriptions of the existence of the Pa Kua. The Pa Kua
was simply a combination of two opposite symbols. The Pa Kua
presented eight fundamental classifications such as K'un kua   ,
combining three negative elements which indicate or represent
earth, mother, pot, miserly, balance, cow, a big chariot, decorated, mass, handle, and the black color of the earth. From this
example it can be seen that the Pa Kua had a symbolic reference
and was far from writing.

The use of the knotted strings as a means of calculation
still exists among the Tibetan and Miao tribes and among a certain class of merchants in Shansi province. The small merchants
of Shansi province, when carrying their merchandise, attach

to their cases of wares thongs of leather which they knot to record their credit system. This method is common to primitive people all over the world. It was an aid in remembering only a certain number and had nothing to do with writing.

Cheng Hsüan's commentary to Chih jen of Chou li noted, "The shu ch'i is the tally for the exchange of merchandise. The form of the tally was to write on two wooden slips and then carve marks across the two edges." His commentary to the Hsi tzu   of I ching contains a similar statement but adds that one of the wooden slips is given to each of the persons as a check for a later time. This is the original meaning of ch'i, which was combined with two slips. The marks on the slips were called 'teeth', and the number of the 'teeth' indicated the size, in number, of the contract. The wooden slips of the Han dynasty which were unearthed in recent years had such tallies included among them. They were exactly like the form described by Cheng Hsüan, with the transaction or contract written on the flat surfaces and the edges scored with the appropriate number of marks. It is my belief that in primitive times people using the 'tally' carved only the 'teeth' to keep the number recorded, while the contract as such was oral. There is a pair of jades recorded in Yeh II: 2.28 which has four parallel marks carved across the edges; these are probably ancient tallies. It may be conjectured that the bone plates described by Anderson are also tallies of this type. The Miao tribes still use a tally on which only the 'teeth' are carved, but which omits the writing of the contract.

From the above we know that the knotted strings, the Pa Kua, and the tally were not writing, but were either symbols, as in the case of the Pa Kua, or numerical indicators, as in the other two cases. Chinese writing was simply derived from pictures. As Hsü Shen wrote, "Ts'ang Chieh first made characters by imitating the forms according to the unit of each class.... Hsiang-hsin, imitation of pictures, is that completed drawing of the thing following its shape and curves." So we know that the earliest writing was derived from pictures. This can be proved now since we have many early inscriptions which bear pictographic characters that resemble the likeness of the idea conveyed.

II. The Basic Types of Chinese Characters

Each character has three facets, structural form, sound, and meaning. The relations among these three are not equal. The meaning of a character was derived from the form or the sound. The diagram below illustrates this important point more graphically:

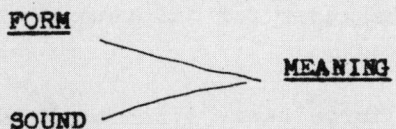

FORM

MEANING

SOUND

There are three ways to express an idea:

1. By form, such as the character nü   , simply a picture of a woman. This is called a pictograph. It may be noted here that this character was written on the oracle bones in a very definitely pictographic fashion.

2. By sound. As we know, we have no phonetic symbols but we do have a sound for each character, such as the character for 'woman' which has the sound nü. We have no character to write for the idea of 'you',

the second person pronoun. But in the spoken language, the sound nü was used as the second person
pronoun. Hence, in writing, the character for
'woman' already pronounced nü, was borrowed for this
pronoun because their sounds were the same. This is
phonetic borrowing. After the Ch'in dynasty this
latter nü was written as   instead of   to make
the distinction more certain.

3. By both form and sound, such as the character
   ku   , meaning 'mother of one's husband' (i.e.,
   mother-in-law). It is a combination of two parts:
   (a) the left side, nü   meaning 'woman' for the
   obvious reason; and (b) the right side, ku   ,
   originally meaning 'ancient', here used only as a
   phonetic symbol because in the spoken language the
   wife called her husband's mother ku, the same sound
   as the character for 'ancient'. This is s phonetic-
   compound.

These are the three basic types of Chinese characters,
and at the same time they indicate the three stages of the development of Chinese characters. By studying the ancient characters
from the beginning, it is clear that the pictograph is first and
the phonetic-compound is last. Between these two is the class of
phonetic borrowing. Although phonetic borrowing is the transitional stage from the pictograph to the phonetic-compound, the
method of phonetic borrowing was still used after the phonetic-
compound had become established. For example, a certain character
A is a pictograph, and is used as B, because A and B have the
same sounds, so that B is the phonetic borrowing. This B added
to a pictographic element forms a phonetic-compound C, with the

same meaning as B.   Then C is used as D, D and C have no relationship in meaning but they have a similar sound.   D has no relationship with A and B, but has a sound similar to C and is a new
phonetic borrowing.

The following diagram indicates the development of these
basic types:

Pictograph (still used as pictograph)-----Pictograph-----Pictograph

   Used as Phonetic Borrowing-----Phonetic Borrowing-----Phonetic
                                                             Borrowing

                        Phonetic-compound-----Phonetic-compound

Phonetic-compound------Phonetic-compound

                                         Phonetic Borrowing

This diagram shows that some pictographs always remain
pictographs, some become phonetic borrowings, and some combine
with another element and become phonetic-compounds.   A phonetic-
compound may be used as a phonetic borrowing.

III. Pictograph

The reasons for the retention of pictographic writing are
found in the very nature of the Chinese language itself.   The following points make this important fact clear:

   1. The early spoken language was monosyllabic and uninflected.
      Because of the extraordinarily high number of homo-
      phones, expression by a phonetic writing was almost im-
      possible.

2. The spoken had and has many dialects; hence, phonetic writing was and is impossible. Within the dialects many local varients are found, and a phonetic writing would, if at all possible, then create different languages. Again it is clear that the retention of the pictographic writing was a necessity due to the nature of the Chinese language.

3. There were in the early history of China certain political influences which tended to enforce the natural evolution. Although Shang and Chou were originally from different tribes, they were quite close. At any rate, close enough for the Chou to adopt the written language of the Shang completely. During the reign of Chou the states were forced by the central authority to use the unified writing.

We have already pointed out the three basic types of Chinese characters, viz., (1) the pictograph; (2) the phonetic borrowing; and (3) the phonetic-compound. If all of the Chinese characters are considered together the majority will be found to be phonetic-compounds. However, each phonetic-compound is made of half pictograph and half sound component, and when considered from this point of view the pictograph becomes the overwhelmingly larger class. In the literary style fu   was used during the Han dynasty, as for example, in the essays dealing with descriptions of mountains or rivers, the phonetic-compounds used for the descriptive purpose are so largely made of the pictographs for mountain or river that the characters themselves present to the eye a prospect of rocks and streams. Of the modern characters there are two examples which can be separated and explained.

The first one is derived from the ancient pictograph but has
become greatly deformed in the process and requires the imagination to aid the eye in finding the picture and in understanding
it. Such a character is   ch'üan, meaning 'dog'. $\bigcirc N$ a
quick inspection it seems closely related to   ta, a picture of
a standing man. However, if the eye, aided by visual imagination,
sees the dot in the right corner as a dog's ear and extends the
lower right-hand stroke to form part of the body, the character
is quickly recognized as a deformed picture of a dog. The second
one has no pictographic source, but long familiarity often assigns
a picture-value to such a character. The character is hsiao   ,
meaning 'smile'. The more rational approach is to consider the
upper part chu   , since it employs that classifier as a bamboo,
but to the Chinese it has the picture-value of 'a pair of smiling
eyes' and carries no denotation of 'bamboo'. Obviously, in a
strict sense, this is a pseudo-pictograph, nonetheless it carries
its own peculiar picture sense. These two examples are cited
mainly to illustrate the point that pictographic representation
and sight are psychologically Chinese qualities.

It might seem that the pictographic nature of Chinese
characters would only create large groups of substantives, but,
because of the lack of inflection, a character can be used to
function as a verb, an adjective, an adverb or a particle. The
syntactical relation indicates the specific use. Examples taken
from the oracle bones are as follows:

The ti   of Shang Ti   means 'supreme power above'
or 'supreme god'. When this character is used as in the above
example, it is clearly a substantive. When ti is placed before
a preposition and the latter is followed by the proper name of an
ancestor, then ti is a verb with the meaning 'to sacrifice'.

When _ti_ is placed before a character like _shih_   meaning 'recorder' or 'messenger', then _ti_ is used as an adjective meaning 'god's recorder'. The character _yü_   , originally a pictograph for 'rain', when placed after the adjective _ta_   'great' becomes a noun. When it is placed after the negative _pu_   'not' or 'no' it has a verbal sense. The character _ch'ang_   , originally a picture of a man with long hair, is used as the adjective 'long' but also as the verb 'to grow'. Hence it is clear that the pictograph is not limited in sense to the noun, but it can also express motion and be used in description. It is very important to note that Hsü Shen's three classes: (1) _chih-shih_, indicative of affairs; (2) _hsiang-hsin_, imitation of pictures; and (3) _hui-i_, assembly of ideas, were called (1) _hsiang-shih_, imitation of affairs; (2) _hsiang-hsin_, imitation of pictures; and (3) _hsiang-i_, imitation of ideas in Pan Ku's work. Pan classed them all as _hsiang_, that is 'imitation', thus indicating their basic pictographic quality with 'affairs' and 'ideas' carrying the verbal and adjectival values (cf. the appendix).

      I will now treat the pictograph in a broad sense, including the three classes mentioned above. The classes of the pictograph can be subdivided into six sections, each of which will be discussed in some detail.

     1. Simple pictograph. This section is called the 'simple pictograph' in order to distinguish it from the 'complex pictograph'. They are the characters which are simple pictures of the substantives such as _jih_   'sun' and _yüeh_   'moon'. These are the elements which are variously treated to form the characters of the following five sections.

2. Generalization. The pictographs which express a generalization for certain objects, i.e., a character which
   can be used as a picture of a quality possessed by a
   group of objects. For example, the characters for one,
   two and three are written with parallel strokes as
   . They represent a quantity of anything, wood, stone,
   jade, etc. The character hsiao   'small', 'scanty',
   originally a picture of grains of sand, is used for anything with the notion of drops, i.e., drops of blood,
   raindrops, the drops of juice from meat, etc. The characters shang   and hsia   , meaning 'upper', 'above'
   and 'lower' or 'below' respectively, simply indicate
   something above or something below, originally taken
   from the level of a vessel as the standpoint.

3. Simplification. This group includes the pictographs
   written in a form simplified from a more eleborate
   and detailed origin.   Examining those characters
   on the early bronzes, which were listed in the first
   part of the appendix to the Chin wen pien, it is very
   evident that they are quite close or similar to actual
   pictures. Most of them were clan names or family names.
   Because of a seeming conservatism in the writing of
   such patronymics, the old forms were retained a long
   time. A simpler form of the same character is sometimes
   found on the oracle bones, which indicates that the
   bronze form is from a source earlier than the oracle
   bones. Since the use of the character on the oracle
   bones was not a patronymic, it could easily be written
   in a simple form while the bronze inscriptions held on
   to the earlier form.

In the matter of writing, and with regard to the materials for
writing, the oracle bone characters were cut in quickly so that
erasures and corrections were not possible. The entire piece
was of a temporary nature. When a bronze was cast it was a
serious occasion, and the characters of the inscription, often
cast with the vessel, were carefully fixed and corrected in the
mould, thus giving the opportunity for use of this type of
character. So the same character used on the oracle bones may
be simpler in form than that found on a bronze and yet have been
written earlier, and the same character written on a bronze cast
at a time later than the oracle bones may retain an older form.

The tendency to simplify is most important in the development of Chinese characters. Except for a few characters from
the Shih chou p'ien this tendency is general. The three general
tendencies in the evolution of form in Chinese characters are:
(1) simplifications in form; (2) an increase in the number of
characters; and (3) the continuing combinations of characters.
Because of this natural type of growth certain terms were applied
to the various scripts in different eras. Again, the changes in
form were conditioned by the materials for writing.

4. Reduction. This section includes those pictographs
   in which the whole character was reduced, and of the
   parts, some were retained and some were omitted. There
   are three types:

   a. Reduced in half by cutting the character into two
      equal parts and omitting half. This often happened
      to the symmetrical characters.

   b. Characters reduced into several parts and one of the
      parts omitted in the writing. Such as the pictograph

of a man holding two weapons being reduced to two
weapons only with the man omitted. Often a character
of a man holding something was reduced to a hand
holding something.

   c. Characters in which the pictographic combination
in the original was reduced by separation but nothing
was omitted.

Many of the characters listed as hsing-sheng or hui-i by
Hsü Shen were so classified because he could not trace the pictograph back far enough to see that they were really one of these
three types of reduction.

   5. Indicative. This section is the one which creates the
emphasis. There are three types:

   a. Emphasis made by adding a part or by accenting a
part in a particular or special way. For example,
jen   meaning 'the edge of a knife' has a dot
added on the left side to point out the very edge
of the knife. This dot has a function of generalization, it signifies a piece of meat or a drop of
blood on the edge, and in this combination is indicative. Ch'i   , in which the foot of the man is
deliberately written under the jen   'man' to indicate someone 'standing on tip-toe looking for or
at something'.

   b. Emphasis created by an omission. The character tzu
was originally the picture of a small child with
two arms on both sides. When the same character is
written without the arms, as niao   it means
'armless'. The character mu   means 'a complete tree'

but when the head of the tree is cut off it gives

nieh   (the old script of   , note Shuo wen,

Chüan 6, part one) meaning 'the top of a tree'.

c. Emphasis effected by a change in position. For

example, ta   meaning 'great', originally a pic-

ture of a gentleman, when turned upside down be-

comes nieh   (this is the oracle bone form; later

the classifier ch'o   was added and the modern

form is nieh   ) meaning 'inverse' or 'reverse'.

The character jen   meaning 'man' when written up-

side down becomes hua   meaning 'to change, to trans-

form', and by extension comes to mean 'death'.

The strong tendency towards stabilization in the writing

of characters was the result of a slow growth. When a character

was a combination of several parts, the position of the parts

was not fixed but was changeable. In later times the classifier

was most often placed to the left or at the top of a character.

During the Shang period there were already certain characters

which could not be changed, such as tso   and yu   (modern

   ,   ) meaning 'left' and 'right'. A simplified picture of

the left and right hands. These were not changeable.

6. Assembly of ideas. In the preceding sections it was

made clear that the pictograph when considered was

itself a unit in which the parts had been added to or

had had their positions changed. In this section we

have those pictographs which are a combination of two

or more units. It falls under two categories:

a. A combination of different units

b. Duplication of the same unit

An example of <u>a</u> is <u>ming</u>   meaning 'bright, shining',
a combination of the sun and the moon. The quali-
ties of the component parts being essentially the
same, the meaning was expressed by a repetition of
the quality of 'brightness'. Another example is
<u>ming</u>   meaning 'to cry out, to sing', which is a
combination of a mouth and a bird. In this example
each part modifies the other and limits the sense.
The 'bird' part indicates the type to be not animal
nor human nor otherwise, but a bird, and the mouth
particularizes both the part of the bird and the
action, hence the meaning, 'to cry out, to sing'.
Examples of <u>b</u> are <u>lin</u>   , 'forest'; this is a
combination resulting from the reduplication of
<u>mu</u>   , 'a tree'; <u>shan</u>   , 'the rank odour of
sheep or goats' very graphically presents a combination of three sheep, a reduplication of <u>yang</u>   ,
meaning 'sheep'; <u>ts'ung</u>   (modern   ), 'to follow'
combines two men facing the same direction, a case
of simple duplication.

Two important points must be noted: first, the combination
of different units should be carefully distinguished from the
complex pictograph. The complex pictograph is more or less an
actual picture while many of the characters in the preceding
sections are combinations artificially contrived from original
pictographs. Second, in the indicative class of characters the
special meaning is made clear by the part of the character
emphasized, and this special meaning is retained only so long
as the character stands by itself. The special meaning is lost

as soon as such a character is made part of a combination; as in
the character ch'i   , different from jen   because it emphasizes the foot, but in the combination found on the bronzes,
the element ch'i is used as equivalent to jen with no special
meaning. This is also true in the duplicative processes just
considered. As pointed out above, when mu   is duplicated the
combination gives lin   , a character with a different meaning, the difference being the difference between a tree and a
forest. However, if it is combined with another element
it becomes ch'u   . It has been found on the bronzes written
either   or   ; the latter used   instead of   without
changing the meaning of the compound character.

From the above discussion, pictographs can be broken
down into six groups with their subdivisions:

1. Simple pictograph

2. Generalization

3. Simplification

4. Reduction

   a. Character cut in half

   b. Character is reduced to parts, one of the parts
      being omitted in writing

   c. Separation without omission

5. Indicative

   a. Emphasis by adding

   b. Emphasis by omission

   c. Emphasis by change in position

6. Assembly

   a. Combination of different units

   b. Duplication of the same unit

Chinese characters may also be divided into the following groups:

I. Simple characters

    A. No changes in position

    B. Changes in position

II. Non-simple characters

    A. Complex

    B. Compound

        1. Combination of two or more units
                                a. Phonetic-compound

                                b. Assembly

        2. Combination by adding a part to a unit

Group IIA may be called the 'complex pictograph'; a group of characters theoretically earlier in form, which did not pass through the evolution involved in simplification, generalization, etc. Group IA includes those characters which were originally simple, or which were made so by the process of simplification. These are discussed in sections 1, 2, and 3. Group IB is the same as IA, but in which the position has been changed. These are discussed in section 5c. IIB2 is of section 5a. IIB1 is a group according to Hsü Shen's definition, called tzu   which he defined as 'the combination of picture and phonetic'. The difference between a and b of IIB1 is obvious, but as we have mentioned before, one of the units of b may be used as the phonetic element. In this case there is no difference in form between a and b; b has been discussed in section 6, and a will be discussed below. 5b, emphasis by omission, is an exception of Group I.

IV. Phonetic-compound

Hsü Shen wrote, "When the picture form and the phonetic
are combined it is called tzu   ."   This can be explained as
(1) the combination of form and phonetic; (2) the combination
of form and form; and (3) the combination of phonetic and phonetic. We may define these three kinds of characters as tzu.
According to Hsü Shen's definition wen.   is the imitation of
the forms according to the units of each class. Both the complex and the simple pictograph were covered by this definition
for they imitated something which existed before the character
was created. These wen then became units which were used in the
combinations of the tzu. Tzu were combined according to ideas
logically possible. There are two types of meaning, an 'inner'
and a 'surface' meaning. We may apply these distinctions by
considering tzu as being related to the 'inner' and wen as being
related to the 'surface'.

In the three types of tzu given above the usual terms
applied are: to (1) hsin-sheng; to (2) hui-i; and to (3) chia-
chieh with an additional phonetic. We have already discussed
hui-i under the assembly section and since the type of chia-
chieh can be subsummed under hsin-sheng, the phonetic-compound,
we shall treat this category only.

As we know, the general development of characters begins
with the pictograph and the phonetic-compound. In the evolution
between these two types, there was a great struggle between form
and phonetic, and though they were compromised, form still held
a dominant position. Here, we may point out that the important
shifts from the pictograph to the phonetic-compound, corresponding

to the three facets, are first, the changing of the form; second, the borrowing of phonetics; and third, the extension of
the meanings.

The changing of the form followed two principles: (1)
a drive toward simplification making the strokes as simple as
possible; and (2) limitations created by the materials and
tools of writing. The result of which is a trend away from the
pictograph; such as   ,   ,   ,   , which in modern
forms are seen to belong to a single classifier, but if we trace
them to their archaic forms they will be seen to have been derived from different forms. In modern characters when yüeh
and jou   were written individually they were different, but
when the latter was in combination it was written in just the
same form as yüeh, i. e.,   . This kind of confusion is the
failure of the pictograph, but fortunately such cases are not
too frequent.

The borrowing of phonetics was really a great danger
to the fate of the pictograph. The reason why the phonetic system can not be substituted for the pictograph has already been
discussed. The use of borrowed phonetics was and is sometimes
necessary, as when a writer found it impossible to create a new
character or when he forgot a pertinent character already in
use. The phonetic borrowing can be only temporarily used for it
makes further confusion if the same character is borrowed for
many uses. There was a natural tendency towards limitation for
the sake of a sharp distinction. The additional form, or classifier, was added to make the new meaning clear. With regard to

the extension of the meaning, the same confusion existed in that
the same character had multiple and different uses. It also
naturally needed an additional form or phonetic to impose a
limitation on the new meanings of a new character. From the
above we know that both the phonetic borrowing and the extension
of meaning were the result of an indulgence of a free and easy
use of pictographs. The endpoint was a confusion in meaning.
The clarification and restoration of order was achieved by adding
form-elements or phonetic-elements. The phonetic-compounds were
gradually made under these circumstances. It was a natural result of the conditions and other reasons such as the increasing
of the categories of classifications, the dialects, and the
development of a philosophical terminology, etc.

The principle of phonetic-compound is simple and logical.
It was combined from two parts, namely, form-element and phonetic element. The former can also be called classifier. The
character was so made that the form-element indicated the category to which the character (or the meaning of it) belonged, and
the phonetic-element was the phonetic symbol of the spoken language by which they called the object of such character. Such
as the character for goose is 鵝   , the form-element   meaning
'bird' or 'fowl' being at the right and the phonetic-element
(originally meaning I) being at the left. Goose in the spoken
language is e, therefore the character   pronounced as e was
used as a phonetic symbol here, and because goose is a fowl
the form-element   was added. Thus the form-element is the
classifier of the character and the phonetic-element is the pronunciation.

The majority of characters fall into the class of phonetic-compound. In later times when the phonetic-compound was established as one of the most conventional and convenient methods of expressing meaning, it was used to make new characters when new events required them.

V. Script

In the appendix I have translated a chapter from the Han shu i wen chih and the preface to the Shuo wen chieh tzu. The "Six Scripts" of the Han dynasty listed in the two books are nearly the same. The "Eight Scripts" of the Ch'in dynasty listed in the preface to the Shuo wen have two scripts duplicated with the Han "Six Scripts." Therefore there are ten types of script for both Han and Ch'in. They are:

1. Great seal

2. Bird and reptile script

3. Small seal

4. Old script

5. Rare characters

6. Li script

7. Curved seal script

8. Script on credentials

9. Script for titles of books or signs

10. Script on staves and handles of weapons

The last four scripts are those scripts which were written on special articles as seals, credentials, etc., but it has been found that the script on the seals or credentials of the Ch'in-Han period are either Small seal or Li script or sometimes

in the Bird and reptile script. Therefore these four scripts
can not be considered as a special script. The Rare characters
are said to be a branch of the Old script yet they are somewhat
different. They should be considered as Old script. Therefore
there are only five scripts to be discussed in the following
pages.

According to the above mentioned two sources, the Small
seal is the Ch'in script, so it was sometimes called Ch'in seal.
The characters 'great' and 'small' do not mean the size of the
character but rather they mean the age of the character. Great
seal is thus older than Small seal of the Ch'in dynasty. It has
been a great mistake for nearly 1800 years to attribute the
maker of the Great seal to a chief-recorder named Chou   of
Chou Hsuan Wang's time. This happened when scholars misinterpreted a sentence in the Shuo wen. It says, "And then at the time
of Hsuan Wang the chief-recorder compiled and wrote fifteen chapters of Great seal quite different from Old script." The character for 'compile' is chou. This sentence is derived from Pan Ku's
own commentary to his Han shu i wen chih which says, "The chief-
recorder of Chou Hsuan Wang made the (book called) Great seal."
In both Pan and Liu the character for 'made' is tso   and Shuo
wen first changed this character into a more archaic and refined
character chou   . Later scholars neglected the sources of
Shuo wen and read the character chou as the personal name of the
chief-recorder. The fifteen chapters of Great seal supposed to
have been compiled during the Late Western Chou period were in
the book which the recorder of the Chou dynasty used to teach
the young students. During 25-56 A.D. six chapters were lost

but when Hsü Shen compiled the <u>Shuo</u> <u>wen</u> he still had the advantage of using the remaining nine chapters. In his book he
quoted 223 characters from it. I compared these 223 characters
with the oracle bones and bronze inscriptions and got the following results:

       1. Similar to Shang oracle bones and bronzes 35%

       2. Similar to Western Chou bronzes   45%

       3. Similar to Eastern Chou bronzes   20%

This shows that the fifteen chapters of the Great seal were
actually compiled during Late Western Chou. The pre-Ch'in bronze
inscriptions could in general be called Great seal.

    According to <u>Ch'in</u> <u>shih</u> <u>huang</u> <u>pen</u> <u>chi</u> of <u>Shih</u> <u>chi</u> and
the preface to the <u>Shuo</u> <u>wen</u> after the unification under Ch'in
Shih Huang Ti the Prime Minister, Li Ssu   suggested to the
Emperor to put a stop to the use of scripts not uniform with the
Ch'in script. The government published three official Rhyme
books compiled by Li Ssu and other high officials to be used as
a standard book in writing by school boys. This book was mostly
adopted from the Great seal but greatly adapted and simplified.
This is the so-called Ch'in script or Small script. The writing
during the Chan Kuo period was very much confused. Each state
had its own style of writing. I have discussed in the chapter
on Geographical Distribution the fact that the Ch'in took over
the old territory of Chou in the western area, and since Ch'in's
culture was very low at the time she adopted the official writing
from Chou and preserved it longer and more strictly than the
other states. The unification of writing under Ch'in Shih Huang
Ti was simply a revival of a unified official writing which was
used throughout Western Chou and was weakened during the Ch'un

Ch'iu period and was very much disturbed during the Chan Kuo
period. The revival of the official writing was not the same
Great seal. The writing itself changed into a more simple form
owing to governmental affairs being more complicated. The inscriptions found on stone monuments and measurements of the Ch'in
dynasty after the unification were very uniform. This can be
called the Ch'in seal or Small seal. But if it is compared with
the following Ch'in inscriptions made before unification it shows
that there is little difference between them:

1. Measurement   **Chou chin:** 6.124

2. Weapon   **San tai:** 20.21

3. Weapon   **San tai:** 20.29a

4. Credentials   **Meng i:** 2.26

5. Credentials   **Hsiao chiao:** 14.90α

It is obvious that Li Ssu did not create a new script
but made the Ch'in official writing the only writing for official
affairs.

It is generally recognized that the Li script was first
used during the Ch'in dynasty, but it is very difficult to define
what kind of writing the Li script is. It was called Li script
because it was a simpler script used by low officials for legal
matters and garrison affairs. In the Small seal it preserved
the strokes in a round form and the Li script was in a square
angular style. The strokes of the Li script are much more simple.
They were used more often on bamboo or wooden slips. For monuments and other important events, the Small seal, or sometimes
the Great seal was used during the Ch'in dynasty. From Han and
later the Li script became the official writing. The Seal scripts

were used only on special important occasions. Thus the Great
seal was simplified into Small seal and the Small seal was simplified into the Li script; it is the continuous development of
the official writing from Shang to Han. The writing of today is
still the Li script.

The Bird and reptile script, sometimes called Bird script
or Reptile script, was found on many weapons and on some musical
instruments of Wu, Yüeh and Ch'u States. It covered a period
from Late Ch'un Ch'iu to the end of Chan Kuo. The characters
were written in the form of either birds or reptiles, or had one
or two birds added to them. There were bronzes, but comparatively
few, other than those of these three states which also had the
Bird script. The Bird script is often inlaid with gold. It is
obvious that this script was used in Southern China on some particular bronzes. The reason for using such script is unknown
to us.

The term ku-wen or 'Old script' first appeared in Shih
chi. It may possibly have appeared during the Ch'in dynasty and
referred to those writings before the unification and was discontinued afterwards. It was said that during the time of Han Wu Ti
many books in Old script were found in the walls of Confucius'
house. This discovery was not recorded in the Shih chi, but was
related both in Han shu i wen chih and the preface to the Shuo
wen. Ku-wen aroused more attention before and during the Wang
Mang reign when Liu Hsiang and his son, Liu Hsin, argued with
scholars that the study of Ku-wen should be listed in the official
school. It was first used to mean the Old script itself and
later was used to refer to the books found in Confucius' walls

and finally became the name of a school of which the two Liu
were the leaders. Wu Ta Ch'eng in his preface to Shuo wen ku
chou pu first considered Ku-wen as not being the script of Confucius' time but rather the script of the Six States, that is,
of the Chan Kuo period. Later Wang Kuo Wei suggested that the
fifteen chapters of the Great seal were the scripts used in the
Western States and the Old script was used in the Eastern States.
One thing is certain, that the date of the Old script is not
earlier than the Chan Kuo period. From these characters recorded
in Shuo wen as Ku-wen we get the impression that they are similar
to the inscriptions found on seals, coins, pottery and weapons of
the Chan Kuo period. They are similar because: first, they were
contemporary and second, they were not made by the officials.
Therefore I consider Ku-wen as a script of the Chan Kuo period
used by the scholars and the common people. The script is less
formal than the seal script and more free and simpler.

The above is a short survey of the scripts mentioned in
the Han dynasty. For the study of palaeography the bronze inscriptions are most important because: (1) they covered a long
period, from Shang to the end of Ch'in; and (2) they not only
covered official writing but also the unofficial writing as
shown on the Chan Kuo weapons. For this long period the bronze
inscriptions may be divided into four periods:

1. Shang inscriptions. The ends of the strokes are sharp.

2. Western Chou inscriptions. The characters were written
   carefully in a square and a round shape.

3. Ch'un Ch'iu inscriptions. The characters became lean and
   slender.

4. Chan Kuo inscriptions. The characters are loose and more
   free.

Appendix I

Translation of I wen chih of Han shu

The I says, "In ancient times (the ruler) regulated
affairs by means of knotted strings; in later times writing was
substituted by the sages. The hundred officers were controlled,
the myriad of classes were manifested. It was inspired by chüeh."
(the 43rd.of the 64 diagrams) "Chüeh, spread in the king's court,
means, 'it was spread and disseminated in the audience-halls of
the king." Its (the character's) usage was very great . In
ancient times when (a boy) was eight years old (he) went to the
primary school. So the Book of Chou Kuan (same as Chou li in the
chapter of) Pao Shih said, 'His (Pao Shih's) duty was to teach
the royal sons the liu shu   ' (six types of characters)
They were:

1. hsiang-hsin   (The imitation of pictures)

2. hsiang-shih   (The imitation of affairs)

3. hsiang-i   (The imitation of ideas)

4. hsiang-sheng   (The imitation of sounds)

5. chüan-chu   (Literally 'Turning and pouring')

6. chia-chieh   (Phonetic borrowings)

These are the fundamental methods of making characters.

At the beginning of the Han (when) Hsiao Ho made a
regulation which states, "The chief Recorder shall examine youthful students (to determine whether they are) able to recite and
write more than nine thousand characters. (If so they) are
therefore to be recorders. Again (they shall be) examined

tha Six Scripts. The best shall be chosen for appointment as a
secretary   in the Department of Secretaries   , or
in the Department of Yü-shih   . (If the) officers' and
the peoples petitions are not correct in writing they shall be investigated."

The Six Scripts are: (1) Ku-wen   (Old script)   (2)Ch'i-
tzu   (Rare characters in Old script), (3) Chuan-shu
(Seal script), (4) Li-shu   (Li script or lower officials'
script), (5) Miu-chuan   (Curved Seal used for writing on
seals), (6) Ch'ung-shu   (Reptile script). These were used
for fully comprehending ancient and modern characters, for drawing
seals, and for writing banners and credentials.

The ancient statutes said that writing must be in the
regulation script. If (it) is not known, then leave it aside and
inquire of the elders. During decadent times (there was) no
standard of right and wrong, people used only their own opinions,
so Confucius said, "I yet had the opportunity to touch fragments
of History. They are now gone." (Lun yü, Wei Ling Kung),

The Shih chou p'ien   was the book which the Recorder
of the Chou dynasty used to teach the youthful students. Its script
was different from the "Old script" which came from the walls of
Confucius' house. The seven chapters of the Ts'ang chieh
were made by Li Ssu, the Ch'in Prime Minister; the six chapters
of Yüan li   were made by Chao Kao, the Chief Officer of the
Chariots; the seven chapters of Po hsüeh   were made by Hu-wu
Ching, the Chief Recorder. These characters were mostly adopted
from the Shih chou p'ien but the Seal script (in these three books)
was quite different. It is the so-called 'Ch'in seal'. At that

time the Li script was created because officers' affairs and legal matters were greatly increased. (Therefore the strokes of
the characters) tended to be simplified, and (made) easy. It
was used in the affairs of prisoners.

In the beginning of the Han dynasty the school masters
of the common people combined the Ts'ang chieh, the Yüan li, and
the Po hsüeh, the three p'ien, into one, making sixty characters
to the chapter. There were fifty-five chapters altogether called
the Ts'ang chieh p'ien. In the time of Han Wu Ti, Ssu-ma Hsiang-
ju made the Fan chiang p'ien   without duplicated
characters. In the time of Han Yüan Ti, Shih Yu, Chief of the
Palace Eunuchs, made the Chi chiu p'ien   . In the
time of Han Ch'eng Ti, the Chief Architect, Li Ch'ang made the
Yüan shang p'ien   . These books utilized only the
characters in the Ts'ang chieh p'ien, but the Fan chiang used
some other characters. During Yüan shih (the Emperor) ordered
each scholar who knew the Hsiao hsüeh (palaeography), more than
a hundred of them, to come to court to record the characters.
Yang Hsiung picked out the most useful characters and made the
Hsüan ch'uan p'ien   continuing the Ts'ang chieh, but
changing the duplicated characters in the Ts'ang chieh. Altogether there were eighty-nine chapters. I (Pan Ku) continued
Yang Hsiung, another thirteen chapters, making one hundred and
two chapters without duplicated characters. The characters in
all of the books of the Six Arts are nearly complete here.

Ts'ang Chieh had many ancient characters (but) the
common school masters lost the pronunciations. In the time of

Han Hsüan Ti a man of Ch'i who could pronounce correctly was ordered (to the court) and Chang Ch'ang studied with him. (Chang Ch'ang) transmitted to his daughter's grandson, Tu Lin, who made a commentary (to the Ts'ang chieh p'ien)which is listed (in this catalogue).

Pan Ku's I wen chih is one of the volumes in Han shu which is a catalogue of books in Arts and Letters. This section is taken from the section of Hsiao hsüeh category in which he listed a group of word-books and made the statement above. The I wen chih is said to have been a copy of the catalogue by Liu Hsin called the Ch'i lüeh with some new materials added. The work of Liu Hsin was itself adopted from another work by his father, Liu Hsiang, called the Pi lu . This work is known only from quotations. Two of these fragments which are important for comparison with Pan Ku's work are as follows:

1. The Chief Recorder of Chou Hsüan Wang made the Great Seal.

2. All of the Classics (were written) in Old script. All writing has six fundamentals (that is, can be analysed in six classes : (1) hsiang-hsin; (2) hsiang-shih; (3) hsiang-i; (4) hsiang-sheng; (5) chuan-chu; (6) chia-chieh. There are six scripts: (1) Old script; (2) Rare characters in the Old script; (3) Seal script; (4) Li script; (5) Curved seal; (6) Reptile script. In Ch'in times legal officials' affairs were greatly increased and) the characters were simplified and made easy (to write). It (the Li script) was used in the affairs of prisoners, so it was called the Li script. (Li means 'prisoners').

Appendix II

Translation of Preface to Shuo wen chieh tzu

In ancient times when Fu Hsi was ruler of the empire, he
looked up and beheld the phenomena of the skies, down and saw the
colour and design of the birds and animals and that which was
proper to the soil. He took forms from the human bodies near
himself, and took forms from objects distant. Then (he) made the
I's Eight Trigrams to be symbols of the real world. Up to Shen
Nung, affairs were regulated by means of a knotted string. When
matters became more complicated, falsities appeared in abundance.
Huang Ti's recorder, Ts'ang Chieh, seeing the tracks of the birds
and animals, knew how to distinguish them (from one another) by
their signs, and first created writing. The hundred officers
were controlled, the myriad of classes were manifested. It was
inspired by chüeh. "Chüeh, spread in the king's court" means that
the culture was disseminated and made bright in the audience-halls
of the king. By means of it gentlemen obtained a salary, but it
is forbidden to have culture alone without virtue.

Ts'ang Chieh made characters by imitating the forms
according to the unit of (each class). Therefore they were called
wen   . Later when the picture and the phonetic were combined
it was called tzu   . (The character) tzu means 'to increase'
and 'become abundant'. Recorded on bamboo and silk cloth it was
called shu   . Shu means 'as'. To the time of the Five
Emperors and the Three Kings, the script changed to different
forms. The seventy-two kings (who went to) make a sacrifice at

T'ai Shan (left inscriptions on stone) which were not alike (in the scripts).

The Chou li says, "At eight they entered the primary school, (and) the Pao shih taught the royal sons first, the liu shu."   (They are:)

1. Chih-shih   : (indicative of affairs). Chih-shih is seeing (the character) and being able to know (it); observing and recognizing its meaning. Shang   (and) hsia   are examples.

2. Hsiang-hsin   : (imitation of pictures). Hsiang-hsin is a completed drawing of the thing following its shape and curves. Jih   (and) yüeh   are examples.

3. Hsing—sheng   : (form and sound in compound). Hsing-sheng is taking the affair as (part of the) character and completing (it) by adding a similar sound. Chiang   (and) ho   are examples.

4. Hui-i   : (assembly of ideas). Hui-i is units put together and meanings combined in order to bring out the point. Wu   (and) hsin   are examples.

5. Chuan-chu   : (the turning and pouring). Chuan-chu are characters which have been built up with the same classifier and so have a similar meaning passed on to each other. The example is k'ao   (and) lao

6. Chia-chieh   : (borrowing and lending). Chia-chieh (means a character) originally lacks its written form, and to carry out the affair (an already) established character with a similar sound is followed. Ling (and) chang   are examples.

And then at the time of (Chou) Hsüan Wang, the Chief

Recorder, compiled and wrote fifteen chapters of Great Seal quite
different from Old script. When Confucius wrote the Six Classics
and when Tso Ch'iu Ming made the Ch'un ch'iu chuan they both used
Old script. Their reason (for using the Old script) can be explained. Later on the feudal lords assumed power and were not
controlled by the king. Disliking the Ritual and the Music as
obstacles to them, they all rid themselves of the books and records.
Separated into the Seven States, the land-measures were different
in size, the roads were different in track-widths, the laws were
different in formulation, the garments and head-coverings were
different in style, the languages were different in sound, and the
characters were different in form. When Ch'in Shih Huang Ti first
unified the empire, the Prime Minister Li Ssu then memorialized
(to make all writing) the same, and put a stop to the use of
scripts not uniform with Ch'in script. Ssu made the Ts'ang chieh
p'ien; the Chief Officer of the Chariots, Chao Kao, made the
Yüan li p'ien; the Chief Recorder, Hu-wu Ching, made the Po hsüeh
p'ien. These were mostly adopted from the Shih chou (p'ien's)
'Great seal', but greatly adapted and simplified that which was
the so-called 'Small seal'. At that time Ch'in burned the
Classics and the books and swept away the old records, and sent
a great number of prisoners and troops to garrisons and forced
labour; (so) the duties of officers and legal officials were
greatly multiplied. Then the Li script first came into use in
order to make (the characters) simple and easy, and from that
time on the Old script was discarded forever. Since then Ch'in
had Eight Scripts: (1) Great seal, (2) Small seal, (3) Script on
credentials, (4) Reptile script, (5) Script on seals, (6) Script
for titles of books or signs, (7) Script on staves and handles of
weapons, and (8) Li script.

At the beginning of the Han the manuscript-style (called ts'ao shu) came into use.

The codified law said, "The youthful students who are more than seventeen years of age may begin to take an examination in reciting, reading, and writing nine thousand characters; then they may be a recorder. Again, they shall be examined in the Eight scripts. They shall be sent from the commanderies to the Chief Recorder (of the Imperial Government) to be examined together, and the best shall be chosen for appointment as a secretary in the Department of Secretaries. The writing, if not correct, shall be investigated." Now, although there is still the codified law, the examination is not held. Hsiao hsüeh was not cultivated, (and) its theory was not fully comprehended for a long time.

At the time of Hsiao Hsüan (someone) was called to the court who could read the Ts'ang chieh (p'ien) and Chang Ch'ang studied with him. The governor of Liang-chou, Tu Yeh, and Jüan Li of Pien, and the Chief-of-the-Teaching-Officials, Ch'in Ching were also able to understand (the Ts'ang chieh p'ien). At the time of Hsiao P'ing, (Jüan) Li and more than a hundred scholars were ordered to explain (and to record) characters at Wei-yang court. (Jüan) Li was entitled 'First Scholar of Hsiao hsüeh'. Yang Hsiung, High Attendant of the Imperial Palace, collected (the characters) to compile the Heüán ch'uan p'ien, together with Ts'ang chieh (making) fourteen p'ien, totalling five thousand three hundred and forty characters. The characters in all of the books are nearly all listed here.

At the time of the perished Hsin (Wang Mang's dynasty) the regency (of Han) ordered Chen Feng, the Ta-ssu-k'ung, and others to collate the written materials. (Wang Mang) himself seemed to create systems, changing and correcting the 'Old script' greatly. At that time there were six types of writing:

1. Ku-wen (Old Script), books from the wall of Confucius'
   house.

2. Ch'i-tzu (Rare characters), is Old Script, yet somewhat
   different.

3. Chuan-shu (Seal script), is small seal.

4. Tso-shu (Lower officials' script), is Ch'in's (dynasty)
   Li Script.

5. Miu-chuan (Curved seal) is used for drawing seals.

6. Niao-ch'ung-shu (Birds and Reptiles script), is used for
   writing on banners and credentials.

The 'books-from-the-wall' were found when Lu Kung Wang
pulled down Confucius' house discovering the Li chi, Shang shu,
Ch'un ch'iu, Lun yü, and Hsiao ching; and Chang Ch'ang, Marquis
of Peip'ing, offered the Ch'un ch'iu tso chih chuan (to the throne).
Also, commanderies and states often recovered ting and (other)
vessels from mountains and rivers. Their inscriptions were in
the 'Old script' of earlier dynasties, and all were alike.
Although the sources can not be found, the general situation can be
surmised.

But the people criticized them greatly .   (They) believed
it was those who had a fondness for the peculiar who changed
treacherously the original text, and falsified without evidence
the books whose sources were unknown (and) who rebelled against
the conventional way in order to be conspicuous in the world.
Those scholars who vied with each other in explaining and in commenting on the meaning of the Classics said, "The Li script of
Ch'in was the script of Ts'ang Chieh's time," and again (they) said,
"(Since) this was passed on from father to son, how could it be

moved (from the truth)?" They ranted saying, "The horse's head
and a man" was (the character) ch'ang   , "A man holding ten"
was (the character) tou   (a dry measure, a peck), and ch'ung
     was a curved chung   A judge of the court explaining
the law sometimes had recourse to characters in his explanations
of the law; (such as) "The K'o   (modern   ) people could
receive money because the character k'o   is made up of
'stop'   and 'hook'   (that means 'to stop a man and hook his
money')." Examples such as these are many and none are compatible
with the Old script of Confucius, and are in error with the
Shih chou p'ien. Vulgar scholars, those rustics, displaying
what (they) knew and hiding their ignorance, neither comprehended
thorough scholarship nor enquired of the fundamental principles
of characters. (They) were strange to the old arts and familiar
with wild talking, (they) considered what they knew to be
mystical, and that (they) had penetrated the hidden ideas of the
sages. (They) saw in the Ts'ang chieh p'ien the sentence, "The
younger son received the Imperial mandate." So they said, "This
(i.e., Ts'ang chieh p'ien) was made by an ancient emperor, and
its words have the tricks of the Immortals!" They strayed into
error and were not aware of it. How then could they not be
perverse! The Shu (ching, the I chi part of Kao yao mu) said,
"I wish to see the ancient men's symbols;" it means, "I must
follow the ancient culture and practice it, but yet not per-
vert it." Confucius said, "I yet had the opportunity to touch
fragments of History. (They are) now gone." For (those who)
reject what they do not know and yet do not inquire of other
men, (who) use only their own opinions, (who) are without a

standard of right and wrong, (who) have a smooth tongue and de-
vious expressions, lead all scholars away from the truth. The
character is the fundamental of both Classics and Arts, and is
the prime factor of government, and by means of them (our) forerunners have passed tradition on, and future generations can
understand their heritage. So it was said, "If the Fundamental
is established then the Tao (Principle) is brought forth" (Hsüeh
er of Lun yü) and "To know the world's utmost principle and yet
not disturb it." (Hsi tzu of I ching)

        (I am) now compiling (this work) with Seal script and
with both Old script and the Chou(-script, i. e., Great seal).
(This book) widely adopts from thorough scholars, in much and in
little. (It is) thrustworthy and offers evidence, it explains
and comments its statements. This (book) is the means to order
many groups, to dissolve errors, to enlighten scholars and to
disclose abstruse meanings. (The characters) are divided into
orderly groups and there is no confusion within the arrangement.
If a meaning is obscure then it has been made clear by means of
explanations.

        The editions are, Meng Hsi's I; K'ung An-kuo's Shu; Mao
Kung's Shih, the Li, the Chou kuan ; Tso Shih's Ch'un ch'iu, the
Lun yü, and the Hsiao ching. All were 'old script' (i. e., of the
Ku-wen school). That which I did not know, thereupon I left it
aside.

        Hsü Shen's preface to Shuo wen chieh tzu is now listed
at the end of his book (Vol. 15) before the table of Classifiers.
According to the second preface made by his son (now listed
after the table), he presented his father's work in 100 A.D. to
the throne when his father was sick in his old age. Shuo wen is
the first work which can properly be titled an 'Old Dictionary'

L 343

and both in method and in content it differs greatly from the
earlier word-books. The following points show the advance made
in _Shuo_ _wen_ over earlier works:

1. A great increase in the number of characters,
   altogether 9353 in number.

2. These 9353 characters are ordered under 540 classifiers.

3. Each character has an analysis of its form

4. Each character has a commentary on its meaning.

5. A pronunciation is given, and the phonetic element
   of compounds is noted where possible.

6. All scripts available are recorded.

7. The subject is given systematic treatment and presentation.

∠ ᴣ94

CHAPTER X
INSCRIPTIONS

The inscription on the vessels was called K'uan-shih in Feng shan shu of Shih chi. Inscriptions not only show facts of history, but they also reveal the style of composition, grammar, and dialects which help in determining the date and geographical distribution of the vessels. It is obvious that the inscriptions on bronzes are monuments for the study of ancient history. They are first hand materials, whereas the written histories were reconstructed and recopied from the earlier texts which are no longer extant. The written histories, especially those of the pre-Han period, are incomplete and full of contradictions. Therefore, while the critical study of written histories still helps us in dating the bronzes, the inscription on bronzes often supplement and check what was unknown or misconstrued in written documents.

In the previous chapter we discussed the different types of script. Script is the style of writing or the form of the characters. The differences in style are due to (1) the change of periods, (2) the geographical distribution, (3) the use of different tools, materials, and methods of writing, and (4) the different classes of writers. Both script and inscription can be arranged, just as shapes and decoration, according to periods and geographical distribution. This is in the field of palaeography. The results of which can be used as criteria to ascertain the date, geographical distribution and the class of writers.

Generally, the inscription was carved on the mould together with the decoration, so it was cast when the vessel was made. In later periods, however, the inscription was carved directly on the vessel after the vessel was made. Therefore we can divide inscriptions under the following heads:

      1. Cast

          a. incised inscription, intaglio, concave

          b. raised inscription, relievo, convex

      2. Carved or engraved

The early inscriptions were only names of the ancestors for whom the vessel was made to offer a sacrifice, the name of a person or family by whom the vessel was made, and the name of the vessel. The sacrificial vessel was the property of a family or a clan rather than that of a certain person. Therefore during the Shang period the inscriptions were mostly the clan name, the ancestor's name and the common name for the vessel. The ancestor's name was T'ien-kan   , the so-called temple name which is one of the ten day-names . On this day their descendants offered the sacrifice to the deceased ancestors. During this period there was no special name for the special type of vessel, so the vessel was called tsun   or I   or both. Usually the inscription was very short, not longer than twenty characters. In special cases the inscriptions were longer than the aforesaid, and the date and events were also given.

The criteria for a Shang inscription are:

      1. The script is earlier than that found on the
          Western Chou bronzes and similar to that on
          the oracle bones.

      2. The syntax is similar to that on the oracle
          bones.

3. Historical facts refer to Shang

4. Provenance is the An-yang site or other areas

   occupied by the Shang people.

It is not true that simple inscriptions must be Shang, for
the Early Western Chou inscriptions inherited many of the characteristics of the Shang style. Such as the Shang inscription begins with the day-name and ends with the year-name. Some of the
Early Chou inscriptions adopted this formula. The clan names were
used not only in Early Western Chou but they even appeared on
Middle Western Chou vessels. But, in general, the style of the
inscription changed at the beginning of Early Western Chou. The
personal name of the donor, although its use began during Late
Shang, was more popularly used in Early Western Chou. The length
of the inscription greatly increased until the end of Late Western
Chou when the inscription had five hundred characters—the same
length as some of the chapters in Shang shu. The contents of the
inscriptions in Western Chou may be divided into five groups:

1. Records of warfare

2. Ceremonial events

3. Rewards and commendations from the king

4. Appointments from the king

5. Records of disputes about land

All of these inscriptions were made by the officials
who were connected with the government. These inscriptions may
be treated as official documents or historical records. Five is
very rare and one to three are sometimes written in the Shang
inscription. Most of the inscriptions are prose, but during the
Late Western Chou rhymes were used in most inscriptions on the
musical instruments. The grammar of these inscriptions show
little geographical differences. Therefore I believe, that during

Western Chou a unified official writing was used in the official
documents. This was probably the Chou writing in the western area.
The character ke   meaning 'come' was often used in Western Chou
inscriptions. Fang yen, vol. I, says that besides ke, six other
characters were used in other areas to indicate the meaning 'come'
and ke was used in that area of the southern part of Shansi where
the river curved eastward. This is the old place where the Chou
people lived before they moved to Shensi province. Therefore the
ke is the Chou dialect while the Shang people used the lai
and chih   dialects instead of ke, which can be found on the
oracle bones.

The vessels of Western Chou were mostly limited to the
officials of the royal government. During the Eastern Chou period
the vessels were mostly made by the rulers or officials of the
different states. The inscription became formalized and shorter.
Rhymes were used quite often on musical instruments and other vessels. The contents of the inscriptions during the Eastern Chou
period may be divided into four groups:

1. Records of warfare

2. In praise of ancestral deeds

3. Vessels made for dowries

4. Names of donors, ancestors and vessels

Four returned to the old form but added formal expressions
of goodwill. During the Late Chan Kuo period the volume, weight,
and measurement of the vessels were recorded in the inscription
as well as the name of the caster. The inscription became very
short and simple in the Chan Kuo period.

During the Eastern Chou period the local characteristics
of the inscriptions can be found in the inscriptions. In Western
inscriptions the possessive case of the first person pronoun,

chen   was used throughout the period, but during Eastern Chou
in the inscriptions of Hsü[2], Chü, Ch'u, and Ch'i[2], t'ai was used
instead of chen. The apposition was used during this time, such
as, "I, the grandson of so and so." In Hsü[2] and Ch'i[2] the character yü   was used to indicate the first person pronoun in both
the nominative and the possessive cases.

  Generally, a vessel without a lid always has one inscription (which may be one or more characters), and the vessel with
a lid has two inscriptions which is called pair inscriptions or
tui-ming   in Chinese. The latter had the same inscription
both on the lid and on the body. But there are some exceptions:
(1) On the yu in Fogg 43.52.89 there is a third raised inscription
underneath the base; (2) On the yu in Chou chin: 5.85; Shuang
chien I: 1.32; Hakkaku: 12 and Shan Chai: 111, the inscriptions
on the lid are shorter and different from the inscriptions on the
body; (3) On the ting in San tai: 4.40-41 and San tai: 4.45b-46a
there are two long inscriptions on each vessel; (4) On the kuei
in San tai: 9.33b-34 the main cast inscription begins on the lid
and ends on the body and there are two carved inscriptions of
the later period on the outside of the lid and the body; (5) the
musical instrument, pien-chung has its inscription continued
from one bell to the other in the set.

  In most cases, the inscription of a particular class was
cast in a particular place on the bronzes. The most common
examples are:

    1. Ting   inside the wall underneath the rim
         between the ears. The inscription
         is generally on the large wall on
         rectangular ting.

    2. Li   as on ting except during the Late

Western Chou period when it was on the **rim**.

3. <u>Hsien</u>   as on <u>ting</u>

4. <u>Kuei</u>   inside the body in the middle of the bottom and inside the lid.

5. <u>Hsü</u>   as on <u>kuei</u>

6. <u>Fu</u>   as on <u>kuei</u>

7. <u>Tou</u>   as on <u>kuei</u> except during the Late Eastern Chou when it was on the stem.

8. <u>Tun</u>   as on <u>kuei</u>

11. <u>Chia</u>   inside the body in the middle of the bottom

12. <u>Ho</u>   underneath the handle and inside the lid

13. <u>Chüeh</u>   underneath the handle, sometimes on the pillar also.

14. <u>Chiao</u>   as on <u>ho</u>

15. <u>Tsun</u>   inside the body in the middle of the bottom, sometimes underneath the base.

16. <u>Chih</u>   inside the body in the middle of the bottom and inside the lid, sometimes underneath the base.

17. <u>Ku</u>   underneath the base

18. <u>Yu</u>   inside the body in the middle of the bottom and inside the lid.

19. <u>Fang-i</u>   as on <u>yu</u>

20. <u>Kuang</u>   as on <u>yu</u>

22. <u>Hu</u>   inside or outside the mouth. In Late Western Chou the inscription of the lid was on the tongue.

23. <u>Fou</u>   outside the belly

24. <u>Ling</u>   outside the shoulder

25.	Ts'ung	inside or outside the mouth
26.	Ying	inside the body
27.	Tan	outside the shoulder
28.	Min	outside the shoulder
29.	Cheng	inside the wall underneath the rim
33.	Yu	as on kuei
34.	P'an	inside the body in the middle of the bottom.
35.	I	inside the body in the middle of the bottom.
36.	Chien	inside the wall underneath the rim

Generally, the characters in one column run from top to bottom and the columns run from right to left which is the same as the Chinese writing today. But there are exceptions. On oracle bones, the columns and characters run either from left to right or from right to left according to the rules. There are two yu in our catalogue which have the same inscriptions. The columns of one of them (R. 330) run from left to right while the other (R. 229) runs from right to left.

The inscriptions on bronzes can be classified under four categories:

      I. Names

     II. Recordings of Events

    III. Names and Good-will Endings

     IV. Maker, owner, and the volume and weight

Shang bronzes have only I and II; Chan Kuo and Han bronzes have mostly IV. Western Chou and Ch'un Ch'iu bronzes have II and III. The names can be divided into six elements:

A. Clan name—one or two characters, or combined with
yü (R. 123-152), ts'e (R. 101-17), etc.

B. Ancestor's name—the name of the deceased person for
whom the vessel was made.

C. Donor's name—the name of the person who ordered the
making of the vessel.

D. Owner's name—the name of the person who owned the
vessel which was given by others as a gift, usually a
bridal gift.

E. General or specific names for the vessel.

F. Maker's name—the name of the craftsman who cast the
vessel.

The establishment of the "clan name" can be well shown
on several sets of bronzes in our catalogue. For instance, the
vessels in the Ling set (U.S. 652) were made by two generations
which had the same clan name. In the Tun set (U.S. 467), the
vessels were made by more than one donor of different generations,
but they had the same clan name. In the case of the Tun set some
vessels which were made by that clan mentioned only the clan
name and the ancestor name but they had no donor's name. In the
case of the Ch'en-ch'en set, U.S. 341 and 637, the clan name,
the ancestor name and the donor's name are mentioned, while
U.S. 54, 609, and 612 do not mention the donor's name.

The Ch'en-ch'en set (U.S. 341 and 637) has long inscriptions recording names and events, while U.S. 54, 609, and 612
record only names. This shows that the length of the inscription
has nothing to do with the date because both of them were made
about the same time.

The clan name was not used in Shang exclusively. We found vessels of Late Western Chou with clan names at the end of the inscriptions, but there are only a few or no vessels of that time which have the clan name only. The inscriptions having only clan names are mostly of the Shang or Early Chou period.

The ancestors included the senior and junior generations. The senior generation included both female and male. If the vessel were made for an ancestor for sacrificial purposes, the ancestor must be deceased. If the vessel were made for a person for entertaining purposes the person was alive when the vessel was made.

In the short inscriptions of Shang and Early Chou, while only the names were mentioned, the verb "made" was usually omitted. If the character "made" appeared it had to be immediately after the clan name or the donor's name, and immediately following "made" was the ancestor name or the general or specific name of the vessel. In longer inscriptions, this rule was also true: the donor's name must be before "made," the ancestor name and the name of the owner of the gift must be after "made" and before the name of the vessel. The clan name may be at the beginning of the inscription (R. 314) or at the end of the inscription (R. 166, 284) or at the top of the columns (R. 101) or at the bottom of the columns (R. 265, 377).

The donor's name can be either a personal name (R. 319, 328), or a title and a personal name (R. 334, 343), or a fief name and a personal name (R. 341, 442), or a fief name and a rank (R. 391, 413), or a personal name and the order among brothers (as Po, Chung, Shu, Chi, etc.); sometimes the personal name is

added to fu (R. 407-410) and others. The names which are combined with fu are of the Chou period. Sometimes the Shang inscriptions mentioned the donor's personal name, but not as often
as in the inscriptions on the Chou vessels. The donor's name
was at first the name of the person who ordered the vessel. Beginning in Late Western Chou, the vessels were often ordered by
the parents' family for their daughter's dowry. In this case,
the daughter was the owner of the bridal vessel. An exceptional example is
the yu in our catalogue (U.S. 571, 188) which was made by a King
(in the Shang dynasty) for his lady. In this case, the lady,
whose name is mentioned in the inscription, was the owner.

The maker's name was not mentioned until Late Chan Kuo
and it was usually mentioned in the inscriptions on the Han
vessels.

With few exceptions, Shang inscriptions seldom mentioned
the specific names of the vessels; only general names of the
vessel (tsun, i, or tsun-i) were mentioned. After the first
part of Early Chou both the general and the specific names for
the vessels were mentioned.

The different forms of the short inscriptions (with
names A-F) of Shang and Early Chou are listed below to show the
development of the inscription in that period:

    1. Clan name   A

      a. Shang

        Clan name only - R. 1-2; 3-4; 5-8; 9-12;
        13-15 and 456; 457; 16-18; 19-23; 24-26;
        30-37; 38-40; 41-43.
        Clan name at the end of the inscription, R. 153.

b. Early Chou

Clan name only - R. 277-279

Clan name at the end of the inscription - R. 284,
304, 305, 313, 315, 360, 377.

c. Late Western Chou

Clan name at the end of the inscription - R. 414,
415.

2. Ancestor's name   B

a. Ancestor's name only - R. 206, 212, 214

b. Plus "made" - R. 285

3. Clan and Ancestor's name   A, B

a. For Father - R. 36, 305

b. For Mother - R. 91

c. For Grandfather - R. 83, 241

d. For Grandmother - R. 246, 247

e. For Brother - R. 280, 281

f. For son - R. 98, 385

g. Omit "Father" etc. - R. 62, 79, 200

h. Plus "made" - R. 85, 249, 252, 311

4. Clan and general name for vessel   A, Ea

R. 301

5. Ancestor's and general name for vessel   B, Ea

R. 238, 300, 338, 351, 370.

6. Clan, ancestor's and general name for vessels   A, B, Ea

R. 144, 164, 273, 278.

7. Clan, Ancestor's and specific name for vessels   A, B, Eb

R. 297.

8. Clan, donor's and ancestor's name   A, C, B

R. 101

9. Clan, donor's ancestor's and general name for
   vessels   A, C, B, Ea
   R. 97, 314, 265, 266, 360, 377.

10. Clan, donor's and general name for vessels A, C, Ea
    R. 166.

11. Clan, ancestor's and general name for vessels C, B, Ea
    R. 318, 319, 324, 325, 331, 333.

12. Donor's and general name for vessels   C, Ea
    R. 289, 294, 344.

13. Donor's, ancestor's and specific name for
    vessels   C, B, Eb
    R. 362, 388.

14. Donor's and specific name for vessels   C, Eb
    R. 288, 375, 382

15. Donor's name only   C
    R. 386.

16. General name for vessels only Ea
    R. 363-369.

17. Specific name for vessels only   Eb
    R. 372

With the exception of 1c, the above examples are of the
Shang or Early Chou period. All of the inscriptions have "made"
except 1a (clan name only), 1b (clan name only), 2a and 3a-g.
Examples under 7-17 are Early Chou except 8. Examples under 1-3
are Shang and Early Chou. Examples under 4-6 are mostly Early
Chou; some might be Shang. From the above we may draw the following conclusions:

L. 406

Shang

    A Element only

    AB Combination

    AEa, BEa, ABEa, combinations (not often)

Early Chou

    A Element only

    AB Combination

    AEa, BEa, ABEa, combinations

    Combinations with C element

    Combinations with Eb element

    Ea element only

    B element only.

∠ 407

CHAPTER XI
Forgery and Casting

Forgery should be distinguished from imitation and copy. A forged vessel is a false reproduction of a vessel represented as itself the original vessel. A copy is a faithful reproduction of an object and represented as such. Imitation is the act of producing an artificial likeness of the original object. Thus in the study of bronzes a vessel that is an imitation should be catalogued in its own age, and a copy, though made later, could still be used as the authentic one.

The following specimen are examples of imitations which, quite often, had the dates inscribed:

1. Chung - Ontario: NB 4114
2. Chung - Tsun ku: 1.7
3. Chung - Ku kung: 41.14
4. Chung - Hsi ch'ing i: 17.18
5. Chung - Walters 54.2185
6. Chung - Hsiao chiao: 13.83.1
7. Chung - Hsiao chiao: 13.83.2
8. Tsun - Ku kung: 40.17
   Dated 1113 A.D.
9. Fu - Chin so
10. Hu - T'ao chai II: 2.46
    Dated 1114 A.D.

11. Tou - Shan chai: 174. Dated 1146 A.D.

12. Hsi - T'ao chai I: 7.46. Dated 1153 A.D.

13. Fu - Chin so. Dated 1304 A.D.

14. Chüeh - Ch'ing i: 8.17. Dated 1365 A.D.

15. Chüeh - Ch'ing i: 8.18. Late Ming dynasty

16. Chüeh - Nelson 44.8.3. Dated 1541 A.D.

17. Ting - Ch'eng ch'iu: 78. Dated 1635 A.D.

18. Ku - Hai wai: 81. Dated 1636 A.D.

Numbers 1-7 form a set of musical instruments which were
made in 1104 A.D. According to Yüeh chih of Sung shih in 1104 A.D.
the Emperor ordered a new set of chung to be made and the set
was called t'ai ch'en   . According to Yüeh chih of Chin
shih, during the Chin dynasty when T'ai Tsung captured K'ai-feng,
the capital of Sung, he got all of the musical instruments which
were made in 1104 A.D. Because the character ch'en was the
tabooed name of Chin T'ai Tsung, his officials at first used
yellow paper to cover the two characters t'ai ch'en, and in
1174 A.D. these characters were deleted and t'ai ho   were
carved in their place. On the other side of the chung, the
original characters remained which indicated the different tone
names. Thus in the inscriptions on the chung from 1 to 7, we
have the Sung inscription on one side and the Chin inscription
on the other side.

The above examples show the imitations of the Sung, Yüan
and Ming dynasties. These imitations were recorded in history
and in literature. However, during the Sung dynasty there were
not many deliberately made forgeries. Therefore, with but a
few exceptions, the vessels catalogued in the Sung works are

reliable. After Sung, forgeries were made in many places. In
the Ming dynasty, Kao Nien   in his book, Tsun sheng pa
chien   ; 1428 said that during the Yüan dynasty a
woman named Chiang Niang-tzu   of Han Chou and a man
named Wang Chi   of Ping-chiang (both in Chekiang province)
were experts in forgery. He also said that during his time, in
Shantung, Shensi, Honan and Nanking forgeries of sacrificial
vessels were made. The forgers used authentic vessels as their
models so the size, decoration and inscription of the forged
vessels were very similar to the real pieces.

    Many forged vessels are included in the four Imperial
Catalogues of the Ch'ing dynasty. Some of them might have been
handed down from the Ming dynasty. Among those forgeries, quite
a number were excellently made such as the one in Pao yün: 53.
Before the Ch'ien-lung period the false vessels and the false
inscriptions were cast at the same time, therefore if the inscription is a fake the vessel is also a fake. In the early
period of the Ch'ing dynasty, the false inscriptions were often
copied from the vessels drawn in the Sung Catalogue. Frequently,
the forged vessels in the Shang or Early Chou style were inlaid
with silver and gold which is a technique that did not exist
during the Shang or Early Chou period. For examples, the hsien
in Ku kung: 26.7 (London: No. 6) and the kuei in Pao yün: 60
were made with the above mentioned technique and they are definitely fakes. Yung Keng, however, included them in his
Shang chou (Nos. 178 and 309) and considered them genuine. The
kuei was probably copied from a kuei in Liang lei: 6.28. Both
the shape and the inscription seem to indicate that it was

copied from the Liang lei one, but the false one changed the base
and added pendants to the ears. When Yüan Yüan edited the Chi
ku, a catalogue of Bronze inscriptions, he included many false
inscriptions from the Imperial Collection.

After the Ch'ien-lung period, forgeries can be grouped
under two categories: (1) false inscriptions are added on authentic vessels; (2) vessels are recast by using authentic vessels
as models. The former was unknowingly encouraged by scholars
who bought only bronzes with inscriptions. Liu Hsi-hai, for an
example, was stationed in Shensi and bought bronzes only when
they had good inscriptions. The famous forgeries were made in
Wei Hsien   in Shantung province, the native district of
the famous collector Ch'en Chieh-ch'i who was an authority on
the authenticity of antiquities and an expert on the making of
rubbings. Sometimes the dealers who were sent by him to collect
bronzes copied the authentic bronzes for recasting. Because
Wei Hsien was famous for the excellence of its forgeries, even
those forgeries not made in Wei Hsien have been often attributed
to these industrious hard working people. As a matter of fact
the super forgers are fairly widely scattered. The famous
makers during this period were as follows:

    Shensi province: Su brothers, Chou family (most probably
               in Ch'ang An).

    Shantung province: Chi Nan: Hu family

                Wei Hsien: Chao, Fan and other families

    Chiangsu province: Suchow: Ku family

    Hopei province: Hen-shui: Chang family

The technique of making forgeries has greatly improved
in recent years because of the very fine publications of the
collotype catalogues which enable forgers to copy more accurately.
Furthermore, more tricks are used in forgery, such as the
authentic patina which is used to cover a false surface or the
authentic lid of one vessel is put on an authentic vessel whose
lid was missing. When parts of a vessel are missing they easily
pick up some authentic broken parts of another vessel and add
them to the vessel in question. They have a knowledge of dating
so they make Shang inscriptions on Shang vessels. The best
forgeries and restorations were done in Peiping and Shanghai.

A bronze may be forged in many ways. Below we list
some of the very common catagories and illustrate them by
examples from our catalogue or from other sources:

I. Complete forgery - both vessel and inscription

I have discussed in details, in our catalogue, the
forged body of the Mo-tzu yu (Pillsbury Collection; U.S. 634).
Besides this, I am quite uneasy about vessels in U.S. 141, 249,
344, 392, 453 and 569. Because of over cautiousness, I have
excluded some vessels from our catalogue which might be authentic.
In Shang chou: II, 138, Yung Keng reproduced a rectangular ting
whose inscription appeared in Hsü k'ao ku: 4.17. When we compare this ting with the one in the Sung catalogue we find that
the designs are very different. As a rule, the vessels catalogued in Sung times were all lost, so the one in Shang chou is,
no doubt, a complete forgery.

After carefully handling the following vessels in

American collections, which have been illustrated in various
catalogues, I have found that they are fakes or doubtful pieces:

1. Ku - Shina kodo: 16; Foreign Collections: 38;
   Chicago 25.359.

2. Yu - Shina kodo: 72; Holmes: B29

3. Kuang - Shina kodo: 144; Fogg 44.57.3

4. Yu - Yin and chou: pl. 26, A64; Freer 11.55

5. Tun - Foreign Collections: 11; Walters Gallery

6. Kuei - Foreign Collections: 21; Buckingham: 80-82;
   Chicago 31.12

7. Hu - Foreign Collections: 52; Walters Gallery

8. Hu - Foreign Collections: ᵗ⁸; Buckingham: 77-79;
   Chicago 31.10

9. Hu - Boston 29.1079

10. Hu - Foreign Collections: 61; Walters Gallery

Vessels 8 and 9 are gilded hu and 6 was made by the
same technique. Chicago's gilded hu and Boston's gilded hu
are about the same size and, with the exception of their ears,
are alike in every way. In my draft for Buckingham I noted,
"This vessel is particularly puzzling because adequate materials
for comparison are lacking." However, if we compare this pair
with the gilded incised hu in U.S. 737 (also of the Art Institute
and those the gilded hu listed under 737 u.s.
of Chicago) we must feel that something is wrong with this pair.
My personal opinion is that vessel 8 should not be included in
the catalogue because there is still a question in my mind about
its authenticity.

A huge bell in Brundage's Collection has an inscription
that is an imitation of that on the Tsung Chou chung in the

Palace Museum (fig. 49 in our catalogue, discussed under U.S. 259).
Brundage's inscription was reproduced in Chou chin: Vol. I,
supplement 11-12 and Hsiao chiao: 1.94-95 and differs from the
Palace's (San tai: 1.65-66a). The design on Brundage's chung
is also different from that on the Palace's. Brundage's chung
was formerly in Sheng Ping-ch'eng's (1823-1895) Collection and
was brought to America in 1928 by Li Wen-ching, a Shanghai dealer.
It is probably the same one that is catalogued in Chi ku: 3.8-11
and Chün ku: 32.56-57.   Chi ku was published in 1804.

If a bell had a long inscription it was divided into
several parts and written in several places on the bell. The
different places were:

       a. Lower right of the front

       b. Upper center of the front

       c. Lower left of the front

       d. Low right of the rear

       e. Upper center of the rear

       f. Lower left of the rear (front and rear are the
          two sides of the bell).

The general rule was for the several parts of the inscription to run in one of the following orders:

       I. b, c

         b, c, d

         b, c, d, e, f, a

      II. a, b, c

     III. c, d

The inscription on the Palace chung runs, b, c, d; while that on
Brundage's runs, b, c, a which is certainly wrong. Furthermore,

the missing strokes on the Palace's are also missing on Brundage's and there are more mistakes on the latter because the forger carved the forged inscription from a rubbing which was not very clear. Even so, the forged inscription on Brundage's <u>chung</u> was nicely done. So before 1804 there were good forged inscriptions which were faithfully copied from those on authentic vessels.

I have seen a <u>kuei</u> in America, first catalogued in <u>Chi ku</u>, with an inscription that seems to be perfect. Yet the vessel is a very doubtful piece even though the inscription looks like a genuine one.

II. Part Forgery

    A. Part or parts added to authentic vessels which did not belong to them.

    B. Forged inscriptions added to authentic vessels.

    C. Authentic inscriptions inserted in forged vessels.

IIA. The lids of U.S. 603 and 680 were added by dealers. The lid of U.S. 680 has the same inscription as that on the authentic body; both the lid and the inscription on the lid are fakes. In our catalogue U.S. 243 (a lid) and U.S. 244 (a body) have the same designs but different inscriptions, and so they do not belong to the same vessel as they are supposed to. The handles of the <u>kuei</u> in U.S. 151 were added by a dealer. It was originally a <u>kuei</u> without handles with an all over decoration. When the <u>kuei</u> had handles the craftsman usually left a plain part underneath the handles. On this <u>kuei</u> (U.S. 151) the added handles cover a part of the decoration which proves that the handles were added later. The lid of the <u>kuei</u> in U.S. 246 was added later and the inscription is a copy from the authentic body.

IIB. There are only a few examples which have forged
inscriptions added to authentic vessels. The best speciman is
the yu in Hsi ch'ing: 15.20 which was destroyed when the Allied
troops burned the Palace Yüan-ming-yüan during the Boxer Rebellion
in 1900. A piece of the body with the inscription was saved and
was at one time in the Collections of Wang I-yung and Liu Ê. A
dealer took it and built it into a new yu. It is illustrated in
Shan chai: 116. If we compare the picture in Shan chai with the
drawing in Hsi ch'ing we will find out that the new one has a
different style and design from the authentic one. The latter
had the same design as that on a kuei in the same set (Shang
chou: II, 271). Without any doubt, Shan chai's is a forged vessel with an authentic inscription. Another example is a kuei
in Meng yi I: 1.25 which was originally a fragment with an
authentic inscription that was built into an old vessel.

IIC. Forged inscriptions can be divided into two groups:
(1) a forged inscription that is added to an authentic inscription; and (2) a thorough forged inscription carved into a vessel
which never had an inscription. There are only a few examples
of the former. A ting in Yeh Chih-hsien's Collection had nine
characters when it was found as shown in Chia chai: 6.13.4. A
dealer named Su of Shensi asked a forger named Chang to add one
hundred and thirty characters as shown in Ching wu: 1.32.
Another example is the tsun in Ch'eng ch'iu: 28 which had three
authentic characters but eight characters were added on both
sides of the authentic inscription.

The thorough forged inscription has been discussed in details by Shang Ch'eng-tso in an article entitled "A Study of Forged Inscriptions on Chinese Bronzes," Nanking Journal, Vol. 3, no. 2. Forged inscriptions can be classified under three catagories: (1) the early period of the Ch'ing dynasty when the forgers copied the inscriptions directly from the Sung catalogues. The beginning and the ending of the strokes were very sharp because the Sung catalogues were reprinted many times and the characters were far from the original inscriptions. (2) The inscriptions are composed of sentences and phrases taken from different inscriptions. The forgers did not have a formal education, therefore the false inscriptions were poorly written and ungrammatical. Vessels in U.S. 157, 202, 793 and 795 are of this kind. (3) Inscriptions forged in recent years. The forgers knew that copying inscriptions from the Sung catalogues, altering certain characters from authentic ones and composing sentences and phrases from various inscriptions were out of date and could be very easily detected so their technique of false carving has greatly improved. They just copy faithfully the inscriptions from authentic vessels and carve them on vessels that never had inscriptions. In our catalogue, the inscription on the p'an in U.S. 820 was copied from a fragment of a p'an in Shan chai: 94. The original fragment was of the Ch'un Ch'iu period, but the forger took it and carved it on an Early Chou p'an (U.S. 820). The same mistake was made in U.S. 798.

An ultra-violet examination might help us, to a certain extent, to detect whether the vessel is in tact and whether new parts have been added. A chemical analysis and a microscopic

examination are also useful in determing authenticity by studying the surface, the crystallographic texture and the composition of the alloy. Poor qualities or coarse techniques do not
mean that the vessels are fakes. Such vessels are vessels that
were ordered by the middle or lower classes and/or made for
burial purposes. Generally, they were simple, thin and coarse.

The connoisseur of bronzes needs an accumulation of
knowledge concerning every aspect of the bronze—techniques of
casting, styles of writing, and the various designs, and the
long experience of handling the bronzes. One of the best ways
to become a connoisseur is not to condemn a fake if we are not
quite sure and admit that we often make wrong judgments.

There are two different theories about the method of
casting Chinese bronzes. One is the cire perdue or lost wax
process which is held by Professor Yetts in his "Techniques of
Bronze Casting," Eumo, Vol. I, pp. 34-39. The other method is
the direct process which is discussed in O. Karlbeck's "An-yang
Mound," BMFEA, no. 7, pp. 39-60. From the discovery of cores,
models and moulds in An-yang in the thirteenth expedition by
the Academia Sinica, certain facts reveal that more arguments
support the view of direct casting. A model was first fashioned
in the form of the vessel to be made. The model was made of
solid clay and was baked , hence the inner part became reddish
and the surface shiny black. The designs were drawn in red
on the surface and then the unpainted parts were engraved. The
result was the red painted designs remained on the surface and
the incised parts were black, the original color of the surface

L 41

of the model. The mould pieces were made from the model. The
number of the mould pieces in one vessel differs in different
types of vessels. When casting, the solid cores were surrounded
by clay mould pieces with a little space, the required thickness
of the bronze to be made, between the cores and the mould pieces.
The clay mould pieces were connected by means of mortise and
tenon. On the outside (the undecorated side) of the mould pieces
were grooves and holes to be fastened by clay belts. The mould
pieces could be used only once that is why many bronzes in one
set are never identical. In the process of casting, the molten
liquid bronzes were poured through the center of the core on the
base (the mouth of the vessel facing downward). That is why on
the base of the kuei, p'an, etc. there are two holes on both
sides of the base which served as exists for the liquid bronze
to pass through and fill up the space between the cores and the
mould pieces. In some cases small clay plates with engravings
were inlaid in the main model. The long feet of the chüeh and
the ears on the large ting were sometimes cast separately.
During the Eastern Chou period many parts of the vessel (like
the ears and legs) were often cast separately and soldered to
the main body.

L419

CHAPTER XII

CULTURAL BACKGROUND

I. Shang*

From an archaeological point of view Chinese history may
be divided into three periods: (1) pre-historic, i.e., before the
Shang dynasty when no authentic written records existed; (2) from
the Shang dynasty (1300 B.C.) to the unification of China by the
Ch'in dynasty (221 B.C.) when written histories in very incomplete
forms existed; and (3) from the Ch'in dynasty to the present day.
For this period we have detailed and authentic written histories
for more than twenty-one centuries. Chinese scholars consider
the first two the ancient or archaic periods (ancient history begins with the so-called "Three Dynasties") and the last the
modern period.

During the past twenty years both Chinese and Western
scholars have made significant excavations of Neolithic sites
from various places in North China. They found many pieces of
pottery, bones and stones but no writing or architecture, and
there is no written record to identify the date of these finds.
We have no chronology for the pre-historic period. The whole
period is shrouded in myths and legends and we can not rely upon
them. For this reason we are leaving it out of our treatment.
Our knowledge of the Hsia, the first of the Three Dynasties, is
equally limited, so much so that we can never place any object

---

*A lecture delivered in the Anthropology Department,
University of Chicago, April 15, 1946. Published in Human Origins,
Selected Readings, series II, second edition, 1946, University of
Chicago.

with certainty in that dynasty. Even knowledge of the Shang (or
Yin) dynasty, the second of the Three Dynasties, remained obscure
until the discovery of the oracle bones at the end of the nineteenth century. The oracle bones are the tortoise shells and
scapulae of animals which royal diviners of the Shang kingdom
used in divinations and on which they incised their records.
These records were the questions from the kings or the diviners
asking about war, sacrifices, hunting, harvest, weather and so
forth. The answers were supposed to have come from the spirits.
Chinese scholars have tried to read and decipher these archaic
inscriptions for forty years and now at last can understand them
but yet with some little difficulty. From them we can reconstruct
a table of the kings which is the same as that recorded in the
Yin pen chi of Shih chi made some fifteen centuries later. So we
have been able to use archaeological materials together with written documents to reconstruct the outline of the beginning of
Chinese culture.

From 1928 to 1937, the National Central Research Institute
made several scientific excavations in the old Shang capital, called An-yang. Besides the oracle bones the excavators recovered
white and grey pottery, carved jade, bones, ivory and marble objects, shell objects, and bronze and stone objects. They also
unearthed architectural remains and hundreds of tombs and from
this we know how our ancestors lived and also how they were buried.
Basing my facts on this first-hand material, I shall try to describe the Shang civilization.

On the origins of the Shang tribe we can but make conjectures. Concerning the derivation of the original ancestor,
both the Shang and the tribes of the area to the northeast had the

common myth that this person was hatched out of a bird's egg.
Both areas in their divination procedures made an extensive use
of scapulamancy. In recent excavations held by Japanese scholars
the oracle bones were found near Port Arthur. Finally, it will
be recalled that the dolmen structure was known to both the tribes
of the northeast and to the Shang people. It then seems probable
that the Shang people came from the northeast near the sea known
as Pei Hai, and moved southward into what is now present day
Shantung province. About 1600 B.C. the king of Shang, named T'ang,
moved westward and came into contact with Hsia. The earliest historical references note that T'ang conquered Hsia. After nine
generations, ca. 1300 B.C., P'an Keng established his capital at
An-yang in Honan province. Since the name of the capital was Yin
later people called this half of the Shang dynasty the 'Yin' to
distinguish it from the earlier part. The Chou people, as we
learn from the bronzes, used 'Shang' as a place-name and 'Yin' as
the name of the people. Of the discoveries, both fortuitous and
scientific, nothing dates before the time of P'an Keng.

        Strictly speaking it is inaccurate to call the Shang cul-
ture the beginning of Chinese culture, for at that time the
technique of bronze casting had reached such a peak of high
quality that it not only surpassed all succeeding dynasties, but
even in the whole world it is not easy to find material for comparisons. So also was the standard of the carved jade, ivory,
bones and the marble sculptures. The writing had already developed
to such a degree that we can hardly call it primitive. The Shang
State was not a tribe, it was a kingdom. The state was divided
into five quarters, one in the center called middle Shang and four
quarters in the four directions. In the middle was the capital

called the Great City of Shang. The borders to the four directions were within three to five hundred miles. Within and on the borders were smaller cities. Although we do not know where the borders were located we have records that these were east and west borders. Inside, these four borders were controlled by the king of Shang; outside, there were feudal lords and allies. Under the king were officials who may be divided into three classes: (1) priests, (2) historians, and (3) military officers, whose names have been found on the oracle bones. The king often gave orders to his officers and officials , to his feudal lords and to his allies.

The rule of succession, which we may call fraternal succession, was at first from elder to younger brother and thence to the sons of the elder brother. At a later period the succession, which we may call primogeniture, was from father to son, probably to the eldest son. Sacrifices were made to the direct ancestors all the way back to the beginning. For the collateral ancestors, sacrifices were offered only to those within five generations. The former were called the Great Ancestors and the latter were called the Small Ancestors. The brothers of the father or grandfather were called father and grandfather respectively. In sacrifices the female ancestors were treated just like the male ancestors. They also received fiefs from the king and commanded armies to fight, if needed. The king had more than one wife, but only those whose sons became kings received the offerings from their descendants. These are the facts about the family relationships of the royal family found on the oracle bones. The common people might have had a similar system although we do not have it on record.

The feudal system existed at that time. There were the ranks of duke, marquis, earl, viscount, sir and so forth. Some of

these names were derived from the names of relationship. They were
the relatives of the royal family and they were given fiefs and
made the landlord or ruler of a certain area. There were also
feudal lords outside the royal family who, under the protection of
Shang, defended the borders for the Shang. We have some clues as
to the slave system. The slaves were probably the defeated foreign
tribes. These slaves had a special kind of braided hair on top of
the head. They were found in a thousand small tombs near the
Royal Tombs, buried in groups of five or ten with the heads buried
separately from the bodies. These may have been slaves who were
killed and used in a "companionate burial." They were also killed
as sacrifice during the great ceremonies.

The important affairs of the kingdom were dominated by the
priests. It is more accurate to say that the priests were the real
rulers. They functioned as the intermediaries between the gods of
nature and the ancestors and the living king. They were supposed
to receive the mandate from above through the oracle bones. As
we know, whenever the king intended to do anything he had to ask
the diviners to make the request of the god or an ancestor.first.
They were also closely affiliated with the historians. All of
them held important positions in deciding sacrifices, wars and
with regard to the calendar. It is probable that aside from the
royal family they were the only part of the aristocratic class
who could write and who knew all the rituals, the calendar and the
history of their nation.

We may divide the religious practices into two parts; the
worship of ancestors and the worship of the spirits. The Shang
people held the belief that their ancestors still had their powers
above, that the ancestors might act harmfully or beneficially

toward their descendants and the reign. Therefore, on special
occasions, such as during a great war, harvest, or flood, a report
would be made to the ancestors. As to the spirits, they worshipped
the Spirit of Earth, of the Sun and the Moon, of Fire, Wind, Rain,
Rivers and Mountains. The most powerful spirit was called Shang-
Ti   (Shang meaning 'above' and Ti having a meaning somewhat
close to God), whose life was conceived of as being similar to
that of an ideal king having a court and high officers and having
direct influence with the earthly king and his reign. Shang Ti
held the sovereign power to give rain and various blessings and to
grant an approval of actions. He could also dispense sickness,
calamity and famine and reject courses of action. There is no
hint that Shang Ti was thought of as a person or as one of the deceased kings. He was only a God of Nature.

Dancing, accompanied with music, was used exclusively in
appeals for rain. From theirfrequent requests for rain we know
that the Shang people's main occupation was agriculture. The pro-
duce included grain, panicled millet, black millet (or probably
glutinous rice) and wheat. In the Ontario Museum there is a food
vessel, unearthed at An-yang, in which there are remains of some
rice. Wine was made from the rice and spirits from the wheat and
millet. From the black millet they made a special spirit which was
mixed with herbs. They used the ploughshare and the plough which
were drawn by an ox and sometimes by an elephant or a dog. The
kings practiced hunting quite often and they divided the hunting
land into four quarters and fired it during the hunts. The people
used nets to catch birds and fish, though fishing hooks were also
used. It is interesting to point out that the Shang people had
two meals per day; the heavy meal in the morning and the light

meal in the afternoon. It is still the custom among most modern
Chinese peasants to have the heavy meal before they go to work.

It is quite an astonishing fact that not only linen but
also silk was used at that time. We can draw a simple form of the
dress from a jade sculpture: a high hat, a short coat with a cross-
collar and the lapel of the coat buttoned under the right arm, a
short petticoat, puttees or leggings, and shoes with a sharp toe
turned up. The peculiar point of buttoning the coat under the
right arm, which persists to the present day, is a pure Chinese
custom. In earlier times Confucius pointed out that the barbarians
buttoned their coats on the left and did not dress their hair.
The Shang people used combs to dress their hair and they used hair-
pins of carved bone or ivory. They also wore jades. They sat on
mats and therefore the tables were very low. The rectangular-
shaped house always faced south. The gabled roof was supported by
wooden pillars and the wall was built of pounded earth. When
building the wall a wooden board frame was used, loose earth was
piled into it and then pounded down. The pillar base was placed
between the raised platform and the pillar. In the case of the
palace, a bronze base was used instead of the natural round stone.
When we found the chambers of the royal tombs the walls and ceil-
ings were painted and carved marbles were used as decoration. It
may be suggested that the palace also had such decorations. The
decorated bronze vessels for containing and heating food and wine
were daily used by the royal family.

The army was divided into three columns, one in the center
and a left and right wing. Sometimes there were armies numbering
as high as ten thousand men. The chariot used in war was driven
by four horses and these chariots had four yokes. The basket of
it was shaped like a Chinese dustpan with a high front. The

chariot was made with wooden frames and had bronze fittings. On
the head and back of the horses were trappings and harness made
of both bronze and leather. The main weapons were the bronze
dagger, axe and spearhead on a long wooden pole, the bronze arrow-
head and bow, and the knife-shaped weapon. The elephant was also
used during the fighting. The warriors wore helmets and possibly
armor.

The musical instruments were hand bells without clappers,
three of different tones forming a set, which were struck on the
outside with a mallet; musical stones, leather or serpent skin
drums on wooden frames; flutes and an ocarina-like instrument
made of pottery, bone or stone.

The only established fact of the Shang economy is that
they used cowrie shells and perhaps these cowrie shells had the
significance of money. Although the character for the Shang
dynasty has the meaning of merchant, we are not in a position to
suggest that there were merchants at that time. However, since
the turquoise, jade, cowries and tortoises were not produced in
the Shang area, they must have had some exchange with frontier
tribes.

The patterns on the white pottery has little relation
to those found on Neolithic pottery. They are more advanced and
are affiliated with the bronzes. These most beautiful bronze
vessels came into use suddenly. They were cast by the direct
method, although the moulds were made separately *in pieces* and put together
when casting. A vessel was made as a whole piece in one single
casting operation. The decorations used on the bronzes were also
used on the jades, bones, ivory and marbles. Carved bones,
bronze weapons and chariot fittings were often made with a tor-

quoise inlay.   The factories were found in the Shang capital.

The Shang calendar seems to be of a luni-solar type. The
year was solar, which gave 365 days to the year, but the month,
which we still call 'moon', was a lunar month measured by the complete revolution of the moon. Therefore the twelve lunar months,
which made a year in Shang, was shorter than a solar year. For
this reason after a certain period, an intercalary month was added
to the year. It was called the 13th month. In the later part of
Shang, this intercalary month was added, not after the last month,
but under certain considerations, could follow any month. If it
followed the third month, there had to be two 'third' months in
that year. The long months had 30 days and the short months had
29 days. They were often so arranged that one alternated with the
other. On the oracle bones only the seasons of spring and autumn
are mentioned. The Shang people divided the month into three
cycles, each lasting for a period of ten days. A day was divided
into day and night; for the day there was a further subdivision into dawn, early morning, large meal time, noon, small meal time, and
twilight or evening. The Shang diviners recorded some of the con-
stellations and solar and lunar eclipses.

There is no trace of writing on any of the Neolithic pottery found in North China. On the black pottery, which is supposed to be a little earlier than the Shang grey pottery, no
writing was found except for a few marks. On the oracle bones,
the bronzes, and on the white and grey pottery we have found writing made by means of the brush, the stylus and by casting. They
are all within the Shang period. Therefore until the present,
with all of the materials available, we know that the Shang writing
is the earliest. On those materials there are about 2000 characters, of which more than half have been deciphered. The structure

of the character can be simplified into three basic types. First
is the pictograph, but the character itself is much simpler than a
picture. Second is the phonetic borrowing in which the pictograph
was used as a phonetic symbol which had no relation to its pictographic origin. Thus a pictograph of a woman, when it was used to
indicate the second person pronoun 'you', was only because in the
spoken language 'woman' and 'you' had the same pronunciation.
Third is the phonetic compound, which is a combination of two elements; one functioned as a pictographic element and the other was
a phonetic symbol. This last type later became the most important
method for creating new characters. The Chinese character, through
the long period of 3500 years still preserves its original construction and function, only changing in the less important matter
of the style of writing, making new characters by the old ways
and simplifying the strokes for convenience in writing.

Together with the spoken language it represents a special
thinking method derived from the whole cultural background. It is
the central nervous system of the culture, and by means of it we
conquer the many different dialects and the vast areas broken and
interrupted by high mountains and deep waters. This nation has
been unified as a cultural whole from Shang to the present day.
Only by studying the Chinese language can we better understand the
genesis of the Chinese civilization.

So far I have not fulfilled the assignment on the question
of "How much of the Chinese Civilization was borrowed from the
West?" I do not think that I am qualified to answer the question
since my knowledge of the West is meagre. I am not in a much better position than those Western scholars who try to find western
influences in Chinese culture with so very little knowledge of

China or the Chinese language. It is both fortunate and unfortunate for a Chinese scholar that the study of Chinese culture involves vast and extensive materials for about 4000 years, with a continuous and fully developed and complicated history of language, literature, art, and thought. Only from industrious research can we deduce facts and create theory. It is easy to make conjectures but it is dangerous to do so without proper research. The theory that Chinese culture came from the West was first made in the nineteenth century when Chinese military and political integration was at its lowest ebb. Western visitors with little idea of Chinese culture or history may perhaps have been unconsciously influenced by an imperialistic tendency and not a little sense of racial superiority which led them to draw conclusions not wholly scientific. The scientific excavations of recent years which uncovered the long obscure Shang culture must correct the conception that China was a nation lacking a very high and refined standard of culture. Even with great admiration for its excellent art, some scholars still endeavor to find the origins of the Chinese civilization in western sources. They neglect the migration and communication situation of that time, of which we know practically nothing. They neglect the fact that units of culture developed independently might have fortuitous similarities. They neglect the philosophy, religion and literature, important as these factors are. Imagine a western hero riding on a horse, with a set of weapons, pottery, bronzes and the tools for casting, invading our land and benefiting us with these materials but leaving no traces in the language and writing. I myself have specialized in the latter for many years and I have not yet been able to find any such traces of western influence. Therefore I believe much research will have to be done before any sort of theory could be

established. My personal feeling is that the Shang culture is
typically Chinese with little or no western influences.

II. Chou*

The history of the power and decline of the House of
Chou covers the longest single dynastic period in Chinese history.
Within the limits of this dynasty are to be found many developments and changes, which are part of the foundation that became
the edifice of Chinese culture and civilization.

If the entire period is viewed as a unit, the complex of
Chou development is more easily comprehended in four general points.
The first period in its history shows a series of feudal states
clustered around and centered in the Royal House of Chou. Two and
a half centuries later, Chou had been reduced in power to the position of a nominal kingship; the real forces of government were held
by feudal lords. Second, we see that, although Chou originated
from a western border area, the dynastic culture pattern was even-
tually Chinese, as handed down from the Shang. Into this pattern
the Chou gradually absorbed other border states and tribes, originally non-Chinese. The third general factor is concerned with the
growth of government and its administration. At first the political organization was limited to the nobility, but in time admitted
the common man to governing power. Finally, archaeological researches indicate that the culture at the beginning of the Chou
made an extensive use of bronze, and that towards the close of the
dynasty this shifted to iron. The Five Hegemonies of the Ch'un
Ch'iu period (722-481 B.C.) and the leadership of the Seven States

---

*Published in China, The United Nations Series, University
of California Press, 1946.

among a host of lesser powers, during the time of the Chan Kuo
period (480-222 B.C.) were symbols of the collapse of Chou power
and the forerunners of the unification achieved during the Ch'in-
Han period.

Unfortunately, source materials for a detailed history of
the Chou dynasty are not available. Except for the Chou pen chi
and the Chronological Tables, the earliest historian, Ssu-ma Ch'ien,
in his Shih chi gave no information for this period. Ssu-ma's
uncritical use of so-called pre-Han sources and his conjectural
filling of gaps renders necessary a reconstruction of Chou history.
For this, two main sources exist: first, the inscriptions on the
bronze vessels, which often supply accurate and detailed records
for the periods with which they are concerned; and second, the
known pre-Han documents when critically treated. It is not sur-
prising that the results yielded are often at variance with the
traditional history.

The Chou tribe was originally located in western China at
the great bend of the Yellow River, in what is now southern Shansi.
Later the tribal leaders established their power in the Wei valley
of present day Shensi. The southern part of Shansi is called Ta
Hsia, the home of the Hsia tribe. Here the Yellow River flowing
from the north turns eastward in a great bend. Inside the curve
of this bend is the great plain on which were laid the foundations
of Chinese culture. Anciently, this was a stronghold of many barbarian tribes, one of which was most probably the Chou. The Chou
are reported to have intermarried with the Chiang tribe. Tradition
makes Hou Chi, God of Millet, the first Chou ancestor. The character for Chou represents a square field divided into quarters on
which plants are marked. It is therefore a major probability that

the Chou tribe practised an agricultural economy.

Toward the close of the Shang there were already contests
in warfare between Chou and Shang. On the oracle bones of Wu-
ting's time the records state that "Shang attacked Chou." A fragment of another record contains part of a sentence beginning,
"Order the Marquis of Chou..." The Chu shu chi nien or Bamboo
Annals report that at the time of King Wu I of Shang, King Chi of
Chou came to court. At the time of King T'ai Ting of Shang, King
Chi was ordered to be Master of the herdsmen and later he was
killed. At the time of King Ti I of Shang, the Chou people attacked
Shang. In the Shih ching is found the statement, "T'ai Wang
attacked Shang." T'ai Wang was the father of King Chi, who had
been slain by Shang. From this, and the considerations stated in
the preceding paragraph, two points of major importance stand out:
first, that the Chou were in the west, in Shansi; second, that
though Chou was vassal to Shang, there were occasional passages
at arms between vassal and master.

For the reign of Ti I of Shang, the Chu shu reports that
the Chou people attacked Shang. This was most probably during the
time of Chou Wen Wang. Concerning Wen Wang, the Shang shu writes,
"Wen Wang exterminated the Yin (Shang) dynasty." The Shih ching
reaffirms this point in a passage of similar content. Tradi-
tionally, the conquest of Shang was completed by Chou Wu Wang. We
know it to have begun with Wen Wang. In several different places
both the Shih ching and the Shang shu writes that "Wen Wang received the mandate (of Heaven)." The Shih ching further states
that "Wen and Wu received the mandate (of Heaven)." Inscriptions
on the bronzes of Western Chou say, "Wen and Wu received the mandate of Heaven." The formula "received the mandate of Heaven" can
be explained in at least two ways; it can mean "to be king by the

order of Heaven," or it can mean "to succeed in possession of the kingdom." Either way, it denotes that Wen Wang began the conquest of Shang.

It is reported in the <u>Shih</u> <u>ching</u> that before the 'extermination' of Shang, Wen Wang, king of Chou, had attacked two states, Yü and Ts'ung, and had begun to build a city at Feng.

From information supplied on the oracle bones and the Shang bronzes it is clear that Chou Hsin, the last king of Shang, had moved most of his troops eastward in order to attack the Eastern Barbarians. Successful in this venture, the last Shang king was at a tactical disadvantage in meeting the attack of the Chou tribe, which came from the west, under Wu Wang before the Shang armies could return. The last Shang king fell in battle. Wu Keng, heir to the Shang throne, was captured by Wu Wang and placed under the guard of his (Wu Wang's) two brothers, Kuan and Ts'ai. Although he was now in possession of the city of Shang, Wu Wang yet feared the Shang armies in the field.

The political developments of the ensuing five years are of great importance. Again, the inscriptions from the bronzes of Western Chou are the chief sources of reconstruction. Two years after his conquest of Shang, Wu Wang died. His son Ch'eng succeeded him, but another of Wu Wang's brothers, Chou Kung, the traditional hero of this period, often incorrectly referred to as regent, held the real power among the Chou. Meanwhile, Wu Wang's two brothers, Kuan and Ts'ai, who had been charged with the guarding of the Shang heir-apparent in the interest of Chou, had come to identify their interests with those of Shang and were ready to support it by action. The Shang army, still powerful and at large in the east, had induced the barbarians of both east and south to ally themselves with Shang and stand against Chou.

At this point Chou Kung, in three strategical moves,
justified his later fame. History does not, however, admit for it
the same reasons as are assigned by later tradition. Chou Kung's
first step was to attack the Shang capital again, and then to
execute his brother Kuan and the Shang heir, Wu Keng, and to exile
Ts'ai. He then made one of the descendants of Shang figurehead
in the state of Sung, and placed his youngest brother, K'ang Hou,
in power at the Shang capital in northern Honan. Second, he moved
his army eastward into the territory yet strongly Shang. Here,
in present day Shantung province, he utterly defeated the Shang
allies and pushed the remnant of the barbarians far eastward to the
coast. Thus he cleared the way for his own son, Po Ch'in, to become governor of this area. The result was a mixture of eastern
Shang and western Chou.

The state created in the east, and latter called Lu, came
to be accepted as the archetype of Chinese culture. Its great
philosophers of a subsequent period, Confucius and Mencius, con-
trasted the rule of Chou Kung with the confusion of their own times
and considered him the heroic figure of classical antiquity.

Finally, Chou Kung built a second capital at Lo-yang in
Central Honan, to stand guard toward the south and the east. The
Shang people were compelled to migrate to the new capital at Lo-
yang, to be more easily watched by Chou Kung's second son, Chün
Ch'en, who had been appointed chief of the eastern capital. This
exploit of Chou Kung is referred to in the bronzes as the "second
conquest of Shang"—and thus it is known that the first must have
been that gained by Wu Wang. The attack on Shang which had begun
with Wen Wang was continued and pressed forward into initial victory by Wu Wang, and finally brought to completion by Chou Kung

during the reign of Ch'eng Wang. The events are rather summarily
reported in two passages of the Tso chuan. The first writes,
"Formerly, Wu Wang conquered Shang and Ch'eng Wang stttled (the
kingdom)." The second says, "Formerly, Wu Wang conquered Yin
(Shang) and Ch'eng Wang made peace in the four quarters." More
accurately stated, Chou Kung settled the kingdom by completely de-
feating the Shang and so was responsible for the "peace of the four
quarters."

The Chu shu notes, "During the period of Ch'eng and K'ang,
the kingdom was peaceful. Punishments were rescinded for more
than forty years and were not used." It seems fairly clear that
the tribes of the eastern and western marches of the kingdom were
quiescent and lived a normal life. During the Shang the main
forces pressing the center came from the northeast and the northwest, but not from the south. The eastern capital of Chou, as has
been pointed out, was built to serve as a bastion against the south.
Concerning the reign of Chao Wang, the Chu shu somewhat laconically
reports that he attacked the southern state of Ch'u and "did not
come back." That he was killed while on this expedition seems a
fair inference. Years of intermittent border warfare, perhaps
supplemented by occasional contacts of a non-military nature,
slowly drew the tribes on the peripheral areas into the sphere of
the already established Chinese culture where they were assimilated.

The reign of Mu Wang (ca. 965-928 B.C.) brings to a close
the early period of Western Chou. After Mu Wang's reign the
shapes and styles of the bronzes are noticeably different, an indi-
cation of new conditions. The inscriptions pertain to developments
in the system of officials and in ritual instead of the continuing
echoes of war. Several chapters in the Shang shu purport to belong to the period ending with Mu Wang. By a comparison with the

inscriptions on the vessels of the time following Mu Wang, however, it is clear that these chapters were compiled at a date later than conservative scholars have generally held.

Kung, I, and Hsiao—the three rulers who in turn succeeded Mu Wang—held the kingdom peacefully for about seventy [60] years. Among the factors which may help to account for changes in the bronzes for this period immediately after Mu Wang were the more settled conditions within the Chou kingdom and at its borders. A further reflection of these conditions is to be observed in the regulation of court rituals and in the balance—both in the structure of the whole and in the making of separate strokes—which now becomes part of the characters.

A branch of the Eastern Barbarians, anciently settled in the area of present day Shantung, had migrated southward into the Huai River valley in the times between Shang and Chou. In the course of the period covered by the three rulers following Mu Wang, the barbarians—the so-called southern Huai—spread into the valleys of the Yangtze and Han rivers. The rebellions of these barbarians began under Chao and Mu Wang. An inscription on a bronze bell relates that "Yi Wang conquered the Southern and Eastern Barbarians, thirty-six states in all." *(a.s.259)* From another inscription comes the information that Li Wang also fought the Southern Barbarians, and history adds that he was defeated. The circumstances attendant on the defeat suffered by Li Wang and the continued pressure of the Southern Huai Barbarians revealed his incapacity to rule under difficulties. Li was then deposed either by the feudal lords or through an uprising of the people, and was exiled.

Following Yi Wang (ca.887-858 B.C.) and Li Wang (ca. 857-842 B.C.), traditional history writes that the Duke of Chou and the Duke of Shao assumed control in a manner similar to a regency.

The bronze inscriptions and the Chu shu present the situation
somewhat differently by naming Kung Po Ho as regent— or, more
strictly, as usurper. Ho's control lasted for fourteen years
after the exile of Li Wang, and is known as the Kung Ho period.
The Chou pen chi of Shih chi relates that in the fourteenth year
of Kung Ho, Li Wang died and his son and heir, Hsüan, became
ruler.

All sources agree that Hsüan Wang was an exceptionally
able king throughout the forty-six years of his reign (827-782
B.C.). That he was successful in his wars against the Southern
Huai Barbarians is recorded both on the bronzes and in the Shih
ching. The Chu shu extends the narrative and notes six expeditions against the barbarians of the northwest. Three of these
were led by the feudal lords of Ch'in and Chin, two states bor-
dering on the frontier territory; these expeditions met with only
one reverse. Two of the three expeditions led by the Royal Chou
were defeated. Clearly, the Chou kings were no longer capable of
carrying on independent warfare against the barbarians. Moreover,
border states such as Ch'in and Chin which continually engaged in
skirmishes to maintain their frontiers were developing formidable
military strength.

In the thirty-ninth year of his reign, Hsüan Wang attacked
the Shen Barbarians of the northwest with success. It is known
that Hsüan's son Yu, the heir-apparent, had married a woman from
a barbarian tribe in the northwest. Since her name was Shen and
since the character for both the tribe and her clan name were the
same, it is conjectured that she was of this tribe. A domestic
turmoil in the royal household during the rule of Yu Wang brought
about a further decrease of the already waning Chou power. Yu
Wang favored the issue of his concubine Pao-ssú, and attempted to

name him the heir-apparent thereby replacing P'ing, his legal heir.
The latter appealed to his mother's people, the Shen tribe, to
support his claims. In a coalition with other west barbarians,
the Shen killed Yu Wang and his concubine's son and placed P'ing
on the throne. At the same time another son of Yu Wang, whose
mother is not known, was established as king in Hsi by the Duke of
Kuo. This king was called Hsi Wang. It would seem that the feudal
lords were split into two groups and the P'ing and Hsi were put
forward as their respective candidates for the throne.

P'ing Wang, supported by the states of Lu and Hsü,[3] moved
eastward to set up his capital at Lo-yang. This move was also
prompted by P'ing Wang's apprehension about remaining among the
northwest barbarians, and the slow encroachment on Chou power
being made by the increasingly stronger Ch'in State. In the
eleventh year of P'ing Wang's rule the Duke of Chin slew Hsi Wang
thus making P'ing the sole ruler. The change of capital marks
the beginning of the period called the Eastern Chou.

During their rule from the western capital the Chou kings,
on the whole, proved equal to the twofold task of controlling the
feudal lords and maintaining a certain level of general culture, as
is shown in the uniformity of grammar and character usage on the
bronze inscriptions. This uniformity was lost in the Eastern
period when the kingship was nominal and control washeld by the
nobles. Inscriptions begin to reflect local variations; hetero-
geneity replaces the uniform pattern of the earlier centuries.

The decline of Chou is adumbrated by the rude behaviour
of the nobles. When P'ing Wang died (720 B.C.), the Duke of Lu
did not attend the funeral ceremonies. In the course of the next
two and a half decades P'ing's successor, Huan Wang, visited Lu
five times in attempts at conciliation. Again, in battle against

the state of Cheng, Huan Wang was wounded. The person of the
king was no longer held in extraordinary honor.

In the seventh century B.C. Ch'i and Chin assumed the hege-
mony successively which supplanted that of Chou, although a nominal
kingship was still maintained. Because the threat of barbarian
expansion was increased by this lack of central authority, the
states were forced to act independently. In this process, the
larger states swallowed the smaller ones. Finally, from among the
most powerful, there emerged the hegemon who was referred to as
the Pa. The functions of the Pa were to repulse increasingly
troublesome barbarians and to enforce respect for the Chou sovereign.
The institution of the Pa prevented another strong state setting
itself up as sole ruler in place of Chou. This delicate balance of
power and the traditional respect for kingship kept a member of
the Chou on the throne.

Briefly summarized, the political system of the Ch'un
Ch'iu period was still aristocratic, since the nobles were of the
royal family and a great effort was made to retain old forms and
to preserve traditions. This formulation of proper behaviour
ceased entirely at the end of the Ch'un Ch'iu with the rise to
power of the Wu and Yüeh—states which evolved from among the barbarians of the southeast.

Throughout the Chou dynasty there were three different
attitudes toward the barbarian tribes. The vigourous power of
Western Chou sought to attack and conquer the border tribes; in
the Ch'un Ch'iu period the states were forced to defend themselves
against the growing strength of non-Chinese clans; finally, in the
Chan Kuo period, contacts with the barbarians were sought and an
assimilation attempted. The influx of barbarians infused the

Chinese pattern with new life and vigour, nor was the unique
character of the firmly established Chinese states lost. Rather
did Chinese culture gradually infiltrate the outlying tribes until
they too were completely Chinese. Out of many states, large and
small, developed seven which were the most powerful. Their strength
was mainly derived from acceptance of the incoming barbarians,
whereas the more conservative states which rejected the new tribes,
rapidly declined.

In the Ch'un Ch'iu period none of the rulers of the Chinese
states used the title 'Wang' (king). Among the barbarian tribes
the head of the state of Ch'u had been designated by this title
since the beginning of Eastern Chou, and when, in the Ch'un Ch'iu,
this state entered the Chinese group, its leader still referred
to himself as king. Toward the close of the Ch'un Ch'iu, in the
sixth and fifth centuries B.C., the leaders of two barbarian
states, Wu and Yüeh, which had just become part of the Chinese
pattern, adopted the title Wang. In the second half of the fourth
century B.C., that is, during the Chan Kuo era, the rulers of the
Chinese states also began to use the title.

Throughout the Chan Kuo era, a series of changes took
place which are of maximum importance to the history of later
China. Hereditary succession to power ended and the high officers
assumed both control and title. This was illustrated in the state
of Ch'i, where the ruler, heretofore always a member of the
Chiang clan, Royal Chou on the maternal side, was ousted by his
high officer, a member of an outside family named T'ien. In the
state of Chin, three high officers, Han, Chao, and Wei, dispossessed
the king and divided the state into three parts, each under the
rule of one of these officers. The state of Ch'in established two

classes of administrative units called <u>chün</u> (commandery) and
<u>hsien</u> (district).   The principles governing the ownership of land
were now radically altered: for the first time officials were
given salaries by the crown and were not owners of the land as in
former days, but only overseers. As a result of these changes, the
common man who had ability could enter the service of a king as an
administrator.

      This brought about other developments. The scholars of the
time began private teaching and thereby opened the way for the
common people to receive an education and enter government service.
This soon gave rise to a class of professional statesmen. Occasionally, a state would hire from the frontier areas a non-Chinese who
was skilled in military matters and would put him in charge of
army affairs. Thus was created a class of professional soldiers.
Ambitious kings surrounded themselves with militarists and political philosophers, who were treated as honoured guests. Appreciation
of the value of public works is shown by the ambitious engineering
projects undertaken by single states. Although the canal system
for this period is not known, it may be pointed out that at the end
of the Ch'un Ch'iu period the king of Wu want to meet Chin at
Huang-ch'i, in present day Honan, by "linking the rivers and making
canals." The Wei state, during the disruption of the Chan Kuo,
built a highway which is mentioned in the <u>Shui ching chu</u> or <u>Commen-
tary to the Water Classic</u>. A project in which many states participated was the building of barriers against the northern barbarians.
These barriers were finally linked by Ch'in Shih Huang Ti to form
the Great Wall.

      The disunity prevalent during the era of Chan Kuo contained
within itself the promise of unification. In time, the strongest

state, Ch'in, imposed its will on the rest of the group and welded
the parts into a whole under a single ruler, Ch'in Shih Huang Ti,
First Emperor of Ch'in. Much of the apparatus of government which
enabled Ch'in toorganize successfully had been developed in the
preceding Chan Kuo period. Much of it was retained and amplified
by the Han rulers. Some of it yet remains. Both inspite of and
because of the furor of internal dissension, China was ready for
unification.

Cultural differences between Western and Eastern Chou are,
in a general sense, of the same type as their political differences.
The sketch in the following pages has treated only the main topics
and has been deliberately limited to subjects for which evidence
is available.

In religious practices there was no difference between
Shang and Chou with regard to ancestor and nature worship. The
development of ancestor worship in the Royal Chou family tended to
form a pattern of the family group which, when transferred to the
state, had a certain practical political value. It is known from
the bronzes that the conception of Shang Ti, originated by the
Shang people, was adopted by the Chou. The inscriptions make it
clear that "Shang Ti orders (something or someone)," and that
after death members of the Chou family go to live at the court of
Shang Ti. At the same time the Chou were developing the idea of
T'ien   (sky) on the same plane with Shang Ti. The bronzes show
that the two were at first interchangeable: some inscriptions
record "The mandate of Ti"; others record "the mandate of T'ien."
At a later date, T'ien superceded Shang Ti as the more powerful.
Two essential notions concerning T'ien are obtained from the
bronzes and the Shang shu: the first is, "Stand in awe of T'ien's

might"; the second, "Respect illustrious virtue (Te)." These are
fundamental in the attitude of Confucius toward T'ien and the human
person. It is rather strange that no mention of kuei (ghost) is
made until the Eastern Chou period, whereas shên (spirit) is recorded earlier. There are, then, two categories of such phenomena:
one is the spirit of the deceased human being, called kuei; the
other, called shên, includes hundreds of nonhuman spirits, and
ghosts which were always disembodied. Bronze inscriptions from
the state of Ch'i, in the period of Eastern Chou, record three expressions belonging to the same class of ideas: one concerns being
"not old" that is, remaining young; another refers to "eternal life";
the third is "not to die". All three ideas are subjects of prayer,
possibly addressed to T'ien, although it is not so stated in the
inscriptions. In the years following Confucius the intrinsic
religious qualities involved in ancestor worship and in the ideas
of both T'ien and Shang Ti were gradually dissipated until they
were practised only as forms by the intelligentsia, and held as a
minor, often misunderstood tenet by the common people. Hencefor-
ward, until the coming of Buddhism there were no practices with a
strict religious content.

For the history of philosophic thought before the time of
Confucius, documents are scarce and not well organized. Confucius
was both a school-master and a statesman, who practiced the con-
victions of moderation, "neither too much, not too little." As a
teacher he emphasized the study of history, which meant the complete range of antiquity. As a statesman he attempted to apply
the principles of his historical knowledge to the practical affairs
of government. At no time in his life was he attracted by the
glamour of either glory or riches. Inwardly firm, failures in
government administration left him free to return to a deep study

of his own heritage. The tradition to which Confucius returned
time and again was the summation of Chou culture as exemplified
in the state of Lu. Both Mencius and Hsün-tzu, as students of
the Master, followed much of his teaching, shifting the accent
as each saw and understood the demands of his own time. Confucius stressed aristocratic government and the regulation of the
common people. Mencius, however, emphasized the importance of
the people and Hsün-tzu developed a doctrine in which the concept of Law held first place.

As the barbarian states entered physically and culturally
into the Chinese world they made their strength felt not only in
the political sphere but also in the realm of ideas. The culture
of the Northern Barbarians deeply influenced both Chin and Ch'in.
Legal structure and concepts of the function of law began to out-
weigh other considerations. The background for this may possibly
be traced to the barbarian emphasis on military matters and discipline which was so integral a part of the Northern Barbarian
life. I believe that the philosophy of Mo-tzu was partly derived
from such influences. The Eastern Barbarians, because they came
from the coastal regions, brought with them ideas which were
associated with long years of observing the character of the ocean,
and tended to concentrate on the importance of change. The in-
land groups, never subjected to the sudden and sometimes terrify-
ing changes of a great body of water, had basic notions of stability. These groups had two different horizons, one of the land
and the other of water, brought a new cosmological picture into
Chinese thinking. The attraction of the ocean is illustrated by
the number of visits made by Ch'in Shih Huang Ti. Impressed by

the instability of the sea and feeling keenly the ephemeral
quality of existence, the coastal peoples populated the sea with
immortals who were always happy and who were not subject to the
vagaries of nature. This free fancy and imaginative invention
caught hold in Ch'i; it was of peculiar importance in the growth
of concepts found in the thought of Chuang-tzu and Lao-tzu.
Among the Southern tribes the patterns of thought were conditioned
by the limitations imposed by geography and climate. Heavy and at
times almost continuous rainfall nurtured the conviction that life
was colourless and drab. There was little or no cultivation, and
horizons were cut short by dense jungle growths. Religious obser-
vances focused on a myriad of ghosts and spirits. This influence
was strongest in the state of Ch'u; though literary production was
small, a heavy, dim and oppressive sense of the tragedy of life
can be felt in the poetry of Ch'u-tzŭ.

          Philosophical activity reached its apogee at the end of
the Chan Kuo era. The school of Mo-tzu, in developing and em-
phasizing the art of disputation, had a very wide range of application in other schools. The tendency of the period, in philosophy
as in politics, was toward unified presentation. The Taoists attempted to bring everything under a single heading, and the systema-
tization which had started in the Eastern Chou was applied to the
problem of ordering everything in a closed structure. The I ching
or Book of Changes was used from early times as a handbook of
divination by means of the tortoise shell and milfoil. It is necessary to emphasize that this handbook had no philosophical content. The scholars of the Chan Kuo or later, however, composed a
commentary on this work giving interpretations which were turned
toward philosophical ideas. The combined text and commentary were
used to create a cosmological picture based on the idea of unity.

The early prose writings are mainly the inscriptions of
the Western Chou bronzes and the Shang shu. The language of the
bronzes, and often of the Shang shu, maintains an economy which
results in terseness and brachyology. Both are characterized by
close adherence to the rules of syntax and, despite the brevity,
a rich vocabulary. The contents were limited to the orders of
the king and a bare statement of facts. The genuine text of the
Lun yü or Confucius' Analects is clear and simple, and continues
the traditional brevity of earlier prose. The writings of Mencius
display more of a conscious striving for literary style. Descriptive passages and interesting anecdotes depart from the tradition
 of austere simplicity. The prose style of Chuang-tzu stands, in
the evolution of style, midway between that of Mencius and that of
Han Fei-tzu. The latter, writing at the time when the art of disputation was at its height, argued various points in his prose
works, and so lengthened the paragraphs that a style more nearly
that of the essay resulted. Much the same is true of Hsun tzu.
The monotonous styles of Han Fei-tzú and Hsün-tzu did not recom-
mend them as models to Han scholars, who revived the style of the
Shang shu.

Inscriptions on the bronzes at the close of Western Chou,
particularly those on bells, make use of rhyme schemes. There is
little doubt that very early ballads were sung with rhymes, but
the use of rhyme schemes in the written language is of much later
origin. The Shih ching has three parts: a series of ballads, a
class of songs called Ya, and a group of Odes. The latter two
were used in court ceremonies. The Odes of Chou can be divided
into two classes: the oldest have no rhymes and lack a pattern;
the second group has both rhyme and pattern, and can not by com-

parison with the bronzes, *Can* be dated ~~before~~ *at* the close of Western
Chou. It is probable that the entire content of the <u>Shih ching</u>
stems from a Chinese source, for when it is compared with the
earliest works written in the Chinese language but outside the
Chinese tradition, sharp differences in style, form, and content
are obvious. Writings which are of particular value in such a
comparison are the Songs of Ch'u. Here terseness is missing in
both sentence and stanza, which are drawn out to great length.
The repetitions characteristic of the <u>Shih ching</u> are absent, and
the tone of moderation familiar in the traditional work is re-
placed by imaginative fancy. The two works are obviously pro-
ducts of two separate groups. Since the <u>Shih ching</u> is by far the
older it is generally agreed to be of the Chinese tradition.

　　　The earliest known written documents in the Chinese language already show an advanced stage of development. The bronze
inscriptions of Western Chou make use of a set of personal pronouns
with case and number distinctions. These gradually disappear
in the Eastern Chou period and are completely nonexistent in the
Han period. The development of certain characters can be traced
on the bronzes as their usage varied; for example, <u>chih</u> 之 appears
first as a demonstrative adjective, then as a sign of the genitive
case, and later as a pronoun of the third person singular. It is
used in present day writing in all three senses—plus later additions. During the slackening of central power under the Eastern
Chou, slight differences in syntax can be detected on the bronze
inscriptions, but the main syntactical pattern never changes.
Variations in the spoken language created dialects of wide dis-
parity, but the written language, because it was controlled by a

central authority, has shown no more than small and negligible
changes in syntax.

Developments in the script of the Chou dynasty mirror
faithfully the shifts in political control. Early Chou script is
sharp and strong, tending to become more balanced and moderate in
Western Chou. It is weakened and slanted in the Eastern Chou and
the Ch'un Ch'iu periods. In the Chan Kuo era, the script is unre-
strained and artificial. Under the leadership of the Seven States
the Ch'in State retained and preserved the traditional script of
Western Chou, which was called Large Seal script, and when, at the
end of the Chan Kuo, Ch'in unified the states, it adopted this
script calling it Small Seal, and enforced its general usage.

The court system of ritual employed in the Chou age is
obscure, but some knowledge of it may be gained from the bronzes.
Royal audiences were usually granted at dawn and occasionally in
the twilight before dawn. For this reason the Chinese character
for "audience" had the original meaning of "early morning." The
practice of holding audiences was continued for two and a half
millenia and ended only with the fall of the Ch'ing dynasty in
1912 A.D. Chou audiences took place either in the royal residence
or temple, although sometimes in the home or temple of the nobles.
The audience chamber was gained through a south gate entering
a courtyard at the north end of which was the T'ai Shih, or Great
Room. Leading up to the T'ai Shih were steps on which the king
stood facing south. At his right was the historian of the Inner
Palace. The officers, standing at the left, were conducted by a
high official called Pin-hsiang, Master of Court Ceremonies, who
approached the king facing north. The orders for the day, previously written on bamboo slips, were announced by the historian
of the Inner Palace, and given to the particular officers, who

made deep obeisance and withdrew. This was the form of ceremony
beginning with Mu Wang and continuing throughout the rest of the
Chou dynasty. The orders on the slips were considered of such
importance that they were often cast as the inscriptions on bronze
vessels, and were thus preserved for posterity. In another
fashion they were compiled and edited to form the Shang shu. It is
because of this preservation of early documents in their original
form that the bronze inscriptions are of unique importance in
modern researches, and are considered more trustyworthy than the
Shang shu. The official called Pin-hsiang was required to know
the Ritual and thus was the only person capable of presenting
others to the king. In the Chan Kuo period, interstate relationships were, for the most part, carried on through the medium of
such rituals; in consequence, great importance was attached to the
position of Master of Court Ceremonies. It was the aim of Confucius to train his pupils so well in the Ritual that they could
fill this position. Since many of the affairs of state were
carried on by the Pin-hsiang, this office grew until it became
the Prime Ministry.

        As an adjunct to the court ritual certain musical forms
were used. It is most probable that there were popular songs and
dances, possibly with accompaniment, but these were not part of
court ceremony and were looked upon as vulgar by Confucius. The
musical instruments used in the ceremonies were bells, drums, and
a small wind instrument made of clay similar to the ocarina. However, many more musical instruments are listed in the Shih ching.
The purpose of the music was to set a rhythm for the performance
of the ceremony. The officials in procession wore, hanging from
their clothing, pieces of jade which were used to keep time with

the bells. Within the sacrificial vessels there were bells, with
clappers, similar to the jades, to provide rhythm. By the time of
Confucius, reaction had set in against this simple traditional
music and the preference for the songs and music from the state of
Ch'eng drew severe censure from the Master. The history of music
in China poses a difficult problem: why, in a culture highly developed in all of the other fine-arts, is music almost always an
importation?

There are few data concerning economic history under the
Chou, but indications of relative values may be gleaned from inscriptions listing gifts given to the nobles and officers by the
king. A comparison of the bronzes of the first half of Western
Chou with those of the second half reveals the fluctuation in
values. Gifts common to both periods were jades, weapons, sacrificial wines, and salt. In the first half of Western Chou, articles mentioned as gifts were cowrie shells, red-gold, bronze,
various animals (such as deer, cattle, birds, and horses and
chariots), and occasionally clothing. For the second half of Western Chou are listed cowrie shells, red-gold, and bronze, but much
less frequently to gifts of horses and chariots, fittings are
added; more gifts of clothing are recorded. Silks are found listed
only for the later period. The barbarians offered tribute of
horses, cowries, metal, silks, and jade. An inscription of the
second half of Western Chou reads, in part: "The Huai Barbarians
formerly were my tribute subjects. They dare not fail to offer
tribute (and men for) service.... The king ordered that the market should be in a definite place, and must not be in the barbarians' territory. The feudal lords and the people must not pay
tribute to the barbarians." Another inscription of the same period

records exchange values in the bartering system: "One horse and
one roll of silk are exchanged for five slaves." The inconvience
of barter on a large scale led to the use of cowries, silks and
metals as money. The actual shift to a money economy did not take
place until the Chan Kuo era. Development of a merchant class in
the Ch'un Ch'iu made this a necessity.

The basic material for agricultural implements and weapons
in the Chan Kuo era is iron of this area, in contrast to the earlier
use of bronze. Art forms still employed bronze and had added silver. The technique of inlay also had been developed. Lacquered
wares appear for the first time in the Chan Kuo period. Stone
monuments and inscriptions had been used by the state of Ch'in
since the time of Eastern Chou.

The calendar of the early Chou did not differ greatly from
that of Shang, which was used for both harvests and sacrifices. In
Chou times, however, the calendar was used for harvests only. The
month was divided into parts corresponding to the phases of the
moon. Under the Western Chou all of the feudal lords used the
calendar of the Royal House; under the Eastern Chou the inscriptions
show that each state calculated its own dates for various events.
Four seasons are mentioned in the calendars of Eastern Chou. The
earlier Western Chou records do not name the four seasons, which
may possibly indicate a continuance of the Shang claendar of two
seasons, spring and autumn. The political confusion of the Chan
Kuo was doubly confounded when both astrology and astronomy were
used in calendrical systems. The result was a maze of complexes
which has not only obscured the chronology of ancient history but
has also complicated the study of philosophy.

The extremes of this period—the Western Chou at the

L 452

beginning and the Chan Kuo at the end—display, for the first, a conservative calm, and, for the latter, disruption and complete confusion. It is clear, however, from the preceding pages, that the evolution was continuous, with no sudden breaks. The final unification under Ch'in was the logical outcome of developments beginning in the early days of Western Chou. The Chinese culture pattern had assimilated all newcomers, had drawn from their life and vigour, and yet had retained its own forceful character. Not until the advent of Buddhism was there a major shift—so firmly established was that quality known as "Chinese."

2 45?

CHAPTER XIII
Chronology

CHAPTER XIII

CHRONOLOGY

It is necessary to spend some time in a detailed discussion of chronology, because without it history has no firm base and the dating of the bronzes becomes impossible. In this chapter I shall not discuss the calendar system in detail. I shall place emphasis on the length of the dynasties and on the regnal periods.

In James Legge's *Chinese Classics* (1865), vol. III, part 1, the Shoo King, there is an appendix on the astronomy of the ancient Chinese by John Chalmers. A table of ancient Chinese chronology appears at the end of this which is based on the traditional schemes and the *Chu shu*. The 'common scheme' was based on Liu Hsin's *San t'ung* and other later materials. The *Chu shu* is the false edition. In 1905 the *Variétés sinologiques*, no. 24 published the *Synchronismes Chinois* of Pere Mathia Tchang. This chronology is similar to the previous work on Chinese chronology. I shall now discuss the general background of pre-Han chronology and make a revaluation of Liu Hsin's system and attempt to formulate a Shang-Chou chronology based on reliable materials.

I. Pre-Han Chronology

The confusion about astronomy and astrology began in the Chan Kuo period. In *Meng tzu*, about 312 B.C. when he left Ch'i in his 70th year, he said, "Every 500 years there should arise a true royal sovereign and during that period there should be men

known in the world." In the last chapter of Meng tzu he gave
examples of the men known in the world every 500 years, and in
T'eng wen kung II he also gave examples of such men. It seemed
to him that 500 years was a cycle for order and disorder. The
Fung shan shu of Shih chi recorded that the Chou historian Tan
told Hsien Kung of Ch'in   (384-362 B.C.)   that "At first
Ch'in and Chou came together and then separated. After 500 years
they will come together again." In T'ien kuan shu of Shih chi
it is recorded that "In the revolutions of the world, 30 years is
a small change 變 , 100 years is a medium change and 500 years is
a great change. Three great changes make a great cycle 紀 and
three great cycles complete everything." During Meng-tzu's
time the five elements' doctrine came into power. Each of the
five elements, metal, wood, water, fire, and earth dominated each
dynasty and alternated with the dynasties. In Meng hsüan li chuan
of Shih chi it is recorded that a man called Chou Yen, who wrote
a book entitled, Beginnings and Endings and Great Sages, said,
"When Heaven and Earth separated the five elements went alternately."
He wrote a book entitled, Revolutions 主運 , and although all of
his works have been lost we know that his theory was somewhat
similar to Meng-tzu's: a cycle of a certain number of years and with
each dynasty having a dominant element.

During this period the calendar system had two characteristics. The first made a solar year 365.25 days per year and so
four years gave an extra day over 365; this was called the 'One-
fourth' or the 'Quarter' system because of the remainder. The
month on a lunar system had 29 499/940 days and seven intercalary
months in 19 years called a chapter   , thus four chapters made
76 years with no remainder. This was the common characteristic

of the so-called Six Calendars including the Yin claendar, said
to have been used during the pre-Han and the early Han periods.
We have some records of these calendars which can be dated, *as a*
conjecture, about 370 B.C. (cf. Chu Wen-hsin, Li fa t'ung chih:
pp. 60-1). At the same time they used a year star, the planet
Jupiter, to record the year. This was recorded in Tso chuan and
in Kuo yü. Tso chuan, compiled late in the fourth century, B.C., is
the commentary to the Ch'un-ch'iu Annals. Chalmers found that
calculation by the planet Jupiter was used in the Tso chuan and
supposed that that system was established in 306 B.C. De Saussueein,
Les Origines de l'Astronomie Chinoise (T'oung Pao ser. 2, vol. 14,
1913, p. 410) says, "C'est en effet aux environs de l'an 380 (et
non pas de l'an 305) que le cycle astrologique se trouve en
concordance avec les positions sidereales de Jupiter...." The
Japanese scholar Shinjo Shinzo in his History of Chinese Chronology
(pp. 340, 354, 400) calculated the establishment of this system
to be in 376 B.C. or later. It should be noticed that we have
reason to believe that the Tso chuan was compiled by a Chin State
scholar. In Kuo yü only the Chin State (except for one case in
the Chou yü) had a system using the Jupiter cycle. Tung kuan yü
lun   , which was written by Huang Po-shih   of
the Sung dynasty, says, "I have seen the imperial collection
Shih ch'un   which recorded the generations of those states
and the twelve zodiacal signs of Jupiter." This Shih ch'un was
unearthed with the Chu shu from a Wei tomb. The Wei State was
separated from Chin. It seems to me that the Jupiter system was
popular in the Chin State during the second half of the fourth
century B.C., which was the time when the Tso chuan was compiled.
I shall discuss this point later.

II. Liu Hsin's Chronology

Liu Hsin died in 23 A.D., late in the Former Han dynasty. The San t'ung li (calendar) was generally attributed to Liu Hsin; this is not correct. In 104 B.C. Han Wu Ti changed the name of his reign from Yuan-fung to T'ai-ch'u and changed the calendar called T'ai-ch'u. This calendar was made by Teng P'ing . Before that year the Han still used the pre-Han 'One-fourth' system. The T'ai-ch'u calendar made a month 29 43/81 and a year 365 385/1539 days long. This was also called San t'ung and is sometimes attributed to Liu Hsin. Liu Hsin just adapted the T'ai-ch'u and his contribution is the Shih ching which is quoted in Lu li chih of Han shu. This calendar was *applied* to earlier history by Liu Hsin.

For the archaic six calendars based on the 'One-fourth' system, 19 years made a chapter , 4 chapters made a section of 76 years, 20 sections made a cycle of 1520 years and 3 cycles made a great cycle of 4560 years. We should notice that these 4560 years are quite near to the great cycle, 4500 years, mentioned in the T'ien kuan shu. However, the latter is only a theory. The San t'ung made 19 years a chapter with 7 intercalary months in this period. In 1539 years the days have no remainders—this was called one t'ung . Three t'ung made a cycle of 4617 years. He also called 9 chapters (171 years) a small ending and 9 small endings (1539 years) a big ending .

The Yin claendar gave a total length from the beginning of the earth to the year of the capture of the unicorn, 481 B.C., the close of Ch'un Ch'iu, as 2,759,886 years which was recorded

in <u>Lü li chih</u> of <u>Hou han shu</u>. In the year 47 B.C. of Yuan Ti of
the Han dynasty the Yin calendar considered this point as the
start of another Yin cycle, a period of 1520 years. From 481 B.C.
to 47 B.C. is a period of 434 years and this added to 2,759,886
is 2,760,320 (Number One) which is the total length from the beginning of the earth to the second year of Yuan Ti, as calculated
on the Yin calendar. Let us call this the remote beginning   .
It is from 605 times the great cycle plus a single Yin cycle that
this length of time is derived.

> From the beginning to 481 B.C.   2,759,886
> From 481 to 47 B.C.   434
> _____
> Total from beginning to 47 B.C.   2,760,320
> $(605 \times 4560 + 1520 = 2,760,320)$

Liu Hsin calculated the cycles of the five major planets
as Jupiter 1728, Venus 3456, Saturn 4320, Mars 13824 and Mer-
cury 9216. From this he determined the common multiple, 138,240,
within which period the five planets had been in conjunction.
Then he found the common multiple of the five planets' conjunc-
tions and the conjunction of the sun and moon and got 2,626,560
(Number Two), which he called the 'conjunction cycle'   .

In the <u>Shih ching</u> it is said, "From the 'One-fourth'
beginning   to the attack of Chieh (the last Hsia king)
there were 132,113 years." (Number Three)

Thus far we have three large numbers which I believe are
the sources from which Liu Hsin determined the first year of the
Shang dynasty. Number One minus Numbers Two and Three is 1647
years:

>   2,760,320
>   2,626,560
>   _____
>   133,760
>   132,113
>   _____
>   1,647

The final remainder appeared in the Shih ching. Liu Hsin
said, "From the San t'ung remote beginning   to the attack
on Chieh was 141,480 years and the first year of T'ai-ch'u (104 B.C.
to the San t'ung remote beginning was 143,127 years." Therefore
the year of the attack on Chieh to 104 B.C. was 1647 years and the
year of the attack was 1751 B.C. The Shih ching says, "From the
attack on Chieh (by T'ang) to the attack on Chou (the last Shang
king) by Wu Wang was 629 years and altogether the Yin dynasty had
31 kings for 629 years. Chou had altogether 36 kings for 867
years." Therefore the year of the attack on Chou by Wu Wang was
1122 B.C. Since the Chou dynasty lasted 867 years, consequently
the last year of Chou was 256 B.C. Liu Hsin also gave the total
length of the Hsia dynasty as 432 years. Therefore the first
year of the Hsia dynasty should be 2183 B. C. It is obvious that
Liu Hsin got 1647 from the three big numbers from three different
systems. The remote beginning of the Yin calendar counted from
the very beginning to 47 B.C., and Liu Hsin's starting point was
104 B.C. The conjunction cycle was made after T'ien kuan shu
and Huai-nan-tzu, because in these the planet Saturn was given a
cycle of 28 years. Liu Hsin gave thirty years which is more
accurate.

After Liu determined the total length of Shang and Chou
he attempted to prove the calculation and supplement the reigns
of the Western Chou kings. I shall now offer some criticisms of
the whole system from the beginning.

It is recorded in Chou yü II of Kuo yü that "When Wu
Wang attacked Yin, Jupiter was in Cancer-Leo." According to his
method this was in the year 1122 B.C. His method for calculating
the cycle of Jupiter was different from the method used before,
which was to take a 12 year period as the exact cycle. He found

that the 12 year cycle was accurate and determined that in a 144
year period Jupiter passed through 145 signs. This method was
called 'jumping a sign' and the older method was called 'not
jumping a sign'. We know that the Jupiter records in the Tso
chuan and the Kuo yü do not jump the sign. The information mentioned in the Chou yü should be considered as an opinion held
during the year 370 B.C. when the Jupiter system was first established. At that time it was believed that in the first year of
Chou, Jupiter was in Cancer-Leo according to the twelve year cycle.

Liu Hsin quoted the record of Jupiter from the Chou yü in
order to prove that 1122 B.C. was the first year of Chou, but
this year was selected according to the length of Chou. In the
Yi wei chi lan t'u   it is recorded that "The Chou
lasted 867 years." This work was based on the Yin calendar
school and was possibly made before Liu Hsin's work. The commentary to Hsi chen fu   of Wen hsüan   quoted the Chan
kuo ts'e, "Lü Pu-wei said,'from the first year of Wu Wang to the
59th year of Nan Wang there were 37 kings and 867 years.'" This
is not in the present edition of the Chan kuo ts'e.

From the above we know that Liu Hsin got his 1647 years
for the length of the period from the opening of Shang to the
first year of T'ai-ch'u as the result of the Yin system's remote
beginning minus the conjunction cycle given in San t'ung and the
'One-fourth' calendar's remote beginning to the first year of
T'ang. After the end of Chou, 255 B.C., to the year before the
first year of T'ai-ch'u, 104 B.C., is 151 years. From this year
to the beginning of Chou is 1018 years, and because he considered
the first year of Shang to be 1647 years before 104 B.C. the
length of the Shang should be 1647 minus 1018, which is 629 years.

Then he tried to collect some of the material from the books which he selected and quoted from with the particular intention of proving that the theory was correct. This material forms the history of the first 56 years of the Chou dynasty. It is as follows:

    a. Chin wen shang shu   Hung fan

                                        Shao kao

                                        Lo kao

                                        Ku ming

    b. Ku wen shang shu   Wu ch'eng

                                        Pi ming

    c. Ku wen yüeh ch'ai p'ien

    d. Tso chuan

    e. Kuo yü

    f. Wen wang shih tzu of Li chi

    g. Shu hsü

Shu hsü is the preface to the Shang shu which was made during the Ch'in-Han period. The Li chi is also late. The so-called Ku wen shang shu is said to have been found in the walls of Confucius' house during Han Wu Ti's time. The Ku wen school was headed by Liu Hsin and his father, Liu Hsiang (77-6 B.C.). The Wu ch'eng chapter was quoted in Meng tzu, chapter Ching-hsin II. It is different from the quotation given by Liu Hsin from the Ku wen shang shu. Therefore the latter was made after the Meng tzu. Even the Meng tzu says, "For Wu ch'eng I take only two or three of them." This shows that Meng-tzu did not accept the Wu ch'eng of his time. The Wu ch'eng quoted by Liu is similar to the Shih fu chapter of the Yi chou shu, but the date has been changed by Liu to fit his own calculations. In other cases he adopted the Yi chou shu's records. Liu says, "This is from the Weh chuan of

Yi chou shu, 'Wen Wang died nine years after he received the mandate.'" Again Liu says, "From the Ming t'ang of Yi chou shu,
'Wu Wang died seven years after he conquered Yin.'"

Sometimes the material he quoted mentioned or recorded
the points of the month. Liu serialised them into the following
system:

First day of the month	So	, ssu-p'o	, chi-ssu-p'o
Second day	P'ang-ssu-p'o		
Third day	Fei		
Fifteenth day	Wang	, sheng-p'o	, chai-sheng-p'o
Sixteenth day	Chi-wang		
Seventeenth day	Chi-p'ang-sheng-p'o		

If we check these names with authentic Early Western Chou
bronzes we find that only three names appear. According to my
conjecture they are: (1) The first half month, chi-sheng-p'o. The
The first ten days of this period were called ch'u-chi   , a
quarter; (2) the second half month, chi-ssu-p'o and chi-wang. As
we know, wang means 'the full moon on the 15th or 16th of a month'
and this point is used to divide the month into two parts. So
these names indicate a certain period of a month and not necessarily
a particular point. Liu Hsin's points of the month were no more
than conjectures and the material he used to reconstruct the first
56 years of the Chou are not reliable. In the T'ang dynasty, the
monk, I-hsing   made 1111 B.C. the starting point of the Chou
and using the same material and method as Liu Hsin to 'prove'
this , made the date fit for a reconstruction of the first 56 years
of the dynasty. Therefore, even if Liu Hsin's method and material
were reliable they could not be used to prove that 1122 B.C. was
the first year of the Chou dynasty.

He reconstructed the first part of the Chou dynasty and
sixteen years of K'ang Wang. Liu says, "Neither the Yin calendar
nor the Lu claendar give the regnal periods beginning with Chao
Wang." Therefore he used the records in the Lu shih chia of Shih
chi until the year before Yin Kung of Lu (722 B.C.), the beginning
of the Ch'un Ch'iu period. Here, if we check his years for the
reigns of Lu we find some of them have been changed to agree with
his theory. He did not give the years of the Chou kings after
K'ang Wang. He gave Wu seven years, Chou Kung seven years, Ch'eng
thirty years and K'ang more than sixteen years. He did not give
the total length of Western Chou, but it can be calculated. He
says, "From Po Ch'in   to Ch'un Ch'iu was 386 years." From
the end of Western Chou (771 B.C.) to the beginning of Ch'un Ch'iu
(722 B.C.) was 48 years. He put the first year of Po Ch'in as the
first year of Ch'eng Wang. Thus 386 minus 48 plus 14 (Wu Wang and
Chou Kung) is 352, which is the length of Western Chou.

III. Traditional Dates of Western Chou Kings

Liu Hsin said that there were no records for the kings
beginning with Chao Wang. Cheng Hsüan's   (127-200 A.D.) preface to Shih p'u   says, "From Yi and Li upward the years are
not clear. Ssu-ma Ch'ien's table begins with Kung Ho." T'ai
p'ing yü lan, vol. 85, quotes Huang-p'u Mi's   (215-282 A.D.)
Ti wang shih chi,"Chou, from Kung Wang to Yi Wang, was four
generations. The years of these reigns are not clear." But the
commentary to T'ung chien wai chi   says, "From ancient
times to Chou Li Wang there is no record for the years of each
reign but Huang-p'u Mi and other scholars all have the dates (in
their works). Their records of the dates are different." It

seems to me that Huang-p'u Mi was the first man to assign years
to the Western Chou kings. After that, during the Sung dynasty,
many scholars tried to assign dates. The two schools are:
T'ung chien wai chi by Liu Shu   (1032-1078 A.D.) and T'ung
chih   by Cheng Ch'iao   (1104-1162 A.D.), and the second school was the Huang chieh ching shih   by Shao
Yung   (1011-1077 A.D.) and T'ung chien ch'ien p'ien by Chin
Lü-hsiang   (1232-1303 A.D.).

Kings	Wu	Ch'eng	K'ang	Chao	Mu	Kung	I	Hsiao	Yi
First school	7	37	26	51	55	10	25	15	15
Second school	7	37	26	51	55	12	25	15	16

Kings	Li	Kung-Ho	Hsüan	Yu
First school	40	14	46	11
Second school	37	15	46	11

The total number of years is, for the first school, 352 and for
the second school, 353 years. These numbers are from the following sources:

a. Mu 55, Li 37, Kung-Ho 14, Hsüan 46, and Yu 11, totalling
   163 years from the Chou pen chi of Shih chi.

b. I 25, Hsiao 15, from the Shih chi quoted in T'ai p'ing yü
   lan, vol. 85.

c. Wu 7, Ch'eng 37 (or Chou Kung 7 and Ch'eng 30) totalling
   44 years from the Shih ching.

d. K'ang 26, Chao 51, Yi 16, totalling 93 years from Ti wang
   shih chi quoted in T'ai p'ing yü lan, vol. 85.

The total of a through d is 338 years excluding Kung Wang.

Because the Sung scholars accepted Liu Hsin's 352 years as
a total, by substraction they gave Kung Wang a period of 12 years.
The years were superficially given and this is not proved by the

inscriptions on the bronzes which mention the fifteen years of Kung Wang.

I have mentioned that Huang-p'u Mi was the first to give regnal periods to the kings of Western Chou. He died in 282 A.D., one year after the discovery of the Chu shu. It seems to me that he was influenced by the Chu shu. He gave the following regnal periods:

Chou Kung	7
Ch'eng Wang	7
K'ang Wang	26
Mu Wang	55
Wu Wang	6
Chao Wang	2
Total	103 years

The first four references are quoted in T'ai p'ing yü lan, vol. 85. In this volume from the Ti wang shih chi, Chao Wang is given 51 years. The last two references are from T'ung chih: 36, quoting Huang-p'u Mi. It seems to me that in the Ti wang shih chi he gives Chao Wang 51 years. In his later years, when he had seen the Chu shu, he corrected his own calculations to make Ch'eng and K'ang altogether 40 years, and to make the total from Wu Wang to Mu Wang about 100 years to accord with the Chu shu. His total length for Chou was 867 years as in Liu Hsin.

IV. Total Length of Western Chou

Now I shall reconstruct the Western Chou period. I believe that it is impossible to find out the accurate dates of this period because: (1) the claendar system changed several times be-

fore the Han dynasty and our knowledge is insufficient to solve
these problems; (2) even the Eastern Chou chronology is still
confused and there are many small problems concerning the exact
length of each reign waiting to be solved; (3) the length of each
king's reign can not be found out because information is lacking
both in written documents and in bronze inscriptions. Therefore
we accept 841 B.C. as the first year of Kung Ho only for convenience. It has been generally recognized that after that year
there is no question about the dates that followed.

Starting in the last year of Chou, 256 B.C., the total
length of Eastern Chou is 515 years. Therefore the first year of
Eastern Chou should be 770 B.C. The 515 is the total number of
years of the twenty-two kings beginning with P'ing Wang and ending
with Nan Wang. The length of the reign of each king is given by
Ssu-ma Ch'ien in his Chu hou nien piao and Liu kuo piao as follows:

1.	P'ing Wang	51
2.	Huan Wang	23
3.	Chuang Wang	15
4.	Hsi Wang	5
5.	Hui Wang	25
6.	Hsiang Wang	33
7.	Ch'ing Wang	6
8.	K'uang Wang	6
9.	Ting Wang	21
10.	Chien Wang	14
11.	Ling Wang	27
12.	Ching[3] Wang	25
13.	Ching[4] Wang	43
14.	Yuan Wang	8

15.	Ting Wang	28
16.	K'ao Wang	15
17.	Wei-li Wang	24
18.	An Wang	26
19.	Li Wang	7
20.	Hsien Wang	48
21.	Shen-ch'ing Wang	6
22.	Nan Wang	59

Total - 515

For the length of each king, Ssu-ma Ch'ien in his Chou pen chi gives different figures:

	Table	Chou pen chi
Hsiang Wang	33	32
Ching[3] Wang	25	20
Ching[4] Wang	43	42
Li Wang	7	10

For some reigns Huang-p'u Mi gives different figures:

	Ssu-ma	Huang-p'u
Hui Wang	25	24
Ching Wang	43	44
Yuan Wang	8	28
Ting Wang	28	10

It is obvious that these differences are caused by some sort of error although, as yet, there is not enough information to determine its source. I can not help but accept 515 years as the total length for Eastern Chou and I believe that the total length of Western Chou should be 257 years as recorded in the Chu shu; thus making the total length of Chou 772 years beginning in 1027 and ending in 256 B.C.

For this, though it can not be proved with direct evidence, I
shall try to point out the possibilities as follows:

the three paragraphs from Meng-tzu have been translated
(cf. Appendix III) and the last two paragraphs seem to me to be
the commentary to his theory of 500 years in a cycle. They probably belong to the same time but were also probably written by
different disciples. It is quite reliable to believe that he left
Ch'i about 312 B.C. His dates are about 390 to 305 B.C., and he
would have been about 70 at that time. He said that from Wen Wang
to K'ung-tzu was 500 years and more and from K'ung-tzu to his
time (312 B.C.) was 100 years and more. Because he said that from
Chou (that is, Wen Wang) to now is 700 years and more, therefore
the 'more' of the first two cases should be at least 50 years,
that is, 550 plus 150 is 700, a minimum figure. K'ung-tzu's dates
are about 551-479 B.C. From the last year of K'ung-tzu to 312 B.C.
is 167 years. From the first year of Eastern Chou (770 B.C.) to
the last year of K'ung-tzu (479 B.C.) is about 290 years. From
the first year of Eastern Chou (770 B.C.) to the time of Meng-tzu's
leaving Ch'i (312 B.C.) is about 460 years. Thus we arrive at
two results:

1. From Wen Wang to the last year of K'ung-tzu   550

   From the first year of Eastern Chou to K'ung-tzu 290

   Western Chou, including Wen Wang   260

2. From Wen Wang to the year Meng-tzu left Ch'i   750

   From the first year of Eastern Chou to the
       year Meng-tzu left Ch'i   460

   Western Chou, including Wen Wang   290

From this rough calculation, the Western Chou period (including Wen Wang) is between 260 to 290 years and not more than

300 years.   Therefore Liu Hsin's 352 must be wrong and the Chu
shu's 257, which is exclusive of Wen Wang, is within the range.

In the Tso chuan it was predicted that Chou would last 30
generations or 700 years.   This can not be considered as the real
record made during Ch'eng Wang's time.   It is mostly the beliefs
of the compilers of the Tso chuan who observed the symptoms of decay toward the end of the Chou dynasty.   It is now for us to determine the date of the compilation of the Tso chuan which scholars
generally believe was compiled sometimes in the fourth century B.C.
I have already stated that the Jupiter system mentioned in the
Tso chuan was established about 370 B.C.   Therefore the Tso chuan
must have been compiled after that date.   The Chu shu was compiled
between 297-296; its records are similar to the Tso chuan.   Also
the book Shih ch'un was found with the Chu shu.   The Shih ch'un—
the records of the divinations by tortoise and milfoil is said to
have been the same as the Tso chuan, and the Shih ch'un seems to
have been copied from the Tso chuan.   Therefore, the Tso chuan
must have been compiled between 370 and 300 B.C.

In the Tso chuan, Hsi Kung's thirty-first year (629 B.C.),
it is recorded that during that winter the barbarians beseiged Wei.
Wei moved to Ti-ch'iu and got the divination that the dynasty
would last for another 300 years. The Wei State actually ended in
209 B.C., but in 320 B.C. the Wei State gave up the title of Marquis and was called Chün   . It became a very weak and small
state occupying only P'ö-yang. The tradition of 300 years was probably calculated before 329 B.C. or sometimes near 320 B.C. when
the author of the Tso chuan saw symptoms of decay in the Wei State.

Until this period, except for the barbarians such as Ch'u,
Wu and Yüeh who called their leader 'king', the title 'king' was

exclusively used by the royal Chou family. During the second half
of the fourth century they either called themselves 'king' or the
states agreed to call their respective leaders 'king' on a re-
ciprocal basis. The important facts are given in the Shih chi as
follows:

    334 B.C.   Both Ch'i and Wei (Liang) reciprocally adopted
                     the title Wang.

    325 B.C.   Ch'in adopted the title

    323 B.C.   Both Han and Yen adopted the title as they
                     joined in a group of five states using it re-
                     ciprocally. The five states were Wei, Chung
                     Shan, Ch'in or Chao, Han and Yen.

    322 B.C.   Six major states had already adopted the title.
                     They were Ch'u, Ch'i, Ch'in, Han and Yen.
                     About this time the state of Chao most probably
                     adopted the title also, but the histories do
                     not state the exact year.

      During this period several states called their leader
'king'. Chou was so weak that the states did not consider the Chou
King the sovereign ruler. This act broke off even the pretense of
continuing the nominal relationship of subject and master with the
royal house of Chou. If we take 325 as the year in which the Tso
chuan was compiled, which also fits the supposition of its compilation in the period between 329 and 320, it is the 44th year
of Chou Hsien Wang. According to the Shih chi, Hsien Wang was of
the thirtieth generation from Ch'eng Wang, which is also 700 years
from this time to the first year of Ch'eng Wang if we take the
Chu shu's 257 as the period of Western Chou. Therefore the com-
piler of the Tso chuan, who made the prediction during 325 B.C.,

had in mind the total length of years from Ch'eng Wang to this time,
about 700 years in 30 generations of Chou kings. The first year
of the Kung Ho period was 841 B.C., and since he held power for
fourteen years the first year of Hsuan Wang must have been 827 B.C.
Prior to Hsuan, from Ch'eng Wang to Li Wang, there were eight
generations. Assuming four generations to a century, this dates
the beginning of the Chou dynasty circa 1027 B.C.

We can now draw the tentative conclusion that the total
length of Western Chou should be 257 years as recorded in the
Chu shu and that the first year of the Chou dynasty was 1027 B.C.

V. The Date of the Piao Bells

I shall now show, with the aid of the bronzes, that the Chu
shu is more accurate in its dates than the Shih chi. On the famous
Piao bells, found in Chin-ts'un of Lo-yang in 1930/31 (cf. Lo-yang:
no. 502 and Shan chai: 12), the inscription tells us that in the
22nd year Piao Ch'iang followed his master of the Han State and
attacked Ch'in and Ch'i, then entered the great wall and met other
allies at P'ing-yin   . He was favoured by the masters of
Han and Chin and was presented to the Son of Heaven. There has
been a great deal of confusion about the date of the bells. The
three theories concerning the date are:

1. 550 B.C., the 22nd year of Chou Ling Wang. This date was
        by Wu Ch'i-ch'ang   , Hsü Chung-shu
   , Liu Chieh   and Karlgren. According to the
   Chin shih chia and Chu hou nien piao of Shih chi in the
   13th year of Ling Wang (559), Chin with allies attacked
   Ch'in. According to the Ch'un ch'iu, in Hsiang Kung's

18th year (Ling Wang's 17th year, 555 B.C.) the Duke of
Lu "met Chin with Sung, Wei, Chen, Ts'ao. Chü, Chu, T'eng,
Hsüeh, Ch'i and Hsiao Chu Tzu, and besieged Ch'i." In the
Tso chuan for the same year it is recorded that "The
allies entered P'ing-yin." From these records we see that
first, the Chin attacked Ch'i and entered P'ing-yin. This
seems to accord with the inscription but it was not in the
22nd year of the Chou king. Second, the above records
show that the two attacks were made four years apart, one
in 559 and the other in 555, but the inscription seems to
place both in the same year. Third, the Han State was not
mentioned among the allies because at that time Han was
still a part of Chin and not yet an independent state, but
in the inscription it stood together with Chin as an independent state. From these points together with the pattern which was discussed under the date of the Hsin-cheng
finds, the dating of these bells to the Ling Wang period
is certainly wrong.

2. 380 B.C., the 22nd year of An Wang. This date is given
   by Kuo Mo-jo. Kuo quotes the T'ien shih chia and the
   Liu kuo piao of Shih chi. In this year Ch'i was attacked
   by Han, Chao and Wei at Shang-ch'iu   . First, according to the T'ien shih chia, in that year Ch'i
   attacked Yen and captured Shang-ch'iu so the other feudal
   lords attacked Ch'i at Shang-ch'iu to help Yen. This war
   was in the Yen territory and not in Ch'i and this does not
   agree with the inscription for we know that P'ing-yin was
   in the Ch'i State. During the year 380, Han already had
   the title of Marquis, but the inscription does not mention the title of Marquis. Therefore Kuo's dating is also

not reliable.

3. 404 B.C., the 22nd year of Wei-li Wang. This date is
given by Wen T'ing-chün and T'ang Lan. Wen quoted the
Shui ching chu: 26, which quoted the Chu shu saying, "in
the 12th year of Chin Li Kung the king ordered Han
Ching Tzu   , Chao Li Tzu   , and Ti
Yuan   , to attack Ch'i and they entered the Great
Wall." But Wen found in the Liu kuo piao that the 22nd
year of Wei-li Wang was the 16th year of Chin Li Kung—
there must be something wrong. Ssu-ma Ch'ien's table,
especially for the Chan Kuo period, has errors frequently.
There is even disagreement in the Shih chi between the
Nien piao and the Pen chi. Fortunately, we know that
the 12th year of Chin Li Kung was the 22nd year of Wei-li
Wang. It was recorded in the Chu shu that Kung-sun
Hui   of Ch'i rebelled at Ling-ch'iu   and
surrendered to Chao. This was quoted in Ssu-ma Cheng's
So yin of Shih chi, T'ien shih chia, as the 51st year of
Ch'i Hsuan Kung. It was also quoted in the Shui ching
chu: 24, as the 11th year of Chin Li Kung. Therefore
Chin Li Kung's 11th year is the same as Ch'i Hsuan Kung's
51st year. According to the Liu kuo piao, Ch'i Hsuan
Kung's 51st year was the 21st year of Wei-li Wang (here
the table is correct). Therefore the 12th year of Chin
Li Kung was the 22nd year of Wei-li Wang. In my table of
the Six States, based on the Chu shu, Wei-li Wang 21,
Ch'i Hsuan Kung 51 and Chin Li Kung 11 are all in the
same year.

The following year Han, Chao and Wei were allowed
to use the title of Marquis by the Chou king. This was

probably the result of their victory the previous year.

VI. *Durations of Western Chou Kings*

There is no question about the beginning and end of Chou
in the Chu shu. The first year of Chou was 1027 B.C. when Wu
Wang conquered Shang and established the kingdom. The last year
of Western Chou was 771 B.C., the last year of Yu Wang who was
killed by the barbarians. Using this year, according to the Chu
shu and other reliable written material, I shall trace the line of
Western Chou kings backwards. Both the Shih chi and the Kuo yü
agree that Yu Wang was killed in his 11th year. The Chu shu says,
"In his 10th year apricots grew on the peach trees." This would
seem an omen of his termination. It seems to me that in the Chu
shu Yu Wang lasted only eleven years.

There are more details in the Chu shu about Hsüan Wang.
It listed five events with the northern barbarians four years after
the establishment of Hsüan Wang, that is, it begins in the fifth
year of Hsüan Wang.

1. Hsüan Wang 5.   Ordered Ch'in Chung   to attack the
   barbarians and Ch'in Chung was killed.

2. Hsüan Wang 32. Dispatched soldiers to attack the barbarians of T'ai-yüan.

3. Hsüan Wang 37. Attacked the barbarians at T'iao   and
   Pên   .

4. Hsüan Wang 39. Chin defeated the northern barbarians at
   Fen-shih   .

5. Hsüan Wang 40.   Attacked the barbarians at Shen

6. Ten years after Hsüan Wang 40, Yu Wang attacked the barbarians of Liu-chi   .

This shows that Hsüan Wang 40 is the minimum number of
years for this reign and that 49 is the maximum. The Shih chi
records 46 which fits the range very well, but the Shih chi records the death of Ch'in Chung in the 6th year of Hsüan Wang, one
year different from the Chu shu. According to the Chu shu, in
the 32nd year when attacking the T'iao, Chou was defeated; in the
39th year Chin defeated the barbarians at Fen-shih, but the barbarians extinguished all of the cities of Chiang-hou   .
The latter meant that the king's army was defeated. In Chou yü I
of Kuo yü it says, "In the 39th year they fought at Ch'ien-mu   .
The king's army was defeated by the barbarians at Chiang-shih   ."
In the same year the Chin army was successful, so in the Tso chuan
for the 2d year of Huan Kung it is recorded that "The wife of Chin
Mu Hou   , Chiang Shih   , gave birth to a son during
the war of T'iao. He was named Ch'ou   (meaning 'Revenge').
His younger brother was born during the war of Ch'ien-mu. He was
named Ch'eng-shih   (Meaning 'Complete success of the army')."
This proves that the attack on T'iao was earlier than that on
Ch'ien-mu, in Hsüan's 39th year.

There are two theories about the Kung Ho period. The Chou
pen chi of Shih chi says, "Li Wang fled to Chih....Shao Kung and
Chou Kung were both in control of the government. It was called
Kung Ho." Here Ssu-ma Ch'ien interprets 'Kung Ho' as the name
of a period in which two ministers worked together. This theory
is different from the pre-Han documents including the Chu shu.
The Chu shu said that there was a Kung Po Ho   who usurped
the throne. Kung was the fief, Po was the rank and Ho a personal

name, hence it may also be called Kung Ho. Besides Chu shu, the
following sources also recorded that Kung Po Ho usurped the
throne:

1. K'ai ch'un chapter of Lü shih ch'un ch'iu

2. Lu lien tzu   quoted in Chang's Cheng yi to the
   Chou pen chi of Shih chi.

3. Ssu-ma Piao's commentary to Jang Wang chapter of Chuang-
   tzu.

4. Huang-p'u Mi quoted in Ssu-ma Cheng's Cheng yi to the
   San tai shih piao of Shih chi. The latter may have been
   taken from the Chu shu.

Ssu-ma Ch'ien's theory is certainly wrong, but his assignment
of fourteen years for the Kung Ho period seems all right. Li Wang
was said to have died in the 14th year of Kung Ho.

The Chu hou nien piao of Shih chi begins in the first
year of Kung Ho. In the Chou pen chi he gave Li Wang 37 years. It
seems to me that Ssu-ma Ch'ien was not convinced to accept the 37
years. The events of Li Wang in the Chou pen chi were copied from
the Chou yü of Kuo yü. There were two paragraphs of which the
first was concerned with restrictions on speech. The Kuo yü says,
"After three years the king was exiled to Chih." Ssu-ma Ch'ien
stated this for the 34th year of Li Wang and also said that three
years later the king was exiled. Therefore we know that the 34
years were added by Ssu-ma Ch'ien without any evidence. These 37
years must be wrong because they conflict with his own work in the
Shih chi. The evidences are:

1. Wei shih chia says, "Ch'ing Hou (of Wei) greatly bribed
   Chou Yi Wang and Yi Wang to name him Marquis. Ch'ing Hou
   reigned for twelve years and was succeeded by his son, Li

Hou. In the 13th year of Li Hou, Chou Li Wang fled to
Chih." Therefore Li Wang's reign can not be longer than
twenty-five years.

2. Ch'i shih chia says, "Hu Kung moved his capital to Po-ku
during the time of Chou Yi Wang. Ai Kung's younger
brother, Shan, hated Hu Kung. He, with his group, led
the people of Yin-ch'iu to attack, and killed Hu Kung
and established himself. This is Hsien Kung.... Nine
years after Hsien Kung died and was succeeded by his son,
Wu Kung Shou. In the ninth year of Wu Kung, Chou Li Wang
fled to Chih." From this Li Wang's reign can not be
longer than eighteen years.

3. Ch'en shih chia says, "Shen Kung was at the time of Chou
Li Wang. Shen Kung died and was succeeded by his son,
Yu Kung Ning. In the 12th year of Yu Kung, Chou Li Wang
fled to Chih." According to Ssu-ma Ch'ien's table it is
the 13th year of Yu Kung. Therefore the reign of Li Wang
was not shorter than thirteen years.

From the above evidence Li Wang's reign was probably between fourteen and eighteen years, and I have taken the mean value
of sixteen years for his reign.

The Chu shu records the 7th year of Yi Wang and therefore
the reign must have lasted at least seven years. From the evidences of the bronze inscriptions we know that Yi Wang reigned for
at least twenty-seven years, probably thirty. This has been discussed in the catalogue (cf. U.S. 259).

There are no records of the length of the reigns of Hsiao
and I Wang. I believe that each lasted for not more than ten years.
According to the Chu shu from Wu to Mu was about 100 years. If we

give Yi Wang 30, Li 16, Kung Ho 14, Hsüan 40 and Yu 11, as we discussed before, it totals 117 years—100 and 117 is 217, the total
of Western Chou being 257 years and the remainder for Kung, I and
Hsiao is 40 years. We know from the bronzes that Kung reigned at
least 15 years, and probably 20 years. Therefore I and Hsiao can
have only ten years each.

Scholars have had a great deal of trouble trying to ascertain the exact length of the reign of Mu Wang. The fragments in
the Chu shu about Mu Wang are coloured more by both fiction and
legend than by historical facts. Five chapters of a biography of
Mu Wang and a story telling of the death of his beautiful concubine
were uncovered with the Chu shu. In all of these books Mu Wang
was described like fictional heroes are pictured who travelled vast
distances into the far west and south. I believe that these
stories were told in the fourth century B.C., for they are exag-
gerated stories which can not be accepted as real history. In
Chou pen chi, Mu Wang is recorded as coming to the throne at the
age of fifty and regeining for fifty-five years. Ssu-ma Ch'ien
also attributed the chapter Lü hsin of Shang shu as the order of
Mu Wang. This chapter begins when "Lu Ming Wang was in his hun-
dredth year of rule." This may have been the source for Ssu-ma
Ch'ien's belief that Mu Wang lived 105 years. In the Chu shu, in
his 37th year he attacked Yüeh. This fragment was quoted in
different books. Some say 47th year, some 17th and some 7th, but
due to the fact that this expedition was no more than a legend
we can not rely on it.

The Chu shu says that from the beginning of Chou to Mu
Wang was altogether 100 years. This covered Wu, Ch'eng, K'ang,
Chao and Mu. We can only determine from the Chu shu that Chao

Wang lasted nineteen years.

The Chu shu says, "During the period of Ch'eng and K'ang
the kingdom was peaceful. Punishments were rescinded for forty
years and more, and were not used." This also appeared in the
Chou pen chi and Chu fu yen chuan of Shih chi; the latter quoted
Yen An's   essay. Wang Ch'ung's   Ju chen chapter of
Lun heng   quoted Ju shu as saying the same thing. This
shows that the period of Ch'eng and K'ang was more than forty
years. From the bronze inscriptions we know that K'ang was on
the throne at least 35 years, but we have no reliable records for
the length of the reign of Ch'eng Wang.

Now we must discuss the problem of Chou Kung. According
to tradition he was the regent during Ch'eng Wang's minority.
This idea was derived from a misinterpretation of the Shang shu
which I would like to discuss in detail.

VII. Early Chou Events

Before discussing the problem of Chou Kung, it is necessary to discuss the length of Wu Wang's reign. Written documents
agree that Wu Wang's reign was very short. The Hsiao wen
chapter of Kuan tzu   says, "Wu Wang attacked Yin and conquered it. After seven years he died." This theory was also
accepted in the Ming t'ang   chapter of Yi chou shu. Both
Shang shu ta chuan   and Chou pen chi say that Wen
Wang in his sixth year called himself Wang and died the next year.
The belief that the length of the reign of Wen Wang, Wu Wang and
the regency of Chou Kung was seven years probably derived from
the misinterpretation of the Shang shu. I shall take three years

as the length for Wu. It was recorded in the Chin t'eng chapter
of the Shang shu, the Chou pen chi and the Fung shan shu of Shih
chi that he died two years after his conquest of Yin. If we
count the year of attacking Yin he reigned for three years.

　　　　The Shang style inscriptions always put the day-name at
the beginning of the inscription and this is followed by the events.
Then followed the month, year and the great event of the year. For
example, Academia Sinica excavated an animal head with the following inscription:

　　　　　(On the day) X-X (two characters of the day-name

　　　　　are missing) the king hunted at X Lu. He cap-

　　　　　tured a white unicorn. X (verb) at X X (place-

　　　　　name). In the 2nd month, the king's 10th year,
　　　　　　　　　　　　　　　　　　　　season
　　　　　the period of T'ung jih (name of a sacrifice),

　　　　　the king came to attack the Yü-fang-po.

Now, we may compare this with the Lo kao chapter of Shang shu:

　　　　　(On the day) wu-shen the king was in the new

　　　　　capital. He performed a sacrifice.... In the

　　　　　twelfth month when Chou Kung guarded Wen and Wu's

　　　　　received mandate, the seventh year.

In the same chapter is says that the present king (Ch'eng Wang)
ordered that this be made the first year. This means that the
official first year of Ch'eng Wang was the 7th year after Wen
and Wu received their mandate from Heaven. The idea of the 'mandate received from Heaven' *does exist in Early Chou.*   The
bronze inscriptions from Early Chou to Late Western Chou have
such records. This idea also appear   in the Shang shu and in
the Shih ching. It is recorded that Wen or Wen Wu received the
mandate but not that Wu received the mandate. I shall now give
a table of the seven years according to the Shang shu:

1. Wen Wang's first year, in which he received the mandate.

   Chiu kao: "Your austere father Wen Wang established
   the kingdom in the western land. He ordered those states,
   those officers, chiefs and assistants, and day and night
   reminded them that the spirits should be used (only) in
   the sacrifice. When Heaven sent down the mandate to
   raise our people (this made) the first year." This was
   the order given by Ch'eng Wang to K'ang Hou.

2. The year Wu conquered Shang.

3. The first year after the conquest of Shang.

4. Two years after the conquest of Shang: Wu Wang died.

   Chin t'eng: "Two years after the conquest of Shang, the
   king (Wu) fell ill and was disturbed.... After the death
   of Wu Wang...."

5. Three years after the conquest of Shang: Ch'eng Wang's
   first year in which he attacked Wu Keng.

6. Four years after the conquest of Shang: Ch'eng attacked
   Yen (cf. Meng tzu, Appendix 3).

7. Five years after the conquest of Shang: Ch'eng's third
   year on the throne.

   To fang: "In the fifth month, (on the day) ting-hai, the
   king came from Yen and arrived at Tsung-chou. Chou Kung
   said, 'The king said as follows,I order you states within
   the four boundaries and without, to you the Yin Marquis,
   officers and people I hand down your great order..... I
   order you, the many states, many officers, now you have
   been serving my guards for five years....."

8. Seventh year after Wen and Wu received the mandate which
   is also the first official year of Ch'eng Wang.

   a. Shao kao: "....in the third month..., on the next day

i-mao, Chou Kung came to Lo and thoroughly inspected
the new city being built. The third day, ting-ssu,
(he) used the sacrifice in the suburb with two oxen.
The next day, Wu-mu, (he) made the sacrifice to the
Earth at the new city with one ox, one sheep and one
pig. The seventh day, chia-tzu, Chou Kung, holding
the book of mandates, ordered those Yin Marquis
Hou, T'ien, Nan and Pang-po...."

b. To shih: "In the third month, Chou Kung first went
to the new city Lo. He ordered the Shang king and
officers. The king said as follows, '...formerly I
came from Yen and I handed down the great order to
you people within the states.... Now I make this new
city in this Lo....'"

The book of mandates mentioned in the
Shao kao was read by Chou Kung for the king. Shao kao
records only the events; the whole text of the mandate
is in the To shih. In To shih the king mentioned the
previous order he gave to the Shang people. This was
the To fang chapter in Shang shu.

c. K'ang kao: "In the third month, the first half, Chou
Kung first commenced the foundations and built the
new great city at Lo of the Eastern State.... Chou
Kung ordered, the king said as follows...." (This was
the order given to K'ang Hou by Ch'eng Wang).

d. Shao kao: ".... Chou Kung said.... I order you Yin
people...."

e. Lo kao: ".... I (Chou Kung, on the day) i-mao, came
to Lo camp.... The present king ordered and said,
'To recall success in the ancestral temple, may this

year be the first year because of the success...."

f. <u>Lo kao</u>: Translated above, following the Shang inscription.

From <u>a</u> to <u>e</u> are the orders given in the Eastern capital, Lo,
in the third month of the first official year of Ch'eng Wang, and
<u>f</u> is the same except that it is for the twelfth month of the first
official year. This year was the seventh year after the conquest
of Shang. If the materials quoted above from the <u>Shang shu</u> are reliable, then the duration of the reign of Wu Wang should be three
years and the time after Wen Wang received the mandate can not be
over one year. Some of the late materials give very different
accounts for the duration of Wen Wang and Wu Wang including his
reign before the conquest. As the <u>Shang shu</u> is no doubt earlier
than the other materials, it must be chosen as the more reliable.

We should notice that the tradition of Chou Kung's being
regent was coincident with the story that when Ch'eng Wang succeeded to the throne he was still in swaddling clothes. The latter
tradition appeared in some of the late Chou and Han works used to
support the theory of the regency. From the early Chou bronzes
we know that Chou Kung attacked the Shang and the Eastern barbarians
in the name of the king. It seems that the attack on Shang was
started by Wen Wang. The <u>K'ang kao</u> of the <u>Shang shu</u> says, "Heaven
gave the great mandate to Wen Wang to exterminate the barbarian
Yin and then to receive his mandate." It seems to me that Wen
Wang started the attack but died before fulfilling the conquest.
The 'received mandate from Heaven' should be explained as his
actually controlling the kingdom.

VIII. Evidence from the Bronzes

Sometimes the bronze inscriptions mention the years of the
kings but the materials are too scant to supplement the above and
fill in the blanks. There is only one bronze which can be dated
to Wu Wang and it gives only a day-name. Those assumed to be
Ch'eng Wang's do not mention the year. During the K'ang Wang
period the Yü ting (San tai: 4.44-45a) mentioned the 35th year
and therefore K'ang's reign must have been longer than thirty-five
years. During the Kung Wang period the Ch'io Ch'ao ting says, "At
the 10 and 5 year, 5 month, first half, (on the day) jen-wu, Kung
Wang was at the hsin-kung *New palace* of Chou...." (San tai: 4.25.) Therefore
Kung Wang reigned for at least fifteen years. Under the K'e set
I have stated that Yi Wang reigned for at least twenty-seven years
according to the bronze inscriptions. During the Li Wang period
the Shih Li kuei (Shang chou: II, 334) mentioned the 11th year so
Li Wang must have been on the throne at least during that time.
During the Hsüan Wang period there are many bronzes which give him
more than ten years.

IX. Periods of the Chou Dynasty

I have decided on 1027 B.C. as the first year of Wu Wang
who lasted for three years. According to the bronzes K'ang lasted
at least thirty-five years and I have assigned him thirty-eight
years and this is taken as the length of his reign. Chao Wang
lasted nineteen years according to the Chu shu. Again, according to
Chu shu, from Wu to Mu was 100 years. Therefore both Ch'eng and Mu
are given twenty years, which fill out the 100 year period.

From the bronzes Kung Wang lasted at least fifteen years
and Li at least twenty-seven years. Therefore I have given Kung 20

and Li 30 years. I have given I and Hsiao 10 years each, Li 16,
Kung Ho 14, Hsüan 46 and Yu 11 (cf. table above). This totals
257 years. Except for K'ang all of these rulers have been given
round numbers in order to show that these figures are no more than
conjectures.

For convenience in the study of bronzes I have divided
Western Chou into three parts:

1. Early Western Chou   Wu to Chao   80 years
2. Middle Western Chou   Mu to Yi   90 years
3. Late Western Chou   Li to Yu   87 years

The first year of Eastern Chou began when P'ing Wang
moved his capital to Lo-yang in 770 B.C. After this period scholars
usually divided the Eastern Chou period into Ch'un Ch'iu and Chan
Kuo. The Ch'un Ch'iu period was named after the Ch'un ch'iu
Annals which began in 722 B.C. and ended in 431 B.C. It is proper
that the forty-eight years before the Ch'un ch'iu Annals should be
considered as the Ch'un Ch'iu period. Thus the Ch'un Ch'iu period
is given 290 years while the Annals consist of the events of only
242 years.

The year after the close of these Annals was the beginning
of the Chan Kuo period. Chan Kuo has sometimes been translated as
Contending States or as Warring States. It is named after the
book, Chan kuo ts'e. Chan Kuo is sometimes mentioned as Liu
Kuo   , which were the six most powerful states during that
period. In 256 B.C. the last Chou king died. This was the last
year of the nominal Chou dynasty, but not the end of the Chan Kuo
period because after that year the six major states still existed.
This period really ended in 222 B.C., the year before the unification under Ch'in. The Chan Kuo period lasted 259 years. Together
with the 290 years of the Ch'un Ch'iu period the total is 549 years

but the total length of Eastern Chou is 515 years because after
the close of Eastern Chou there were still 34 years of the Chan
Kuo period. Like the Western Chou period, both the Ch'un Ch'iu
and the Chan Kuo periods may be divided into three parts.

X. Hsia and Shang before P'an Keng

According to the Chu shu, P'an Keng's removal of the capital to Yin was 273 years before the end of the dynasty. Therefore
the first year of P'an Keng's removal to Yin should be 1300 B.C.
The total length of Shang, i.e., from T'ang to its close, is *given*
differently in various records. The Tso chuan gives 600 years,
Meng tzu gives '500 years and more' and the Chu shu gives 496 years.
The latter is the same as that recorded in the Yi wei chi lan t'u
of the Han dynasty. The quotation in the Chu shu must be wrong
because the Chu shu gives the total length of Hsia as 471 years
and Shuo Chih   says, "The years of Hsia were more than Yin."
(Shuo chih chuan of Ching shu.) Shuo was the person who worked on
the Chu shu when it was unearthed in his time. There must have
been something wrong with these quotations. Therefore I have given
Hsia and Shang 500 years each. Meng tzu says, that from Yao and
Shün to T'ang was 500 years and more. Hsia was supposed to have
been contemporary with Yao and Shun.

It is more difficult to reconstruct the length of the
             after P'an Keng
Shang kings than the Western Chou kings.   There
are only four sources which offer a few records of the reigns of
the Shang kings. In the Wu yi chapter of Shang shu and the Wan
                                                  in
chang chapter of Meng tzu and in the Chu shu some of the reigns
are given, and on the oracle bones and the bronzes it was recorded

that Ti Hsin reigned for at least 20 years. The sources are as
follows:

    1. <u>Wu yi</u>

       Chung Chung (Tsu Yi) 75 years

       Kao Tsung (Wu Ting) 59 years

       Tsu Chia   33 years

    2. <u>Meng tzu</u>

       Wai Ping 2 years

       Chung Jen 4 years

    3. <u>Chu shu</u>

       T'ai Chia   12 years

       Wu Yi   35 years plus

       T'ai Ting   11 years plus

       Ti Yi   2 years plus

       Ti Hsin   6 years plus

    4. <u>Oracle bones and bronzes</u>

       Ti Hsin   20 years plus

The <u>Wu yi</u> chapter says, "After Tsu Chia the duration of
the kings was very short; some 7 or 8 years, some 5 or 6 years,
and some 3 or 4 years." This is all we can find. In section
three of this chapter I have listed the traditional duration of
the Western Chou kings according to the Sung books. These books
also gave the duration of the Shang kings, which were the sources
for the chronological systems of Legge and Pere Tchang. In recent
years some scholars have tried to reconstruct the Yin chronology
after P'an Keng with the aid of the numerous fragments of the oracle
bones. These fragments can not be made into a complete table
because they themselves are not complete. Except for the last

Shang king none of the earlier oracle bones give any records of
the years. I have discussed the difficulty involved in arriving
at the total length of Western Chou, how then can the length of
Shang be determined when Western Chou is conjecture? Even if the
arrangements
fragments of the oracle bones made by scholars are correct, how is
it possible to find out the last year of Shang and the duration of
the kings? It is unfortunate that all of this depends on the late
sources which are conjectures without evidence. Furthermore, the
chronological system during Shang changed several times and knowledge of it is very limited. Mr. Tung Tso-pin of the Academia
Sinica published his Yin Chronology in 1944 in 4 huge volumes.
It does not convince of the above reasons. It was a great surprise
to me to compare Tung's regnal periods with those of Pere Tchang
and find more than 50 per cent agreement. This is because they
were all based on the Sung sources.

In my article, "The Names of the Kings of Shang" (Yenching
Hsüeh Pao, 27 (1930), pp. 115-142), I divided the Shang into three
periods. The first eight generations recorded in the Shih chi
are not reliable. Their names often form two characters and are
not from the t'ien-kan as the later ones. The second period of six
generations was found on the oracle bones which used the t'ien-kan.
The last generation of the first period was also found on the oracle
bones, but this together with the four generations of the second
period never offered sacrifices with their wives. The third period
began with T'ang, which is listed in Table IV. We know very little
about the Hsia dynasty. The Hsia pen chi of Shih chi listed seventeen kings for fourteen generations and the Chu shu recorded the
total length as 471 years and assigned some of the kings definite
periods.

TABLE I

General Chronology from Hsia to Han

I. HSIA ....ca. 2100-ca. 1600 B.C.

II. SHANG

        A. From T'ang to the year before
        P'an Keng's removal of the
        capital to Yin ....ca. 1600-1301 B.C.

        B. From P'an Keng's removal of
        the capital to Yin to the end
        of the dynasty...................... 1300-1028 B.C.

III. CHOU

        A. Western Chou .... 1027- 771 B.C.

        B. Eastern Chou......................... 770- 222 B.C.

        1. Ch'un Ch'iu period, from P'ing
        Wang's removal to Lo-yang to the
        last year recorded in the book
        of Ch'un ch'iu .... 770- 481 B.C.

        2. Chan Kuo period, from the year
        after the close of Ch'un ch'iu
        to the year before the unifica-
        tion under Ch'in .... 480- 222 B.C.

IV. CH'IN From the unification under Ch'in Shih
        Huang Ti until the end of the
        dynasty .... 221- 206 B.C.

V. HAN

        A. Former Han (Western Han)............ 206-   8 A.D.

        B. Hsin .... 9- 23 A.D.

        C. Later Han (Eastern Han)............. 25- 220 A.D.

TABLE II

Western Chou

Early Western Chou

Wu Wang	1027-1025 B.C.	3
Ch'eng Wang	1024-1005 B.C.	20
K'ang Wang	1004- 967 B.C.	38
Chao Wang	966- 948 B.C.	19

Middle Western Chou

Mu Wang	947- 928 B.C.	20
Kung Wang	927- 908 B.C.	20
I Wang	907- 898 B.C.	10
Hsiao Wang	897- 888 B.C.	10
Yi Wang	887- 858 B.C.	30

Late Western Chou

Li Wang	857- 842 B.C.	16
Kung Ho	841- 828 B.C.	14
Hsüan Wang	827- 782 B.C.	46
Yu Wang	781- 771 B.C.	11

TABLE III

Eastern Chou

P'ing Wang	770-720 B.C.	51
Huan Wang	719-697 B.C.	23
Chuang Wang	696-682 B.C.	15
Hsi Wang	681-677 B.C.	5
Hui Wang	676-652 B.C.	25
Hsiang Wang	651-619 B.C.	33
Ch'ing Wang	618-613 B.C.	6
K'uang Wang	612-607 B.C.	6
Ting Wang	606-586 B.C.	21
Chien Wang	585-572 B.C.	14
Ling Wang	571-545 B.C.	27
Ching[3] Wang	544-520 B.C.	25
Ching[4] Wang	519-477 B.C.	43
Yüan Wang	476-469 B.C.	8
Ting Wang*	468-441 B.C.	28
K'ao Wang	440-426 B.C.	15
Wei-li Wang	425-402 B.C.	24
An Wang	401-376 B.C.	26
Li Wang	375-369 B.C.	7
Hsien Wang	368-321 B.C.	48
Shen-ch'ing Wang	320-315 B.C.	6
Nan Wang	314-256 B.C.	59

*Huang-p'u Mi called it Chen-ting Wang to distinguish it from the first Ting Wang (606-586 B.C.).

TABLE IV

Shang Kings

1. T'ien I (T'ai I, T'ang)

2. T'ai Ting, 3. Wai Ping, 4. Chung Jen*

5. T'ai Chia

6. Wo Ting,   7. T'ai Keng

8. Hsiao Chia, 9. Yung Chi,10. T'ai Wu

11. Chung Ting,12. Wai Jen,13. Ho T'an Chia

14. Tsu I

15. Tsu Hsin, 16. Wo Chia (K'ai Chia)

17. Tsu Ting, 18. Nan Keng

      Hsin
19.Yang Chia,20.P'an Keng,21.Hsiao ^ 22. Hsiao I

23. Wu Ting

24. Tsu Keng, 25. Tsu Chia

26. Lin Hsin* (Fung Hsin) 27. K'ang Ting

28. Wu I

29. T'ai Ting (Wen Ting)

30. Ti I*

31. Ti Hsin* (Chou)

The numbers indicate the order of succession, based on
the Yin pen chi of Shih chi. Each line represents one generation.
Those on the same line are brothers. The mid-line shows a succession from father to son forming the 'great ancestors' and
those on the sides (brothers) forming the 'small ancestors'. The
asterisk indicates that the names have not yet been found on the
oracle bones. The names are based on the Yin pen chi. They are
altogether seventeen generations and thirty-one kings. Before
T'ang, both Yin pen chi and the oracle bones listed the following
kings:
Shang Chia (Wei) - Pao I - Pao Ping - Pao Ting - Shih Jen - Shih Kuei,

TABLE V

Chou Kings

1. Wu

2. Ch'eng

3. K'ang

4. Chao

5. Mu

6. Kung

7. I,   8. Hsiao

9. Yi

10. Li

11. Hsüan

12. Yu

13. P'ing

   Hsieh-fu

14. Huan

15. Chuang

16. Hsi

17. Hui

18. Hsiang

19. Ch'ing

20. K'uang,   21. Ting

               22. Chien

               23. Ling

               24. Ching[3]

25. Tao   26. Ching[4]

               27. Yüan

               28. Ting

TABLE V

Chou Kings (continued)

28. (see first page)

29. Ai,   30. Szu,   31. K'ao

                          32. Wei-li

                          33. An

                          34. Li,   35. Hsien

                                          36. Shen-ch'ing

                                          37. Nan

One line represents one generation. The table is based on the Chou pen chi of Shih chi, except for Hsiao. Hsiao is listed as Kung's brother in the Chou pen chi, but the San tai shih piao and the Shih pen listed Hsiao as the brother of I Wang which is accepted here. This makes no difference in the number of generations. In the Shih pen Huan is listed as the son of P'ing which would give one generation less. Hsieh-fu died before he got to the throne. Tao, Ai and Szu reigned for only a few months. In the cases of 7-8, 20-21, 25-26, 29-31, 34-35, the younger brothers succeeded the elder ones.

Genealogical / chronological chart of state rulers across the Zhou royal eras.

		Kung Ho 1-14	Hsüan W 1-46	Yu W 1-11
Chen K. 15-28	Chen K. 29-30		Hsiao K. 1-25	Hsiao K. 26-36
Wu K. 10-23	Wu K. 24-26		Wu K. 1-10	Chuang K. 14-24
			Ch'eng K. 1-9 Chuang K. 1-13	
Ching H. 18	Hsi H. 1-13		Shang S. 1-3	Shang S. 4
			Wen K. 1-12	Wen H. 1-10
Ch'in C. 4-17	Ch'in C. 18-23	Chuang K. 1-40		Chuang K. 41-44
			I K. 1-9	Hsiang K. 1-7
Wen Hs.Yung 1-6	Hs. Yen 1-10	Hs. Shuang 1-6	Hs. Hsün 1-22	
			Hs. Ê. 1-9	
			Jo-ao 1-9	Jo-ao 10-20
Hsi K. 18-28	Hui K. 1-3	Hui K. 4-31	Tai K. 1-18	Tai K. 19-29
Hsi H. 14-27	Hsi H. 28-42		Wu K. 1-31	Wu K. 32-42
Yu K. 14-23	Hsi K. 1-4	Hsi K. 5-36	Wu K. 1-14	Wu K. 1-15
Wu H. 23-26	Yi H. 1-10	Yi H. 11-28	Hsi H. 1-28	Hsi H. 29-39
Yi P. 24-30	Yu P. 1-7	Yu P. 8-9	Tai P. 1-30	Hui P. 15-25
Hui H. 24-37		Hui H. 38	Hsi H. 1-36	Ch'ing H. 10-20

Additional era entries:
Li K. 1-9; Hsien H. 1-11; Mu H. 1-27; Hui P. 1-14; Ch'ing H. 1-9; Yi K. 1-3; P'ing K. 1-7.

Headers: Yu W 1-11 · Hsüan W 1-46 · Kung Ho 1-14

```
W.  - Wang
K.  - Kung
H.  - Hou
P.  - Po
C.  - Chung
S.  - Shu
Hs.- Hsiung
* Died in the sixth year of K'ang Wang (based on the Chu shu).
# Killed in the third year of Yi Wang (based on the Chu shu).
```

TABLE VI

Western Chou Feudal Lords

Chou	Ch'eng W. 1-20	K'ang W. 1-38	Chao W. 1-19	Mu W. 1-20	Kung W. 1-20	I. W. 1-10	Hsiao W. 1-10	Yi W. 1-30	Li W. 1-16
Lu	P. Ch'in	K'ao K. 1-4 / Yang K. 1-6 / Yu K. 1-14 / Wei K. 1-8	Wei K. 9-27	Wei K. 28-47	Wei K. 48-50 / Li K. 1-17	Li K. 18-27	Li K. 28-37	Hsien K. 1-30	Hsien K. 31-32 / Chen K. 1-14
Ch'i	T'ai K.*	Ting K.	I K.	Kuei K.	Kuei K.	Ai K. #	Ai K.	Hu K. 1-24 / Hsien K. 1-3	Hsien K. 3-9 / Wu K. 1-9
Chin	T'ang S.	Chin H.		Wu H.	Ch'eng H.	Ch'eng H. / Li H.	Li H.	Ching H. 1	Ching H. 2-17
Ch'in	Wu-lai-ke	Nü-fang		P'ang-kao	Ta-chi	Ta-lo	Fei-tzu	Ch'in H. 1-10	Kung P. 1-3
Ch'u	Hs. I.			Hs. Ai	Hs. Tan	Hs. Sheng	Hs. Yang	Hs. Chü	Hs. Chih-hung Hs.
Sung	Wei-tzu	Wei C.	Sung K.	Ting K.	Ming K.	Yang K.	Li K.	Hsi K. 1	Hsi K. 2-17
Wei	K'ang S.	K'ang P.	Ssu P.	Chieh P.	Ching P.	Chen P.		Ch'ing H. 1-9	Ch'ing H. 10-12 / Hsi H. 1-13
Ch'en	Hu K.	Shen K.		Hsiang K.	Hsiao K.	Hsiao K.	Shen K.	Shen K.	Yu K. 1-13
Ts'ai	Ts'ai S. / Ts'ai C.			Ts'ai P.	Kung H.	Kung H.	Li H. / Li H.	Wu H. 1-6	Wu H. 7-22
Ts'ao	T'ao S.	T'ai P.	C. Chün	G. Chün	Kung P.	Kung P.	Hsiao P.	Yi P. 1-7	Yi P. 8-23
Yen	Shao K.							Hui H. 1-7	Hui H. 8-23

From Shao to Hui, nine generations

Note on Table VI

This table is based on materials from my conjectures on Western Chou which takes 257 years as the total length of time from Ch'eng Wang to Yu Wang and gives the duration of each king as I have suggested. The dates from Kung Ho's first year to the end of Yu Wang were taken from the Chu hou nien piao of Shih chi without alteration. Before the Kung Ho up to Yi, I have taken the duration of each feudal lord from the Shih chia of Shih chi and arranged it under the corresponding Chou reign based on my conjectures. I have also taken some sources from the Chu shu chi nien, viz., "Ai Kung of Ch'i was killed in the 3rd year of Yi Wang," and "T'ai Kung of Ch'i died in the 6th year of K'ang Wang." I also took one reference from the 12th year of Chao Kung in the Tso chuan, "Po Ch'in of Lu, Ting Kung of Ch'i, Chin Hou of Chin, K'ang Po of Wei and Hsiung I of Ch'u all served under K'ang Wang." If we know that one of the feudal lords reigned under a certain king and that his reign was shorter than the reign of the king, then I place him, his forerunner or successor, within the reign of that king. In the case of Ch'i I calculated Hu Kung as about twenty-four years, based on the supposition that Yi Wang lasted thirty years. If we know that one of the feudal lords reigned under a certain Chou king then we place this lord's forerunner or successor before or after that Chou king's reign. With this method I was able to work out a table before Kung Ho and Hsiao Wang. Although they are not quite accurate, they are near the truth for they are consistent for every feudal lord. Between K'ang and Hsiao the histories did not give the duration of each feudal lord, therefore I have placed those feudal lords, only for convenience, in the appropriate places.

In the San tai shih piao of Shih chi, Ssu-ma Ch'ien listed
eleven feudal lords under each Chou king's reign from Ch'eng to
Kung Ho. The arrangement is full of errors which my table might
be used to correct. In the Chu hou nien piao, he listed thirteen
feudal lords, of which I have omitted Wu and Cheng because they
came to power later. This new table is actually a combination
and reconstruction of the Shih piao and the first part of the Nien
piao. The duration of the feudal lords given in the Shih chia and
the table are sometimes at variance. The differences are as follows:

	Shih chia	Nien piao
1. Lu State		
Wu Kung	9	10
Hsiao Kung	27	38

The Shih chia gave Po Yü 11 years before Hsiao Kung.

2. Ch'en State

Here the Shih chia places the 12th year of Yu Kung
as the last year of Chou Li Wang. From then on the
Shih chia is always one year earlier than the Nien
piao but the seventh year of P'ing Kung is given as
the last year of Yu Wang and here the Shih chia and
the Nien piao agree, but according to Ch'en shih chia
Yu Wang lasted only ten years.

	Shih chia	Nien piao
3. Sung State		
Hui Kung	30	31

Between Hui Kung and Tai Kung the Shih chia gives
Ai Kung one year.

These discrepancies make no difference in the total length
of time and are reflected only in the placing of some particular
feudal lord. I have retained the original table after Kung Ho,
although if it is checked against the Chu shu there are still a few

small differences. This new table helps to prove our conjectures,
especially the table for Lu which is more complete in the Shih
chia than for other feudal lords. Unfortunately, we do not have
the duration of Po Ch'in. Based on this conjecture, Po Ch'in
should have twenty years under Ch'eng and six years under K'ang
Wang, a total of twenty-six years. As I have pointed out before
Liu Hsin was based on the Lu shih chia for a reconstruction of
Western Chou. His quotations from the Lu shih chia are different
from the ones we have today, such as, his giving the six years of
Yang Kung as sixty and the thirty-two years of Hsien Kung as fifty;
this is only because his conjecture for Western Chou was for a
longer period.

In Table VI, from the first year of Ch'eng Wang to the last
year of Yu Wang is 254 years, this excluded three years of Wu Wang's
reign. Therefore, from the year when Wu Wang conquered Shang to
the end of Western Chou is 257 years.

TABLE VII

Duration of States

State	Duration	Exterminated by	Source
1. Ch'in	?-206 B.C.	Six states	Ch'in shih huang pen chi
2. Western Kuo	?-687 B.C.	Ch'in	Ch'in pen chi
3. Chou	1027-256 B.C.	Ch'in	Ch'in pen chi
4. Tu	?-687 B.C.	Ch'in	Ch'in pen chi
5. Liang	?-641 B.C.	Ch'in	Ch'un ch'iu (Hsi 19)
6. Jui	?-640 B.C.	Ch'in	Ch'in pen chi
7. Chih	?-453 B.C.	Han, Chao, Wei	Han, Chao, Wei shih chia
8. Northern Kuo	?-655 B.C.	Chin	Tso chuan (Hsi 5)
9. Yü	1027-655 B.C.	Chin	Tso chuan (Hsi 5)
10. Chin	1024-369 B.C.	Han, Chao, Wei	Chu shu; Chin shih chia
11. Han	403-230 B.C.	Ch'in	Ch'in shih huang pen chi
12. Chao	403-222 B.C.	Ch'in	Ch'in shih hunag pen chi
13. Wei	403-225 B.C.	Ch'in	Ch'in shih. huang pen chi
14. Shang	1300-1027 B.C.	Chou	Chu shu
15. Wei	1024-209 B.C.	Ch'in	Wei shih chia
16. Tung Chou	367-249 B.C.	Ch'in	Chou pen chi
17. Hsi Chou	1027-249 B.C.	Ch'in	Chou pen chi
18. Su	?-617 B.C.=?		Ch'un ch'iu (Wen 10)
19. Hsing	1027-635 B.C.	Wei	Ch'un ch'iu (Hsi 25)
20. Eastern Kuo	?-771 B.C.	Cheng	Cheng shih chia
21. Cheng	806-375 B.C.	Han	Cheng shih chia
22. Hsü[3]	?-494 B.C.=?	Cheng	Ch'un ch'iu (Ai 1)
23. Ying	Western Chou		
24. Ch'en	1027-478 B.C.	Ch'u	Tso chuan (Ai 17)
25. Sung	1024-286 B.C.	Ch'i[2]	Liu kuo piao

TABLE VII

Duration of States

	State	Duration	Exterminated by	Source
26.	Tai	?- 713 B.C.	Cheng	Tso chuan (Yin 10)
27.	Yung	1027-1024 B.C.	Chou	
28.	Ts'ai	1027- 447 B.C.	Ch'u	Ch'u shih chia
29.	Shen	1027- 506 B.C.	Ts'ai	Tso chuan (Ting 4)
30.	Chiang	?- 623 B.C.	Ch'u	Ch'un ch'iu (Wen 4)
31.	Huang	?- 648 B.C.	Ch'u	Ch'un ch'iu (Hsi 12)
32.	Teng	?- 678 B.C.	Ch'u	Tso chuan (Chuang 6)
33.	Jo	?- 504 B.C.	Ch'u	Tso chuan (Ting 6)
34.	Yen[1]	1027- 222 B.C.	Ch'in	Ch'in shih huang pen chi
35.	Pei	Western Chou		
36.	Ch'i[3]	1027- 445 B.C.	Ch'u	Ch'u shih chia
37.	Chi	?- 690 B.C.?	Ch'i[2]	Ch'un ch'iu (Chuang 4)
38.	Ch'i[2] (of Chiang)	1027-379 B.C.	T'ien	Ch'i shih chia
	Ch'i[2] (of T'ien)	378- 221 B.C.	Ch'in	Ch'in shih huang pen chi
39.	Chu[4]	1029- 550 B.C.?		Tso chuan (Hsiang 23)
40.	Lu	1027- 250 B.C.	Ch'u	Lu shih chia
41.	Shang Yen	1027-1024 B.C.	Chou	
42.	Po Ku	Western Chou		
43.	Chu[1]	?- 281 B.C.?		Ch'u shih chia
44.	Ni	Eastern Chou		
45.	Shih	?- 560 B.C.	Lu	Ch'un ch'iu (Hsiang 13)
46.	Ts'ao	1027- 487 B.C.	Sung	Tso chuan (Ai 8)
47.	Tseng	?- 567 B.C.	Chü	Ch'un ch'iu (Hsiang 6)
48.	Chü	?- 431 B.C.	Ch'u	Ch'u shih chia
49.	T'eng	1027- 286 B.C.	Sung	Chan kuo ts'e
50.	T'an	?- 281 B.C.?	Ch'i[2], Yüeh	Ch'u shih chia

TABLE VII

Duration of States

State	Duration	Exterminated by	Source
51. Hsüeh	Eastern Chou		
52. Hsü[2]	?-512 B.C.?	Wu, Ch'u	Ch'un ch'iu (Chao 30
53. Ch'u	?-223 B.C.	Ch'in	Ch'u shih chia
54. Wu	?-473 B.C.	Yüeh	Ch'un ch'iu (Ai 22)
55. Yüeh	?-333 B.C.	Ch'u	Chu shu

APPENDIX I

Translation of the Chu shu chi nien

Wei

1. The prince of Yin, Hai, was a guest in the I
   State. (His behaviour was) obscene. The chief of
   I, Mien Ch'en, killed him and quartered him.
   Therefore Shang-chia Wei of Yin borrowed an army
   from Ho Po and attacked the I territory. He con-
   quered it and killed Mien Ch'en.

T'ang
(T'ai Ting)

2. T'ang had seven names and made nine expeditions.

Wai Ping

3. Wai Ping, Shen, succeeded. He lived in Po.

Chung Jen

4. Chung Jen succeeded. He lived in Po. He appointed
   I Yin as Ch'ing-ssu.

T'ai Chia

5. Chung Jen died. I Yin exiled T'ai Chia to T'ung
   and established himself (on the throne).

6. I Yin established himself, exiled T'ai Chia.
   After seven years T'ai Chia secretely escaped
   from T'ung and killed I Yin and ordered his (I's)
   sons, I She and I Fen, to reoccupy their father's
   fields and house and equally divide them into two.

7. T'ai Chia reigned only twelve years.

Wo Ting

8. Wo Ting, Hsün, succeeded. He lived in Po.

T'ai Keng

9. Hsiao Keng, Pien, succeeded. He lived in Po.

Hsiao Chia

10. Hsiao Chia, Kao, succeeded. He lived in Po.

Yung Chi
(T'ai Wu)

11. Yung Chi, Chou, succeeded. He lived in Po.

Chung Ting

12. Chung Ting succeeded. In the first year he
    moved from Po to Ao.

	13. (Chung Ting) attacked the Lan barbarians.
Wai Jen	14. Wai Jen lived in Ao.
Ho T'an Chia	15. Ho T'an Chia, Cheng, succeeded. He moved from Ao to Hsiang.
	16. Ho T'an Chia attacked the Lan barbarians. He again attacked the Pan Fang.
Tsu I	17. Tsu I, T'eng, succeeded; he was called Chung Chung. He lived in Pi.
(Tsu Hsin)	
Wo Chia	18. Ti K'ai Chia, Yü, succeeded. He lived in Pi.
Tsu Ting	19. Tsu Ting succeeded. He lived in Pi.
Nan Keng	20. Nan Keng, Keng, he moved to Yen from Pi.
Yang Chia	21. Yang Chia succeeded. He lived in Yen.
P'an Keng	22. P'an Keng, Hsün, moved from Yen to the south mound called Yin.
	23. From P'an Keng's removal to Yin until the termination (of Shang) under Chou, there were altogether 273 years and the capital was not changed.
Hsiao Hsin	24. Hsiao Hsin, Sung, succeeded. He lived in Yin.
Hsiao I	25. Hsiao I, Lien, lived in Yin.
(Wu Ting)	
Tsu Keng	26. Tsu Keng, Yao, lived in Yin.
Tsu Chia	27. Ti Tsu Chia, Tsai, lived in Yin.
	28. Tsu Chia made an expedition to the east and got Tan Shan.
Lin Hsin	29. Fung Hsin, Hsien, lived in Yin.
Keng Ting	30. Keng Ting lived in Yin.
Wu I	31. Wu I succeeded. He lived in Yin.
	32. In the 34th year, Wang Chi Li of Chou came to

court. The king gave him land of thirty li,
ten pairs of jades and eight horses.

33. In the 35th year, Wang Chi of Chou attacked
the Kuei barbarians of Hsi Lo and captured
twenty barbarian kings.

T'ai Ting   34. In the 2nd year of T'ai Ting, the Chou people
attacked the barbarians of Yen-ching. The Chou
were greatly defeated.

35. In the 3rd year of T'ai Ting the Huan River on
one day stopped flowing three times.

36. In the 4th year of T'ai Ting, the Chou people
attacked the barbarians of Yü Wu and conquered
them. Wang Chi of Chou was ordered by Yin to
be the Master of Herdsmen.

37. In the 7th year of T'ai Ting, the Chou people
attacked the barbarians of Shih Hu and conquered
them.

38. In the 11th year of T'ai Ting, the Chou people
attacked the barbarians of Yi T'u and captured
three high officials.

39. Wen Ting killed Chi Li.

Ti I   40. Ti I lived in Yin.

41. In the 2nd year of Ti I, the Chou people
attacked Shang.

Ti Hsin   42. Ti Hsin, Chou, lived in Yin.

43. In the 6th year of Ti Hsin, Wen Wang of Chou
first made a sacrifice called Yao at Pi.

44. Chou of Yin made a house of precious jades and
established a jade gate.

45. One day the sun was greatly obscured.

46. From T'ang's termination of the Hsia to Chou
    there were 29 kings lasting 496 years.

Wu Wang   47. Wu Wang of Chou led the feudal lords of the
               western barbarians, attacking Yin. He defeated
               Yin at Mu Suburb.

48. Wu Wang himself captured Chou at the altar of
    Nan Tan thereby revealing Heaven's brightness.

49. Wu Wang lived 54 years.

(Ch'eng Wang)

K'ang Wang   50. In the 6th year of K'ang Wang, T'ai Kung Wang
                  died.

51. Chin Hou made a too luxurious palace. K'ang
    Wang censured him.

52. During the period of Ch'eng and K'ang, the
    kingdom was peaceful. Punishments were re-
    scinded for more than forty years and were not
    used.

Chao Wang   53. In the 16th year of Chao Wang, he attacked Ch'u
                 Ching across the Han River and met a large
                 female unicorn.

54. In the 19th year of Chao Wang, the sun was
    greatly obscured; pheasants and rabbits all were
    frightened.

55. In the last year of Chao Wang, in the evening
    there were five colour lights through the Tzu
    Wei constellation. This year the king made an
    expedition to the south and never returned.

Mu Wang   56. In the first year of Mu Wang, he built Tzu
               palace at Nan Cheng.

57. From Chou's receiving the mandate to Mu Wang
    there were 100 years.

58. Mu Wang lived at the Cheng palace and the
    Ch'un palace.

59. The chief of the Pei T'ang came to court with
    a black-tailed bay horse which there gave birth
    to a horse with blue ears.

60. Mu Wang made an expedition to the south and
    went through 1000 _li_ of Liu Sha and 1000 of
    Chi Yü.

61. In the 13th year, he made an expedition to the
    west, to the place where the green birds rest.

62. (The king attacked the Ch'üan barbarians in the
    West) and brought five kings to the east. (The
    king moved the barbarians to T'ai-yüan).

63. In the 17th year of Mu Wang, he made an expedi-
    tion to the west to the K'un Lun mountains to
    see Hsi Wang Mu. In the same year Hsi Wang Mu
    came to court and was guest at Chao palace.

64. In the 37th year of Mu Wang, he attacked Yüeh
    with nine armies, eastward to Chiu-chiang and
    whistled to the terrapin to make a bridge.

65. Mu Wang made an expedition to the south. The
    gentlemen all became cranes and the mean men
    all became flying ospreys.

66. Mu Wang's eastern expedition went through
    202,500 _li_. The western expedition went through
    190,000 _li_. The southern expedition went through
    100,703 li and the northern expedition went
    through 200,007 _li_.

(Kung Wang)

I Wang

67. In the first year of I Wang, one morning the sun rose twice at Cheng.

(Hsiao Wang)

Yi Wang

68. In the 2nd year of Yi Wang, the people of Shu and Lü came to present jades. The king made a sacrifice at the river using a special jade.

69. In the 3rd year of Yi Wang, he assembled the feudal lords and boiled Ai Kung of Ch'i in a ting.

70. Yi Wang hunted at Kuei-lin and got a rhinoceros.

71. Yi Wang ordered Kuo Kung to lead six armies and attack the barbarians of T'ai-yüan extending to Yü-ch'üan. He captured a thousand horses.

72. In the 7th year of Yi Wang there was a great rain and hail as large as whetstones.

Li Wang

73. Kung Po Ho usurped the throne.

Hsüan Wang

74. When Hsüan Wang was established four years, he ordered Ch'in Chung to attack the western barbarians, and he was killed by the barbarians. The king then summoned Ch'in Chung's son, Chuang Kung, and gave him 7000 soldiers to attack the barbarians. He subdued them. The barbarians withdrew a little. Twenty-seven years later the king dispatched soldiers to attack the barbarians of T'ai-yüan without success. Five years later the king attacked the barbarians of T'iao and Pen. The king's army was defeated. Two years later the Chin people defeated the northern barbarians at Fen-shih. The barbarians extinguished the cities of Chiang Hou. The fol-

lowing year the king attacked the barbarians
of Shen and subdued them. Ten years later Yu
Wang ordered Po Shih to attack the barbarians
of Liu Chi. The army was defeated and Po Shih
died.

75. In the 3rd year of Hsüan Wang, there were rabbits dancing at Hao.

76. In the 33rd year of Hsüan Wang, a horse changed
into a wolf.

77. In the 8th year of Yu Wang, he made Pao Shih's
son, Po Fu, heir apparent.

78. P'ing Wang fled to the Western barbarians and
made Po P'an heir apparent, who with Yu Wang
died at Hsi^4. At first Shen Hou, Lu Hou and
Hsu^3 Wen Kung established P'ing Wang at Shen.
After Yu Wang's death, Kuo Kung Han again
established the prince Yü Ch'en at Hsi^1, then
Chou had two kings who reigned at one time.
Twenty-one years later Hsi^1 Wang was killed by
Chin Wen Kung because he was not the legal heir.
So he was called Hsi^1 Wang.

79. In Yu Wang's tenth year, ninth month, apricots
grew on peach trees.

80. From Wu Wang's termination of Yin to Yu Wang
there were 257 years. The sources for these
sections are given below. The volume number
is given in the Roman numerals; the other
numbers refer to the sections as numbered in
the translation.

T'ai p'ing yu lan, II, 67.

                    XIV, 72.

                       XXCIII, 2, 3, 8-12, 14-21, 24-27, 29-32, 35, 40-42.

                       XXCIV, 52, 68, 69.

                       CXLVII, 77.

                      CLXXIII, 58.

                     DCCXXC, 13

                  DCCCLXXIV, 55

                    DCCCXC, 70

                     CMVII, 75

                    CMLXVIII, 79

Ch'un ch'iu chin chuan chi chieh hou hsü, 4-6.

Chin shu, Su hsi chuan, 39, 57.

Ssu-ma Cheng's So yin of Shih chi:

              Lu shih chia, 7.

              Hsiang yü pen chi, 22.

              Chou pen chi, 73.

Chang's Cheng yi of Shih chi:

              Yin pen chi, 23.

Pei's Chi chieh of Shih chi:

              Yin pen chi, 46.

              Chou pen chi, 80.

Commentary to the Hou Han shu:

              Hsi ch'iang chuan, 33, 34, 36, 37, 38, 71, 74.

Kuo's Commentary to the Shan Hai ching:

              Ta huang pei ching, 28, 60.

Commentary to Wen hsüan:

              Tung ching fu and Wu tu fu, 44.

              Hen fu, 64.

K'ai yüan chan ching, CI, 45.

        IV, 66.

        CIX, 76.

T'ung chien ch'ien pien, 43.

Shui ching chu:

    Ch'ing shui chapter, 47.

    Ch'i shui chapter, 48.

Lu shih:

    Fa hui, IV, 49.

    Kuo ming chi, VI, 1.

T'ai kung lü wang mo piao, 50.

Pei t'ang shu ch'ao, XVIII, 51.

Ch'u hsüeh chi, VII, 53, 54.

Kuo's Commentary to Mo t'ien tzu chuan, 56, 59, 62, 63.

I wen lei chü, XCI, 61.

Fragment of T'ang MSS of Hsiu wen tien yü lan from Tun-huang, 65.

K'ung's Commentary to the Tso chuan:

    Chao Kung's 26th year, 78.

The Chu shu chi nien, the Bamboo Annals, were unearthed
about 281 A.D. in the Chi   commandery of northern Honan from
the tomb of a Wei king. The robber, Pu Chun   , got numerous
bamboo documents of which the Chu shu was one of the most important. They were the histories made by the Wei (Liang) historians.
The Annals ended at the "20th year of the present king" which referred to Wei Hsiang Wang   who was called Ai Wang by
Ssu-ma Ch'ien. According to the Wei shih chia of Shih chi, Ai Wang
died in the 23rd year of his reign. Therefore this book must have
been made after Hsiang Wang's 20th year and before his 23rd year.
According to the Liu kuo piao of Shih chi, Hsiang's 21st and 22nd
years were Chou Nan Wang's 18th and 19th years, which we can date
as 297-296 B.C. After 281 A.D. this book was quoted in numerous
works until the Sung dynasty. It seems to me that it was lost
after the Sung dynasty and a work was compiled which was called
the Chu shu chi nien which is the present day edition. This work
had added to it many materials other than those contained in the
original and it was ordered in a chronological system invented by
Liu Hsin of the Han dynasty which was in conflict with the original
Bamboo Annals.

     In the Ch'ing dynasty there were more than twenty scholars
who worked on this problem. Chu Yü-ts'eng   was the leading
scholar and he determined that the present edition contained many
late interpolations. Professor Wang Kuo-wei added to and corrected
Mr. Chu's book and also worked on the present edition determining
the sources from which that edition had been compiled. Unfortunately he did not dig out all of the original materials which
were scattered in many commentaries and books. For the Chan Kuo
period he did not try to use these materials to make a table
similar to that for the Six States in the Shih chi. Professor

Ch'ien Mu worked on the chronology of the pre-Han philosophers
and endeavoured to reconstruct a chronological table for that
period. This was very valuable, but he did not utilize the materials
from the Eastern Chou bronzes and the work was not thoroughly done.
I myself have found the original sources once again and have tried
to make a table from these materials. This work will be published
in the future. The part of the Chu shu dealing with the later
reigns has been tested by the bronze inscriptions and found to be
more reliable than the Shih chi, but the results are as yet too
complicated for immediate publication, therefore only the early
parts, on the Shang and the Chou, are translated here. In 1865
James Legge published his translations of the Chinese Classics
and in the Prolegomena to the Shang Shoo, chapter 4, translated
The Annals of the Bamboo Books, based on the present day edition.
If the reader compares the above translation with Legge's he can
readily determine which parts were added later.

APPENDIX II

Translation from the Tso chuan

Hsüan Kung, 3rd year.

Ch'u-tzu attacked the barbarians of Lu-hun and came to Lo
where he reviewed his army in the Chou territory. Ting Wang sent
Wang-sun Man to laud Ch'u-tzu. When Ch'u-tzu asked about the size
and weight of the ting he replied, "It is on virtue, not on the
ting. Formerly when Hsia had virtue, the distant regions presented
the pictures of objects and nine pastors presented metals and the
ting were cast with pictures of these objects. All the objects
were pictured, so that people might know the spirits and devils.
Thus the people who went to the river, marshes, hill and forest
would not meet the improper things; the spirits of the mountains
and the marshes, the woods and the stones would not be able to meet
the people. Hereby harmonizing the high and the low, to receive
Heaven's blessing. Chieh (of Hsia) had a vicious behaviour. The
ting were transferred to Shang. They lasted for 600 years. Chou
of Shang was tyrannical and unfeeling. The ting were transferred
to Chou. If the virtue is beautiful and illustrious(although the
ting) were big they would be light. Heaven blazes illustrious
virtue. Its favour rests on it. Ch'eng Wang fixed the ting at
Chia-ju and divined that (the kingdom) should last for 30 reigns,
and divined that (the dynasty) should last for 700 years. This is
the mandate from Heaven. Though the virtue of Chou is decayed,
the mandate of Heaven is not yet changed. Therefore the weight of
the ting may not be asked. "

Chao Kung, 12th year.

The king of Ch'u told told Tzu-kê saying, "Formerly our deceased king Hsiung-i with Lu-chi (of Ch'i), Wang-sun Mao (of Wei), Hsieh-fu (of Chin) and Ch'in-fu (of Lu) all served under K'ang Wang."

Chao Kung, 26th year.

The prince of Ch'ao announced to the feudal lords, saying, "Formerly Wu Wang conquered Yin and Ch'eng Wang made peace in the four quarters, and K'ang Wang rested the people (from troubles). They all established their brothers to be fences and screens to Chou, and the kings said, "We should not complacently accept the achievements of Wen and Wu and should not allow our descendants to be led astray, to be defeated, or to be over thrown, or being plunged into calamity require the succour of others." At the time that Yi Wang felt unwell in his body the feudal lords all hastened (to make sacrifices in the mountains and rivers) in their locality to pray for the king's health. At the time of Li Wang, the king's heart was cruel and unfeeling, but the myriads of people could not harden their hearts against him and therefore made him live in Chih. The feudal lords gave up their own places to substitute for the king's affairs. And when Hsüan Wang showed his ability, they surrendered all their offices to him. At the time of Yu Wang, Heaven gave no good to Chou. The king was vicious and improper and therefore lost his throne. When Hsi Wang usurped the throne the feudal lords set him aside and established the King's legal heir and moved (the capital) to Chia-ju (i.e., Lo-yang)...."

Ting Kung, 4th year.

Tzu-yü (Chu T'o of Wei State) said, "Formerly Wu Wang

conquered Shang. Ch'eng Wang settled it. He chose and established
those who had illustrious virtue to be fences and screens to Chou.
So Chou Kung advised the royal family in administering the kingdom,
choosing those closely related to Chou. Lu Kung was given a grand
chariot, a grand flag, the jade of the Hsia sovereign, a bow of
Fung-fu and six clans of the Yin people: the T'iao, the Hsü, the
Hsiao, the So, the Ch'ang-shao and the Wei-shao. They were ordered
to lead their kinsmen, to collect their branches, to control the
multitude of the common people and to follow the principle of Chou
Kung. They took orders from Chou and performed duties at Lu,
making the illustrious virtue of Chou shine. (Lu Kung) was given
lands and fields and dependant fiefs, prayers and genealogists,
diviners and recorders, tablets of historical records and the sacrificial vessels. To have the people of Shang-yen, (Lu Kung) was
given the order of "Po-ch'in" and took his fief at the ancient
site of Shao-kao. K'ang-shu was given a grand chariot, a vari-
coloured flag, a red flag and a plain flag, ornaments of feathers,
a great bell, and seven clans of the Yin people: the T'ao, the Shih,
the Po, the I, the Fan, the Chi and the Chung-k'uei. The boundaries of his territory were from the south of Wu-fu to the north
territory of P'u-t'ien, taking a portion of Yu-yen to serve the
king's duty, taking the eastern capital of Hsiang-t'u to attend the
king's hunting in the east. Nan-chi was ordered to administer the
land, T'ao-shu was ordered to administer the people. K'ang-shu
was given the order of "K'ang-kao" and took his fief at the ancient
site of Yin. Both (Lu and Wei) were to lead their people according
to the custom of Shang and control them under the rules of Chou.
T'ang-shu was given a grand chariot, the drum of Mi-hsü, armor, a
bell, nine families with the clan name Huai, and officials and five

heads of departments. (T'ang-shu)was given the order of "T'ang-kao"
and took his fief at the ancient site of Hsia. (Chin State) was to
lead by the Hsia custom and control under the rules of the barbarians. These three were younger uncles (of Ch'eng Wang) and
possessed of good virtue, therefore they were distinguished by
grants of territory and things. If not so, there were many other
elder uncles of Wen, Wu, Ch'eng and K'ang who did not receive their
grants, showing it was not years which were valued. Kuan and Ts'ai
instigated Shang, poisonously to disrupt the royal house. The king
therefore killed Kuan-shu and banished Ts'ai-shu with seven
chariots and seventy attendants. His son, Ts'ai-chung, changed his
behaviour pursuing virtue. Chou Kung raised him up to be a minister of his own, presented him to the king and gave him the order of
"Ts'ai." The order read, "The king said, 'Hu, be not like your
father, disobedient to the royal family.'"

APPENDIX III

Translations from Meng-tzu

I. Kung-sun Ch'ou II

When Meng-tzu left Ch'i, Ch'ung Yü said to him on the
way, "Master, you look as if (you are) uneasy. The other day I
heard you saying, 'The gentleman never complains to Heaven nor
grouches to men.'" Meng-tzu replied, "That was one time and this
is another. Every 500 years there should arise a true royal
sovereign and within that period there should be men known in the
world. From Chou until now there were 700 years and more. For
the number, it is more than (500); examining the time, it should
be now. Yet Heaven does not wish to have the kingdom in peace.
If it wishes to have the kingdom in peace, in the present time
who else besides me (is there to fulfill it)? How should I be
otherwise than uneasy?"

II. T'eng Wen Kung II

Kung Tu-tzu said, "Other people all say that our Master
is fond of disputation. May I ask why?" Meng-tzu said, "Am I
fond of disputation? I can not help doing it. The world has
been for a long time; a period of order, a period of disorder. At
the time of Yao the waters ran uphill and flooded the Middle Kingdom.
The snakes and dragons occupied it and the people had no place to
settle. In the low lands they made nests, in the highlands they
made caves. The Book says, 'The flood warned me.' The flood was
the wild waters. Yü was ordered to repel the waters. Yü dug the
earth and diverted the waters to the sea and forced the snakes and

L 52

dragons to be banished to the marshes. The waters ran through the
country; they were the Chiang, the Huai, the Ho and the Han. The
dangers and obstructions were far away. The birds and the beasts
which injured the people disappeared. Then men could find a level
place to settle. After Yao and Shun had already died, the principle of the sage decayed, the tyrannical sovereigns arose one
after another pulling down the palaces and houses to make ponds so
that the people had no place to rest in quiet. The farm lands were
given up to be gardens and hunting grounds so that people could not
get clothes and food. The improper theories and tyrannical affairs
arose, gardens, hunting grounds, ponds and marshes became more
numerous and birds and beasts came. At the time of Chou (of Shang) the kingdom was again in great disorder. Chou Kung advised Wu Wang to
kill Chou and to attack Yen³. After three years he put the
(sovereign) of Yen³ to death. He forced Fei Lien to a corner of
the sea and killed him. He extinguished states to the number of
fifty. He drove tigers, leopards, rhinoceroses and elephants far
away. All the people were greatly delighted."

III. Chin-hsin II

Meng-tzu said, "From Yao and Shun to T'ang there were
500 years and more. As to Yü and Kao Yao, they had seen and knew
them. As to T'ang, he heard and knew them. From T'ang to Wen
Wang there were 500 years and more. As to I Yin and Lai Chu, they
saw and knew him. As to Wen Wang, he heard and knew him. From Wen
Wang to K'ung-tzu there were 500 years and more. As to T'ai Kung
Wang and San I-sheng, they saw and knew him. As to K'ung-tzu, he
heard and knew him. From K'ung-tzu downward until now there were
100 and more years. From the sages' time it is not as far away as
this; near the sages' house is as near as this. But yet is there
no one? Is there no one?"

CHAPTER XIV
Style and Decoration

We have used the words "decoration," "design" or "pattern" in this work to indicate the decorative parts of vessels. The decoration might have more than one motif or unit on one vessel, but in most cases a single unit or two units appear repeatedly, successively or alternately on a certain zone. Some vessels, like the kuang, have designs which are a combination of many motifs. We may divide the decoration, according to the degree of the decoration and the area or space occupied by the decorative zones, into three catagories:

1. Ornate style, all over decoration. The decoration occupies the full section or three-fourths of the vessel.

2. Moderate style, frieze decoration. The decoration occupies several narrow zones, such as under the neck, on the base or on the far most circular zone of the lid. This leaves the major section undecorated.

3. Simple style, no decoration or only a simple decoration such as bow strings or animal-heads.

From the An-yang finds we know that the three styles were used in the Shang period. Probably, the simple styles were used for mortuary vessels or for the common people's ves-

sels. But sacrificial vessels were also made in this style.
The mortuary type vessels are simple in style and coarse in
casting. There is no doubt about the fact that the refined,
ornate style vessels were made for sacrificial use. The co-
existence of these three styles is also true on Western Chou
and Ch'un Ch'iu bronzes. However, we do not find many Chan
Kuo vessels with a frieze decoration, and the Han vessels are
mostly undecorated.

The early ornate style decorations with a high relief
give us a suffocative feeling. They were inspired by a strong
religious emotion and piety mixed with fear. No matter how
skillful the craftsmanship the Chan Kuo vessels, except those
with beasts, birds or hunting scenes, are too florid and me-
chanical. It is the frieze decoration o f the Western Chou
bronzes that fit our traditional idea of moderation. There is
a quiet and peaceful beauty in the harmonious relationship of
the decorated to the undecorated areas. The blank space is
not wasted; it is so well arranged that one can meditate while
looking at it.

Generally, the decoration is on the exterior surface of
a vessel, on both the body and the lid. But sometimes on vessels with wide open mouths and shallow bodies the interior is
decorated like the p'an. There is a frieze decoration on the
raised rim of the tun in U.S. 293.   There is a kuei, in a private collection in New York, with a decoration inside the rim
of the mouth. These are exceptions. Quite often there are
raised cross lines underneath the bottom of the vessel. Sometimes,

there are different raised designs underneath the bottom, such
as whorl circle, U.S. 177, 519; cicada, U.S. 609, 613; dragon,
U.S. 167, 199; and dragon and cicada, U.S. 207. In U.S. 179
raised cicadas are underneath each ear. These were probably
added by the craftsman in order to fill the blanks which were
not designed in the original blue print.

The decoration was usually cut off between the lid and
the body, but the yu (U.S. 639) has its decoration continued
from the body to the back of the lid as shown in Freer Catalogue; pl. 14. This is a rare case. The pattern on the lid and
on the socle is usually the same as that on the body, but sometimes the socle's is different from that on the body. The lids
of the early vessels, those which have rectangular mouths like
the fang-i and lei, always have their decoration upside down,
that is, the t'ao-t'ieh has its mouth on the top and its eyes
and horns under it.

Vessels with bulged bodies have their decoration either
on the belly or on the neck. We call the decoration on the
belly the "Major" because it occupies the major section; we
call the frieze decoration on the neck, base and the lid the
"Frieze." Vessels with hyperbolic arcs, like the ku and tsun,
have their decoration on the three even registers with demarcations between them. We call this "Register" and consider
the middle register as major. The upper register, sometimes
undecorated, usually has a row of triangular blades which point
upward. We call this "Leaf." The low register is the base
which is considered a frieze.

The above discussions do not include the vessels made
in the form of birds and owls, such as the owl yu and the niao-
shou-tsun. When the whole vessel (body and lid) forms a unit
we call it the "Whole shaped decoration." Sometimes birds or
dragons were inserted in the designs. We call this "Inserted."

The motifs fall under two catagories; (1) geometrical
lines, circles, squares or lozenges; and (2) the motifs which
took their forms from birds, reptiles, animals, fowl, etc.
The latter underwent the process of simplification, dissolution,
split, condensation, deformation and stylization. Furthermore,
one motif might take a part of another motif and blend it with
its own and become a new unit.

Let us now take the t'ao-t'ieh for an example. This
decoration is either in graphic or in relief. The main figure
is an animal's head with eyes, eyebrows, horns, ears, mouth,
teeth, nose and feet on both sides. The t'ao-t'ieh on different
vessels has different styles for each part. Below we list the
varieties:

a. With round eyes, feet, recumbent C-shaped horns, no
   eyebrows

        U.S. 1-3

b. With oblong eyes, feet, recumbent C-shaped horns,
   eyebrows

        U.S. 4-5

c. With oblong eyes, feet, C-shaped horns, and no eyebrows

        U.S. 6

d. As b but it has no eyebrows

        U.S. 33

e. As <u>b</u> but it has buffalo horns

      U.S. 42

f. As <u>b</u> but it has frilled recumbent S-shaped horns

      U.S. 57

g. As <u>f</u> but it has no eyebrows

      U.S. 58

h. As <u>a</u> but it has frilled recumbent S-shaped horns and
a wide mouth and a row of teeth.

      U.S. 55

i. As <u>b</u> but it has ~~recumbent S-shaped horns~~ *no eyebrows*

      U.S. 153

j. As <u>e</u> but it has round eyes

      U.S. 689

k. As <u>f</u> but it has round eyes

      U.S. 590

l. As <u>b</u> but it has recumbent S-shaped horns

      U.S. 166

m. As <u>b</u> but it has no feet

      U.S. 126

n. As <u>m</u> but it has round eyes

      U.S. 46

o. As <u>m</u> but it has buffalo horns

      U.S. 139

p. As <u>o</u> but it has no eyebrows

      U.S. 137

q. As <u>b</u> but it has no horns and feet

      U.S. 59

Thus, the above examples show the varieties of each

part as:

    Eyes   round or oblong

    Horns   C-shaped, recumbent C-shaped, recumbent

                     S-shaped, frilled recumbent S-shaped,

                     buffalo.

    Eyebrows   With or without

    Feet   with or without

    Teeth   a row (see h) or on both sides of the nose

This list is not complete. However, it indicates that
the t'ao-t'ieh are in various forms. Besides these minor differences, the t'ao-t'ieh can be classified under several other
types which will be listed later. Now, we shall list the vessels with Shang, Early Chou, Middle Western Chou and Late
Western Chou designs:

I. Shang

S1. Realistic t'ao-t'ieh

    Major   U.S. 1-9, 38-53, 137-139, 147, 153, 166,

                310-314, 324, 327, 329, 416-421, 431,

                432, 593, 594.

    Frieze U.S. 13, 2

S2. Simplified t'ao-t'ieh

    Major   U.S. 122-124

    Frieze U.S. 25, 523

S3. T'ao-t'ieh in spirals

    Major   U.S. 162, 321-323, 379, 408

    Frieze U.S. 137, 138, 162, 408, 533 (neck)

S4. Stylized t'ao-t'ieh or Dragonized t'ao-t'ieh

    Major   U.S. 75

Frieze U.S. 14, 34, 36, 148, 152, 155, 314, 315, 428

S5. T'ao-t'ieh leaves

U.S. 431, 432

S6. Owls

Major   U.S. 603,650

Whole shape   U.S. 580-582

S7. Elephants

Frieze   U.S. 522, 643, 665

S8. "Tigers"

Frieze   U.S. 147, 152, 155, 417, 643

S9. Animals with a long beak

Frieze   U.S. 32, 157, 164, 593

S10. Horned animals kneeling on the front feet

Frieze   U.S. 440

S11. Small birds

Major   U.S. 596, 656, 657, 661

Frieze   U.S. 65, 72, 538, 571, 596

S12. Small birds like dragons

Frieze   U.S. 7, 17, 60, 147, 153, 156, 161, 166, 327,
329, 425, 431, 35 (winged).

S13. Turned small birds like dragons

Frieze   U.S. 153, 156, 157, 163, 164

S14. Stylized turned dragons

Frieze   U.S. 207

S15. Open mouth dragon, facing forward

Frieze   U.S. 29, 44, 66, 159, 566, 594

S16. Open mouth dragon, facing the ground

Frieze   U.S. 30, 59, 593

S17. Vertical cicada leaves

    Major   U.S. 13, 14, 17

    Frieze U.S. 147, 327

S18. Successive cicadas

    Frieze U.S. 11, 38

S19. Triangular leaves

    Major   U.S. 19, 143

    Frieze U.S. 148, 166, 328, 329, 366, 367, 420, 425

S20. Fish

    Frieze U.S. 796

S21. Snakes

    Frieze U.S. 416, 603

S22. Crescents

    Major   U.S. 439, 440

    Frieze U.S. 432

S23. Whorl circles

    Frieze U.S. 780, 781

S24. Whorl circles and t'ao-t'ieh

    Frieze U.S. 15

S25. Whorl circles and birds

    Frieze U.S. 19, 779

S26. Whorl circles and "tigers"

    Frieze U.S. 20, 21

S27. Whorl circles and deformed dragons

    Frieze U.S. 175, 200, 418

S28. Whorl circles and crescents

    Frieze U.S. 200

S29. **Vertical ribs**

    Major   U.S. 175, 200, 571

    Frieze U.S. 596

S30. **Bow strings in three lines**

    Frieze U.S. 402, 403, 556, 566

S31. Chevron lines

    Major   U.S. 330-332

S32. Interlocked T's

    Major   U.S. 10, 65, 66, 161

S33. Spikes

    Major   U.S. 65, 66

S34. Compound lozenges

    Frieze U.S. 567

           U.S. 601, 604 (handle) In single line.

S35. Spikes in lozenges

    Major   U.S. 11, 155

S36. Spirals

    Frieze U.S. 534, 551, 604. In two rows

           U.S. 602 (base). In one row

S37. Eye and diagonals

    Frieze U.S. 74, 545

S38. Eye and spirals

    Frieze U.S. 178

S39. Eye and Dragon's body

    Frieze U.S. 33, 71, 149, 570

S40. Small circle's band (on both sides of the frieze)

           U.S. 24, 425

The above catagories do not include the inserted

vertical birds (U.S. 39), buffalos (U.S. 662) and rabbits (U.S.
665, 666).   We call S12-13 birds rather than dragons because
they have beaks like birds. The term 'dragon' only applies to
those with long S-shaped bodies and broad open mouths.   The
rear parts of U.S. 72 and U.S. 35 are divided into two sections.
The birds on U.S. 65 and 72 are longer than the usual "small
birds."

Among S1-40 many motifs use only a frieze decoration.
This is also true of the Early Chou style, with a very few exceptions. We know that there is a close affinity between the
motifs on white pottery and those on Shang bronzes. The former,
discussed in the chapter on Classification, is earlier than that
on the Shang bronzes. Specimen of white pottery may be found in
Umehara's three books, **An-yang Finds**, **An-yang Treasures** and
Hakushoku (Study on the White Pottery from An-yang). From these
three books we list the motifs that resemble the Shang patterns:

S3. T'ao-t'ieh frieze

Finds: 1, 2, 5, 16; Treasures: 60

S4. Stylized t'ao-t'ieh major

Finds: 17

S15. Open mouth dragon, facing forward

Finds: 6, 7 (on both lids)

S19. Triangular leaves

Finds: 17 (neck); Treasures: 60 (neck)

S23. Whorl circles major

Finds: 1, 2, 5

S32. Interlocked T's major

Finds: 20

S34. Compound lozenges

    Frieze   Finds: 6, 7 (lid); 20 (lower)/ In single line.

    Major   Finds: 6, 7 (body); Treasures: 57, 59;

    Hakushoku: 13

S36. Spiral frieze

    Finds: 3; Treasures: 58, 59, 60; Hakushoku: 5.1-3;
5.5-7; 7.7-11; 12.11-12; 17.4-8.

S39. Eye and Dragon's body frieze

    Finds: 8, 9, 12, 14, 22 (Lei in Freer Gallery)

S40. Small circle's band

    Hakushoku: 5.8

The eyes of the t'ao-t'ieh on white pottery are oblong, and the horns are either made of spirals or are in the shape of the recumbent C (Finds: 17). It seems to me that the oblong eyes are earlier than the round eyes. The eyebrows on the bronzes were added in the latter part of the Shang period. With regard to the horns on the t'ao-t'ieh, it seems to me that the recumbent C came first and the frilled recumbent S-shaped horns came last. The other three styles, that is, the C shape, the recumbent S-shape and the buffalo horns came between the first and the last. These three styles are contemporaneous because on the Shang ku and tsun two of the types often appear on two registers of the same vessel.

The spiral on bronzes and white pottery is very complicated. It has at least three forms: (1) small T shape (U.S. 604); (2) square shape (U.S. 601); and (3) rectangular shape (white pottery).

With the few exceptions of dragons and t'ao-t'ieh, the

basic pattern on white pottery are geometric. Whorl circles,
lozenges and the rectangular spirals played the important parts.
The latter, angular volute fret or meander, are continuous rectangular spirals which are always combined with the broad flat
plain bands in at least three forms: (1) they follow the complicated broad band's pattern with a M-shaped band ending with
"paws" (usually on the belly under the neck) as in Finds: 9, 12,
13; Treasures: 60▾1; 60.2 (right); (2) they follow the parallel
zigzag as in Finds: 22; and (3) they follow the interlocked T's
broad band as in Finds: 20. The interlocked pattern on bronzes
originated from the latter. In the cases of (1) and (2) the
spirals functioned as background. I believe that this is the
source of the "spiral ground" on Shang bronzes.

The "t'ao-t'ieh" of S3 is what Professor Karlgren called
"dissolved t'ao-t'ieh." If there is a "dissolved t'ao-t'ieh,"
I prefer to call them those t'ao-t'ieh on the middle and lower
registers of the Type Ia ku. This can be divided into two
groups: (1) the t'ao-t'ieh pattern raised from the spiral ground
and with incised lines within the design (U.S. 475-477};and (2)
the t'ao-t'ieh pattern in the same level as the spiral ground
(U.S. 493, 503, 508).

II. Early Chou

S1. Realistic t'ao-t'ieh

    Major   U.S. 54, 126, 169, 223-225, 338, 341, 442-445,
              449

S4. Stylized t'ao-t'ieh or Dragonized t'ao-t'ieh

    Major   U.S. 389, 396

    Frieze   U.S. 181, 190, 341. The "triple band."

S7. Elephant

    Major   U.S. 226, 232

S8. "Tigers"

    Frieze U.S. 232, 619, 620

S11. Small birds

    Frieze U.S. 70, 180, 223, 456, 609

S12. Small birds like dragons

    Frieze U.S. 224-226, 338

S14. Stylized turned dragons

    Frieze U.S. 226, 456, 464, 578, 612, 620, 624, 637

S15. Open mouth dragon, facing forward

    Frieze U.S. 168, 169

S16. Open mouth dragon, facing the ground

    Frieze U.S. 209

S19. Triangular leaves

    Frieze U.S. 236

S21. Snakes

    Frieze U.S. 177, 224, 637

S23. Whorl circles

    Major   U.S. 232

    Frieze U.S. 236, 536, 537

S27. Whorl circles and deformed dragons

    Frieze U.S. 177, 181

S28. Whorl circles and crescents

    Frieze U.S. 193

S29. Vertical ribs

    Major   U.S. 70, 177

S30. Bow strings in two lines

    Frieze U.S. 196, 342, 441-447, 636

S31. Chevron lines

    Major   U.S. 340

S32. Interlocked T's

    Major   U.S. 67

S33. Spikes

    Major   U.S. 67, 70

S34. Compound lozenges

    Frieze U.S. 470, 632.   In single line.

S35. Spikes in lozenges

    Major   U.S. 179-181

S37. Eye and diagonals

    Frieze U.S. 183, 233, 234, 635

S38. Eye and spirals

    Frieze U.S. 620

       The above examples were selected more strictly than the Shang examples. According to their inscriptions, provenances and sets, all can be dated in the first part of Early Chou. There is only one simplified t'ao-t'ieh of this period in our catalogue and that is on the base of U.S. 180. The so-called "Triple band" is derived from S3. A good example is the Major and the Frieze on U.S. 162. The "Small birds" on U.S. 70 are longer than usual, but at that time the Chou style "Long bird" was about to be born. The two "Dragonized t'ao-t'ieh" major on two chüeh are very similar to the one found at Chün Hsien (Chün hsien: 180) which can be dated, from its set, Early Chou.

       It is obvious that during the first part of Early Chou a large number of Shang styles were inherited by Chou craftsmen or by Shang craftsmen who worked under Chou. However, some of the Shang motifs were not used and some changes took place in others. Examples:

    1. Few cicadas

    2. Few owls

    3. Few S2, 3, 9 and 10

    4. Elephant, changed from frieze to major

    5. Bow strings changed from three lines to two and
       sometimes there were animal heads in the middle
       of the two lines as in U.S. 191, 344 and 636.

    6. S3 frieze crystallized into "Triple band."

    7. Spikes became sharper and longer

    8. Less combination of whorl circles

The above statements are certainly not conclusive because our examples are limited to those in our catalogue and we do not include "Shang or Early Chou" vessels.

The first part of Early Chou covered, approximatley, the Ch'eng Wang reign and the K'ang Wang reign. It is possible that some motifs, which are not included in the above lists, were in the Shang style and extended to Early Chou. After the first half of the K'ang Wang period, there were new styles which could be considered as the Chou style. Below, we are marking "C" before the number and listing both catagories:

    C1. Open mouth dragons with large whirl as the body
       Major   U.S. 209, 202

    C2. "Phoenix"
       Major   U.S. 209 (socle), 435
       Frieze   U.S. 435 (base)

C3. Stylized "elephant"

Frieze U.S. 574, 575, 589, 619, 621

C4. Snakes with two bodies

Frieze U.S. 652

C5. Overlapped vertical scales

Major U.S. 334

C6. Turned dragons

Frieze U.S. 179, 237, 468, 469, 565

C7. Long birds

Frieze U.S. 194, 199, 626-628

C8. Long bird with detached tail

Frieze U.S. 77, 78, 195, 237, 405, 406, 467, 630, 638

C9. Turned birds

Major U.S. 182, 198, 199, 469, 565, 638

Frieze U.S. 198

C10. Deer

Frieze U.S. 634

Probably, C1 to C4 are the Late Shang styles which still
existed during the early part of Chou. The earliest datable
example of C1 is the T'ien Wu kuei (fig. 20 in our catalogue)
which was made in Wu Wang's time. The design on C3 also appeared
on the vessels excavated from Tomb 60 in Chün Hsien (Chün hsien:
12-16) which can be dated in the first part of Early Chou, probably Ch'eng Wang. We call C3 stylized "elephant" because it
has a trunk. It might have some connection with S8 and S9.
The example (U.S. 652) of C4 is of the Ch'eng Wang period; the
same motif was preserved on the vessel made by the son of the
donor of U.S. 652. After the first part of Early Chou C1 to C4
disappeared.

C5 (U.S. 334) is a rare speciman. It has an"Eye and spirals." With the exception of U.S. 179 (first part also has frieze like U.S. 334), the rest of the examples under C6 are later than the Ch'eng Wang period. The long birds (C7) were derived from the "Small birds." As we have stated before, the "Small birds" of the Shang style sometimes have lengthened bodies. With the exception of 199 (second part), the rest of the examples under C7 are probably of the first part of Early Chou. C8 is the late style of C7. The earliest examples of C8 (U.S. 406, 630, 638) are of the latter part of the K'ang Wang period. The other examples are: fig. 10 of the K'ang Wang period; figs. 13 and 24 of the K'ang or Chao Wang period. C9 may have been derived from S13, only the former has a lengthened body like C7. The earliest example of C9 (U.S. 638) is of the K'ang Wang period; the rest can be dated in the second part of Early Chou. C10 has only one speciman that we know of. The donor can be identified as the donor of a __kuei__ (fig. 74 in our catalogue) which has a design like C9.

We might sum up the characteristics of the Early Chou style as follows: (1) Chou style inherited a large number of the characteristics of the Shang style; (2) the cicada disappeared; (3) __t'ao-t'ieh__ lost its dominating position; (4) birds and dragons became more important, hence new styles were derived from these two; (5) more frequent use of the frieze decoration; and (6) more incised presentation than plastic.

III. Middle Western Chou

C6. Turned dragons

Frieze   U.S. 165, 197, 239, 339

C9. Turned birds

Frieze   U.S. 196, 242, 343

C11. Horizontal grooves

Major   U.S. 240, 241

Except for the t'ao-t'ieh (U.S. 130-132) the Shang
style was completely banished during this period.
Below we list two motifs of Early Chou and a new one:
The examples under C6. are about the Kung Wang
period. Other examples are as follows:

Fig. 19   Mu Wang period

Figs. 15, 17, 36   Kung Wang period

The examples for C9 are of the latter part of
Middle Western Chou. For examples for C11, cf. U.S.
240.

IV. Late Western Chou

C11. Horizontal grooves

Major   U.S. 244-248, 250, 251, 259-261

C12. Successive scales

Frieze   U.S. 81-83, 133, 247-249, 255, 262, 263,
707, 708. In one row.
U.S. 247, 248. In two rows.

C13. Vertical scales

Frieze   U.S. 250, 251, 704

C14. Vertical lines

Major   U.S. 133, 134

C15. Wavy band

     Major   U.S. 255, 698, 699, 704

     Frieze   U.S. 262, 263, 700, 701, 707

C16. K'ê _ting_ pattern

     Major   U.S. 702, 703

     Frieze   U.S. 238, 243-246, 254 (neck)

C17. K'ê _hsü_ pattern

     Frieze   U.S. 136, 254 (base), 259-261

C18. Sung _kuei_ pattern

     Frieze   U.S. 250, 251, 702, 703

C19. Spiral dragons

     Major   U.S. 135, 254 (socle)

C20. Double dragons

     Major   U.S. 144, 254 (belly), 259 (top, see

               Buckingham: 33), 707 (belly).

     Frieze   U.S. 244-246

With the exception of C11, the rest are new patterns.
The first two examples under C13 can be dated in the Hsüan Wang
period. C12 was born earlier. The datable vessels with a
wavy band are vessels in a set of K'ê ting (fig. 45; U.S. 259)
which were made about 865 B.C. This style, like other patterns
of the Late Western Chou period, extended to Ch'un Ch'iu.

It seems to me that C16 was derived from double or
spiral dragons; C17 may have been derived from the turned birds
(compare U.S. 242 with U.S. 259). The examples under C16 and
C17 are about the Yi Wang period. The first two examples under
C18 can be dated in the Hsüan Wang period, which is later than
C16 and C17.

There are still a few t'ao-t'ieh in this period as on
U.S. 257, 700, 701 which are quite different from the earlier
style. This period marked the end of the once powerful dragons
and birds which were substituted by simple repeated units.

V. Ch'un Ch'iu

The style of the vessels made by the various states in
the Early Ch'un Ch'iu period is the continuation of the Late
Western Chou style. Let us take the early group of the Hsin-
cheng finds as examples:

C11 Hsin cheng: 69-78 kuei; 109-113 hu

C12 Hsin cheng: 91 animal tsun; 114 p'an

C13 Hsin cheng: 109-113 hu

C14 None

C15 Hsin cheng: 66 hsien

C16 None

C17 None

C18 Hsin cheng: 69-78 kuei; 109-113 hu

C19 Hsin cheng: 55-65 li

C20 Hsin cheng: 109-113 hu

The above examples show that C16 and C17 of the Yi
Wang period were discontinued. The rest of the examples are of
the Late Western Chou period. However, on the hsien a new
motif of "Interlaced dragons or birds" was added which later
became the principle motif of the Ch'un Ch'iu period.

We may take the delicate "interlacery" as the representative of the Late Ch'un Ch'iu style. The good examples are in
a group of large ting in Hsin cheng: 28-39 and a group of fu

in Hsin cheng; 82-85. The fu in U.S. 268 is the same as Hsin cheng's and also some other fu which were made in the nearby states.

At the very end of this period the Li-yü style came into power. It originated in Northern Chin (now Shansi) and moved down first to Northern Honan and then to Central Honan, the Central plain. The characteristics of the Li-yü finds are: (1) "Interlaced dragons" as on the Li-yü tou (U.S. 260) and the ting (U.S. 96, 97, 99 and 100); (2) "Braided-cord band" in relief as on U.S. 709, 843-845 or incised as on U.S. 269 and 270; (3) "Repeated small turned dragons" forming rows. The dragons are either horizontal as on U.S. 85 or vertical as on U.S. 272 or vertical but interlaced as on U.S. 90. I believe that (3) was the forerunner of the "Comma pattern" which over emphasized the heads of the dragons. Other patterns, besides these three, on the Ch'un Ch'iu can be found on the ting, tou, tun and hu of this period in our catalogue.

VI. Chan Kuo

The vessels of the Late Ch'un Ch'iu and Early Chan Kuo periods found at Li-yü, P'ing-ting and T'ai-yüan in Shansi, and in Hui Hsien and Chi Hsien in Northern Honan have about the same style which we call the "Chin style." During Early Chan Kuo when the Chin State extended its power southward and occupied a part of the Central plain it made the Chin style the principal pattern. And this pattern took the leading position

when the Western Chou style faded out after the Middle Ch'un
Ch'iu period.

The Chin-ts'un finds covered a long period and had
various provincial styles. It was natural for Lo-yang to adopt
the different styles from many directions because it was located
in the center of China. Now we shall list the important styles
of the Chin-ts'un finds which are at the same time the main
styles that existed in the Chan Kuo era:

1. Late Chin style, or the Piao Ch'iang style or the
   "Comma pattern."
2. Yen style or the T'ien Chang style
3. Chin-ts'un style or the inlaid design
4. Shou-hsien style or the Ch'u style

The "Comma pattern" on the Piao Ch'iang bells has been
discussed in the chapter on Chronology. Its date is 404 B.C.
Other examples of this pattern are: U.S. 716-720 and 766-769
which have been dated Middle Chan Kuo.

The T'ien Chang hu, discussed under U.S. 750, was made
before 314 B.C. It is inlaid and has a very complex design of
lozenges which is probably the forerunner of the Chin-ts'un
style.

The best example of the Chin-ts'un style is listed under
U.S. 111. The designs are inlaid in various forms of volutes,
triangles, diagonals, lozenges, etc. and the combination of any
two of the above mentioned units. The other pattern of the
Chin-ts'un style is a double line incised interlaced dragon as
on U.S. 107 which was also found in Shou-hsien. Both styles are
Late Chan Kuo.

The close relationship between Shou-hsien and Chin-ts'un has been discussed under U.S. 109 and 110. Not only the "Incised interlaced dragons" were found in Shou Hsien but also the "Inlaid design" and the "Comma pattern." Usually, the Shou-hsien bronzes are not inlaid. They are Late Chan Kuo.

Inlay of turquoise and black composition, whose nature is unknown to us, were very popular in the Shang dynasty. With a few exceptions, the inlay of black composition died out in Early Chou. At the end of Ch'un Ch'iu, the bird-script and a *of Yueh state* small part of the designs on weapons and musical instruments were inlaid with gold. During Chan Kuo there was a revival of inlay using silver, gold, copper, turquoise and other kinds of jewelry. In the case of copper, the inlay was a very thin sheet of copper which was hammered over the sunk design. Occasionally, the inlay penetrated through the bronze as seen in U.S. 839.

In our catalogue, there are two groups of hu with hunting scenes (U.S. 723, 724) or beasts and birds scene (U.S. 725-728). The latter are inlaid with copper. In the former there are also vessels which are inlaid with copper. We have dated the first group Early Chan Kuo, and the second Early or Middle Chan Kuo. These are two new styles which might have originated from the boundary tribes in the Northern areas.

VII. Han

In the Late Chan Kuo period we have many decorated vessels and many plain, undecorated vessels. The Han vessels are mostly undecorated, but the craftsmen often used the gold

or silver gilded method. A good example is U.S. 737. The Han
vessels were usually cast without designs and inscriptions. So
both the designs and the inscriptions were incised after the
vessels were made. There are a few specimen of gilded bronzes
in Early Chou and Middle Western Chou, but the process might
not have been the same as that used in the Han dynasty. Therefore, I consider the gilded technique as the characteristic of
Han bronzes, although it might have been used at the end of Late
Chan Kuo.

The above is a primary study on style which is the result of three studies: (1) the study of the various groups of
finds; (2) the study of the classification of motifs; (3) the
study of the dates of the bronzes in this catalogue according
to comparisons with datable bronzes, or to their provenances,
types and inscriptions which indicate the approximate dates.
This chapter was written after I had finished the catalogue,
and I found little or no contradiction between the stylistic
arrangement in this chapter and the dates of the 850 vessels
which have been given in the catalogue. We have ventured to
distinguish the Chou style from the Shang style among the Early
Chou vessels. The results seem to be very promising.

It seems to me that in the first part of Early Chou,
the Shang style still existed. After that, there are Chou
styles which differ from the Shang styles. The earliest provincial style was the Chin style. I consider the Hsin-cheng
style a continuation of the Chou style. During Chan Kuo the
mutual influences on and the blending of styles are very conspicuous.

It is my belief that several styles, old, new or
different, existed in the same period. When a new style was
in force, the old style remained for a certain length of time.
It is not necessary to have a strict dividing line between the
time when the old styles disappeared and the new comers became
powerful. The old styles persisted longer than we would expect
because of the conservative tendency. We found many cases
showing the overlapping of the two styles.

So far we have not touched the problem of the symbolism
of the design, the religion to be inferred therefrom and the
possibility of foreign influences. It is my opinion that the
significance of these studies is very important but is too
early to begin while materials are not available. I started
to study pre-Han Chinese religion years ago and found that it
was impossible without some knowledge of oracle bones and
bronzes. Mr. Kuo Mo-jo also started his work in this field
because he was interested in the ancient social organization.
His earlier work failed through lack of reliable evidence and
then he turned to the documented field of oracle bones and
bronzes, in which he has succeeded in making many contributions.
As it is, we know very little about ancient religions and no
records exist which can be used for the study of the symbolism
shown on the bronzes. There is also no authenticated record
of an influx of foreign culture. Primarily, in any case, not
until we can delineate an absolute Chinese culture can we de-
marcate foreign influences. That there is an exotic influence

L 547

in the Chan Kuo bronzes is obvious, but it has been incorporated
from a boundary tribe which is held to be "Chinese." It is
possible, of course, that this tribe may have felt strong
foreign influences, but this must remain in the realm of conjecture at the present time.

CHAPTER XV

Dating

The dating of early bronzes is compelled to be relative
rather than absolute because (1) we do not have a well established Western Chou chronology; and (2) very few bronzes have
the year recorded in their inscriptions. They record only the
years of certain undecided kings. In the old days, bronzes
were dated only as Shang, Chou or Han. Kuo Mo-ju listed some
two hundred and fifty Western Chou bronzes under each reign.
This initiative work was done with some success, but there are
errors. This, however, is natural in a pioneer work that
could not have the benefit of discussion and criticism. Besides listing bronzes under the Western Chou reigns, Kuo listed
the bronzes of feudal lords according to geographical distribution which contains many Eastern Chou bronzes as well as a few
Western Chou bronzes. Professor Karlgren, in his valuable
work, "Yin and Chou in Chinese Bronzes," divided the inscriptions
of the Royal Chou bronzes into the first half and second half
of Western Chou, and Western Chou in general. In dealing with
style, he divided the bronzes into four periods:

  1. Yin

  2. Yin-Chou (i.e., Early Chou)

  3. Middle Chou (i.e., second half of Western Chou)

  4. Huai (sixth century to the Ch'in dynasty)

Karlgren's divisions have been erroneously applied by
some people who accept Huai as meaning Late Chou, that is,

Late Chan Kuo, and Middle Chou as being between Early Chou and
Late Chou. Since the term "Huai" was derived from the vessels
which were first found in the Huai valley, we can use it only
as a name to refer to a certain style. Middle Chou as a period
does not exist in history. Furthermore, the division into four
periods, as Karlgren said in his article, is a very rough and
summary division. Therefore, I make the following four major
divisions with their subdivisions according to the periods recorded in history:

1. Shang

2. Western Chou

   a. Early

   b. Middle

   c. Late

3. Eastern Chou

   a. Ch'un Ch'iu

      (1) Early

      (2) Middle

      (3) Late

   b. Chan Kuo

      (1) Early

      (2) Middle

      (3) Late

4. Han

   a. Western Han

   b. Eastern Han

Thus the term, Late Chan Kuo is limited to the third century B.C.
before the unification under Ch'in. Hsiao, Yi, Li, Kung Ho and

Hsüan are names of kings who reigned in Western Chou, nineth
century B.C., but Hsiao and Yi reigned in Middle Western Chou
while the rest reigned in Late Western Chou. So we do not take
the nineth century to indicate a date, but rather we take the
names, Yi, Li, etc., of the kings in order to indicate a more
exact date.

  "Consistency" is the safest yard-stick for us to use in
determining the date of a bronze. The shape, the decoration and
the inscription of a certain bronze should be of the same period.
If they do not belong in the same period, then the vessel is a
fake, the inscription is a forgery or our judgment is not right.
Concerning the latter, it is important to point out that some
scholars who have found vessels that did not fit into their
categories have denounced them as forgeries in order to save
their theories. This is most unfortunate. It is my belief that
under scientific and objective study, that is, through stylistic,
epigraphic and typological studies, we might be able to ascertain the date of a certain bronze which would be in accord with
every aspect of the vessel. In dating a bronze, other aspects
or phases such as the provenance, the technique of casting, and
the surface treatment should also be considered. So we have
listed below the epigraphic criteria which we have used in
dating the bronzes in our catalogue:

  1. Historical events—to compare the events recorded in
the inscription with the written historical documents which have
been critically treated. For example, history recorded that
during the reign of Ch'eng Wang there was great fighting against
the revolting Shang allies in the Eastern territory. Therefore,

the vessels which recorded this event should be dated in the
Ch'eng Wang period (cf. Hsiao-ch'en Lai kuei and Hsiao-ch'en
Chai kuei, U.S. 77). Another example from history is the invasion of Yen by Ch'i in 314 B.C. Therefore the hu in the
University Museum (U.S. 750) should have been made before that
year. The hu was made before the war and was among the prizes
of loot by the Ch'i army in the year 314 B.C. so the inscription was carved either in 314 B.C. or later.

2. Historical persons—to identify the persons mentioned
in the inscriptions with those mentioned in written documents
and to find out their dates. For example, the T'ien Wu kuei
(U.S. 209) was made by the king for his father, Wen Wang. The
son of the latter who succeeded him was Wu Wang, therefore the
vessel was made in Wu Wang's life time. The rectangular ting
in the Nelson Gallery (U.S. 70) was made for the sacrifice to
Ch'eng Wang so it must have been made after the Ch'eng Wang
period. The Ling set (U.S. 652) and the Ch'en-ch'en set (U.S. 54)
were made during Chou Kung's life time, who lived during
Ch'eng Wang's time. Therefore, with a few exceptions which will
be discussed in the next paragraph, both sets should be dated
Ch'eng Wang.

3. Genealogy. In the Ling set, the rectangular Ta ting
were made by the second generation of Ling. Since Ling was
in the Ch'eng Wang period, the Ta ting should have been made
about the K'ang Wang period. We used the same method in dating
the Tun set (U.S. 467) which was made by three generations.

4. Capitals—Chou moved to the Eastern capital, Ch'eng Chou, in the year 770 B.C., therefore the vessels which mention the Western capitals, Tsung Chou, Chou, or P'ang Ching should be dated in the Western Chou period. It is possible for an Eastern Chou bronze to mention Ch'eng Chou, yet all of the bronzes that mentioned Ch'eng Chou are of the Western Chou period.

5. Extermination—the Chiang family controlled the Ch'i State until the throne was usurped by the T'ien family in 379 B.C. So the vessels that were made by Ch'i Hou could be dated before 379 B.C. (cf. Ch'i Hou set, U.S. 296), and the vessels that were made by the T'ien family (written as Ch'en on the bronzes) could be dated after 379 B.C.

6. Script—in the Ni set (U.S. 338) we selected several common characters which appeared on all of the vessels of that set in order to determine which style of writing was earliest. From that we can date the vessels that were made first and last in that set.

7. Commonly Used Phrases—the phrase, "sons and grandsons" never appeared on Shang vessels. Sometimes on Early Chou vessels it appeared in the form of "grandsons and sons." On Middle and Late Western Chou bronzes, the usual ending was "always treasure [and] use [it]." Then in Late Western Chou it changed to "always treasure and use [it] in ceremonies" (U.S. 251), and in Ch'un Ch'iu it changed to "always preserve and use it" (U.S. 266-267 and 296). Thus certain phrases and idioms were used in certain periods.

8. Composition. There is a clear distinction between the Chou inscriptions and the long Shang inscriptions. The long

2 663

Shang inscriptions, discussed under U.S. 200, usually began with the day name and ended with the year. On the contrary, the Chou inscriptions, after Ch'eng Wang, began with the year, the month, and the day name. Furthermore, the Chou people divided the month into several parts and the Shang people used a kind of "sacrificial season."

9. Gifts—the gifts mentioned in the Shang and Early Chou inscriptions were mostly cowries and metals while after Middle Western Chou the gifts were articles for the chariots and garments.

It is understood that when an inscription is used as a criterion for dating it should be an authentic inscription and it should be interpreted in the right way. The wrong interpretation often leads to the wrong dating as seen from the Kansas rectangular ting (U.S. 70) which was made for Ch'eng Wang after his death therefore it should not be dated Ch'eng Wang. For the same reason, the rectangular ting in Tsun ku: 1.24 was not made by the Great Prayer Ch'in, who can be identified as the eldest son of Chou Kung and the first Lord of the Lu State, but it was made for him after his death. Thus this ting should not be dated earlier than the first part of K'ang Wang since history records that Po Ch'in served under K'ang Wang.

The stylistic and typological criteria were discussed in the chapters on Classification, Typology and Decoration and will not be repeated here.

Chen Mengjia: Chinese Bronzes, Western Collections, International Perspectives

Elinor Pearlstein

On September 16, 1944, Chen Mengjia 陳夢家 and his wife Zhao Luorui 趙蘿蕤 boarded a flight from Kunming to Calcutta, the first leg in their two-month journey to the United States. Chen, Associate Professor of Paleography, History, and Ancient Literature at Tsinghua University in Beijing—then consolidated within Xinan-Lianda University 西南聯大 in Kunming—and Zhao, Lecturer in English Literature at nearby Yunda 雲大 (Yunnan University), were setting out from that remote academic refuge from the Second Sino-Japanese War for the University of Chicago. Upon award of Chen's fellowship from the Rockefeller Foundation, both he and Zhao had been appointed research associates in the university's Department of Oriental Languages and Literatures.[1] Their invitation demonstrated admirable foresight by foundation and university administrators, who recognized that World War II underscored America's urgent need to learn about East Asia—particularly China—and that Chinese intellectuals were preeminent sources of information and understanding.

Chen and Zhao's projected nine-month leave would extend, respectively, to three and four years and contribute significantly to Chinese academic studies in Chicago. It would also allow both young scholars to realize impressive intellectual goals: for Zhao Luorui, an MA and PhD in English Language and Literature;[2] for Chen Mengjia, an encyclopedic survey

---

[1] The University of Chicago's department of Oriental Languages and Literatures had focused exclusively on ancient Near Eastern and Mediterranean studies before 1936, when Professor Herlee Glessner Creel, a scholar of classical Chinese language and literature, established a program in Chinese Studies. The university's current Department of East Asian Languages and Civilizations, an outgrowth of that program, was founded in 1966.

[2] Zhao Luorui had been awarded a fellowship by Bryn Mawr College, but University of Chicago administrators persuaded her to come to Chicago as a research associate. She simultaneously enrolled in graduate courses in English literature and earned a modest salary by teaching conversational Chinese and working in the Far Eastern Library. John Albert Wilson to John Marshall, November 27, 1944, Rockefeller Foundation records, Projects, Record Group 1.1 (FA386), Series 216R: Illinois, Humanities and Arts, Box 19, Folder 264: University of Chicago Visiting Scholars-(Chinese Studies), 1944, 1946. She returned to China in December 1948, more than a year after Chen, upon receipt of the PhD. Her dissertation, "The Ancestry of The Wings of the Dove," focused on the American novelist Henry James.

of ancient Chinese bronze vessels in museums, galleries, and private collections throughout the United States.

Chen's survey, funded primarily by two grants from the Harvard–Yenching Institute at Harvard University, culminated in a pioneering work titled "Chinese Bronzes in American Collections: A Catalogue and Comprehensive Study of Chinese Bronzes." Chen's wide-ranging perspectives and systematic methodology presented both a synthesis of Chinese and Western scholarship and a practical guide to cataloguing for Western professors, curators and collectors.

In early July 1947—three months before his return to Beijing—Chen submitted his typescript and images to Professor Serge Elisséeff, Director of the Harvard–Yenching Institute at Harvard University. With the subsequent deterioration of Sino-American relations, however, these documents were abandoned and their whereabouts left unknown. This loss of what was certainly a paramount achievement for its time makes vitally important the preservation of a second copy of that typescript at the Kaogusuo—the Institute of Archaeology at the Chinese Academy of Social Sciences in Beijing. Although the Kaogusuo issued an adaptation of the Catalogue portion in 1962, the Comprehensive Study was kept in reserve until scholars were able to publish a Chinese translation of the entire manuscript.

In recognition of that long-awaited volume, this paper attempts to provide a narrative history of events that inspired Chen Mengjia to pursue and enabled him to complete this remarkable work of investigation and analysis, which he informally termed the "Corpus." Also addressed will be Chen's broader aims and achievements during his tenure in the United States—late December 1944 through August 1947—a period that included brief research trips to Toronto and to western Europe. Finally, it describes some of the groundbreaking academic programs at Tsinghua University that Chen was vital in initiating upon his return to Beijing and that were largely inspired by his experiences abroad. Primarily sources include Chen's correspondence, lecture notes, and unpublished papers that are preserved at the Kaogusuo, as well as substantial files archived at the Rockefeller Foundation in Sleepy Hollow, New York. Additional documents include those provided by the Harvard–Yenching Institute at Harvard University, the Oriental Institute at the University of Chicago, and other American universities and museums.

Why America?

Chen's exploratory mind and determined spirit reflect the strengths as well as the challenges faced by many Chinese intellectuals during a complex and somewhat paradoxical era
of nationalist and internationalist currents then sweeping their nation's preeminent educational
institutions and liberal arts. Born of Christian parents in Shangyu 上虞, Zhejiang, Chen at-
tended elementary mission schools in Nanjing and Shanghai. He first achieved youthful fame
as a member of the avant-garde Crescent Moon Society (Xinyue She 新月社) founded in
Beijing in 1923 by prominent writers who introduced aesthetic principles of Western literature
to Chinese poetry. Those most inspirational to Chen included the poet Xu Zhimo 徐志摩; the
poet, artist, and philologist Wen Yiduo 聞一多; and the historian, philosopher, and theorist Hu
Shi 胡適. Together, those brilliant and charismatic scholars of classical Chinese thought, all of
whom had studied in the United States, led China's spirited literary renaissance in the 1920s
while seeking modernist forms of expression in their respective disciplines.[①]

In 1931, following his graduation from Zhongyang University 中央大學 with a degree
in law—a discipline that he never pursued—as Zhao Luorui later recalled, "not even for one
day"[②]—Chen began studies of classical Chinese literature at Qingdao University in Shandong
under Wen Yiduo, his former Zhongyang professor of modern Chinese poetry and Western lit-

---

[①] Both Wen Yiduo and Hu Shi had spent significant time in Chicago. Wen Yiduo arrived in August 1922 to study
painting at the School of the Art Institute of Chicago. During his year in that city, Wen lived on the University
of Chicago campus and became an avid student of British romantic poetry while composing his own verse. His
literary circle included some of Chicago's most eminent writers, as well as a young English instructor, Robert
F. Winter. With Wen's encouragement, Winter began a teaching career at Tsinghua University in 1923 and later
became one of Zhao Luorei's most influential professors. After Wen Yiduo's assassination in 1946, Winter was
entrusted with Wen's ashes by the martyr's family.

For Wen's life in Chicago, see Sheng huo, du shu, xin zhi san lian shudian 生活‧讀書‧新知三聯書店, *Wen
Yiduo jinian wenji* 聞一多紀念文集 [Collected works commemorating Wen Yiduo] (Beijing: Xinhua shudian
faxing, 北京：新華書店發行, 1980), 53–64. For Winter, see Bert Stern, *Winter in China: An American Life*
(Bloomington, Ind.: XLibris, 2014). In 1947, Winter purportedly joined Chen Mengjia and other professors in
founding a department of art history at Tsinghua (see below).

In 1933, Hu Shi delivered a series of lectures at the University of Chicago that described the pivotal role
of *baihua* 白話 writers in revitalizing modern China. Hu Shi, *The Chinese Renaissance*: The University of
Chicago Haskell Lectures (Chicago: The University of Chicago Press, n.d. (1934). At the university's convo-
cation of June 13, 1939, he was awarded an honorary Doctor of Laws.

[②] Zhao Luorui, "Yi Mengjia 憶夢家 [Recalling Mengjia]," *Chen Mengjia shi quan bian* 陳夢家詩全編 [Com-
plete collection of Chen Mengjia's poems] (Hangzhou: Zhejiang wenyi chubanshe 杭州：浙江文藝出版社,
1995), 234, commenting on Chen's disinterest in law.

erature. Wen had turned his academic focus to the Classics and was beginning to publish icon-oclastic interpretations of ancient poetry and prose. In summer 1932, Chen accompanied Wen on a journey to Mount Tai in Shandong, a sacred site of ancient Daoist and Confucian ritu-als—a pilgrimage that may have inspired or strengthened Chen's decision to pursue graduate studies of ancient Chinese religion, mythology, and ceremonial. That autumn, Chen entered the School of Religion at Yanjing University, where his future father-in-law Zhao Zichen 趙紫宸 (T. C. Chao) served as Dean.

Like Tsinghua—a secular university then strengthening its American ties, Yanjing—a Protestant university founded by American missionaries, had emerged in the 1920s and the early 1930s as a major bilingual center for multidisciplinary "national studies" (*guoxue* 國學)— Chinese history, archaeology, epigraphy, philosophy, religion, and literature. Liberal and farsighted administrators educated in both China and the United States—John Leighton Stuart (Situ Leideng 司徒雷登), President of Yanjing (1919–46) and Mei Yiqi 梅貽琦, Pres-ident of Tsinghua (1931–49)—appointed to their faculties dynamic Chinese scholars in early history and culture—some trained exclusively in China but many in the United States as well. At Yanjing's School of Religion, the latter included Hong Ye 洪業 (known in the West as Wil-liam Hung), initially recruited for his graduate and theological training in the United States but soon appointed Dean of Arts and Sciences. Hong's undergraduate expertise in classical Chinese literature inspired him to initiate ambitious research and publication projects at the university's Harvard–Yenching Institute 哈佛燕京學社—established in 1928 with its admin-istrative headquarters at Harvard and primary academic center at Yanjing.[①]

Among the many renowned and promising Sinologists appointed by Leighton Stuart and William Hung, Rong Geng 容庚 perhaps figured most prominently in Chen's early ac-ademic career. Rong, author of the *Jinwenbian* 金文編 [Dictionary of Bronze Inscriptions of the Shang and Zhou] of 1925 (rev. 1929), served as professor of Chinese paleography at Yanjing and editor-in-chief of the *Yanjing Xuebao* 燕京學報 [*Yenching Journal of Chinese*

---

①Phillip West, *Yenching University and Sino–Western Relations, 1916–52* (Cambridge, Ma.: Harvard Universi-ty Press, 1976), 187–94, provides a history of the Harvard–Yenching Institute and its offices in Cambridge and Peking as well as biographical notes on these scholars. See also Dwight W. Edwards, *Yenching University* (New York: United Board for Christian Higher Education in Asia, 1959), 173–83; and Susan Chen Egan, *A Latter-day Confucian: Reminiscences of William Hung* (Cambridge, Ma.: Harvard University Press, 1987) , esp. 116–17 on the founding of the Harvard–Yenching Institute.

Studies, originally the *Yanjing Journal*]. Chen's research on ancient Chinese religious beliefs and practices inspired him to seek primary sources in oracle bone and bronze inscriptions,[①] to study under Rong, and to keep apprised of bronzes in private and museum collections as well as those steadily being unearthed—some excavated and documented by archaeologists at sites including Anyang, but most discovered accidentally or pillaged. Chen's early graduate career coincided with Rong's 1935 publication of *Haiwai jijin tulu* 海外吉金圖録 [Pictorial record of bronzes in overseas collections]—a survey of bronzes in Japanese collections that Rong had envisioned as someday encompassing the United States and Europe as well. The Japanese invasion of north China, however, abruptly ended those plans.[②]

As he studied and analyzed seminal reference works by Rong Geng as well as Sun Haibo's 孫海波 *Jiaguwen bian* 甲骨文編 [Compilation of oracle bone characters] of 1934—Chen also familiarized himself with the publications of Li Ji (Li Chi) 李濟 and other pioneering archaeologists in China as well as sinologists in America and Europe—notably, Professor Herrlee Glessner Creel of the University of Chicago, Bernhard Karlgren of the Museum of Far Eastern Antiquities in Stockholm, and Walter Perceval Yetts of London University. Chen's early perspectives on Western scholarship, which he later recollected in letters to all of these men,[③] was undoubtedly facilitated by strong research facilities at both Yanjing and Tsinghua,

①In chapter I of his 1947 English-language manuscript "General Study of Chinese Bronzes," Chen recalled: "About fifteen years ago the writer became interested in ancient religion and then realized that comparative anthropology alone could not solve the problem. It needed the two tools of paleography and archaeology, especially for the study of the original materials, the oracle bones and the bronzes."

②Several biographical tributes to Chen refer briefly to his studies with Rong Geng. See, e.g., Zhou Yongzhen 周永珍, "Wo de laoshi Chen Mengjia 我的老師陳夢家 [My teacher Chen Mengjia]," Lishi: Lilun yu piping 歷史：理論與批評 [History: Theory and Criticism],190; and Wang Shixiang 王世襄, "In Memory of Mengjia," *Journal of the Classical Chinese Furniture Society*, I, 3 (Summer quarter 1991), 57.

Rong Geng compiled his *Haiwai jijin tulu* from seven Japanese catalogues of private collections, primarily that of Baron Sumitomo Kichizaemon 住友吉左衛門(1864–1926).

③Chen's familiarity with the works of Creel, Karlgren, and Yetts is documented in his correspondence with these men that is archived in the Kaogusuo. This includes a handwritten draft to Creel, datable to mid-December 1944, noting his familiarity with Creel's books; and a letter to Karlgren of October 29, 1945, expressing admiration for Karlgren's work on Chinese phonology, and noting that he had reviewed Karlgren's "Grammatic Serica" for the *Tsinghua Journal* and found Karlgren's work valuable for his own research on non-Chinese dialects of southwest China.

Chen to Yetts, April 19, 1946, noting that he had read Yetts' volume, *The Cull Chinese Bronzes* (London: Courtauld Institute of Art, 1939), while in China and was "delighted" that Yetts agreed with him about the *hu*. Chen clearly referred to the pair of *hu* vessels (inscribed and dated 482 BC) then owned by the Cull brothers of London, which he published in "Yu Han Wang hu kaoshi 禹邗王壺考釋 [A study of Hu of King Yu Han]," as well as the new National Library of Beijing, then directed by one of its founders, Yuan Tongli 袁同禮 (T. L. Yuan). Yuan had earned graduate degrees in New York, catalogued Chinese books at the Library of Congress in Washington D.C., and studied at the Institute of Historical Research in London.[①]

Chen retained a research associateship at the Harvard–Yenching Institute after receiving his master's degree from Yanjing in 1936; in 1937, he joined the faculty of Tsinghua, where Wen Yiduo was establishing preeminence in classical Chinese studies. That July, invading Japanese armies forced the Tsinghua community to flee south to Changsha and establish a temporary College of Arts in nearby Hengshan; in February 1938, the university was exiled west to Kunming. At that remote mountain outpost, Tsinghua's faculty joined their colleagues from Beida 北大 (National Beijing University) and Nankai Daxue 南開大學 (Nankai University) in Tianjin in founding Xinan Lianda .

Throughout his post-graduate year in Beijing (1936–July 1937), three months in Hengshan 衡山 (October–December 1937), and six years in Kunming (1938–44, initially in the nearby village of Mengzi 蒙自, Chen lectured on paleography and classical literature while publishing important articles on Shang and Zhou texts, artifacts, and belief systems in the *Yenching Journal, Ts'ing-hua [Tsinghua] Journal* 清華大學學報 and the National Library of Beijing's *Tu shu ji kan* 圖書季刊 [*Quarterly Bulletin of Chinese Bibliography*]. As later recalled in the preface to his Corpus, Chen initially drafted several issues discussed in that manuscript under distressed wartime conditions in a simple hut in the outskirts of Kunming.

Yanjing xuebao 燕京學報 21 (June 1937), 207–29, 351–52. After summarizing issues of political patronage surrounding the commission of these vessels, Chen identified a group of *hu* with similar "flower covers" (*hua gai* 華蓋). See also *The Chinese Exhibition: A Commemorative Catalogue of the Exhibition* (London: Faber, 1936), cat. no. 133.

　　Then in the collection of Edgar Worch in Geneva, both vessels were subsequently purchased by Anders Eric Knos Cull and his brother James K. Cull. Yetts acknowledged Chen's comprehensive study of these vessels in *The Cull Chinese Bronzes*. Yetts also published the vessels in "A Datable Pair of Chinese Bronzes," *Burlington Magazine* 70 (January 1937), 8–11. Mrs. U. E. K. Cull gave both vessels to the British Museum in 1972.

　　In his Corpus ten years later, Chen ascribed these *hu* to the site of Liyu 李峪, Shanxi; recounted alleged reports of their discovery as well as previous studies by Chinese and Japanese scholars; and related them stylistically to vessels in Japanese and other Western collections—notably an impressive *jian* basin in the Freer (1939.5).

①For Yuan Tongli, see Yuan Cheng 袁澄, *Si yi lu: Yuan Shouhe xian sheng ji nian ce* 思憶錄：袁守和先生紀念冊— *T. L. Yuan: A Tribute* (Taipei: Commercial Press, 1967) and K. T. Wu, "Yuan T'ung-li," Howard L. Boorman, ed., *Biographical Dictionary of Republican China* 4 (New York: Columbia University Press, 1971), 89–92.

In October 1938, soon after re-settling in Kunming, Chen wrote to Hu Shi, then recent-ly appointed Ambassador to the United States. After reflecting on his recent teaching and re-search, Chen expressed his desire to work and study at an American university. Recognizing his era as a historical juncture, he affirmed that a comprehensive understanding of China's past requires that her scholars integrate Western disciplines of archaeology and anthropology with China's traditional text-based fields of study: history, paleography, and literary criticism. Such Chinese specializations were essential but inadequate; if studied in isolation, he argued, they lacked dynamism and creativity. Chen's ideal, as articulated to Hu, was to go abroad and glean perspectives on Western modes of inquiry— either with fellowship support or in a work-study position in a university museum or library, where Zhao Luorui could simultane-ously pursue her studies of Western literature and linguistics.[1]

Chen was acutely aware that Chinese bronze vessels of historical and artistic signif-icance were steadily entering American and European collections and that those vessels—particularly inscribed examples among them—merited careful analysis and publication.　In 1936, he followed several senior colleagues—Luo Zhenyu 羅振玉，Wu Qichang 吳其昌，Guo Moruo 郭沫若, and Tang Lan 唐蘭—in publishing a study of one of the Freer Gallery of Art's most notable acquisitions—an early Western Zhou (c. 11th/early 10th c. BC) Ling 令 *fangyi*, (1930.54) cast with a detailed historical text and reportedly found at Mapo 馬坡, near Luoyang, in 1929[2]; in mid-1937, he addressed the pair of inscribed and dated Eastern Zhou *hu*, described in fn.③, pp.573. Both articles demonstrated Chen's interdisciplinary approach that would distinguish his later research: Focusing on linguistic and historical interpretations of inscriptions, he simultaneously addressed questions of function, decorative style, and re-ported provenance.

Many of Chen's references were likely provided by Yuan Tongli, who was then direct-

①Chen to Hu Shi, October 30, 1938. Du Chunhe 杜春和, Han Rongfan 韓榮芳, Geng Laijin 耿來金, ed., *Hu Shi lunxue wanglai shuxin xuan* 胡適論學往來書信選 [Compendium of Hu Shi's scholarly correspondence], Shijiazhuang: Hebei renmin chuban she, 1998. See, e.g., 770:"……要注意訓練自己的新方法、新態度，而研究古代文化，西洋的考古學、人類學尤爲急需。因此，總願意有機會出國一次……我總覺得自己處此際會，也極難得，總可以盡其所能，略有貢於學術……"

　　　Chen's firm belief in the integration of artifactual and textual evidence dovetailed well with Hu's advoca-cy of Western methods of scientific inquiry for the study of ancient Chinese history and intellectual thought.

②Chen Mengjia, "Ling yi xin shi 令彝新釋 [New interpretation of the Ling *yi*],"*Kaogu shekan* 考古社刊 4 (1936), 27–39. Chen discussed this vessel at length in his Corpus (cat. 652).

ing the National Library's wartime branches in Chongqing and Kunming and beginning to re-establish library services at Xinan-Lianda.[①] Having developed research and archival facilities at Beijing's new Palace Museum and been instrumental in founding the Museums Association of China, Yuan also sought to document a broad range of important Chinese artifacts in Western collections and to avail Chinese scholars of Western publications. He had begun to collect photos and publications of Chinese bronzes while on a nine-month furlough to North America and Europe in 1934–1935; after returning to China, he and his library staff pursued their search with letters of request to museums and private collectors—written initially from Beijing; and after its Japanese occupation, from Shanghai and Kunming. Yuan's photo archives—and perhaps sale records of Chinese art dealers as well—undoubtedly alerted Chen to the quantity and quality of Chinese bronzes—vessels, weapons, mirrors, sculptures, and fittings—that were steadily entering Western collections.[②]

In spring 1940, Yuan enlisted Chen's assistance in annotating those bronze photos with historical, literary, and archaeological references. Chen prefaced his first 150 catalogue entries with similar but not identical essays in Chinese and English: "Zhongguo tongqi gaishu" 中國銅器概述 and "Outline Study of Chinese Bronzes." Together, these studies addressed issues of historiography, typological classification and style of ritual vessels and other bronze forms, and content and calligraphic styles of inscriptions. The 150 bronzes described in this first volume include 57 from three American collections: the Nelson Gallery-Atkins Museum,

---

① Tsuen-Hsuin Tsien, "Yuan Tung-li and International Exchange," *Collected Writings on Chinese Culture* (The Chinese University of Hong Kong, 2011), 260–66.

② Yuan visited several American and European cities while en route to Geneva, Switzerland to represent China at the Commission on Intellectual Cooperation of the League of Nations in July and the International Museums Conference in Madrid in October 1935. WWB, Librarian, to Dr. Andrew Keogh, Yale University Library, March 9, 1935, Rockefeller Foundation records, Record Group 1, Series 601, Box 47, Folder 388: National Library of Peiping; "Notes and News: National Library of Peiping," *Quarterly Bulletin of Chinese Bibliography*, I, 1 (March 1934), 24.

  Preserved in the Archives of the Freer Gallery of Art are several letters written from Beijing in 1936 and Kunming in 1940 by Yuan Tongli and his staff, in which they requested photographs and publications documenting the Freer's collections of Chinese art. The earlier requests refer broadly to "antiquities" in the Freer. (M. Y. Mok, National Library of Peiping, to Carl Whiting Bishop, Freer Gallery, September 25, 1936; Lodge to Mok, September 25, 1936. Freer Gallery of Art and Arthur M. Sackler Archives, Smithsonian Institution, Washington, D.C.) In 1940 acknowledging books previously received from Yuan, Freer curators John Ellerton Lodge and Archibald Wenley mailed him photos of 41 Chinese bronzes. (Bishop to Yuan, February 2, 1940, Lodge to Yuan, March 30, 1940, Yuan to Lodge, May 22, 1940). Freer Gallery of Art and Arthur M. Sackler Archives, Smithsonian Institution, Washington, D.C.

Kansas City (18); the Walters Art Gallery, Baltimore (4); and most prominently, the Art Institute of Chicago (35).[1]

Yuan's preface, quoted and translated below, follows a title page inscription by Rong Geng:[2]

我國古物歷年流失於國外者，不可勝記。近人雖有《海外吉金圖録》諸作，迺收藏既限於一隅，徵訪更非朝夕所克奏功，偶獲吉光片羽，誦覽者猶以未窺全豹爲有憾也。民國二十三年適有歐美之行，爰從事調查列邦所藏之中國古器物，稿已盈尺，未克刊布。二十五年復承中央古物保管委員會之委托，乃繼續徵集；本擬將影片記録，分類刊行，工作未竣，而盧溝變作，進行事宜，胥受影響。本年春乃將銅器部分，重行整理，並承陳夢家先生之贊助，編成圖録，分集印行。今後仍當繼續采集，蕲成全帙。先民遺物，縱不獲睹其真形，亦應識其影象，承先考古，因質見文，非僅爲藝術玩賞而已。惟是散布既廣，兼有遷移，展轉訪徵，頗需時日；且原器之款識文飾，既不獲一一攝取，色彩斑斕，合金成分，又非影片所克具傳，安得遍叩公私藏家之門，而一一爲之摩挲鑒別耶？是可憾也。然海外諸收藏家，不秘所藏，惠然示以影片，俾斯集得以印行，其盛意良可感矣。

民國二十九年六月　袁同禮

---

[1] Chen Mengjia, *Haiwai Zhongguo tongqi tulu* 海外中國銅器圖録: Chinese Bronzes in Foreign Collections [First Series] (Beijing and Shanghai: National Library of Peiping and Commercial Press, 1946). Chen's Foreword, dated April 1940, focused on the value of bronze inscriptions as historical sources; his Postscript, dated March 31, 1941, explained the differences between his Chinese and English essays. Chen proposed a functional classification of bronzes : (1) Food Vessels: A. Heating Vessels, B. Receptacles (2) Wine Vessels: A. Heating Vessels, B. Receptacles, C.Spoons (3) Supports (4) Water Vessels (5) Musical Instruments (6) Military Implements (7) Chariot and Harness Fittings (8) Measurement Standards (9) Agricultural and Hand Tools (10) Dressing and Other Daily Use Articles (11) Miscellaneous. He revised and refined this classification in the 1947 Corpus.

A few additional bronzes (no. 90, chariot fittings and no. 106, *ling* jingle) are erroneously cited as belonging to the Art Institute. The remaining 91 bronzes are attributed to dealers, private collectors, and museums in London, England; Berlin, Munich, Cologne, and Freiburg im Breisgau, Germany; Gothenburg, Sweden; and Amsterdam, Netherlands.

[2] Ibid., vol. 1, 1.

In 1934, I went to Europe and the United States to inquire about collections of ancient Chinese objects in those locales. I had prepared more than a foot of manuscript copy, but the materials that I collected could not be published. In 1936, I continued to collect materials under the auspices and at the request of the Central Committee for the Protection of Ancient Artifacts. For publication, I planned to annotate and classify the objects in photographs. Before I finished, circumstances changed due to the outbreak of the Sino-Japanese War, and all progress on this work was halted. In the spring of this year [1940], I reviewed the section on bronzes and with Chen Mengjia's encouragement and help, compiled a catalogue for publication in this series. We coordinated the pictures and text in different volumes. After this, [we intend] the project to continue and develop into a comprehensive set. Even if we do not have the opportunity to personally see [these] objects left by our ancestors, we should at least know their images by heart. To inherit our ancestral heritage and examine its tradition, we can see the culture through those objects and regard them not merely as playthings. These objects have been sporadically dispersed over a wide area. Collecting information about them requires a great deal of time. Moreover, we do not have the opportunity to gather individual inscriptions and decorative patterns, and the richness of color and the [metallic] alloy cannot be documented in black-and-white photos. How can we visit all of these private and public collections and make a complete survey of each and every piece? We cannot; this is a great pity. Nonetheless, I am most appreciative of the generosity of overseas collectors, who have not kept their collections secret and have agreed to share photos of their objects so as to facilitate the compilation of this catalog.

Yuan Tongli, 29th year of the Republic, 6th month [June 1940]

Chen later described this book—*Haiwai Zhongguo tongqi tulu* 海外中國銅器圖録: *Chinese Bronzes in Foreign Collections* [First Series]— as the first of several projected volumes, together envisioned to comprise a series on Chinese bronzes and other archaeological artifacts that he had been appointed to edit for the National Library.[1] But the outbreak of the

---

[1] Chen to Alfred F. Pillsbury, January 2, 1945, describing *Chinese Bronzes in Foreign Collections* as one of a series of books on Chinese archaeology of which he was the editor-in-chief; Chen to Hu Shi, February 17, 1945, stating that this book had been sent to Shangwu [Press, Shanghai] in 1944; and Chen, unpublished paper: "Im-

Pacific war postponed publication of that first volume until 1946.

Chicago

Yuan Tongli's ideal—to examine firsthand important Chinese bronzes that had entered Western collections—could be realized by Chen Mengjia only when financial assistance facilitated his extended stay in the United States. Chen's first grant materialized in early 1944, when a distinguished Tsinghua colleague took action on his behalf. Jin Yuelin 金岳霖, China's preeminent professor of formal logic, had returned to his Harvard alma mater on a pioneering exchange program sponsored by the State Department's new Cultural Relations Division, chaired by Wilma Fairbank.[1]

In his capacity of Far Eastern Representative of the Library of Congress, Wilma's husband, the Harvard historian John King Fairbank, had worked closely with Yuan Tongli to support the research of Chinese scholars whose academic livelihood was threatened by wartime deprivation. Together, they had cited Chen as worthy of fellowship support for projects in

---

portant Publications and Researches in China During 1937–1946," noting that the National Library of Peiping in 1941 "prepared to publish a series of archaeological researches edited by the writer. About ten works have been put in press but with the single exception of the writer's 'Chinese Bronzes in Foreign Collections' none have been published." This document is Chen's reply to a memo from Professor Robert Braidwood of the University of Chicago's Oriental Institute (May 23, 1946) seeking information on important archaeological events in China during the years 1937–46. Chen to Yetts, May 29, 1946, noting that "My book 'Chinese Bronzes in Foreign Collections' was finished in 1941 but because of the war was never bound. I myself had only a proof of it in China. Dr. T. L. Yuan of the National Library told me last month that when he was in China he saw the book but couldn't bring a single copy for me because of the airline restrictions. I believe these books are on sale at the Commercial Press in Shanghai, but I don't know how to get them since the Press is always on strike." The outbreak of the Pacific war had incarcerated Yuan in Hong Kong (1941–42) and imposed Japanese control on the Shanghai harbor. All of these documents are in the Kaogusuo.

In his Corpus (p. 20), Chen noted that "the second series, still in the press, contains 160 bronzes."

Collections represented in this second unpublished manuscript or incomplete third draft may include the Freer Gallery of Art (see fn.[2], pp. 576) as well as that of the German-Swiss banker Baron Eduard von der Heydt, whose letter of November 19, 1940 to Yuan is included in Chen's papers in the Kaogusuo. Chen was able to include four of von der Heydt's bronzes in the Corpus, as the collector kept them on loan to the Buffalo Museum of Science.

[1]See Wilma Fairbank, *America's Cultural Experiment in China, 1942–1949*, Department of State Publications 8839, Cultural Relations Programs of the U.S. Department of State, Historical Studies: Number 1 (Washington, D.C.: Bureau of Educational and Cultural Affairs, U.S. Department of State, 1976), especially ch. 4: "Chinese Educators and Artists Visit the United States." For Jin Yuelin, see 91–93, and John Israel, *Lianda: A Chinese University in War and Revolution* (Stanford, CA: Stanford University Press, 1998), 157–58.

both the United States and in China.[1] Jin now recommended Chen Mengjia to David Harrison Stevens, director of the Rockefeller Foundation's Humanities Division and former associate dean at the University of Chicago:[2]

> While in New York last time I mentioned to you the desire of a colleague of mine by the name of Chen Meng Chia to come to the United States. He is young and brilliant in his field, namely ancient Chinese history and language. He will be on furlow [sic: furlough] for the next academic year, but he wants to stay here longer than that to get himself more in touch with what is done in this country and elsewhere along his own field as well as to acquire more technique and method. I wonder if you know of any vacancy in the Chinese department of various universities. Anything you can do to help him will be greatly appreciated by both him and me.

Stevens proposed that Jin submit Chen's name to the University of Chicago, where Herrlee Glessner Creel, then on wartime leave with the United States Intelligence Service in

---

[1] While researching his doctoral thesis for Harvard in 1933–34, Fairbank had taught classes in Economic History; Renaissance and Reformation; and the subject of his thesis, History of the Chinese Maritime Service. See John Fairbank, *Chinabound: A Fifty-Year Memoir* (New York: Harper & Row, 1982), p. 103. In 1942–43 as a Harvard professor assigned to the Office of Strategic Services in Washington, D.C., he returned to China, initially on assignment with the American Publications Service to collect, microfilm, and distribute Western scientific publications for Chinese universities and Chinese publications for Western libraries. The American embassy and major Chinese government offices were then based in Chongqing. See Fairbank, "Yuan Tung-li as I Knew Him," in Ch'eng, *T. L. Yuan: A Tribute*, 18–19; and Yuan and Fairbank, "Sino-American Intellectual Relations," December 31, 1942, Archives, Harvard–Yenching Institute, Harvard University; and "Preservation of Chinese Scholarly Personnel," March 6, 1943., ibid., especially 86.

Among other projects, Fairbank and Yuan cited Chen's research on bronze rubbings in the National Library as worthy of funding, but how if at all these rubbings related to those that Yuan Tongli had gathered for *Haiwai Zhongguo tongqi tulu* is unclear. (Yuan and Fairbank, "Preservation of Chinese Scholarly Personnel," March 6, 1943.) John and Wilma Fairbank's concurrent memos to Serge Elisséeff confirm support for this and other grants (John Fairbank, Chungking, to Elisséeff, June 3, 1943; Wilma Fairbank, Department of State, Washington, D.C., to Elisséeff, June 3, 1943.) All documents cited here were filed in the Archives of the Harvard–Yenching Institute in 1999. Funds may have been approved but not awarded; similar grants had been vetoed by China's Ministry of Education, whose members believed that Chinese professors should not receive American charity. (Paul M. Evans, *John Fairbank and the American Understanding of Modern China*. New York, 1988, 78.)

[2] Y. L. Chin [Jin Yuelin] to Stevens, January 1, 1944, Rockefeller Foundation records, Record Group 1.1, Project Files, Series 216R, Illinois, Humanities, Box 19, Folder 264: University of Chicago Visiting Scholars.

Washington, D.C., shared Chen's specialization in paleography and Bronze Age literature:[1]

> I value your direct suggestion of your colleague Chen Meng Chia for a study pe-
> riod in the United States. I have two suggestions to offer, quite apart from any possible
> later interest in the Rockefeller Foundation: one is that you canvass the question with
> Dr. Serge Elisséeff, and then later with the people at the University of Chicago. Your
> friend is a specialist in the field of Professor Creel, and consequently would find the
> tools of his study available in Chicago almost as adequately as in Cambridge.

On June 30, 1944, John Albert Wilson of the University of Chicago cabled Chen to
offer him a nine-month research associateship beginning in October 1944:[2]

> I have today sent you the following cable:
> "UNIVERSITY OF CHICAGO OFFERS YOU RESEARCH AND TEACHING POSI-
> TION BEGINNING OCTOBER FOR NINE MONTHS WITH LIVING ALLOWANCE
> AND TRAVEL FOR YOU AND YOUR WIFE. LETTER FOLLOWS."
>
> The Chicago position would provide for teaching and study. We should like to
> have you do a limited amount of teaching with reference to current conditions in the Far
> East. If you wish also to give work in your own field of Ancient Literature this may be
> arranged. There may also be a certain amount of necessary work in relation to our li-
> brary of Chinese books. However, I can assure you that we should like to guarantee you
> adequate time for your own studies so that the time you spend here may be profitable

---

[1] Stevens to Jin, January 11, 1944, Rockefeller Foundation records, Record Group 1.1, Project Files, Series
216R, Illinois, Humanities, Box 19, Folder 264: University of Chicago Visiting Scholars. Shortly after his
arrival at Harvard, Jin had met several University of Chicago faculty members, including Chen's former
colleague at Yanjing, Deng Siyu 鄧嗣禹. In August 1943, Jin spoke at a University of Chicago roundtable
conference, "*Voices from Unoccupied China,*" organized by Chicago's professor of modern Chinese history,
Harley Farnsworth MacNair. See MacNair, ed., *Voices from Unoccupied China* (Chicago: University of Chicago Press, 1944), 81–99.

[2] Wilson to Chen, 30 June 1944, John Albert Wilson Papers, The Oriental Institute Archives, Oriental Institute,
University of Chicago. Ch'en's Special Grant-in-Aid (Humanities, RF4404) of $6500 was awarded on 21
June 1944. Rockefeller Foundation records, Record Group 1.1, Project Files, Series 216R, Illinois, Humanities, Box 19, Folder 264, University of Chicago Visiting Scholars. The University of Chicago supplemented
this with a salary of $1200, divided between the Division of Humanities and the Library.

for you personally.

The position will be characterized as a Research Associateship for nine months beginning October 1, 1944. The sum of money involved is $7,700 (American) out of which must come round-trip travel for Mrs. Chen and yourself. I assume that you will wish to begin negotiations about travel immediately, and I shall try to find how to allocate for you the necessary funds to secure this travel for Mrs. Chen and yourself.

At the University of Chicago you will be associated with Dr. Teng Ssu-yu [Deng Siyu 鄧嗣禹], who is in charge of our Chinese teaching and research program. I should be grateful if you would wire to me, Wilson, University of Chicago, Chicago, the word "accepted."

Chen wired his acceptance on August 14th.[1]

Wilson was Professor of Egyptology and Director of the university's Oriental Institute—a renowned museum and research center that had been established in 1919 for the study and exhibition of the art and archaeology of the ancient Near East, but whose academic curriculum had then recently expanded to encompass East Asia as well. Wilson and Stevens had judiciously drafted terms to bridge divergent requisites—Chen's expertise in ancient history and literature, the Rockefeller Foundation's focus on contemporary Asia, and the nationalistic interests of China's Ministry of Education: Chen's scholarship was needed in Chicago "to promote the teaching of present-day China as an outgrowth of its past" and to organize the university's Far Eastern library. As a service to China, he would be expected to return to Xinan-Lianda within one year.[2] Chen, however, keenly wished to stay longer in America—in

---

[1] YOUR KIND OFFER ACCEPTED CHINESE GOVERNMENT WANTS TO KNOW LIVING AND TRAVELING ALLOWANCES YOU OFFER US IN ORDER TO FIX FOREIGN EXCHANGE RETURN CABLE CARE OF Y T KU TELEGRAPHIC NUMBER 7526 CHUNGKING CHEN MENG CHIA. Archives, The Oriental Institute of the University of Chicago.

[2] Stevens to Wilson, March 9, 1944; Wilson to Stevens, March 24, 1944; Marshall to Wilson, April 4, 1944; Wilson to Marshall, April 6, 1944. In the last letter, Wilson noted that he added the "protecting clause, 'as an outgrowth of its past,' so that he [Chen] may not feel constrained to work solely in a single area which is not thoroughly his own." Rockefeller Foundation records, Record Group 1.1, Project Files, Series 216R, Illinois, Humanities, Box 19, Folder 264: University of Chicago Visiting Scholars.

Jin's words— "to acquire more technique and method."

Wartime transport postponed Chen Mengjia and Zhao Luorui's arrival in Chicago to November 24, well into the university's autumn academic quarter. As research associates in the Department of Oriental Languages and Literatures, both would teach part-time—Chen, seminars in Chinese paleography and Zhao, conversational Chinese. Owing to their delayed arrival, the university administration would extend their stay through the summer quarter—ending mid-September 1945.[1]

Chen earliest letters from Chicago indicate that he wished to extend his stay well beyond that date, having arrived with a survey of Chinese bronzes in American collections firmly in mind but still exploratory in scope. To Creel—who would remain in Washington D.C. on government and then academic leave until September 1946—Chen drafted his preliminary objectives:[2]

> My furlough begins from 1945–46, so I might stay in your country for a longer time. In the last seven years, I completed some works on Bronzes, Shangshu [Classic of Documents], and Ancient Chronology. Few of them were published, but I have brought my manuscripts with me and wish you could read them over if we have a chance to meet. My project in staying here is to continue my research and to have a chance to look over all the Chinese bronzes and oracle bones here in your country. Would you kindly introduce me to those collectors and directors of museums so that I could call on them?

Creel responded affably but without offering to mediate:[3]

---

[1] Zhao Luorui detailed their travel itinerary: Kunming- Calcutta (air)-Bombay (train)-Los Angeles (ship)-Chicago (train). They spent ten days in Calcutta and eighteen days in Bombay. Zhao to Wilson, November 24, 1944. Archives, The Oriental Institute of the University of Chicago. Like other institutions that followed the quarter system, the University of Chicago had four academic quarters (trimesters) per year during World War II rather than the conventional three quarters and summer break followed during peacetime.

[2] Chen to Creel, handwritten draft, n.d., late November / early December 1944. Kaogusuo.

[3] Creel to Chen, December 17, 1944. Kaogusuo. Creel concluded by recommending that Chen contact the Art Institute of Chicago; Minneapolis Institute of Art; Nelson Gallery, Kansas City; Freer Gallery of Art, Washington D.C.; Metropolitan Museum of Art, New York; Museum of Fine Arts, Boston; and the Fogg Art Museum, Harvard University, Cambridge. Creel did not return to campus until 1947. Although Chen's records mention only one encounter—that for an academic roundtable in mid-April 1947 (Sol Tax to Chen, April 2, 1947. Kaogusuo)—he and Creel would have met earlier that month, at the Princeton University Bicentennial Conference described below.

It is good to know that you are now at the University and will be able to lighten the load which Prof. Teng [Deng Siyu] is carrying... Now, with a distinguished colleague, he will not have the same excuse for overworking....

It is indeed sad for me to sit here in Washington and think about what interesting talks we could have about all sorts of problems connected to ancient China if I were there. … As far as private collections of bronzes, etc., are concerned, I have seen almost none in this country. I have a peculiar and probably reprehensible reticence about asking to see them. And I'm afraid that most museum curators I know are away because of the war. You will find, however, that museums are almost always cordial to visiting scholars…

Two months later, Chen described his work and his objectives more concretely to Hu Shi: [1]

現在我在此地的工作非常清閑，下學期（正月二日起）只教一門文字學，其他自己研究。我想整理一下舊稿以外，多去聽一點歷史學，人類學和埃及學的課。我自己想要做的事，大約有三項：

一、把我的文字學講義改編成一本英文的課本；

二、把我研究上古史（偏重金文，"尚書"和古年代的）寫成一個英文本；

三、看一看所有在美國的古銅器，作詳盡的記錄和考訂。

[I have a lot of leisure time in my current job. In next semester, which starts the second day of the First month of the lunar year, I will teach only a paleography class. The rest of the time, I can do my own research. Besides making revisions to my old papers, I am thinking to audit some classes of history, anthropology, and Egyptian studies. There are three things I am planning to do. First is to rewrite my lectures on Paleography as an English textbook. Secondly, to write an English version of my research in ancient Chinese history, focusing on bronze inscriptions, the Book of History, and ancient chronology. Thirdly, to tour around to see all the bronzes in the States, make detailed records, and examine and do research on them.]

---

[1] Chen to Hu Shi, February 17, 1945. Kaogusuo.

Aside from his third and main objective, which culminated in the Corpus, Chen would fulfill all of these plans. Soon after arriving at the University of Chicago, he began auditing classes in anthropology and archaeology. He participated in seminars for the Department of Anthropology and developed especially collegial friendships with its most eminent specialists in the civilizations of the Near East and the Americas. Some of these professors were pioneers in anthropology as a mode of scientific inquiry, and many had done archaeological fieldwork in their respective areas.①

---

①Chen mentions auditing these classes in a handwritten draft of a letter to John Fairbank, undated but probably January 1945. Kaogusuo. These professors include Robert J. Braidwood, a pioneer in prehistoric archaeology of the Near East; Sol Tax, an anthropologist of Native American cultures; and Robert and Margaret Park Redfield, specialists in Mexican and Central Asian civilizations. Chen's archives at the Kaogusuo include drafts for two lectures given for an Anthropology class on "Human Origins" —one titled "Shang Culture," the second, "On the Genesis of Civilization in China."

Especially noteworthy is one memo from Braidwood asking Chen's advice on the ten most important archaeological events in China during the period 1937–46, as requested by editor of the *Britannica*, an American encyclopedia (Braidwood to Chen, "Help!" May 23, 1946. Kaogusuo). Amid Chen's papers, this list (abbreviated and romanized in pinyin below) is presumably his reply:

Academia Sinica: Publication of the monograph *Liutong bielu* (1945) on excavation work at Anyang.
National Central Museum: Excavations in Dali, northern Yunnan.

Han Bamboo Slips: Discovery in Ningxia and publication by Lao Gan

Dunhuang Expedition: Work by Academia Sinica and other research institutes; discoveries yet unpublished.

Chronology: 1944 publications by Dong Zuobin on Yin dynasty based on oracle bones and by writer on Western Zhou chronology based on bronze inscriptions and the *Bamboo Annals*.

National Library of Beijing: "In 1941 they prepared to publish a series of archaeological researches edited by the writer. About ten works have been put in press but with the single exception of the writer's 'Chinese bronzes in Foreign Collections' none have been published."

Harvard–Yenching Institute: Publication in 1940 of Rong Geng's *The Bronzes of Shang and Zhou*; sponsorship of the writer's *Corpus of Chinese Bronzes in American Collections*.

Henan Provincial Gazette [sic]: Catalogues of Xinzheng (1937) finds discovered in 1923 and of Xunxian finds (1938) excavated in 1932 by Academia Sinica.

Changsha finds: Excavation (1936–37) and publication (1937).

Han Tombs: Discovery of Han tombs in Sichuan province.

In late 1948, the Redfields would live briefly in Chen's home while working with the sociologist Fei Xiaotong 費孝通 to develop Tsinghua University's teaching and research programs, but military unrest forced them to leave in December. Robert Redfield's letters describing Chen's home are in the archives of the Regenstein Library, University of Chicago. See also Redfield's "Visit to China," *University of Chicago Magazine* 42 (1949) 9, 19–20. Lothar von Falkenhausen pointed out to the author that Redfield's latterly famous juxtaposition of "Great vs. Little Tradition" within civilizations, which he articulated in a book written soon after his return from China, is one of the rare instances in the mid twentieth century American science in which a major theoretical concept was decisively based on Chinese data. Personal communication, January 17, 2017.

Two copies of Chen's seminar lectures on paleography, titled "An Introduction to Chinese Paleography," are preserved in the Kaogusuo. These clearly represent a draft of his textbook on paleography. The lectures comprise two main parts: I. Historical Survey and II. Construction, with each subdivided into chapters. Each manuscript copy (112 pages) includes handwritten annotations by one of his students. Similarly, many of his historical insights on the Bronze Age are detailed in his Corpus, especially in Chapters IX and X. Some of these were more broadly reiterated in an essay, "The Greatness of Chou" for an anthology published by the University of Chicago.[1]

A fourth, unanticipated project arose in March, when Charles Fabens Kelley, Curator of Oriental Art at the Art Institute of Chicago, invited Chen to co-author a catalogue of the museum's collection of Chinese bronzes. Kelley was a brilliant and dynamic scholar but had no academic background in Chinese language or history; he had been trained in architectural design and printmaking. Their collaboration was productive: Kelley contributed descriptions of shape and surface design accessible to the general reader, and the collection's significant number of Shang and Western Zhou inscribed vessels provided subjects apt for Chen's expertise. In addition to annotated translations of inscriptions, Chen provided a brief but wide-ranging "Commentary" in which he addressed issues of dating as well as function and nomenclature of vessel types that he would tackle in greater detail in the Corpus.[2] His meticulous scholarship would earn Chen widespread renown among Chinese bronze specialists in the West, as well as the enduring friendship of one of the most eminent among them—Ludwig Bachhofer of the University of Chicago. Writing to Wilma Fairbank in April 1945, Chen noted that he and Bachhofer engaged in a serious intellectual game: "We try to start from different angles, Professor, from design and decoration, and I from the inscriptions and history, to see if we may not arrive at the same results with greater accuracy of dating. We have worked on about a hundred bronzes with very interesting results." Chen noted that he and Bachhofer focused exclusively on inscribed Western Zhou vessels and that their debates were held "with the sty-

[1]Harley Farnsworth MacNair, *China* (The University of Chicago Press, 1951), 54–71. Although published after his return to China, Chen wrote this essay in 1946. Chen is also acknowledged by Ignace Jay Gelb, an eminent Assyriologist at the University of Chicago, in his *A Study of Writing* (1952).

[2]Charles Fabens Kelley and Ch'en Meng-chia, *Chinese Bronzes from the Buckingham Collection* (Chicago: Art Institute of Chicago, 1946), 143–46. In contrast with the vague stylistic periods of Zhou dynasty bronzes then outlined by most art historians in the West, Chen (and some of his contemporaries) argued for finer chronological subdivisions bracketed by or within the reigns of specific kings.

listic and epigraphical studies on bronzes, although begun from different angles, would merge
as if both were founded on and pursued with Euclidean precision."[1]

Initiatives and Funding

Chen's priority nonetheless remained a comprehensive survey of Chinese bronzes in
American collections, and he had begun his reconnaissance almost immediately after arrival
in Chicago. In late December 1944, he and Zhao Luorui visited New York, where Han Shoux-
uan 韓壽萱, Junior Research Fellow in Chinese art at the Metropolitan Museum of Art, conducted them through the museum's Chinese galleries. Their mutual friend Hu Shi had likely
arranged Chen's meeting with Han.[2] Important introductions followed. These included Alan
Priest, Curator of Chinese Art at the Metropolitan; Alfred Salmony, Professor at the Institute
of Fine Arts, New York University; and Roswell Sessoms Britton, Professor at New York University—all of whom had significant experience in China—as well as C.T. Loo (Lu Qinzai)
盧芹齋, whose New York and Paris galleries distinguished him as the preeminent dealer in
America and Europe. These men, in turn, clearly referred Chen to one of America's most
prominent collectors of early Chinese art, Alfred Fiske Pillsbury of Minneapolis, for Chen
visited him en route home to Chicago.[3]

Encouraged by such enthusiasm for his survey, Chen contacted Yuan Tongli, who was
then working at the Library of Congress in Washington, D.C. Yuan, in turn, strongly recommended Chen's proposed catalogue to Serge Elisséeff, director of the Harvard–Yenching
Institute in Cambridge. In February 1945, Chen sent a detailed proposal to Elisséeff, in which
he envisioned a comprehensive and well-documented study of ancient Chinese bronzes in
American collections—vessels, bells, mirrors, and weapons—that would serve as "a source-
book for Western museum curators and private collectors." By analyzing paleographic criteria together with typological features of shape and design, Chen asserted, he would date the

---

[1] Chen to Wilma Fairbank, April 1, 1945; Chen, "Some Notes on Chinese Bronzes," ms. draft, 1. Kaogusuo.

[2] Following a brief career at the Library of Congress, Han worked at the Metropolitan's Department of Far
Eastern Art between 1937 and 1946, before returning to Beijing to accept a professorship at Peking University,
where he taught classes in art history and museum training. He later served as director of the National Historical Museum. Personal communication, Professor Qi Dongfang 齊東方 Peking University, April 8, 2001.

[3] Chen to Priest, December 30, 1944 and Britton to Chen, December 29, 1944; Chen to Pillsbury, January 2,
1945, noting that C.T. Loo, Alfred Salmony, and Roswell Britton had encouraged him to see Pillsbury's collection. All correspondence in Kaogusuo.

vessels among them—which he estimated to total five hundred —with greater precision than his predecessors, notably Umehara Sueji 梅原末治 of Kyoto University. Chen undoubtedly referred to Umehara's magnificent opus of 1933: *Ōbei shūcho Shina kodō seika:* 歐米蒐儲 支那古銅菁華 *Selected Relics of Ancient Chinese Bronzes from Collections in Europe and America* —then the most complete pictorial record of bronzes in Western collections, public and private.[1]

In early April 1945, trustees of the Harvard–Yenching Institute awarded Chen a grant of $3000 to extend his stay in Chicago one year (July 1, 1945–June 30, 1946) for that ambitious undertaking. On Elisséeff's recommendation, this grant incorporated $1000 from the American Council of Learned Societies, a prestigious consortium of scholarly organizations.[2] Chen was finally launched on his systematic quest for Chinese bronzes in American collections.

Already in hand or firmly promised were a substantial number of photos from C. T. Loo, Alfred Pillsbury, the Metropolitan Museum of Art, and the Freer Gallery of Art. Perhaps through introductions by Yuan Tongli or Charles Fabens Kelley, Chen first met Archibald Gibson Wenley, director of the Freer Gallery of Art, in Chicago in April 1945. Even before the grant was operative, Chen also pursued his quest by visiting another major collection at the

----

[1] Yuan Tongli had been dispatched to the United States by China's Executive Yuan. In 1945, he was based at the Library of Congress, to which rare books of the National Library of Beijing had been sent for wartime safekeeping. Chen's proposal is summarized in minutes of the Board of Trustees Meeting of the Harvard–Yenching Institute, April 9, 1945, 212. Archives, Harvard–Yenching Institute, Harvard University. Chen cited this numerical estimate in a letter to Wilma Fairbank of April 1, 1945, and his expectation to supersede Umehara's scholarship in a letter to Elisséeff of February 19, 1945. Kaogusuo. Umehara's extensive (1926–29) study trip through Europe and the United States culminated in this seven-volume set, published in Kyoto by Yamanaka & Co.

Typed on the reverse of his letter to Elisséeff, Chen's incomplete title: "Project for a Complete Catalogue of Chinese Bronzes and Other Antiques in American and Europea" [sic] suggests that he initially contemplated a survey more expansive in content as well as geographic scope than Chinese bronzes in American collections.

[2] Minutes of the Board of Trustees Meeting, Harvard–Yenching Institute, April 9, 1945, 212, in which the Director [Elisséeff] noted Yuan Tongli's high recommendation for Chen's project. "VOTED T-885: That a grant of $3,000 for Mr. Ch'en Meng-chia be granted in the budget for 1945–46 for the preparation of material for a catalogue of Chinese bronzes in American collections… The Director felt that the publication of this material should be made by the American Council of Learned Societies, who have already sponsored the *Corpus Vasorum Graecorum*, and he said he had written to Mr. Graves to see if the Council is interested in joining in publication." The *Corpus Vasorum Graecorum* documented primarily ancient Greek painted pottery throughout the world.

Nelson-Atkins Gallery in Kansas City.[1] He also expanded his scope beyond the United States with a letter to William Charles White, Keeper of the East Asiatic Collection at the Royal Ontario Museum Toronto, requesting photos of both oracle bones and bronzes in advance of his visit. In his role as Anglican missionary in Henan province, Bishop White had collected vast numbers of artifacts from undocumented archaeological sites. Recognizing the importance of Chen's scholarship, White replied with an immediate offer of a temporary staff position, if financial help could be secured through the Rockefeller Foundation, to enable Chen to study the museum's vast collections.[2] Other Western curators and professors soon echoed that confidence in Chen's scholarship.

Pursuit and Documentation

Survey 1: June 30–ca. August 10, 1945

In July and early August 1945, Chen embarked on his first systematic reconnaissance of east coast and mid-Atlantic collections. His itinerary—insofar as it can be reconstructed from correspondence, expense reports, and museum guest registers—indicates that he quickly secured appointments with the majority of collectors, curators, and dealers who would prove essential to his research over the subsequent two years.

July 2–5: Washington, D.C. Freer Gallery of Art. Chen had a second meeting with director Archibald Wenley— one of the few American museum professionals who had visited Chinese sites of Bronze Age discoveries and whose intensive training in language and epigraphy enabled him to undertake detailed studies of bronze inscriptions. Wenley was then completing the first scholarly catalogue of the Freer bronzes and appreciated the importance of Chen's project.[3] Chen's visit was the first of four to the Freer, from which he selected 51 vessels for the Corpus.

---

[1] Chen to Loo, April 20, 1945. Kaogusuo. Both Wenley and Yuan had visited the Art Institute a few days earlier. Diary of Charles Fabens Kelley, loan of James Love, Ryerson Library, Art Institute of Chicago. Chen visited the Nelson–Atkins Museum of Art during the weekend of June 8–10. Curator Laurence Sickman was then stationed in Japan; his research assistant and acting curator, Lindsay Hughes, reviewed the bronzes with Chen. She subsequently enrolled in his classes at the University of Chicago.

[2] Chen to White, April 20, 1945, citing Yuan Tongli as reference; White to Chen, April 27, 1945. Kaogusuo.

[3] *A Descriptive and Illustrated Catalogue of Chinese Bronzes Acquired Under the Administration of John Ellerton Lodge.* Oriental Studies, no. 3, Publication 3805. Washington, D.C.: Freer Gallery of Art, 1946.

July 5–6: Philadelphia, Pennsylvania. University of Pennsylvania Museum of Art and Philadelphia Museum of Art. Chen met with Jean Gordon Lee, research associate at the University museum and curator at the Philadelphia Museum of Art. Throughout Chen's stay in the United States, Lee provided Chen with museum and sale catalogues, wrote inquiries on his behalf to private collectors and foundations, and expedited some of his research trips.[4]

July 9–20: New York. The Chinese Gallery. Its secretary-treasurer, Harald G. Wacker, had acquired the inventory of the renowned Dutch dealer Jan W. A. Kleijkamp. Chen selected 30 vessels for his Corpus from this short-lived gallery, which, despite its title, focused on Western art.

Chen also met with C. T. Loo on this trip, and clearly with some frequency thereafter. Of all persons that Chen met in New York, Loo would prove most instrumental to Chen's quest, providing hundreds of photos from the files of his New York and Paris galleries and extensive address lists as well as introductions, oral and written, to major collectors, individual and institutional.[5] He also provided access to bronze vessels closeted away by their European owners for wartime safekeeping.[6] Over the next two years, Loo's assistant Frank Caro photographed hundreds of ink rubbings of bronze inscriptions as well as numerous vessels in public and private collections, which their owners shipped to Loo's New York gallery expressly to

---

[4] Lee had been recommended to Chen by Professor Derk Bodde of the University of Pennsylvania. Bodde, a scholar of Chinese philosophy, had studied under Feng Youlan at Tsinghua University (1934–35). Bodde and Chen maintained contact throughout Chen's stay in America.

[5] Loo refers to these address lists in letters addressed to his secretary, Mrs. Bertha Oliver, of February 14 and 20, 1946, both to be forwarded to Chen. Kaogusuo. But Chen's annotations on an undated "Museum List" suggest that Loo prepared this for him in 1945. The list cites 74 institutions, divided into three categories: "museums which have a department of Oriental art, or which consider Oriental art as their main field;" "which have smaller collections of Chinese bronzes than the above;" and "which have only a few pieces, or which have Chinese antiquities the details of which are unknown." Several institutions cited match those from which Chen received his first completed questionnaires, described below, in September 1945. Chen generously acknowledged Loo and Caro in the prefatory Acknowledgements of his Corpus. The Corpus includes 130 vessels then in the collection of Loo's New York gallery and 159 vessels that Loo had previously owned.

[6] These European collectors included the French museum official and Jewish exile from the Vichy government, D. David-Weill. Loo kept David-Weill's bronzes in a New York storage vault through part of World War II. He and Caro arranged for Chen to see the bronzes and provided Chen with photos. (Chen to Mme. Levy, Librarian, Musee Guimet, February 19, 1946. Kaogusuo; Loo to Chen, August 5, 1947. Kaogusuo). Chen acknowledged Caro as photographer of the David-Weill bronze in the Acknowledgement to his Corpus, where he cited two of these vessels as comparative references (cat #652).

meet Chen's need.[①]

Late July-early August. Cambridge and Boston, Massachusetts: Chen concentrated his visit at the Fogg Art Museum at Harvard University, Cambridge. Here he studied the extraordinary bequest of Grenville Winthrop, from which he would select 29 bronzes (almost all of the vessels) for publication.[②] In Boston, Chen met with Tomita Kojiro 富田幸次郎, Curator at the Museum of Fine Arts, who began to document all the museum's bronzes to Chen's specifications—registration numbers, dimensions, names of former owners— and later assisted with locating and annotating a bibliography of Japanese reference books. Chen then made side trips to the Rhode Island School of Design, whose museum provided one vessel, and to Springfield, Massachusetts for the first of several visits to Mr. and Mrs. Raymond Bidwell. The Bidwells made available five vessels for his Corpus, as well as photos of their extensive collection of Chinese bronze mirrors and ceramics.[③]

Altogether, Chen spent more than two weeks at Harvard, where he finalized a detailed questionnaire to be mailed to curators, collectors, and dealers in the United States for immediate reply and to White and Karlgren for future reference:[④]

Dear Sir:

I am taking the liberty of writing to enlist your cooperation in the compilation of a corpus of Chinese bronzes (excepting those made for Buddhist use) which is now in

---

①In September 1946, Chen noted that he would ask Caro to photograph 300–400 rubbings (Chen to Elisséeff, September 14, 1946). As Chen's deadline approached, he offered to work evenings as "apprentice" in Caro's home darkroom (Chen to Caro, October 10, 1946). Kaogusuo.

Frank Caro also coordinated the duplication and shipment of Loo's photos [Loo to Chen, January 29, 1945; Chen to Loo, February 29 (1945); Loo to Chen, August 30, 1945 and November 14, 1945.] All letters in Kaogusuo. The last two letters refer to photos in Loo's Paris files, which were duplicated and shipped by Loo's Paris manager, his nephew Yusen Shen.

②To these he added 37 bronzes from an anonymous gift to the Fogg. Chen's correspondence with the donor on April 19 and April 23, 1946 identifies him as Mr. F. L. Higginson. Kaogusuo. Chen included this in his annotations to the 1947 manuscript. Mr. Higginson is named in the 1962 edition.

③Chen also requested and received a portrait of Bidwell (Bidwell to Chen, December 31, 1935). He did the same for Alfred Pillsbury (Chen to Pillsbury, June 1,1946), and requested biographical information on Charles Lang Freer (Mrs. Eugene Meyer to Chen, February 20, 1946). Kaogusuo.These requests suggest that he may have had planned some type of biographical index for a Chinese edition of the Corpus.

④Chen to Elisséeff, September 16, 1945, noting that he had spent sixteen days in Cambridge; Chen to White, September 23, 1945, and to Karlgren, October 29, 1945, both expressing hope that his Corpus would expand to include their collections. Kaogusuo.

course of preparation under the auspices of Harvard–Yenching Institute.

You will find enclosed blanks which you will oblige us greatly by filling out and returning to me at the above address.

It is also a matter of prime importance in this work that adequate photographs be made of each object, and in some cases more than one view and additional details. For these photographs I am, of course, prepared to pay. Glossy prints are desired.

While I quite realize that some of the items cannot be filled in, in every case, and that I am making demands on your good will, I do not hesitate to take your cooperation for granted as a contribution to international scholarship.

Believe me,

Very sincerely yours,

Ch'en Meng-chia

For each bronze, Chen requested description of shape and decoration, assessment of condition, and historical references: publications, former collections, and known or alleged provenance. For each inscribed vessel, he also requested a photo, ink or carbon rubbing, or hand copy of the text. Date and geographic distribution were to be left blank. (see the attached table)

Upon receipt of his first questionnaires in mid-late September 1945, Chen realized his six-month timetable for collecting his data to be woefully inadequate; he had anticipated neither the quantity of bronzes in American collections nor the post-war shortage of museum curators, photographers, and photographic paper to furnish his data. Some mailed available photos, rubbings, and partially completed questionnaires; others, feeling academically inadequate or overwhelmed by the size of their collections, returned incomplete questionnaires and encouraged Chen to conduct his research on site.[1]

---

[1] Photographic paper was rationed by the U.S. government through 1946 owing to wartime needs, and several curators noted a consequent delay in meeting Chen's requests. Major museum personnel had concurrently been called away for military and intelligence service.

Archibald Wenley of the Freer Gallery of Art replied promptly and with characteristic whimsy: "I am in receipt of your letter together with some 250 questionnaire forms … we have something like 684 bronzes … what you propose would be tantamount to our recataloguing the whole collection... and answering some 8, 208 questions … We should be happy to have you come to the Freer yourself and fill out your own questionnaires." Wenley to Chen, September 20, 1945. Kaogusuo.

By early November 1945, Chen also realized that American collections of Chinese bronzes far exceeded his expectations and truly warranted "a systematic study of forms and patterns, chronology, and geographic distribution." He may have decided by then to restrict his catalogue to vessels (and perhaps bells as well), but nonetheless continued to request photos of all non-Buddhist bronzes, including mirrors, small sculptures, and miscellaneous fittings.

Survey 2: late November 1945–early February 1946

Over the subsequent fifteen months, Chen's intensive pursuit of objects took him on three additional surveys of the mid-Atlantic and New England states that generally followed his initial itinerary. His second journey added public and private collections in Georgetown and Baltimore, Maryland; Cambridge and Worcester, Massachusetts; New Haven, Connecticut; Buffalo, New York; and Cleveland, Ohio.

Very early in that trip, on November 30, 1945, Chen lectured at the Metropolitan Museum of Art in New York on "The Style of Chinese Bronzes." For inscribed vessels, he advocated the integration of stylistic analysis with epigraphical study; and for those documented or alleged from specific sites, for investigation of provenance as well. His lecture was proposed by Loo and sponsored by the Chinese Art Society of America—a private organization then recently founded by some of America's most prominent scholars, collectors, and dealers. As many members of the Society would provide vessels for Chen's Corpus or refer him to others who did, the meeting proved mutually beneficial.[1]

By late 1945, the unexpected quantity of bronzes that Chen had seen in about thirty American museums compelled him to re-evaluate his timetable as well as expenses for photography and travel. In late February 1946, he requested that his Harvard–Yenching grant be renewed for a third year in the United States. On Elisséeff's recommendation, the Harvard–Yenching committee awarded Chen that second research grant, effective July 1946–June 1947.[2] His academic leave from Tsinghua was correspondingly extended, and he maintained

[1]Loo to Chen, May 9, 1945; Florence Waterbury to Chen, May 23, 1945, both Kaogusuo. Ch'en Meng-chia, "Style of Chinese Bronzes," *Archives of the Chinese Art Society of America* I (1945–1946), 26–52.

[2]Chen to Stevens, February 19, 1946, describing his meeting with Elisséeff: "Both he and [Langdon] Warner agreed that I better extend my work one more year so that I could work out all the Chinese Bronzes in America. They are going to discuss this possibility in April at the meeting of Educational Committee of Harvard–Yenching Institute," Kaogusuo. At that meeting, Elisséeff noted that Chen had visited about thirty museums but had underestimated the number of bronzes in American collections; Chen now calculated that he would

an office at the University of Chicago, teaching part-time as honorary (non-salaried) Research Associate.

Surveys 3 (mid-June–mid July 1946) and 4 (late October–early December 1946)

By April 1946, Chen had already collected more than two thousand photographs of Chinese bronzes in American collections. Yet having seen so much made Chen keenly aware that more remained to be seen. With steadfast focus, he aimed to revisit some collections, locate new ones, and document as many additional vessels as possible. This second grant facilitated his third and fourth surveys of collections in the eastern and mid-Atlantic states in the summer and fall of 1946. The third took him, sequentially, to New York, Princeton, Philadelphia, Washington, D.C. and Cambridge; and the fourth to Princeton, Philadelphia, New York, Cambridge, and Washington, D.C.

But Chen's net was not cast only eastward; he devoted weekends and intervals in his teaching schedule to surveying or reviewing major midwestern collections, public and private. In addition to frequent calls on the Art Institute, the Field Museum (then the Chicago Natural History Museum), and Avery Brundage in Chicago, Chen's correspondence details his visits to Minneapolis, Kansas City, St. Louis, Cleveland, Detroit, and Ann Arbor (The University of Michigan), as well as other cities.[1]

Princeton University Bicentennial Conference on Far Eastern Culture and Society, April 1–3, 1947

Chen's three trips to Princeton in 1946 aimed primarily to advise Professor George Rowley in organizing the university's 1947 Bicentennial Conference on Far Eastern Culture and Society—a comprehensive series of multidisciplinary panels that would focus exclusively on China. The meeting was envisioned by Rowley—an art historian—and his co-organizer David N. Rowe—a Yale University political scientist—to explore the challenges and potential of Chinese scholarship in the postwar world by juxtaposing historical topics of Chinese art

require the remainder of the grant year [ending June 1946] to collect data and another to organize and prepare the manuscript. The Harvard–Yenching trustees awarded a grant of $5500: salary, 3600; research assistant, 1200; travel, photos, and office expenses, 700. Grant T-889, Harvard–Yenching Institute Meeting of Trustees, April 1, 1946, Minutes, 246, Harvard–Yenching Institute, Harvard University.

[1] In 1966, Brundage would present his collection to the city San Francisco, where it formed the foundation for the Asian Art Museum.

and archaeology with current developments in philosophy, anthropology, geography, politics, and economics.[1] Rowley sought Chen's recommendations for academic panels and loan exhibitions.

Sharing an art and archaeology panel with Alfred Salmony, Chen addressed "Some Suggestions for the Study of Chinese Bronzes." He emphasized the importance of integrated studies of epigraphy, geographical distribution, and sets of vessels that had been cast together under common patronage, and of using those sets to analyze variations in form and surface design—all issues that would be reiterated in the Corpus. He concluded with the hope for further scientific excavations in China and for greater international cooperation by Sinologists of diverse disciplines.[2]

Chen also worked with Yuan Tongli and other contacts at the National Library of Beijing to help Rowley organize the first American exhibition of the library's books and manuscripts, primarily on art and music, which in 1941 had been shipped from Japanese-occupied Shanghai to the Library of Congress in Washington D.C. for wartime safekeeping. He simultaneously assisted Rowley in coordinating an exhibition of Chinese bronzes, which Rowley had long contemplated but deferred to Chen's selection. In addition to pieces from the Metropolitan Museum of Art, Nelson Gallery-Atkins Museum, and Buffalo Museum of Science, Chen negotiated the loan of twenty vessels from the Royal Ontario Museum in Toronto, and with C. T. Loo's cooperation, from dealers and private collectors who had contributed to his Corpus. This exhibition is partially documented in gallery photos; a catalogue was planned but did not see publication.[3]

---

[1] Rowley noted in his proposal to the Rockefeller Foundation. "Through twenty-five years of teaching and preparing men for museum work, I have found that Chinese art is one of the most effective approaches to China for Western students. However, this field is a newcomer and desperately needs sound scholarly foundations. David Rowe and I feel very strongly that the discipline must come first, even before training in the language. The History of Art has been too long in the hands of philologists and missionaries who have lacked sound training in this humanistic discipline." Rowley to George Burton Fahs, Administrator Of East Asian Programs, Rockefeller Foundation, February 4, 1947. Rockefeller Foundation records, General Correspondence, Record Group 2, 1947–1951 (FA759), Series 1947/200: Box 371, Folder 2507: United States - Princeton – Bicentennial Conferences, 1947. Papers and events of this conference are summarized in *Far Eastern Culture and Society*, Princeton University Bicentennial Conferences, Series 2, Conference 7 (Princeton University, 1947).

[2] Copies of Chen's brief symposium paper are included in his archives at the Kaogusuo as well as in the Rockefeller Foundation records file cited in fn. [1].

[3] A partial list of lenders to the bronze exhibition is citied in *Far Eastern Culture and Society*, 2. See also "Chinese Conference Held at Princeton University," *The Museum News*, vol. 24, no. 20 (April 15, 1947), 1.

For Chen, the conference was both collegial and timely. It occasioned reunions with his Tsinghua colleagues—notably, the philosopher Feng Youlan 馮友蘭 and architectural historian Liang Sicheng 梁思成, who were then teaching, respectively, at the University of Pennsylvania and at Yale. The meetings provided introductions to some of the most eminent Sinologists in Europe as well as America and—perhaps most importantly—leads to yet more collections of Chinese bronzes.[①]

Completion and Submission

Upon his return from Princeton, Chen spent 2-1/2 intensive months completing the manuscript, even as curators, collectors, and dealers continued to send him photos of their recent acquisitions. An inscription on one of those vessels—a *liding* 鬲鼎 tripod that had been purchased in March from C. T. Loo by the Museum of Fine Arts, Boston, enabled Chen to precisely date the piece within the six-year reign of the fourth Duke of Lu (994–989 BC). Chen promptly added it to his Corpus and submitted his study to Alfred Salmony, who published it in the following issue of *Artibus Asiae.*[②]

In early July 1947, three years after receipt of his first Rockefeller grant to work and study in Chicago, Chen made a final trip to Harvard to deliver his manuscript—complete with photos, comparative figures, rubbings of inscriptions, and detailed "Directions for Printing." The remarkable endeavor that Chen had termed the "Corpus" comprised a text ("Comprehensive Study") of almost 600 pages and a Catalogue documenting 850 bronzes from 37 institutions and 76 private collections and galleries.[③] With the accompanying publication, Chen's

---

According to a preliminary outline of conferences and exhibitions (February 21, 1947), the bronzes were to be organized by archaeological site. The few exhibition views provided to me by Professor Robert Bagley of Princeton University, however, do not indicate this.

①Sickman, then recently returned to the Nelson Gallery from his wartime service in Japan, referred Chen to several of his new acquisitions for the Nelson Gallery as well as to bronzes owned by the German dealer Otto Burchard, who in 1927 founded a gallery in Berlin and moved it, successively, to Beijing, New York, and (later) London. Professor James Marshall Plumer of the University of Michigan directed Chen to two vessels at a most unexpected location: the Romanian Episcopate (Church) in Grass Lake, Michigan. (Plumer to Chen, April 21, 1947.) These bronzes appear only in the Chinese edition of the Corpus, described below.

②Ch'en Meng-chia, "A Datable Early Chou-Bronze," *Artibus Asiae* 10, no. 2 (1947), 106–7. It was published as no. 126 in the 1947 edition of the Catalogue and A123 in the 1962 edition. Chen described the vessel as a "recent find."

③In order of the quantity of vessels represented, the major collections are as follows: C. T. Loo: 130; Alfred F. Pillsbury (on loan to Minneapolis Institute of Art): 54; Metropolitan Museum of Art, New York: 53; Freer Gallery of Art: 51; unnamed bequest, Fogg Art Museum, Harvard University: 37; Boston Museum of Fine

true achievement—paramount in its time—is first made available to scholars in both China
and the West.

Here it should be noted that Chen's appreciation of his intended Western readership is
especially evident in his annotated bibliography of Chinese, Japanese, and Western sources;
his historical and cultural overviews; and, for advanced scholars, his detailed discussion of
paleography and inscriptions. The last was based largely on the work that Chen had formu-
lated as a university textbook in Chicago. For museum curators, the chapter on terminology
provided a standardized, visually descriptive vocabulary of unprecedented precision.

The catalogue comprised almost exclusively vessels, but also included chime-bells and
a few implements such as spoons and ladles. Although uninscribed bronzes were documented with only brief registration data, inscribed bronzes—particularly those that by inscription
could be identified as components of "sets" commissioned by a single patron—were exten-
sively annotated. Provenance in Chinese and foreign collections, both private and commercial,
was recorded when known, and those records cross-referenced in an index. Entries were completely illustrated and supplemented by 79 comparative figures and more than 450 rubbings of
inscriptions and surface designs.

Royal Ontario Museum, Toronto (March 1946)

Chen's plans for an even more comprehensive Corpus had been clear by April 1945,
when he first requested photos of both bronzes and oracle bones in the Royal Ontario Museum (ROM) from its curator, Bishop William Charles White. As noted above, White replied
with an immediate offer of a temporary staff position to enable Chen to study the ROM's vast
collections. But upon receipt of Chen's questionnaire in early October, White lamented the
enormous staff resources required to access, inventory, and photograph the material. Chen—
then expecting to complete his research for the American corpus by year's end—proposed to
White, as well as to Serge Elisséeff at Harvard and David Stevens at the Rockefeller Foundation—that he subsequently focus on a comprehensive survey of the ROM's collections. As
Stevens and his associate director, John Marshall, considered funding Chen's new proposal,

Arts: 35; Harold G. Wacker, Chinese Gallery, New York: 30; Grenville Lindall Wintrop Bequest, Harvard University: 29; Art Institute of Chicago: 29; Nelson Gallery of Art-Atkins Museum of Fine Arts, Kansas City: 29;
Avery C. Brundage, Chicago: 28.

White urged Chen to visit Toronto, survey the museum's vast holdings, and narrow his focus.[1]

In March 1946, Chen and White conducted a preliminary survey of the museum's Shang and Zhou bronzes as well as oracle bones, jades, and ceramics that reportedly had been unearthed in association with them at sites in Henan including Anyang 安陽, Luoyang 洛陽, Jincun 金村, Huixian 輝縣, and Xunxian 濬縣. As the depth and documentary importance of these collections impressed Chen, Chen's methodology convinced White to endorse Chen's proposal for further research and publication. Midway through Chen's survey, White wrote to Marshall:[2]

> he [Chen] is a hard and fast worker, very careful and thorough in his investigations, and has good judgment concerning facts and is not given to surmising, so he is making good progress. I am greatly enjoying my association with him and I am delighted with the progress he is making. In my opinion, Professor Chen is outstanding in the field of Chinese Archaeology and I have not yet met anyone that I feel is his equal in this particular work.

White, optimistic of Harvard–Yenching and/or Rockefeller Foundation support, approved Chen's request for about five hundred photographs of the museum's bronzes. Anticipating his own imminent departure for postwar missionary work in China, White also suggested that Chen consider concurrent one–year appointments at the museum and at the University of Toronto. And in a gesture bespeaking unqualified trust, White also proposed that his 1934 tome on Jincun, *Tombs of Old Lo–yang*, be updated and revised by Chen.[3]

---

[1] See fn.②, pp.589. Chen to Elisséeff, October 29, 1945; Stevens to Mortimer Graves, American Council of Learned Societies, December 5, 1945, reporting on his meeting with Chen on December 4 (presumably in New York); White to Chen, October 1, 1945. Kaogusuo.

[2] White to Marshall, March 13, 1946, Rockefeller Foundation records, Record Group 1.1, Project Files, Series 216R, Illinois, Humanities, Box 19, Folder 265: University of Chicago Visiting Scholars. Chen's Corpus incorporated numerous comparative references to ROM vessels and to these sites. Chen included a detailed description of the problematic Jincun "site," for which he acknowledged White's account of the tomb discoveries as related to the bishop by his primary dealer and by local witnesses (Chapter IV, Excavations and Finds, 22–28). But he questioned some of White's conclusions—the coherence of the finds, identity of the tombs' patrons, and dates of key pieces (particularly the so-called "Biao" bells) in relation to textual accounts of contemporary rulers.

[3] Ibid. White's interest in a new edition of his *Tombs of Old Lo-yang* may have been prompted in part by Umehara's attribution of additional finds to Jincun in his *Rakuyo Kinson kobo shuei* 洛陽金村古墓聚英 of 1937.

After returning to Chicago, Chen realized that he could not complete his Corpus while holding dual appointments in Toronto. Writing with regret to White and avowed boldness to both Elisséeff and Marshall, Chen requested funds from the Rockefeller Foundation to support a one-month residence at the Royal Ontario Museum to gather more data. After returning to Beijing, Chen proposed, he would assimilate and document this material for a future catalogue to be published in America or in China.[1] Marshall was agreeable, "particularly in that it will make known to scholars in China much material in this country and Canada to which they do not have ready access." In October 1946, he and Elisséeff jointly ratified a grant-in-aid of $1000, to be issued by the Rockefeller Foundation and administered by the Harvard–Yenching Institute at Harvard, for Chen to complete his survey at the Royal Ontario Museum within the following year.[2]

But Chen could not see this plan to fruition. White had left for China in April 1946 to pursue his Christian missionary work and with sincere promise of facilitating Chen's research in both Canada and China. His intent went so far as to assist in one or more of Chen's publications.[3] But upon return in mid-July 1947—perhaps exhausted by his year away, realizing the demands of Chen's project on his relatively small staff, and anticipating his own retirement—White withdrew his earlier commitment to allow Chen to re-examine the objects off display, access the museum files, and obtain new photographs for future study and publication. As the photos previously provided were, in White's words, "taken in such haste that the prints were not as good as we could desire," Chen's plans for research and publication came to an abrupt end.[4]

---

[1] Chen to Elisséeff, May 14, 1946. Kaogusuo; Chen to Marshall, March 15, 1946 and July 25, 1946. Kaogusuo. See also fn.[2].

[2] Chen's revised proposal and consideration by the Rockefeller Foundation and Harvard–Yenching Institute is documented extensive correspondence between White, Marshall, and Chen in the Rockefeller Foundation records, Record Group 1.1, Project Files, Series 216R, Illinois, Humanities, Box 19, Folder 265: University of Chicago Visiting Scholars. The grant is recorded in Rockefeller Foundation records, Record Group 1.2, Series 200R, Box 344, Folder 3142: Grant In Aid to the Harvard–Yenching Institute, Chinese Bronzes, October 14, 1946, signed John Marshall.

[3] White to Marshall, Rockefeller Foundation, March 13, 1946. White noted that he was taking a leave from the ROM and University of Toronto, as "My Church is sending me at the request of our Chinese Christians to help them in their post-war problems." Rockefeller Foundation records, Record Group 1.1, Project Files, Series 216R, Illinois, Humanities, Box 19, Folder 265: University of Chicago Visiting Scholars.

[4] White to Chen, July 19, 1947. Kaogusuo.

Europe (August 1947)

Even before receipt of White's letter, Chen had resolved to further widen his Western horizons. Since autumn 1945, he had expressed a desire to see Europe in letters to the Palace Museum director Ma Heng 馬衡 as well as to several European scholars, including Bernhard Karlgren in Stockholm and Sir Percival Yetts in London.[1] In January 1947, Chen wrote to David Stevens at the Rockefeller Foundation:[2]

> The unexpected wealth of objects both here and in Toronto encourage[s] me to wish to extend my work to England and the continent, so that I might complete a survey of such materials all over the world. I hope such materials when collected and edited will be of value to both Chinese and Western scholars. Although I was asked to resume teaching in Ts'ing-hua next autumn, I have talked over my plans with [Dean of Humanities] Dr. Fung Yu-lan about another short extension of leave for six months. He was in complete agreement and saw the importance of the work and therefore was willing to do whatever in his power to facilitate me.

While completing his American corpus that spring, Chen began to seek information for museum and private collections in post-war Europe. Dorothy Blair—assistant curator at the Toledo Museum of Art and author of the *Preliminary Survey of East Asiatic Art in the Museums of Europe*—provided him with an extensive list of museums, private collections, and scholars in Great Britain, France, Holland, Belgium, Denmark, Sweden, and Norway—and offered letters of introduction. C. T. Loo, who had supplied photos from the inventory of his Paris gallery to Chen, similarly promised to advise European collectors and curators of the trip.[3]

Having received a priori approval for an extension of his three-year academic leave from Tsinghua, Chen—even before receipt of Bishop White's disappointing letter—asked the Rockefeller Foundation to divert funds previously awarded for research in Toronto to his

---

[1]Chen to Ma Heng, February 25, 1946, quoted below. See fn. [3], pp.601 for correspondence with these European scholars.

[2]Chen to Stevens, January 11, 1947, Rockefeller Foundation records, Projects, Record Group 1.2 (FA387), Series 200R: United States–Humanities and Arts, Box 344, Folder 3142: Harvard–Yenching Institute–Chinese Studies–(Chen Meng-Chia)–(Chinese Bronzes in Canada).

[3]Blair to Chen, June 19, 1947; Loo to Chen, June 16 and August 1, 1947. Kaogusuo.

long-awaited trip to Europe. In late July, the Foundation agreed to amend terms of that grant.[①]
On August 1, 1947, Chen flew from New York to London with the intent to visit Great Britain, France, Switzerland, Holland, Denmark, and Sweden. But he apparently curtailed his itinerary to one week each in Paris and Stockholm, bracketed by two weeks in London and surrounding cities — perhaps because Loo and others had advised him that Europe's major collectors would be away on vacation or had yet to retrieve their collections from wartime storage, perhaps owing to budget constraints as well.[②]

Soon after his arrival at the Chinese Embassy in London, Chen received welcoming letters from Herbert Visser in Amsterdam and from Ernest Richard Hughes, Oxford University's eminent historian of Chinese literature, philosophy and religion. Hughes, who had spoken at the Princeton Bicentennial Conference, invited Chen to examine Chinese books in Oxford's Bodleian library and to visit the university's Ashmolean and Pitt Rivers museums. Chen's follow-up correspondence indicates that he also met with Percival Yetts, and that Geoffrey Hedley accompanied him to several public and private collections in London and its environs. Hedley, a Chinese ceramic specialist and painting collector, was then working for the British Council, which had been established by the government of the United Kingdom to promote international cultural and educational relations.[③]

C.T. Loo arranged for his nephew Yusen Shen to schedule Chen's appointments in Paris, where major museums were only then beginning to reopen after World War II. In Stockholm, Chen enjoyed stimulating meetings with Sweden's most eminent collectors and scholars: Crown Prince Gustaf VI Adolf; Bernhard Karlgren; and Orvar Karlbeck, who took him to see the collection of Axel Lundgren.[④]

---

①Interviews: DHS (David H. Stevens) and Mr. Ch'en Meng-chia, July 14, 1947; Amendment of Grant in Aid "to obviate the restriction of place of study," July 21, 1947; memo to David H. Stevens from MPH, July 31, 1947. Rockefeller Foundation records, Projects, Record Group 1.2 (FA387), Series 200R: United States-Humanities and Arts, Box 344, Folder 3142: Harvard–Yenching Institute-Chinese Studies-(Chen Meng-Chia)-(Chinese Bronzes in Canada).

②Loo to Chen, June 16, August 1, and August 5, 1947. Kaogusuo.

③Visser to Chen, August 7, 1947; Hughes to Chen, August 6, 1947; Yetts to Chen, August 30, 1947. Kaogusuo. Hedley's meeting is alluded to in detailed correspondence of September 1948. Kaogusuo. See below.

④For Gustaf VI Adolph, Karlgren, and Karlbeck, see below. Karlbeck to Chen, November 22, 1947, noting Karlbeck's promise to send photos of the Lundgren collection. Kaogusuo. For this collection, see Bo Gyllensvard, "Axel and Nora Lundgren's Bequest of Chinese Bronzes," *Bulletin of The Museum of Far Eastern Antiquities*, 49 (1977), 1–16.

Departure for China

Upon his return to Chicago, Chen summarized highlights of this his trip in his farewell letter to David Stevens at the Rockefeller Foundation:[①]

I am glad to report to you that my trip to Europe was very successful. I spent a whole month in England and Europe (Aug. 2 – Sept. 4, 1947), two weeks in London and one week each in Stockholm and Paris. During my stay in England, I visited all the museums in London, Oxford and Cambridge, and many private collectors such as Mrs. Seligman, Mrs. Sedgwick, Sir Alan Barlow, Sir Neil Malcolm and Sir Herbert Ingram. In Stockholm, I had the pleasure of discussing my corpus with Prof. Karlgren for six days and spent all the time in the Far Eastern Museum. I was received by the Crown Prince [Gustav VI Adolph] in his castle to see his own collection and had the honour of talking and discussing with him for two hours. I was surprised to see the newly opened Musee Guimet and Cernuschi with their fine arrangement.

I have brought back many photographs and rubbings which I hope some day I may be able to publish. I only regret I could not stay in Europe longer to visit the smaller countries and museums outside the three capitals. I know there are many small but quite important collections which need to be surveyed.

I must tell you again how thankful I am for all you have done for me. I am going home loaded with riches which will occupy me for a long time to come. I sail from San Francisco on September 19 and hope to be in Peiping before the end of October. Please accept my deep gratitude and best wishes.

Those "riches," according to Stevens' final report on Chen's fellowship, included four trunkfuls of photographs of Chinese bronzes and other artifacts in Western collections. Several letters by Rockefeller Foundation personnel—as well as American and Canadian curators and professors—had strongly supported Chen's wish to avail these research materials to his colleagues in China. Chen's correspondence indicates that his extensive photo files included

---

[①]Chen to Stevens, September 7, 1947, Rockefeller Foundation records, Projects, Record Group 1.1 (FA386), Series 216R: Illinois- Humanities and Arts, Box 19, Folder 264: University of Chicago Visiting Scholars-(Chinese Studies), 1944–1946.

not only duplicate photos of many bronzes originally requested for his Corpus, but also documented additional bronzes, as well as oracle bones, jades, ceramics, sculptures, lacquers, and
perhaps a few paintings as well. Some of this material was undoubtedly represented among
the "712 lantern slides/ glass plates" cited in the customs list for Chen's shipments from Chicago.[1]

Although Chen had repeatedly expressed his desire to visit public and private collections on the west coast of the United States, his return trip to China afforded only a brief stop
in San Francisco. There, he acquired additional photos from Gump's department store—a
long-time purveyor of Chinese art, as well as from Eric Mayell, a collector and former photographer for the *Cathay News* in China. He also met with Elizabeth Huff, newly appointed as
founding Curator of the East Asiatic Library at the University of California, Berkeley. Chen
had likely met Huff at Harvard; in autumn 1946, she had returned from six years in Beijing to
complete her PhD in Chinese literature under Elisséeff.

On September 18th, the day before his scheduled departure from San Francisco, Chen
wrote a farewell postcard to Avery Brundage, asking that the Chicago collector forward
photos of all newly acquired bronzes to his office at Tsinghua University.[2] One week later,
Chen's ship docked in Honolulu, enabling him to survey his last collection of Chinese bronzes on American territory. Robert P. Griffing, Jr., recently appointed director of the Honolulu
Academy of Arts, showed Chen the museum collection and promptly mailed him photographs
of bronzes that supplemented those already included in the Corpus.[3]

The Corpus at Harvard

In late October 1947, Chen Mengjia resumed his professorship at Tsinghua University,
anticipating that the fully illustrated manuscript that he had submitted to Elisséeff in June
would be imminently published. But it was not, and the fate of Chen's original materials may
never be reconstructed from surviving documents. To my knowledge, only three letters that
crossed Elisséeff's desk between late September and mid-October 1948 refer to that work.
The earliest of these, from Elisséeff to Stevens, notes that Elisséeff had appointed a Harvard

[1]Inventory, Tianjin Garrison Headquarters, September 15, 1948. Kaogusuo.
[2]Avery Brundage Papers, Archives, Asian Art Museum of San Francisco.
[3]Griffing to Chen, October 3, 1947. Kaogusuo.

graduate student to edit the text.

Chen simultaneously expressed concern at this delay in publication. Through the inter-mediary of Chen Guansheng 陳觀勝 (Kenneth K. S. Chen), then newly appointed Professor of History and Executive Secretary of Yanjing's Harvard–Yenching Institute, Chen suggested in late September 1948 that his manuscript might be printed more economically in Beijing. But that would have required that more than one thousand photographs be shipped to China, a course that Elisséeff firmly rejected owing to the country's political instability. Noting that Harvard's trustees had approved funds for publication, Elisséeff added that he expected to receive the edited manuscript by December, to review it promptly, and that publication by the Harvard–Yenching Institute in Cambridge would probably begin in 1949. This letter, dated October 19, 1948, appears to be the last firsthand reference to Chen Mengjia's manuscript and photos.[1] To my knowledge, no institutional or personal correspondence indicates when plans for publication by the Harvard–Yenching Institute were finally abandoned or to whom Chen's work was last entrusted.

Chinese (1962) and Japanese (1977) Editions

But Chen's research had not been altogether lost. Together with a carbon copy of his manuscript, he had returned to China with duplicaniversitte photos of most bronzes and rub-bings represented in the Corpus, as well as with materials gathered after his deadline had drawn the project to a close. His correspondence indicates that these materials had been ear-marked not only for future research, but also for a Chinese edition of the Corpus.[2]

---

[1]"Memo, "excerpt from letter Serge Elisséeff to DHS, September 29, 1948, Rockefeller Foundation records, Projects, Record Group 1.2 (FA387), Series 200R: United States-Humanities and Arts, Box 344, Folder 3142: Harvard–Yenching Institute-Chinese Studies-(Chen Meng-Chia)-(Chinese Bronzes in Canada).

Kenneth Chen to Serge Elisséeff, September 30, 1948; Serge Elisséeff to Kenneth Chen, October 19, 1948 (Archives, Harvard–Yenching Institute, Harvard University). In March–April,1998, administrators at the Harvard–Yenching Library, Harvard University's Pusey Library, and Harvard University Press each confirmed that its archives preserved no additional record of Chen's manuscript. The only subsequent reference located by the author was a report of March 4, 1949 to Stevens from Ernest Cadmun Colwell, then President of the University of Chicago: "During his [Chen's] stay at the University, he was at work on a catalogue of Chinese bronzes in American collections, which, as far as we know, has not yet appeared in print." Rockefeller Founda-tion records, Projects, Record Group 1.1 (FA386), Series 216R: Illinois-Humanities and Arts, Box 19, Folder 264: University of Chicago Visiting Scholars-(Chinese Studies), 1944–1946.

[2]For example, Chen to Mrs. Huc Mazelet Luquiens, Honolulu, September 26, 1946, in which he requested a second set of photos, specifically for a Chinese edition.

In 1962 and clearly under political pressure, officials at the Kaogusuo published a Chinese edition of Chen's catalogue entries *only* under the title *Mei diguo zhuyi jielüede wo guo Yin Zhou tongqi jilu* 美帝國主義劫掠的我國殷周銅器集録. The book was published anonymously, without citing Chen as its author. In the absence of his Comprehensive Study and with his name mentioned solely in a condemnatory preface of December 1960, Chen's role in this publication is enigmatic to me. The book first reached Western scholars fifteen years later, in a Japanese edition prepared by Matsumaru Michio 松丸道雄 of Tokyo University, *In Shu seidoki bunrui zuroku*: 殷周青銅器分類図録—*A Corpus of Chinese Bronzes in American Collections,* published in Tokyo in 1977. Professor Matsumaru prefaced those entries with a Japanese translation of Chen's 1945 lecture to the Chinese Art Society of America, as well as with his own laudatory tribute to Chen's pioneering scholarship. My notes on the Chinese edition below are based on Matsumaru's translation.

Although the most detailed catalogue texts in Chen's English manuscript are considerably abbreviated or deleted in the Chinese edition, the vast majority of bronzes are represented in both documents. These bronzes undoubtedly represent the pieces for which Chen had received duplicate photographs while in America. We may surmise that bronzes that are limited to the English manuscript represent those for which he received only the single photo that he submitted to Harvard, and that those limited to the Chinese manuscript, those for which he received photos after finalizing the manuscript.[1] Colleagues at the Princeton conference of 1947 had clearly been instrumental in providing leads to private collections that are represented only in the Chinese edition.

Canadian and European Manuscripts

Also preserved in the Kaogusuo are Chen's notes and photographs documenting Chinese bronzes in the Royal Ontario Museum as well as British and other northern European collections. Pursuant to the latter, we know that Chen maintained contact with Geoffrey Hedley as late as September 1948, when Hedley mailed Chen the names of major British curators and collectors whom Chen had been unable to visit. The former included curators at the British Museum and Victoria and Albert Museum in London; Fitzwilliam Museum in Cambridge; and Burrell Collection in Glasgow. Hedley proposed that Chen write directly to these persons

---

[1] 25 bronzes appear to be limited to the English edition and 56 to the Chinese.

and specify his requests; Hedley would then forward the available photos to Chen and expe-
dite payment in Chinese currency.[1] Chen's photo files may clarify whether or not he was able
to pursue Hedley's leads.

Chen's research on one vessel in London, however, did realize publication in the West.
In November 1947, the British scholar William Cohn wrote to Chen in Beijing, informing him
of plans by prominent collectors, several of whom Chen had met in London, to establish the
quarterly journal *Oriental Art*.[2]

A group of people who are interested in Far Eastern studies (Sir Neill Malcolm,
Sir Alan Barlow, Sir Herbert Ingram, Mrs. Seligman, Mr. R. Bruce, Mr. A. Clark, Mr. P.
Palmer, Mr. H. N. Spaulding, Mr. Denis Cohen, and others) have decided to inaugurate
a new journal dealing with Art and Archaeology of the Far East and India, and that I
should be the Editor.

It is to be a kind of revival of Ostasiatische Zeitschrift.

I should be very pleased to include you amongst our contributors. I have just
read your highly interesting article in Archives. If you have further studies ready on
this subject, please send them to us for publication. But let us have, anyway, everything
you publish. We shall report on it in the O.A.

What a pity that we did not meet in England.

With kind regards,

Yours sincerely,

William Cohn

In reply, Chen proposed and promptly submitted an article on the Kang Hou *gui* 康侯
𣪘—an important Western Zhou vessel then in the collection of Sir Neil Malcolm. Chen had
described the vessel in *Haiwai Zhongguo tongqi tulu* and examined it at Malcolm's home in
August. That article would be Chen's last Western publication.[3]

---

[1] Hedley to Chen, September 22, 1948. Kaogusuo.

[2] Cohn to Chen, November 17, 1947. Kaogusuo.

[3] Ch'en Meng-chia, "Malcolm's K'ang Hou Kuei and its Set," *Oriental Art* I, no. 3 (Winter 1948), 111–116.
Chen dated this vessel early in the reign of Cheng Wang and postulated that it had been designed by a Shang
craftsman. The vessel is now in the British Museum.

Reflections in Chicago, Agendas in Beijing

Writing from Chicago in late February 1946, Chen acknowledged a letter from Ma Heng by summarizing progress on his own research and relating his personal impressions of Chinese art in the United States. Preserved in rough draft in the Kaogusuo, Chen's reply underscored his distress at the quantity and quality of Shang and Zhou bronzes that had entered American collections, as well as his desire that the Chinese government would enforce laws to restrict the export of these treasures. But in a note of extraordinarily broad vision, he also proposed the sanctioned exchange of works of art between Chinese and Western countries: "I hope that there will be a means of exchange in the future," Chen wrote, "by which duplicates in China may be exchanged with Western works of art. This would be good for international cooperation and exchange and establish the foundation for museums of Western art in China, with mutual benefit." Although disparaging their ignorance of Chinese history and classical literature, Chen commended American curators for their approach to museum installations as well as their educational programs at elementary, secondary, and university levels. He also recognized American university professors for their specialized courses in Chinese bronzes and painting. And observing the expressed desire of Western specialists for a major exhibition of Chinese art comparable to that shown at Burlington House in London in 1935–36, Chen proposed that overseas loan exhibitions with sharper chronological and geographical focus— supplemented by informative labels and discussions would enhance respect for China's cultural history and by extension, China's international stature.[1]

Together with fellow professors with extensive academic experience in the United

---

[1] 叔平先生賜鑒：昨奉一月二十四日手教，拜悉一一。欣聞貴院將大肆開展，前途無量，可預祝也。晚離國來美忽忽一載有半，去夏今春兩度赴東部各博物院參觀，爲期四月。此邦華夏古物集中東部與中部公私藏家，所見已在七八成之上，以銅器一項而論，數逾千數，玉器等是，石刻亦不在少數，惟書畫不多，其品質亦屬平常。近十年來銅器流入此間數量之大，至足驚人，而商周及戰國精品之多，觀後每多興歎。以管見所及，其數量品質已遠過英歐，亦可與日本舊藏抗衡。國家瓌寶爲少數商估博厚利，言之至堪痛心。晚在紐約時，骨董商已以禁令勢在必行，稍具戒心。甚盼政府藉此良機嚴格屬行，將來可以交換辦法與外國博物院將中國複製品易西方藝術品，如此既可收合作流通之效，並可建中國之西方博物館之基礎，實屬利。晚去夏以還，準備編作存美中國銅器，收集材料已在一千五百品左右。現在編作。本擬今秋返國，但因工作未能如期告畢，或將展延一年。於參觀各博物院時亦時時留意其組織，其陳列方法及研究方針和教育意義，可資借鏡之處不少。有若干博物院如華府及哈佛頗側重中國古物，尤以近年爲甚。惟主其事者於中國歷史典籍究屬隔閡，彼等常願我國政府來美舉行如倫敦之展覽會。此事若預立規程，選以精品，分期分地，劃成數組，附以詳細說明，分類講演，對於西方人之了解中國文化並提高國家地位，收效必宏。來美後甚感此邦人士對我國之超越感，而其惟一尊敬中國之處厥爲古物，以如此精美之文物必有甚高甚遠之文化。因勢利導，甚盼。

States and Europe— most notably, Liang Sicheng and the historian of art and aesthetic theory Deng Yizhe 鄧以蟄, Chen set about implementing ambitious, methodical, and innovative plans for the university. As preface to their formal "Proposal for Establishing a Research Division of Art" 設立藝術史研究室計劃書 submitted to President Mei Yiqi in December 1947, Chen and his colleagues acknowledged the Princeton Bicentennial conference for having demonstrated the achievements of Western scholars in Chinese art history as well as the potential for Chinese scholars to similarly develop this academic discipline. Commending the former for having established East Asian departments in their art museums and Chinese art history courses in their universities, they proposed a methodical four-point agenda for Tsinghua:[1]

(1) An interdisciplinary humanities curriculum, consolidating courses offered by different departments. That curriculum would evolve into a formal department of History of Art 藝術史系, offering classes in Chinese art history, archaeology, connoisseurship, and art appreciation, as well as comparative studies of Western art and primitive art, which would address both historical and theoretical issues. Graduate-level classes would provide opportunities for study abroad.[2]

---

[1]*Liang Sicheng quanji* 梁思成全集 [The Complete Works of Liang Sicheng]. (Beijing: Zhongguo jianzhu gongye chubanshe, 2001), vol 5, 3–4. I am grateful to Lai Delin of the University of Louisville and Lin Zhu 林洙 (Mrs. Liang Sicheng) for this reference.

[2]Records available to me differ in their description of this department of History of Art and its exact date of establishment; its founding members seem to have evolved from (and sometimes been identified with) a planning committee. In a grant application of May 1948 submitted to Charles Burton Fahs of the Rockefeller Foundation, Mei Yiqi noted that a "Committee for Instruction and Research in Chinese Art and Archaeology" had been organized about six months earlier with the objective of developing a museum and research library. Mei to Humanities Division, Rockefeller Foundation, May 19, 1948, Rockefeller Foundation records, Record Group 1, Series 601, Box 50, Folder 415: Tsing Hua University.

In early 1948, Robert Winter (see fn.[1], pp.571) apprised the Rockefeller Foundation: "I have just been notified that a new department has been created [at Tsing-hua University]. It is called History of Art. Liang Ssu-ch'eng is the chairman. Other members are Teng I-chih [Deng Yizhe], Ch'en Meng-chia [Chen Mengjia], Chu Tzu-ch'ing [Zhu Ziqing] and myself." (Winter to Fahs, January 9, 1948 [misdated January 9, 1947], Rockefeller Foundation records, Record Group 1, Series 601, Box 50, Folder 415: Tsing Hua University.) For Zhu Ziqing 朱自清, see Boorman, ed., *Biographical Dictionary of Republican China*, vol. 4, 465–467.

Cao Shuqin 曹淑琴, "Ji women kandaode yipi chuanshi Shang Zhou tongqi 記我們看到的一批傳世商周銅器 [Reflections on a group of Shang and Zhou bronzes handed down by generations that we have seen] ,"*Kaogu,* 1986/9, p. 834, identified Chen as founder of the Committee as well as the museum and art history department. According to a brief report to *Oriental Art* magazine likely submitted by Chen, this Committee (there cited as Committee for the Study of Art and Archaeology) comprised ten members, including Liang, Deng, and F. L.

(2) A "Research Room," furnished with books and lantern-slides, together with studios for photography and the production of models. Initially, this space would serve several functions—library, seminar room, photography studio, lecture hall, exhibition gallery, and administrative meeting room.

(3) A university art museum. "The study of art requires a museum; this goes without saying. The purpose of a university museum is to collect . . . for teaching . . . representative examples from each period and each region."

(4) International scholarly cooperation, its features concretely defined: "We should encourage research reports from throughout the country, as well as the exchange of materials and exhibitions. We should invite scholars and professors from outside the country and accept foreign students who specialize in Chinese art."

On May 2, 1948, the Tsinghua University Exhibition Gallery of Cultural Relics 清華大學文物陳列室 opened to the public. Together with an impressively wide-ranging series of inaugural exhibitions, Chen mounted a photographic survey of Chinese bronzes in American, Canadian, British, French, and Swedish collections. Consistent with goals that had been supported by administrators of the Rockefeller Foundation and scholars at the Harvard–Yenching Institute in Cambridge—as well as by curators, dealers, and collectors who had availed their collections to him—Chen had indeed begun to make available to his colleagues in China the fruits of almost three years of intensive research in the West.[①]

As documented by President Mei Yiqi, the Tsinghua University collection then comprised "1200 objects of interest to Chinese students of art and archaeology, about 500 vol-

Yuan, a scholar of prehistoric ceramics. See "Museums and Exhibitions," *Oriental Art* 1, no. 2 (Autumn 1948), 102.

① According to Lin Zhu, this gallery was located on the top floor of the university's biology building. (Lin Zhu to Delin Lai, February 24, 2001.) Chen—together with Liang Sicheng, Deng Yizhi, and the ethnologist Wu Zelin—also organized several exhibitions that included antiquities purchased from the galleries at Liulichang and those donated by private collectors. Chen's exhibitions were impressively wide-ranging: in addition to those in his specialized areas—early metalwork and Shang oracle bones—he organized displays of Chu lacquers, Six Dynasties (stone) epitaphs, Five Dynasties ceramics, and Qing dynasty textiles. Concurrent exhibitions featured Chinese paintings, architectural fragments and drawings, and artifacts of China's ethnic nationalities— the last to celebrate Tsinghua University's newly founded department of anthropology.

During an interview in Chicago in April 2001, Chen Gongrou 陳公柔 informed the author that John Fairbank initially conceived the idea of a university museum for Tsinghua when Fairbank and Chen were in Kunming together and that Fairbank contributed funds for this purpose in 1948.

umes of rare books, including many on Chinese art, and about 3000 articles of ethnological interest." [1] The first group reportedly included more than 100 Shang and Zhou bronzes and more than 1000 oracle bones. Toward that collection, Chen purchased important bronzes from dealers on Liulichang, Beijing's venerable antiquities street. He also persuaded C.T. Loo to donate and ship at least one bronze vessel from his gallery in New York that had appeared in the Corpus.[2]

That autumn, the museum was announced to the West:[3]

The Tsing Hua University, Peiping, has opened a Museum. A committee of ten Professors was formed for the study of Chinese Art History and Archaeology. Among the members are Professor I. C. Teng, an authority on Chinese Painting, Professor S. C. Liang, an authority on Chinese Architecture, Professor F. L. Yuan, an authority on pre-historic Pottery, and Professor Ch'en Meng-chia, the well-known Archaeologist.

This foundation, however, was short-lived. With the government restructuring of Tsing-hua University in 1952 came the dissolution of its humanities departments and the museum's closure. Chen's ensuing career at the Institute of Archaeology produced major studies on

---

[1] These figures are cited by Mei Yiqi in his application of May 19, 1948 to the Humanities Division of the Rockefeller Foundation for a three-year grant to support the activities of this new department as well as the development of a "model, modern museum of art and ethnology that will serve the purposes of instruction, demonstration, and research. " Rockefeller Foundation records, Record Group 1, Series 601, Box 50, Folder 415: Tsing Hua University. The Rockefeller Foundation turned down this application, officially, because all these projects lay outside the scope of Foundation programs; unofficially, because Foundation officials viewed the stability of Beijing with increasing apprehension. Fahs to Mei, 20 August 1948, Rockefeller Foundation records, Record Group 1, Series 601, Box 50, Folder 415: Tsing Hua University.

[2] Loo donated an inscribed Warring States "hua gai 華蓋 [flower cover]" hu, reportedly found at Jincun in 1928–32, which Chen related to a group of vessels that he had published in 1937 (see fn.[3], pp.573). (Loo to Chen, February 13, 1948. Kaogusuo.) The vessel is catalogued as no.715 in Chen's English Corpus and A714 in the Chinese edition. Chen annotated his copy of the English Corpus with a note of Tsinghua's ownership. Paradoxically, Tsinghua University was required to obtain an "import license," presumably from the United States, before receiving the vessel. (Mei to Chih Meng, China Institute, August 18, 1948. Kaogusuo.) This is most likely the vessel mentioned in Cao Shuqin, 曹淑琴 "Ji women kandaode yipi chuanshi Shang Zhou tongqi 記我們看到的一批傳世商周銅器 [Reflections on a Group of Shang and Zhou Bronzes Handed Down by Generations that We Have Seen] ," *Kaogu* , 1986.9, p. 839, where the it is mentioned as then belonging to the Museum of Chinese History, but previously having been in New York and Paris for more than twenty years.

[3] "Museums and Exhibitions," (see fn. [2], pp.608).

paleography as well as political and social history, as many of which have been recognized for their incorporation of Western methodologies. These included his seminal investigation of Western Zhou bronzes: "Xi Zhou tongqi duandai" 西周銅器斷代 published in 1955–56 in *Kaogu xuebao*, on whose editorial committee then he served. Known among scholars as the "Duandai," this study incorporated the political chronology that he had summarized in the Buckingham catalogue and detailed in the Corpus, and further developed his methodology of grouping vessels into associated sets.[①] Chen's experience abroad enabled him to compare vessels in Western collections with those preserved or subsequently discovered in China. These included a few vessels not included in the Corpus and for which he likely received photos after submitting the draft to Harvard (e.g. Avery Brundage's Ran *fangding*), as well in European collections that he had studied in wartime storage facilities in New York (D. David-Weill's pair of Ling *gui*) or gathered during or after his August 1947 trip to Europe.

Chen's experience abroad, however, intensified his vulnerability to campaigns of political thought reform before his tragic death in 1966. His posthumous rehabilitation by Xia Nai 夏鼐 in 1978 has inspired impressive tributes to his efforts to analyze and document his heritage with sinological expertise while remaining open to Western modes of thinking.[②] Addressing issues of history, culture, archaeology, and style, the monumental English-language study that he completed in Chicago seventy years ago remains firsthand testimonial to Chen's comprehensive scholarship and readiness to share it with Western scholars and collectors. That he envisioned a future Chinese translation of this study makes the publication of his manuscript an especially fitting tribute to its author.

Acknowledgements

Wang Rui of the Palace Museum proposed this study during her visit to Chicago in summer 1997. She and I were then provided essential assistance by the staff of the Rockefeller Archive Center in Sleepy Hollow, New York. Over subsequent years, archivists at the Harvard–Yenching Library of Harvard University; the Oriental Institute and Regenstein Library,

---

①Only the first six installments of this study, however, were published during Chen Mengjia's lifetime. 1955, 9, 137–75 (part 1); 1955, 10, 69–142 (part 2); 1956, 1, 65–114 (part 3); 1956, 2, 85–94, (part 4); 1956, 3, 105–27 (part 5); 1956, 4, 85–122 (part 6).

②See, for example, *Jinian Chen Mengjia xiansheng xueshu zuotanhui* 紀念陳夢家先生學術座談會 [Symposium commemorating the scholarship of Mr. Chen Mengjia], *Hanzi wenhua* 漢字文化, 2006.4.

both of the University of Chicago; the Seeley G. Mudd Manuscript Library of Princeton University; and the Freer-Sackler Gallery of Art were unfailingly helpful to me, as were archivists and curators at several other American museums. Li Feng 李峰 suggested the first critical questions that helped direct my research.

In 1999 and with consent of the late Zhao Luorei, Wang Shimin 王世民 and Wu En 烏恩 of the Kaogusuo generously provided Wang Rui and me access to Chen Mengjia's correspondence preserved at that Institute. A grant from the Asian Cultural Council enabled me to join Wang Rui in Beijing to carefully review that material and to first explore the extraordinary insights of Chen's English manuscript, "Chinese Bronzes in American Collections: A Catalogue and Comprehensive Study of Chinese Bronzes" that is published here for the first time. Wang Shimin, the late Wu En, Zhang Changshou 張長壽, the late Chen Gongrou 陳公柔, the late Wang Shixiang 王世襄, and the late Zhou Yongzhen 周永珍 patiently answered my questions, as did the late Tsien Tsuen-hsuin.

Lai Delin 賴德林, Lai Guolong 來國龍, Wang Youqin 王友琴, Margaret Larson, and Chen Yeongfu provided essential translations. Naomi Noble Richard helped structure and articulate what seemed an overwhelming volume of documentation for a broader version of this study. Thomas Lawton, Edward Shaughnessy, Li Feng and, especially, Lothar von Falkenhausen provided encouraging and instructive comments on that draft. Professor von Falkenhausen furnished me with valuable reflections and corrections on this paper as well. Errors of fact or interpretation are my own.

CHINESE BRONZES

A PROJECT FOR A CORPUS OF CHINESE BRONZES IN AMERICAN COLLECTIONS

Under the auspices of Harvard-Yenching Institute,
Boylston Hall 17, Cambridge 38, Massachusetts

Address: Professor Chen Meng-chia
314 Oriental Institute
University of Chicago
Chicago 37, Illinois

*1. Catalogue number

2. Kind of vessel

3. Name mentioned in inscription

Name of person for whom or by whom the vessel was made as recorded in the inscription

4. Present condition

1) Complete. Repaired. Oxidized. Fragmentary. Restored. Parts missing.
2) Weak. Medium. Strong.

5. Descriptions

Shape. Decoration, inlay, fire-gilt, etc.

6. Inscriptions

Original text rubbing, photograph or hand copy

7. Bibliographical references

1) Of pictures, drawings, rubbings of vessel
2) Of pictures, drawings, rubbings of inscriptions
3) Studies in Chinese and other languages

8. Former collections

Former owners where possible

9. Provenance

Area or district where found if known; dealers' information

10. Dimensions

Height, length, width, etc., in centimeters

11. Museum or collection number

*12. Date

*13. Geographical distribution

14. Photographs

15. Miscellaneous

If vessel is authentic no mention is made. If a forgery or doubtful it is to be listed here. Other types of records to be noted here.

*Please leave blank